THE BLOOD IS RACING

THE CANNON AND DAY FAMILY OF DANEBURY

ANDREW AGER

The Blood is Racing

Edited by John Irvine

Copyright @2016 by Andrew Ager

A catalogue record for this book is available from the British Library

Published in the United Kingdom by
Charles Ager Publishing 2016
Paperback ISBN: 978-0-9955008-0-8
eBook ISBN: 978-0-9955008-1-5

Figure 1 Cannon and Day Family outside Danebury 1883 Family Collection

Dedicated to my beautiful mother Patricia Cannon and my amazing
son Charles

My uncles Terry, Thomas, Mornington & Peter
My aunties Sheila, Joan, Nina & Margaret Cannon the children of
Captain Charles Edward Cannon and Dorothy Thrush
To my descendants and relatives I bequeath to you this book, my
legacy

"VERITAS VOS LIBERABIT"

THE TRUTH SHALL SET YOU FREE

Acknowledgements:

To the patience and love of my beautiful creative wife Wahida and our very clever and talented son Charles our greatest creation. Thank you for putting up with me I love you both so much, you are my world.

I wish to thank Tim Cox Trustee The National Heritage Centre for Horseracing and Sporting Art for reviewing this book and for his very helpful comments. The Racing Museum in Newmarket for allowing me access to their library in the early days of writing. The Hampshire Record Office for their assistance over the years. Also the Rothschild Archive for looking after me when I visited thanks to the Cundle family.

Thanks to John Irvine for editing the text and his daughter Katie for proof reading. My brothers Mark Anthony my sister Jaine my uncle Terry and Auntie Rose, my cousin Martin and Sandy Cannon, Family of Alys Cannon, David Cannon grandson of Morny Cannon, David Cannon son of Noel Cannon, and the rest of my family.

Over the years of researching in Stockbridge and Broughton for this book I spent a great deal of time there meeting many of the local people, who were lovely, they made me feel very welcome and who also had

a very great interest in the races of Stockbridge. My family would have lived and worked with theirs for over 200 years, I promised them I would finish this book. When I visit Stockbridge it feels as if I have returned home. I have tried my best over fourteen years to collect as many photos and story's as possible it may come to light after the publication that you may have photos and stories I will create a website please send them in.

Figure 2 Authors Mother and Father Keith Ager and Patricia Cannon 01-04-1976

CONTENTS

ILLUSTRATIONS

PREFACE

ALL I ASK IS THAT YOU GIVE ME THE STAGE and I will tell you the truth as I have discovered it. Over two hundred and thirty years have passed since the first record of my ancestors appeared in horse racing history. As I sit here writing I am aware of their blood coursing through my veins, all of what made them, made me and they stand behind me in a long line reading every word I write.

One of the greatest families in horse racing history, a dynasty of jockeys and trainers whose descendants have accumulated a combined total of 130 Classic wins including 2 Triple Crowns, involved in some of the largest and notorious scandals of the turf claiming such descendants as Lester Piggott arguably the most accomplished jockey of all time, with 4493 career wins champion jockey 11 times, 9 Derby's and 30 Classics. Or John Barham Day marked as one of the first professional jockeys, or his son John Day Junior who trained the most winning horses in one season a record that stood unbeaten for over 120 years, Alfred Day founder of Fontwell Park near Arundel, Tom Cannon superb jockey and trainer of Jockeys the list goes on.

That family managed to take the small town of Stockbridge in Hampshire at the end of the 18th Century and turn it into a horse racing phenomenon of the 19th Century, rivalling Newmarket in popularity, attracting and servicing some of the most powerful patrons within horse racing history, including royalty, yet hardly anything of that is recorded. They simply vanished into history.

In an age before the motor car and football, horse racing was the national sport and the Cannons and the Days of Danebury my ancestors, were its celebrity jockeys and trainers. Celebrated in their day for their skill honesty and integrity left no story behind them to be judged by they believed, *"The fame of great jockeys, like that of great actors, rests upon tradition. They leave nothing behind them by which future generations can judge their excellence"*[1]. But judged they have been by the modern day horse racing establishment who have written and influenced their own version of history.

That version has provided the base for such statements as *"His nickname Honest John Day was ironic, for the Day stables became a centre of controversy over fraudulent betting."* Tate Gallery 2016 or Jack Waterman *"With the main*

---

1 Thormamby (pseud) Willmott Dixon, *Kings of the Turf: Memoirs and Anecdotes of Distinguished Owners, Backers, Trainers*, Hutchinson and Co, London 1898 p. 301-302

exceptions of Hastings and the popular Duke of Beaufort, Day had a crew of crooked owners who would have been more in place aboard a prison hulk. "Good trainer as John Day was, it is pure conjecture whether Henry Cecil will be happy, even obliquely, to be mentioned alongside him." [2] Even more recently Nicholas Foulkes 2010 *"The Days father and son were a picturesque dynasty of rogues celebrated for their lack of scruples when it came to pulling doping nobbling or otherwise making horses safe. They were highly effective and utterly unencumbered by morals, on occasion betraying the owners for whom they worked. While far from alone on the turf in their dishonesty it is fair to say they were among the leaders when it came to fixing a race"* [3] and lastly Marcus Armytage the Telegraph 2006 *"Writing about the painting of Crucifix, the 1840 Oaks winner owned by one of the Jockey Club's great administrators, Lord George Bentinck, and trained by John Day snr, he alludes to the Day's sharp practice and how the owner and the ironically nicknamed 'Honest John' eventually fell out over the trainer's 'devious' handling of Crucifix's breakdown."* [4]

It must be asked of the above authors where is their evidence for those accusations they have laid against John Barham Day for he received the nickname honest John because that is what he was, *"A good name is as a precious ointment and by uniform correct conduct in the saddle John Day a very celebrated Jockey has acquired that of Honest John"* [5] That was recorded in 1833 and John Porter of Kingsclere one of the most respected trainers in Horse Racing History had this to say on John Barham Day *'The name Honest John so often applied to him was indicative of his reputation in the racing world. The most prominent men on the turf were among his greatest admirers."* [6] or maybe Lord William Pitt Lenox *"one of those in which the public placed entire confidence"* [244]

Perhaps I am not the best person to write this book, I am not an author or historian, a jockey or trainer I can barely ride a horse, with over 14 years of research I have uncovered a far different picture of History than what has and is currently being painted of my ancestors. I want to examine and record their story, passing it on to the next generation in a hope that they will celebrate the lives of those that have passed before them.

---

2 Jack Waterman, *Skulduggery at Danebury in the Days of Yore*, The Times, 12 September 1987.
3 Nicholas Foulkes *Gentlemen and Blackguards* Orion 2010 p.36
4 Marcus Armytage Daily Telegraph 8th Dec 2006
5 Quarterly Review. 1833. *Quarterly Review*, XLIX (April & July) p. 398
6 John Porter, Edward Moorhouse, *John Porter of Kingsclere an Autobiography*, (Grant Richards London, 1919, p.10

INTRODUCTION

Their story has never been known until now. I started this journey of discovery with nothing but a few memories my mother told me there was no book to follow. Charting the rise and fall of an illustrious racing empire grown by a gifted family who worked together, with a vision. A remarkable member of that family Anne Day, at the turn of the 18th century had acquired the skills of a veterinary surgeon, the records show her own family owned and bred pedigree sire horses on their farms in Hampshire as far back as the late seventeenth century. She used these skills to help grow the early stables in Stockbridge and was one of the first women to publicly own and breed horses in a time when women were not allowed. Her favourite saying was *"Fear thy God, speak evil of none, Stick to the truth, and don't be done."* [7]

The Day family of Stockbridge dominated racing, attracting prestigious patrons such as the Dukes of Grafton, Portland, Lord Palmerston and even the very fashionable and prestigious Bibury Club moved there, the most secret of clubs, whose members were the rich and connected of the day who bet on races below the line of sight in a subterranean world that would go on to become infested by the Danebury Confederacy, an organized syndicate that moved in and manipulated the world above the line, the trainers, the jockeys, the horses and even the odds for profit. The most important patron of the Bibury Club was King George IV the Club races were a very private affair, not to be spoken off outside its circle of members.

Lord George Cavendish Bentinck son to the 4th Duke of Portland was a patron of my family, and during their early relationship they were unstoppable, but scandal followed and an infection of distrust grew between John Barham Day and Lord George Bentinck of the Bibury Club who had introduced the Danebury Confederacy to the Racecourse, the Confederacy lent vast sums of money in return for securities and its personnel included muscle like the boxing champion John Gully and guile in the form of Harry Hill. They traded in rigged bets, inside information, persuasion and repercussion, and the nobility ran the risk of being ruined at their hands.

The Jockey Club purveyor of standards in racing life did its best to protect its vested interests and punish the powerless, eventually taking away the livelihood of my ancestor John Day Junior who was caught up in a scandal

---

7 Henry Hall Dixon. *The Druid Post and Paddock*. Vinton and Co. Ltd London, 1856.

that one of the Jockey Club's own members had instigated, this controversial decision made by the Jockey Club Stewards brought a huge uproar and outcry for fairness from both the public and the remaining members of the Jockey Club, maybe one of its high born untouchables was out for revenge or maybe there was something else?

In happier times in the last quarter of the 19th Century, my great grandfather Tom Cannon married John Day's daughter and reached his zenith becoming one of the great jockeys and trainers of all time surpassed only by the success of his sons Mornington, Kempton Tom and my grandfather Charles Cannon for Classic wins and influencing riding style. My great uncle Morny Cannon Triple Crown winner became so famous in his lifetime that he even gained a mention in James Joyce's "Ulysses" a book that is regularly voted the greatest novel of the 20th Century. Another child and sister of my grandfather Margaret Cannon known as Meggie married the jump jockey Ernest Piggott they created a racing dynasty of their own becoming Lester Piggott's grandparents.

Which brings us to the final bitter stab, when ownership of some of the land on which the Stockbridge racecourse was built passed to Marianne Vaudrey Barker Mills a very religious noblewoman who strongly disapproved of gambling. The racecourse and a whole town's future had dropped into her hands.

You see I never wrote this book, it was already written I was just its servant, and it revealed itself to me over many years. This story was my family's mystery, our skeleton. So for the first time in history and since my ancestors took up the reigns in the eighteenth century I have the honour and pleasure of telling their story, **THE BLOOD IS RACING.**

Figure 3 Maria Owner George IV John Barham Day Jockey by R. B. Davis 1828

FAMILY TREE

John Day 1767-1828

Ann Barham 1771-1844

John Barham Day 1795-1860

John Day Junior 1815-1882

Tom Cannon 1846-1917

Kemton Cannon
1879-1951

Morny Cannon
1873-1962

Charles Cannon
1884-1968

Tom Cannon Junior
1872-1942

Figure 4 Authors Family Tree Cannon and Day of Danbury

THE DAY FAMILY OF HOUGHTON DOWN

Figure 5 Day Family by Abraham Cooper R.A.1838 Day 1925

JOHN DAY 1767-1828

A GLOOMY DAY.

taken on the STEYNE at BRIGHTON.

Figure 6 John Day on Brighton Pier 1801 by Charles Dighton

HORSE RACING HAS TAKEN PLACE IN Stockbridge since the early eighteenth century.[8] The race course was originally run on Houghton Down Farm a few miles from Stockbridge and a new racecourse was laid out in 1831 to accommodate the Bibury Club one of England's oldest racing clubs, which was moved from Cheltenham to Stockbridge this was a significant move which was about to turn Stockbridge from a sleepy town into a thriving and fashionable horseracing venue a place to be seen at in the nineteenth century, but this transformation did not just happen overnight. It would require intricate knowledge of horses, training, money, influence and the right fashionable connections. Anne Day, my great-great-great-great-grandmother, was one of England's first professional women to publicly train and breed her own horses. Two hundred years ago this information was well known yet in our modern times has never been recognized. Her husband, the first John Day often referred to as "Gloomy Day" by those who observed his maudlin countenance, he presented a rotund silhouette when observing his horses, his silk waistcoat riding up over his paunch, the brim of his hat shading his skilled eyes from the light and his soft fingers wrapped around the top of his twisted cane.

There is a painting by Charles Dighton dated 1801 by which time he was already racing advisor to the then Prince Regent later to be George VI.[22] It is the beginning of the racing scene in Stockbridge and their partnership. We will examine how the early racecourse was started; what caused it, and who was involved. This piece of history to my knowledge has never been explored and we are going back in time to where it all began, to where the first John Day learnt the art of training horses.

The Day family can trace their descent from John Day of Knighton in Stogursey Somerset. This John Day is marked as a gentlemen and held the Manor of Knighton as early as 1616, the manor contained many farms. The Manor of Knighton eventually was split up and there appears to be no direct sons or heirs so the manor was willed to John Day's daughter Elizabeth Day wife of John Holbech who left if to his son Day Holbech who upon his death 15th September 1761 left a proportion of the manor to his cousin John Day who inherited Bullen Farm through this will dated 25th September 1761.[9]

---

8 Carleton, J. W, *The Sporting Review* 1869. p 355 "Grace the Duke of Devonshire, and got by Childers out of a famous mare, called cabbage, daughter of Grantham, in 1748 when five years old he won 50 pounds at Stockbridge."
9 Somerset County Record Office *Will of Day Holbech of Somerset* 15th September 1761 "Bullen Farm in Stogursey and other land in Knighton to John Day" Acland Hood of

THE DAY FAMILY OF HOUGHTON DOWN

The first John Day in our story was born in 1768, to a John Day of Bullen Farm Stogursey (b.1746) and a Miss Hannah Levershaw (b.1742-1768), who was also from Stogursey and a widow of Stogumber. The Day family were yeomen farmers owning and farming land in Meare and Stogursey, John Day had two sisters Hannah and Joan and a brother named Henry Gould Day. Henry was a successful attorney with his own practice in Wickham Market but unfortunately met with an untimely end when he fell from a horse in 1826. Our family records show that John Day's mother Hannah died in 1768 and his father remarried to a Miss Anne Webber soon after. We have a large family book written in 1928 by Leeson Day in which those family records refer to John having had a falling out with his step-mother Miss Webber, probably over inheritance but we will never know. John Day ran away to stay with relatives at North Leach and Lechlade Gloucestershire. Eventually moving in with his uncle Charles Day at Cirencester it is here he was to be trained in the art of horse racing and an early newspaper account written in May 1830 places the Day family all on one page. *"All the world knows that there are seven days in the week, but it is not so notorious that seven Days are also to be found in the Racing "Calendar." There are Mrs. Day (Lady Sophia Kent) and Mrs. Day are the only ladies who breed racers), old Charles Day, and young Charles Day, Isaac Day, John Day, Sam. Day and William Day! The Stockbridge folks have wisely selected the best Day of the seven first and not the seventh."* [10]

Charles Day, John's uncle was a well-respected horse trainer and breeder of Cirencester, *"Oldest son of the much respected Mr. Charles Day, owner of Valentin Snowdrop and other blood horses."* [11] Johns Uncle was also Clerk of the Burford Races, the earliest account I have found for this is in 1793 *"The Colts or Fillies to be named to Charles Day at Barrows Brook on or before the last Day at Burford Races."* [12]. Mr. Charles Day at Barrows Brook farm near Cirencester bred and owned blood horses he also had a stud farm there. *"At Charles Days Barrows Brook near Cirencester and every proper attention paid to Mares and Foals High and Fling at three grand 5s, Petworth at 3gs and 5."* [13] He is described as a well-respected man within horse racing and from all accounts was

Fairfax DD\AH/28/1/9
10 The New Sporting Magazine. London: Baldwyn & Craddock, 1831. p. 206
11 *Sporting Magazine or Monthly Calendar of Sporting Transactions of the Turf* 1810. Volume 36, p. 241
12 J. Wheble *Monthly Magazine or Monthly Calendar of the Transactions of the Turf the Chace.* 1793. London.p.42
13 E.A.J Weatherby, *Racing Calendar.* Volume 34.London 1806.p.411. "

involved heavily with the Cirencester race scene as well as being involved with the Burford course, which is where the Bibury Club was then based. It is worth noting that Charles Day would have been acquainted with the early Bibury Club, and could have been present at its formation.

The Bibury Club is said to be one of the country's longest running horse racing clubs believed to have been formed in 1681. From looking at their website we can see they think this too. *'The Bibury Club, established in 1681, is the world's oldest racing club and the Bibury Club Meeting is one of Britain's longest-running meetings. Originally this meeting was held at the now-defunct courses of Bibury and Stockbridge before moving to Salisbury in 1899."* [14] However, according to other sources, the Bibury Club was more of a renewal of the Burford Races that was held there *"Stockbridge is now in repute, owing to the Bibury Club being held there-a renewal of the Burford Races ."* [15] The formation of the Bibury club that we are concerned with has been recorded to have been formed by General Grosvenor in1798 [16], at Burford and then moved after 1801 to Cheltenham. *'In 1801 the Bibury club races were run over the Burford Course, from this they were removed from Cheltenham and in 1831 to Stockbridge'* [17]

The Bibury Club was one of the most exclusive racing clubs of the day, formed from the wealthiest patrons and owners within horse racing, the membership was very select and by invitation only. Members included the most powerful and influential aristocrats and statesmen of the time including Lord Palmerston, the Prince of Wales and the Duke of Wellington. All the horses ridden in Bibury Club races had to belong to members of the Club and were also only ridden by members of the Club. The weights for the races were never under 10 stone and no professional riders were allowed. The prizes and events varied but all consisted of 3 days of events. *"Racing Stakes of 25 sovs with 50 added by the club over a mile and half, 25 sovs each with 100 added by the club if three horses start last for mile and half"* [18]

It is worth noting at this point that the Day family was a well-established and respected eighteenth century family of trainers. Charles Day, John's uncle, was based at Barrows Brook Farm [19] and like his father he trained and

14 http://www.racenewsonline.co.uk 2002.
15 William Gifford, Sir John Taylor, The Quarterly Review, John Murray, London Vol. XLIXX April and July 1833, p.435
16.Sporting Review Carleton, 1869
17 James Christy White. *History of the British Turf from the Earliest Period to the Present Day.* Henry Colburn London. 1840 p.244
18 James Christy Whyte., *History of the British Turf,* 1840 p. 245
19 E.A Weatherby, *The Racing Calendar* "At C. Days Barrows Brook near Cirencester, Petworth and 3g and 5s grass and accommodation for Mares on usual terms" 1806, p. 412

bred racehorses well into the 1830's. I also have no doubt he continued to be Clerk with the Bibury Club up until their move to Stockbridge in 1831.

John Day had been provided with the best start possible for a career in horse racing and it was here with his uncle Charles that his skills in the training and breeding of horses would be learnt. I am sure that his exposure to members of the early Bibury Club would have allowed him access to some of the most powerful owners and breeders in horse racing at that time.

John Day was married in Stockbridge on 27th December 1790 to Miss Anne Barham. [20] The marriage record refers to him as living at Crawley which is a small village next to Stockbridge and close to the racing scene that was at Winchester. The popular Maddington Club was run in Winchester on Worthy Down. Anne Barham's lineage has been almost impossible to trace due to the fact that there were two quite different families living in Stockbridge with the same name. It was always thought she descended from the Forster Barham's who were the Lords of Stockbridge Manor, but I could find minimal evidence for this. The other family consisted of Ann and James Barham who were the proprietors of the White Swan Inn in Stockbridge where John Day was living in 1796. James and Ann Barham were millers and farmers attached to a family of brewers. According to the Hampshire Chronicle an advert was placed Feb 1779 announcing that *"James and Ann Barham from the New Inn Sheary Well Broughton beg leave to inform the public and their friends in particular that they have taken that well known and capital Inn the White Swann in Stockbridge."* [21] We may allow the romantic notion that John Day moved into the public house as lodgings and fell in love with the landlord's daughter Anne Barham we will cover more of Anne's family as the story progresses.

John Day was based in Winchester Crawley in 1790 and was racing advisor to the Prince of Wales[22] later to become King George IV. It is likely that he was part of the Prince's racing entourage that was based near to Winchester at this time. The Prince Regent had a falling out with the Newmarket Racing establishment due to the Escape Affair of 1791, where he and his jockey Sam Chifney who was the finest in the land, stood, accused of cheating by the Jockey Club as Chifney was the marked favourite in a race

---

20HampshireRecordOfficeMarriageRecordRef:20m61PR5stockbridgem1754-1794
21 Hampshire Chronical 15th Feb 1779
22 Smith., Dictionary of National Biography second supplement, "John Day of Houghton Down Farm, Stockbridge, was racing adviser to the Prince of Wales, afterwards George IV" 1912, p. 484

of which he finished last. The very next day Chifney and Escape raced again and in this race were a few of the horses from the day before that had beaten Eclipse, but this time Eclipse thrashed the field. The Jockey Club Stewards cautiously approached the Prince to investigate why this had happened, on receiving the request for an investigation the Prince was outraged and considered the investigation as a slight against his name and his honour, and with this withdrew all of his horses from Newmarket and sold them and vowed to never race there again. The Jockey Club even tried to entice the Prince back there in 1805 but he was not interested.[23]

The Prince of Wales first attended the Stockbridge races in 1802, with his new trainer Frank Smallman, and had a new training establishment at Albury Grange near Winchester *"Sam and Small- man, that the Prince engaged the latter as his trainer and in 1802 again ranked among English turfites. His new training quarters were fixed at Albury Grange, near Winchester, and his stud consisted, hunters and all, of about sixteen."*[24] The Prince of Wales in contrast to the image of John Day referred to John Day as *"the jolly sort of fellow"* and as *"Lord Cinque Port"*[25] a title which the Prince promised to create for him when he became King, the occasion was a festive evening at Bath in 1799. The Prince appeared to like the fact that John Day could drink *"two more bottles of wine than anyone else, so says the diary of Mrs. Lybbe-Powys at that time"*[26]

John Day was also a renowned brandy drinker, and great entertainer of his wealthy patrons, a scene captured in a James Gilray picture of the Union Club in 1801 where John Day is featured asleep behind the Prince's chair.

23 Geoff Tiballs, *Great Sporting Scandals*, Robson Books London 2003
24 H.H.Dixon *Post and the Paddock with recollections of George IV, Sam Chifney and other Turf Celebrities*, Rogerson and Tuxford London Volume 1 1862, p. 88-89.
25 Lybb-Powys, *Passages from the Diary of Mrs. Phillip Lybb-Poweys of Hardwick House Oxon*, London, Longmans Green and Co. 1756-1808 p.326
26 Alfred. Day, Racehorse in Training 1925 p.180.

Figure 7 the Union Club 1801 by James Gillray

John Day had moved to Stockbridge to set up a training establishment of his own. It could be argued that he took some of the Prince of Wales's stud which was also managed in Kings Somborne, a few miles away by Colonel Leigh. In 1805 we find John Day in Brighton at the Chapel Royal as the report of the victory of Trafalgar service concludes with *"In the pew with his Royal Highness was Colonel Leigh and Mr. Day."* [27]

John was regularly about town with the Prince of Wales as further testified in the book Famous Racing Men. *"The Prince himself would make his appearance in the crowd. I think I see him now in a green jacket, a white hat, and light nankeen pantaloons and shoes, distinguished by his high-bred manner and handsome person. He was generally accompanied by the late Duke of Bedford, Lord Jersey, Charles Wyndham, Shelley, Brummell, and Mr. Day."* [28] William Day one of his grandson's even alluded to this by saying *"he was a roué, always about with George IV."* [26]

As well as attending to the Prince of Wales he was probably orchestrating the move of the popular Maddington Racing Club from Winchester, where he was based, to Stockbridge his new home.

---

27 John. Docwra. Parry *An Historical and Descriptive Account of the Coast of Sussex* London Longman and Co, 1833 p. 83
28 Thormamby Famous Racing Men (James Hogg London 1882, p.53-54)

MADDINGTON CLUB

THE MADDINGTON CLUB ALWAYS RACED AT Winchester Racecourse and had a long history there, running from 1754. The course was laid out on a two mile oval with a six furlong run. In 1805 the Club moved to the course at Stockbridge, close to the main road which is now the A30. [29] The Maddington Club became one of Stockbridge's first organized regular racing scenes. It consisted of a group of gentleman riders in agreement to race before a certain date, usually in May, over three days consisting of varied races for a prize of different amounts over an agreed distance[30]. For example a Match of 100 guineas over 2 miles called the Claret Stakes of 20 guineas per horse with 25 guineas added over 2 and quarter miles. Most of the riders were gentlemen or owners of the horses, this was the tradition up until 1815 when it changed and then professional jockeys or riders were allowed to represent the owners of the racehorses.

John Day had a vested interest in moving, or having the Maddington Club moved, from Winchester where it raced up until 1804 to Stockbridge in 1805. In that year Day took an additional lease on land in Houghton to run the Houghton Down Races and subsequently the Maddington Club. John Day who had recently set up his training yard at the White Hart Inn in Stockbridge guaranteed himself regular business in the training and selling of horses to a select set of notable worthy patrons by now ensuring they raced on his doorstep.

John Day was in Stockbridge prior to the 1798 formation of the Bibury Club, selling and training his horses from the White Hart Inn **Figure 8 White Hart Inn Stockbridge** This can be traced back to 1796, where he is listed as a subscriber in the Weatherby Racing Magazine, his place of abode is the White Hart Inn Stockbridge.[31] We can further substantiate this after review of the land tax records of 1800-1809 which show that John Day is renting the White Hart Inn from a Mr. John Barrett from 1798 until 1809 and paying 11 shillings in tax. [32]

The White Hart Inn is located at the start of the town of Stockbridge and for all intents and purposes was a 15th Century coaching inn in the days when the stagecoach ruled the roads. There is a substantial amount of

29 E. A. Weatherby *The Racing Calendar*, 1805 "First Day of racing is four horses, "Gentlemen Mr. Porter, Mr. Douglas, Mr. Blyndlots, Mr. Powlet"
30 (E. A. Weatherby *The Racing Calendar*, 1804)
31 (E. A. Wetherby *The Racing Calendar*, 1793-1795)
32 Hampshire Record Office Land Tax records Ltaq22/1/1/119

Figure 8 White Hart Inn Stockbridge

stabling close by and at the rear of the White Hart Inn for many horses. In the late eighteenth century the inns or taverns of the towns were where the horses were entered or registered in to a race; there is much evidence for this in early newspaper transcripts from the Stockbridge locality with premises such as the White Hart Inn, The Swan Inn, The Dukes Head and the Ship Inn as recorded by this 1784 transcript *"To be shewn and entered at Mr. Norman's, the Swan Inn at Stockbridge, on Saturday the 22d of July, between the hours of one and eight in the afternoon, paying three guineas entrance, and 5s to the Clerk of the Course, or double at the post."*[33]

We can see John Day racing his horses in both Stockbridge and Winchester starting on 1st July 1801. *"Mr Days Split Pigeon against Mr. Gibbons Filbert 8st 7lb each two miles 50 gns."*[34] We find John Day in 1802 advertising his horses for breeding in the Salisbury and Winchester journal 15th March 1802 *"Young Trumpator will cover at John Days Stockbridge at 2 Guineas a Mare and Half a Crown the Man, he was got by Lord Claremont's the Trumpator his Dam by Trumpator got out of a Herod Mare. Persons wishing to have their Mares covered are requested to send their names to John Day as the horse will not be permitted to cover unless 20 Mares are subscribed for, he will be at Stockbridge on the 1st April."*[35] It appears John Day's early business was a stud farm as he advertises horses to cover (mate) throughout the next decade.

The early business in Stockbridge was starting. In 1804 and 1805, the Land Tax records show Day renting a further establishment or land in Houghton Down Farm and paying 18 shillings Land Tax renting from a Mrs. Powell. As this was for only two years it could be argued this was for the moving of the Maddington Club from Winchester, as in 1806 he returned to renting

---

33 Salisbury and Winchester Journal, (Issue 12th July1784)
34 Salisbury and Winchester Journal, 29th June 1801
35 Salisbury and Winchester journal 15th March 1802

just the White Hart Inn. We can assume that the new course at Houghton Down had been laid out by then.

We know he was using the White Hart Inn for selling horses as can be seen in an early advertisement of 1807 *"To be seen a Chestnut Gelding seven years old by John Bull master of 16 stone a complete hunter and qualified for any stakes. To be seen and Particulars known by applying to Mr. John Day White Hart Stockbridge if by letter post-paid."* [36]

I have rescued from history a very early reference for John Day which shows him in 1804 running a horse with his son, who is said to be 14 years old. However, to my knowledge there was no son 14 years old in 1804 there was only one son of 11, *"the lad is to ride the pony is son of John Day Training Groom at Stockbridge, now in his 14th year and weighs no more than 42lb but straight made and well proportioned."* [37]

By 1806 John Day was both owner and trainer of horses and was racing these horses in his own name at the Stockbridge Races. His wins were recorded in the Hampshire Chronical of 1806[38], Day won a plate on July 9th 1806 worth 50 Pounds with a horse Peggy Rose, £50. in 1806 was an enormous amount of money close to £3,700 for one race in today's money. John Day was still racing horses elsewhere the same year in Newbury.[39]

Day had successfully set up his training establishment in Stockbridge and seduced a notable racing club, the Maddington, to his doorstep. It is evident from the increasing number of horses and the ever growing number of patrons that John and Anne Day would have required more land and a bigger establishment to exercise, house and train their horses. The business was growing, and very swiftly, as they had also established their own race meeting.

On the 25th September 1809 the Days took a lease on Houghton Down Farm close to Stockbridge I have included an account that I extracted from the original lease, the property package, inclusive of a farmhouse with 383 acres of land, that was previously in the Tenure, or leased possession of Mr. Thomas Gudgeon Esq. and a Mr. Joseph Tomkins Esq. of Bath. The lease agreement was for a period of 21 years for £383 per year, about one pound per acre to be paid quarterly with payments starting on 21st December 1809

---

36 Salisbury and Winchester journal 23rd March 1807
37 Bury and Norwich Post 19 December 1804
38 Hampshire Chronicle 14th July 1806
39 E. A. Weatherby, Racing Calendar 1806

Figure 9 Houghton Down House Courtesy Right move website 2015

then 25th March, 24th June and finally on 29th September. [40] Day had additionally moved the original Houghton Course slightly to the lower course in Houghton nearby to the A30. For this, the land tax paid by Day was 18 Shillings and 8 pence; [41] the last record of the Maddington holding meetings there at Stockbridge was in 1821.

John Day now had control of the Stockbridge races it was now his meeting of which he was also presiding Clerk. There is a funny account of John Day in regency England and his ability to find diplomacy in awkward situations even concerning a parson *"Mr. Day my daughter is in the stand, and there is a naughty lady there. Will you have her removed? Standing with his twenty stone figure erect, hardly daring to smile my great grand-parental hero an old roué'-of the spacious days of the Regency, placidly replied; A naughty lady! I have never seen such a thing in my life. Do show her to me."* [42] John Day continued to hold Houghton Down Farm up until his death in 1828. [43] Joseph Foster Barham purchased the property in 1824 and can be seen renewing the lease on the Houghton Down Stables, and extending it for a further 21 years in his name. Houghton Down seems to have digressed to Foster Barham's son John and then after his death through marriage to 4th Earl of Clarendon from where

40 Hampshire Record Office Lease of the Houghton Down Stables1809 Ref8m52/4
41 Hampshire Record office Land Tax records Ref Ltaq22/1/1/118
42 William Day and Alfred J Day, *The Racehorse in Training* London Cassel and Company, (1925, p.183)
43 Hampshire Record Office Renewal of Lease under Joseph Foster Barham 8th/11/1824 for the Houghton Down Stables 8M52/5

it was sold after his death in 1870 at auction.[44] The Day family was still in possession of the farm and residence after this. I have below included some early accounts from history of John Day's Houghton Down Stables at Stockbridge which paints a better picture of the stables. It shows an advert in the Winchester Journal highlighting horses, for sale there on 2nd November 1812.

"Capital Hunters and Brood Mare for Sale. ORMOND, a Brown Gelding, by Ormond, dam by Carbuncle, aged. A Grey Gelding, by Delpina, dam by Sir Peter, six years old. - Both temperate, steady, Hunters, and in good condition for immediate work. The Brood Mare by Revenge, out of a mare by Trumpator, in foal to Witchcraft. Apply for particulars to the Printers; or to Mr. J. Day, Houghton Down, near Stockbridge. Who will say where the above horses may be seen and tried?" [45]

"A few days ago Mr. Day's famous horse Witchcraft was shot, in consequence of his having received a kick from a mare, by which his leg was broken. A little time previous to this misfortune, Mr. Day had been offered 670 guineas for him." [46]

A further account from the Winchester journal of the famous horse Witchcraft which had to be shot explains how this led to Day losing 670 guineas, which was a lot of money from just a kick. It is likely that this bothered him immensely as Witchcraft was a very successful horse in many races, who was put to stud. I have included below some more of John Day's successes in 1812, this helps to establish the early stables and how they were functioning.

Witchcraft, in 1804, won 140gs. At Catterick, and a Produce Stakes of 650gs. At York.—He was sold at Doncaster, to Lord Viscount Sackville, and in 1805, he won 175gs. At Maddington, Ogns. At Bilmry, 50l. At Stockbridge, the King's Purses at Winchester stud Salisbury; also 50gs. And twice lOOgs. At Newmarket. In 180Ö, he won three times 200gs. At Newmarket, 150 gns. At Maddington, also 8Ogs. And 15gs. At Salisbury. In 1807, he won lOOgs. At Newmarket, and was sold to Mr. Martin.—in the same year, he \von 5CЙ. At Newbury, and twice 50l. At Blandford. In 1803, he won twice 50l. At Taunton, and the Gold Cup, value lOOgs. at Exeter.

44 Hampshire Record Office Sale Particulars of Houghton Down Estate 1870 4m92/n122/4
45 Salisbury & Winchester Journal, 1812
46 Salisbury & Winchester Journal, 1813

And in 1800, he won 50l. at Taunton; notwithstanding, be covered that season. He is now a Stallion at Houghton Down, near Stockbridge, Hampshire." [47]

"Stockbridge Races 1812 "A Sweepstakes of 5gs. each, with £25. added by the County Members, for all ages: Mr. Day's b.c. by Ebor, 4 yrs. Old." [48]
"The Ladies Plate of £50 for maiden horses: Mr. Day names Francoui, 4 yrs. old.
June 13th 1825, at Stockbridge Race's, on Thursday, the 50gs. Sweepstakes (6 subscribers) were run for as follows: Lord Palmerston's ch.c. Grey-leg (J.Day) Lord Grosvenor's Achilles" "Coronation Stakes 25 sovs. 3 subscribers Mr. Shard's b.c. Hougomont (J.Day), Mr.Wadham Wyndham's ch.c. by Granicus, Lord Grosvenor's Achilles." [49]

The next record in 1813 shows the hardships of the day endured by the apprentice jockey or stable lad, and to what lengths the trainer or master would go to ensure the jockey did not escape. I wonder if they ever caught the poor fellow and why he ran away initially, one minute working for John Day the next elevated to Lord Palmerston we shall never know.

"ABSCONDED, from the Service of Lord Palmerston, at Broadlands, near Romsey, Hants, on the evening of Wednesday the 17th of November instant, - WILLIAM HALL, Stable Helper, (late in the employ of Mr. Day, training groom, at Stockbridge), about 19 years of age, 5 feet 3 or 4 inches high, brown hair, fresh complexion, with little or no beard, hazel eyes, and of a light make. He carried away with him the following articles, the property of his fellow servants :- a Drab Livery Great Coat, with one cape and yellow gilt buttons, and the name of Brooks written on the inside of the sleeve; a blue strait single-breasted Groom's Coat with yellow buttons, a pair of light coloured Cord

Breeches, tanned Leather Gaiters, a pair of Shoes, two Waistcoats, and a new Hat. Six £1 Notes of the Bank of England, Two £3 Three £1 Notes ditto, marked T. Biggs on the back. Whoever will give information of the above offender, so that he may be brought to justice and convicted of the above offence, shall receive a Reward of TEN GUINEAS, by applying to Mr. Thomas Warne." [50]

John Day was recorded in history as being a famous trainer and one of the finest in the South of England. It is also said that he had more Horses in his stable than any other stable in the South of England.[55] Day additionally was a keen huntsman and bred not only horses but dogs as well *"Coursing and*

---

47 Sporting Magazine or Monthly Calendar of the Chase and Turf. (Volume 42. 1813, p. 58)
48 Salisbury & Winchester Journal, 1812
49 Salisbury & Winchester Journal, Monday 13th June 1825
50 Salisbury and Winchester journal Monday November 30th 1813

hunting the breeding of dogs raced, at the same place and price, got by Captain Lidderdale's Champion (and the last son of his get), out of Mr. Whitmarsh's famous bitch Darling, by White Par- son's Duke, out of Mr. John Day's (the trainer of Stockbridge) celebrated bitch Spite. Mr. Day sold her, after breeding the dam of Racer and of Mr. Coxe's Clio, &c., for 50gs." [51] The breeding of dogs was for coursing and hunting, he had a pack of hounds and a pack of harriers. The harriers became quite famous in the Stockbridge area, and he used to hunt with them. His first pack went on to become known as the Danebury Harriers, and the descendants of this pack eventually were sold and shipped to Austria, in 1861.[52] John Day's stables seemingly were known far and wide from an early point in horse racing history, as written by Tom Cross in his book "Autobiography of a Stage Coachman." [52]

The early stable of the Day Family boasted some very powerful and influential peers of the realm. One of these patrons was Henry John Temple Third Viscount Palmerston who was Prime Minister of England twice. In a time when the aristocracy were considered the ruling elite in England, and as a non-aristocrat, you would have to be careful of your manners or certainly your tone when in their company. However this did not seem to apply to John Day who was noted as able to approach anyone and almost talk with a free will. *"Old John Day was an immense favourite with his Lordship as he was with numerous other noblemen and was in short a privileged character, who could say anything to anybody."* [53] Most of the Day family rode for Lord Palmerston as referred to in 1861. *"His jockeys have been confined to the Day family; and as there is a feeling of pride in having ridden for so celebrated a "prime minister we may be excused enumerating them as John Barham Day, John Day, Alfred Day, William Day, and Walter Day.* [53]

LORD PALMERSTON

THE FIRST RECORDED TIME I HAVE found of the Day Family racing with Lord Palmerston was in 1810 *"As far back as 1810 we find him running at Winchester a filly called Mignonette by Sorcerer who was trained for him by Grandfather Day sire of Old John Day and Grandsire to John Day of Danebury who then resided at Houghton Down which was in an easy ride of Broadlands. With Mignonette old Mr. Day could do nothing for his lordship, but in the following year 1817 he won his maiden*

51Sporting Magazine, or monthly Calendar of the Turf and Chase and Every other diversion interesting to the man of pleasure, (Enterprise and Spirit London Volume 20 1827)

52 Thomas Cross *Autobiography of a stagecoach man* (Hurst and Blackett London Vol 1, p.202 1861)

53 The Penny Illustrated, (Oct 28th 1863)

Figure 10 Lord Palmerston by Francis Cruikshank

race for him with Enchantress a four year old mare likewise by Sorcerer; and in 1818 he paid his bill for him with a plate at the same place with her."[54] Day then went on to try with Mignonette for the Prime Minister around 1813, but could not win anything with him. The Days went on to train horses for Lord Palmerston for forty four years, right up until 1860 when John Barham died. He then transferred his horses to H.Goater at Littleton. During that time the Day family had provided him with victories one of which was Enchantress by Sorcerer in 1817, won 2.5 mile heats of a Maiden Plate at Basingstoke.

From the historical writings I have reviewed, the Day Family had a good relationship with Lord Palmerston. One example of this was when John Day was ill in his later years, suffering from gout; the Prime Minister would ride to Day's house, then at Houghton Down, and sit talking with him at his bedside about the horses and the politics of the time. *'Lord Palmerston has few seniors, inasmuch as he dates as far back as 1816, when we find him running at Winchester a filly called Mignonette, by Sorcerer, who was trained for him by Grandfather Day, sire of old John Day, and grandsire of John of Danebury, and who then resided at Oughton Down, which was within an easy ride of Broadlands. Grandfather Day—whose portrait taken in his greatcoat, on his pony, when he weighed over twenty stone, all visitors to Danebury -will recollect—was a quaint old man, and as perfect an original as Honest John himself. Straightforward in his conduct to his employers, his thorough knowledge of his business, and industrious habits, gained him the entire goodwill of the neighbourhood, and procured for him more horses than were to be found in any other stable in the south of England. With Lord Palmerston he was an especial favourite ; and often when suffering from the gout, to which he was a fearful martyr, would the kind-hearted Minister ride over, and sit by his bedside, discussing his horses, and making him acquainted with the topics of the day.'*[55] So Palmerston and John Day were more than just owner trainer, they were also friends.

Day's friendship with Palmerston was passed down to his son who can be seen from an incident that has been documented through many years. Now

---

54 The Penny Illustrated, (Oct 28th 1863).
55 Bailey Brothers *Baileys Magazine Of Sports And Past Times*, (1861,Vol II, p.230)

as then, the outcome is considered unheard of, both in the manner that it was approached and the time the question was asked and also the location. John Barham Day wished to secure a position for his son Henry as a Coroner, so instead of writing to Lord Palmerston, like everyone else would have to do, he boarded a carriage to the Houses of Parliament in London where he approached the House without expecting to be stopped, but stopped he was by a policeman.

"Wanting to see his Lordship for an appointment for a son whom he bought up in the medical profession he called in at Carlton House Terrace and was told his Lordship had gone to the House of Commons; There John forthwith proceeded and found his way into the corridor and was proceeding to pass the door when he was stopped by a policeman who asked him what he wanted, To his enquiry he replied, "I want to see Lord Palmerston, and I am John Day!" The policeman refused him admittance and told him Lord Palmerston could not be disturbed". It turns out Palmerston was in a heated discussion over the Irish question. This put John out terribly and he was more annoyed because he had got a crowd of people round him. However his patience was not long tried as the present Lord Strafford took compassion on him and see what he could do for him and passing him through the inner door, to the great astonishment of the policeman, and said to him Lord Palmerston would come to him in a few minutes. That he accordingly did, to John's great delight and after shaking hands with him most kindly, asked him what he had come to see him for. "Why Lord, I have got a son I have brought up as a doctor, and he wants an appointment to a poor law union in Hertfordshire; I have had him tried very high and he has won his trial very easy, and I am sure you will give it to him. "To be sure John" answered the kind hearted Premier."[56]

Many other humorous stories have come down to us from this friendship with the Prime Minister. From all accounts they would discuss politics as well as horses. There was a remark made by John Day to the Prime Minister, about not being paid for his training bills, *"Alluding to some employer who had removed his horses from him in a fit of disappointment at not winning a particular race, and left his bill unsettled, he observed, ' Huff and pay was bad enough, but huff and no pay was awful."* [57] An early account of the difficulty a trainer could be faced with for not delivering the goods. These recollections demonstrate the freedom of speech and expression John Day had with the aristocracy which was by all accounts unusual for the time. Another funny remark that was made by him to Lord Palmerston was recorded in 1861 *"On one of these occasions a remark he made to his Lordship, and frequently quoted by him, we shall reproduce, as the amusing truth conveyed in it cannot be gain- sayed.*

---

56 The Penny Illustrated, Oct 28th 1863
57 Bailey Brothers *Baileys Magazine Of Sports And Past Times*, (1861, Vol II, p.231)

Happening to be at Oughton Down when the Ministry were out, his Lordship informed him of the circumstance. ' Yes, my ' Lord,' replied the old man, ' but they tells I, as how you are the ' cleverest up there among them, for it does not signify which side ' goes out, you always manages to keep in." [57]

By 1825 at Salisbury he had won 4 races with three horses, the following year his only four horses won 21 races between them. It was Luzborough, one of his favourite horses who won most of those races. Lord Palmerston then went on to win in 1820 at Blandford, and again in 1823 he won the Queen's Plate at Salisbury with Biondetta. These were mostly small country races. In 1824, Palmerston is seen racing Luzborough, which he bought at Newmarket for 75 guineas out of a Tattersalls sale. This horse was considered a cast off, but John Day's keen eye knew different. *"The Somersetshire at Bath, The Hampshire at Winchester, The Oxfordshire at Oxford, and The Gold Cups at Salisbury and Winchester; and, in short, Luzborough and John Day at that time, in that part of the world, were as formidable as Fisherman and Wells." [57]*

Lord Palmerston and John Day managed to win many exclusive races together. John Day and Luzborough-(by Williamsons Ditto-Foxberry-Hougomont-Escape) were considered amazing. [58] There is a public house in Romsey Hampshire called the Luzborough just outside of Broadlands which was the home of Palmerston at that time; I am sure this pub was named after the horse. Luzborough was sold to Mr Dilly another trainer of the time for 600 Sovs.[57] Mr. Dilly then sold Luzborough to someone in Virginia, America. *"Mr. Editor I send you a short Memoir of the celebrated Racer and Stallion Luzborough, just imported from England in the Ship Equator and landed at city point Virginia on 29th August 1832."[59]* Day then purchased Grey Leg and Conquest, Grey Leg won 13 races with Conquest winning 9 with these horses Day was dominating the country meetings, *"With Greyleg and Conquest also he made great havoc at the country meetings on the circuit, and nothing could stand up against them." [60]* so it was looking good for the Houghton Down Stables and Lord Palmerston.

The image of John Day was that of a *"Bull Trainer" "sitting in his low crowned hat in his brown leggings on his pony Black Jack and with Lord Palmerston at his side, he was completely the model of the old Bull Trainer." [61]* He weighed 22 stone, now

---

58 H.H.Dixon, *Post and Paddock Hunting Edition*. Piper Stevenson and Co London,1856,p.132
59 J. S. Skinner *American Turf Register and Sporting Magazine*.,(Baltimore 1833, p. 273)
60 Baileys Magazine of Sports and Past Times, (Vol II 1860, p.231) "With Greyleg and Conquest also he made great havoc at the country meetings on the circuit, and nothing could stand up against them."
61 Henry Hall Dixon, *Scott and Seabright*, (Frederick Warne and Co, London,1862, p.41)

Figure 11 John Day of Houghton Down on his favourite Cob Black Jack (Harry Hill 1826)

that even by today's standards is no small size of a man, and certainly not one I could imagine on a horse. But I have read of one such instance where he raced Tom Goodison and the outcome was quite amusing.

"Tom Goodison carried the practice to an extreme. Tom suffered from it two or three times on the Heath, and more especially when Grandfather day who was Two and Twenty stone, and always the boy for a lark would, caught him upon the road after Exeter races, and Gammoned him to put on his cap and jacket, fasten his hack to the gig shaft, and ride it for leader for him into Davenport, the crowd which rolled up like a snowball to dee the great sight, frightened the hack by their cheers, and bolting into a shop window, it landed Tom Headforemost among a pile of shawls, he rode no more leaders to the day of his death" [62] John Day would gallop his horses all over, and his favourite gallop according to history was up Chattis Hill which according to history was overgrown with bushes and brambles.

John Day was named as Clerk of the Stockbridge Course for the years 1810, 1812, 1816, 1819, 1820 and 1821. Part of the Clerk's responsibility was to manage the appointment of the steward from the gentlemen class. I have a

---

62 Henry Hall Dixon, *Scott and Seabright*, (1862, p.29)

letter written by John Day on the 15th July 1821 requesting such from a Mr. George Pervois Jervoise from Heriard House Basingstoke. *"Sir as clerk of the course of Stockbridge know it is my duty to inform you that you were named to be Steward at the next races which will take place on the 2nd August, we hope you will be there but if you should be prevented I beg the favour of you to inform me and if you think proper to propose some Gentlemen in you place, I am Sir of Dutiful for John Day signed John Day 15th July 1821 Houghton Down."* [63] JP Jervoise politely declined the invite on grounds of ill health, and further named J.F.Barham in his place.

I stumbled upon an account of a stage coach man who visited Grandfather Day's house before 1820 he had a run in with the local hotelier and then invited him to Day's house to resolve the argument. *"He would find me at Mr. Days. "Let go my horse's head, sir," said I, addressing myself to the ostler; this the fellow instantly did, and, just touching him with the whip, we were soon under Mr. Day's hospitable roof, where I always had a hearty welcome. We had scarcely discussed a good evening's meal, at which I always substituted malt liquor for the lighter and more polite beverage—and my excellent host's home-brewed was of the best quality, and recommended itself strongly to my not very elevated taste—when the subject of our, or rather my, laughter came in. I saw instantly that he was another man; my coolness and self-possession had subdued him. Seeing me, too, a welcome guest at the house of his neighbour and friend, he found reason to alter his tone."* [64]

John Day shared his life with a great woman and she was in her time very remarkable in many ways, I feel it only fitting to include a piece on my great –great-great-great-grandmother and the wife of John Day of Houghton Down Anne Day.

---

63 Hampshire Record Office Letter from John Day Clerk of the Course 15th July 1821 to George Pervois Jervoise of Basing House Basingstoke
64Thomas Cross Autobiography of a stagecoach man (Vol II 1861, p.58)

ANNE DAY (NEE BARHAM) 1770-1844

Figure 12 Ann Day (Nee Barham) Abraham Cooper, R.A

"FEAR THY GOD, SPEAK EVIL OF NONE, STICK TO THE TRUTH, AND DON'T BE DONE"

ANNE DAY (NEE BARHAM) 1770-1844

THE NEXT PART OF THE STORY I have very recently uncovered. For so many years it remained stubbornly hidden but after many hours in the Hampshire Records Office at Winchester with red eyes and caffeine overload the story revealed itself.

Anne Barham was born to Ann and James Barham Esq. of Ashton, who also held the Manor and Mills of Kimbridge and lands and properties in Stockbridge, the Barham's were a very wealthy family of yeoman farmers, millers and brewers. James was the eldest son to John Barham Esq of Romsey whose other son Richard Barham Esq held Knowle Manor and Knowle Farm of 100 acres near Fareham before 1748.

The Barham family came from Titchfield owning and leasing vast areas of land such as Funtley estate in1697, [65] Knowle Farm in 1728, Little Funtley Farm and Mill in 1728, [66] the Manor of Ashton, and the Manor and Mill of Kimbridge in 1768 [70] with extensive land in Curdridge, all in and around Fareham and also land and a mill with a tavern in Nursling near Romsey. The records show that they had held those lands from the early 1600's passed from father to son.

Anne Barham's grandfather John Barham like his ancestors before him farmed the land for hops and barley to make beer. The Barham's also owned inns and taverns such as the Fox Inn located in North Street Gosport from1735, and the Blue Bell Tavern High Street Gosport up until 1776[67] The New Inn Sheary Well Broughton, The White Swan Stockbridge 1779, The White Hart in Stockbridge. A strange story exists from 1752, surrounding Anne's grandmother Sarah Barham and her grandfather the said John Barham, *"Whereas Sarah the wife of John Barham, brewer in Gosport Hants hath made the third elopement from her said husband, and is supposed to be harboured in the house of some Methodist, she being a follower of that set of people, and hath embezzled divers Goods and Stores, the property of her said Husband, this is to give notice to all persons not to give her credit, if they do they will never be paid; and whoever shall harbour the said Sarah Barham, will be prosecuted according to the full extent of the Law, I being willing to allow her a proper Maintenance, as witness my hand John Barham."* [68]

---

65 Hampshire Record Office 5M50/1881 Rents from John Barham for the Funtley Estate in 1697
66 Hampshire Record Office 5M53/1513 Counterpart Lease for 20 years of Farm and Lands called Knowle Farm and Little Funtley Farm Fareham 12/11/1728
67 Hampshire Record Office 26M95/5 Deeds to the Bell Tavern High Street Gosport 1776
68 Salisbury and Winchester Journal , Wiltshire England Monday 24th February 1752 p.57

John and Sarah Barham had two sons James and Richard Barham, James who was the eldest and my 5 times great grandfather married Ann Chandler on 24th June 1766 at Timsbury near Romsey[69]. Two years later on 4th May 1768 James had been assigned the Kimbridge Mills and the Dwelling House with additional land called the Sling Meads[70] and the Mill Meads paid for by an advance from his father. Not long after this, the happy couple had their first child, Sarah Barham, on the 24th October 1768 in Kimbridge named after James Barham's mother. James Barham then assigns the Kimbridge Mills and House with Sling Meads to John Barham Gentleman of Ashton, his father, on 1st August 1769[71] John then sells the mill on the 7th December 1772. *"To be sold by auction Friday 18th December 1772 at three o'clock in the afternoon at the Bell Inn Romsey. A convenient and well accustomed corn Mill having two water wheels three bolting wheels, and three pairs of French Stones, two of which are new and situate at Kimbridge (three miles from Romsey) being well tackled and repaired and never in want of water nor affected by floods, and capable of grinding twenty loads of wheat per week, together with a Dwelling House a new Stable for 5 Horses a Cart House and other buildings and nine acres of good water meadow adjoining (tithe free) and also an advantageous Eel Fishery which generally produces 16l per anum. The premises are held by Lease for three good lives now in being, under a yearly quit rent of fourteen pounds, and may be viewed any day before the sale, and a part thereof is remarkably well situated for a yard of coals deals and iron, The whole may be entered on immediately For further Particulars and condition of sale apply to Mr. John Barham the owner at Kimbridge Aforesaid or Mr. Daman of Romsey."*[72]

After this James and his young family appear to purchase the New Inn Sheary Well in Broughton *"James and Ann Barham from the New Inn Sheary Well Broughton beg leave to inform the public and their friends in particular that they have taken that well known and capital Inn the White Swann in Stockbridge."*[73] Anne Barham was born in Broughton around 1771 and baptized at Mottisfont 7th November 1775. By February 1779 the Barham family, with Anne who was 8 years old, have purchased the White Swan Inn Stockbridge the family own and live in Mulberry House at the top end of Stockbridge.

---

[69]Hampshire Genealogical Society *HAM 30014 Hampshire Baptisms-CD ROM Ref: HCD012,*
[70] Hampshire Record Office 4th May1768 27A01/B1/4/30 *Assignment of Kimbridge Mills with dwelling house and garden and a piece of ground called the Sling and meads called Mill Meads assigned by Richard Trodd of Michelmersh, yeoman, to James Barham of Michelmersh, yeoman*
[71] Hampshire Record Office 1st August 1769 27A01/B1/4/31 *Assignment of Kimbridge Mills with dwelling house and garden and a piece of ground called the Sling and meads called Mill Meads assigned by James Barham ofMichelmersh, yeoman, to John Barham of Ashton, yeoman*
[72] *Hampshire Chronicle* 17th December 1772
[73] *Hampshire Chronicle* 15th Feb 1779

Barham's father John Barham Esq of Romsey died, leaving three thousand six hundred pounds in his will, Appendix 9: Will of John Barham of Romsey Gent 1781 a substantial amount in 1781. There would have been more but as James, his eldest son and heir, had already been paid before his father's death according to the will it states that *'I give to my son James Barham the sum of one Guinea having already advanced for him as much as my circumstances would admit by indenture 25th day of November One Thousand Seven Hundred and Sixty Eight'.* [74] Perhaps James spent his money on Mulberry House in Stockbridge and the White Swan also in Stockbridge, as the assignment date for the houses and land is the same. James also had a brother, Richard Barham of Knowle Manor and Knowle Farm. By 29th January 1783 James Barham was selling all his effects at the Swan Inn Stockbridge and by 3rd February 1783 he had left[75].

James and his family had moved to the White Hart Inn at Stockbridge and devastation was about to strike the family as James was involved in a fire at a booth at Weyhill fair where he was selling hops on 15th October 1784. I will include a transcript from the local paper of the time, as the fire was quite substantial as reported at the time. *'It is with real concern we inform our readers that this fair concluded on Friday night with an event no less dreadful than unexpected; for about half past nine o'clock a large fire having been made with refuse hurdles, in the chimney of the White-Hart booth, kept by Mr. Barham of Stockbridge, the flames caught the roof, which was thatched, and in a few minutes the whole building and its contents were on fire: the flames almost instantly spread to the east and west, and in less than two hours reduced to ashes nearly the whole of the New Farnham Row, also to the number of nine booths up the fair; 540 feet of standing were burnt, and more than 300 bags of Farnham hops, also various goods and furniture, the property of people who kept the fair. The loss is not yet estimated, though it must amount to several thousand pounds. The fire was stopped by communication being cut off, and the amazing alacrity and spirit of the people. The wind was at first rather brisk, but providentially sunk soon after, else, as the fire was become so vast a body, that not even a plentiful supply of water (had there been any) could have prevented its ravages, everything upon the hill must have fallen a sacrifice. Such was the intenseness of the fire, that for some time it could not be approached within more than twenty yards, and flakes thereof fell as far distant as Fifield. The Crandall Hop Row escaped unhurt. There is no reason to suppose this fire was designed, as was reported on Saturday."* [76]

---

74 Hampshire Record office "Will of John Barham ESQ" 1781B/03
75 Salisbury & Winchester Journal, Monday January 27th 1783.
76 Salisbury and Winchester Journal 18th October 1784

Figure 13 Mulberry House Stockbridge High Street

The fire must have been a real blow to all concerned, the losses were staggering, but James recovered and carried on, there is however another entry in the local paper a few years later referring to the fire and goes some way to demonstrate the community spirit of the time, *"WE whose names are under-written, trustees for Thomas Pittard, William New, James Barham, and Sarah Simes, sufferers by the FIRE which happened the 15th October, 1784, at WEYHILL, think it necessary to inform the public, that from the severe losses sustained by the said fire, the Justices at Winchester Sessions were pleased to grant their certificate for a BRIEF; and that the Lord High Chancellor has been also pleased to direct Letters Patent for the same to be collected throughout England and Berwick upon Tweed, as also from house to house in the counties of Somerset, Dorset, Wilts, Hants, Surry, and Berks, from Lady-day 1786 to Lady-day 1787." [77]*

By 1790 James Barham Esq. and his wife Ann have retired, they are putting their feet up, their children are married off. As seen on a plan of Stockbridge held in the Winchester record office dated 1790 [78] they still own Mulberry House, a rather large house at the Longstock end of the Stockbridge High Street over the river. Additionally they own land and houses in Stockbridge, Titchfield, Wickham and Fareham. The Stockbridge houses they rent to a Mr. James Elton and Charles Leake and a Mr. John Grossman, near to the Grosvenor Hotel[78]. They hold the White Hart also at the opposite end of the High Street which is a coaching Inn. I have been waiting many years to say that but never found the evidence until now, it

---

77 Salisbury and Winchester Journal 9th April 1786
78 Hampshire Record Office "A Plan of the Borough of Stockbridge in the County of Southampton surveyed by Rich Randall Romsey Hants dated 1790" 1A03/1

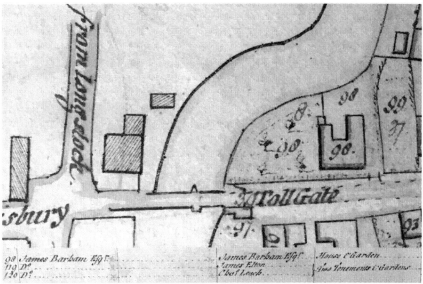

Figure 14 Stockbridge Borough Map 1790 kind permission Hampshire Record Office[78]
feels great to know the story.

John Day is about to get married to Anne Barham on the 27th December 1790 in old St Peter's Church in Stockbridge, with her sister Sarah Barham as witness. Anne Barham's family had a reputation for being far superior to John Day's family as noted in a book from that time. *'A Miss Barham came from a very good family at Stockbridge, as many would say to a much superior one to that of her husband.'* [79] It is evident that the finances for the early stables were provided from Anne's family. This marriage would form the partnership that would launch a dynasty of jockeys and trainers that would span for over two hundred years. The patronage formed by John Day would be of great benefit to their descendants. Anne was described as *"Grandmother Day, with her walking-stick and black crunch bonnet."*[80]

Anne Day had acquired the skills and education to embark on the future venture, the training of race horses. I feel she has been severely overlooked by modern historians because she was a woman. She was very much involved in the stables on a day to day basis and even bred horses of her own. Anne had also, somehow, acquired the skills of a surgeon, which had enabled her to tend to the horses and look after their health equivalent to a vet in a time when there were no female vets allowed. How remarkable she was. It is thought that she was one of the first women to publicly breed racehorses; in a time when this was very much a male dominated sport, as

---

79 Henry Corbett, *Tails and Traits of a Sporting Life*, (Rogerson and Tuxford London 1864, p.57)
80 Enrique Hall Dixon, *Scott and Seabright*, (Frederick Warne and Co, London and New York Second Edition, 1914)

published in 1831. There were only two women who were publicly breeding race horses (Lady Kent) Sophia Day and Anne Day. This has, to my knowledge never been celebrated in modern print until now, but I feel it is a fantastic achievement and deserves to be mentioned here it also shows how the stables were on the front line of the training of horses and inevitably not afraid to challenge the accepted status quo of the age. *"All the world knows that there are seven Days in the week, but it is not so notorious that seven Days are also to be found in the Racing "Calendar." There are Mrs. Day (Lady Sophia Kent and Mrs. Day are the only ladies who breed racers), old Charles Day, and young Charles Day, Isaac Day, John Day, Sam. Day and William Day! The Stockbridge folks have wisely selected the best Day of the seven (first and not the seventh), for "honest" John stands well with all ranks; he is a sober, steady, pains-taking body, and goes to church of a Sun-Day. He has done wonders towards bringing Stockbridge " to the fore," and deserves very great praise ; the " dear boy" (as he is termed by the jockeys), has not only made rich stakes, and erected a new stand, but has seduced many of the principal horses and their masters from Newmarket— but let the sport speak for itself."* [81]

Anne Day also performed all the training duties for the horses when her son John was away riding or attending races, it was also recorded that she mixed her own medicines for the horses as reported in 1840 by an American reporter visiting the family estate Danebury, Anne was by then in her seventieth year. *"One of the most remarkable characters of the age is the senior Mrs. Day, the worthy mother of the aforesaid John. Instigated by the best feelings of maternal affection, her only happiness appears to be centred in the welfare of her family; thus her daily occupations are devoted to their interests; and, although upwards of seventy years of age, she is more active than many women of thirty- five. Having been for many years accustomed to the training and management of horses, she would be unhappy if deprived of her daily attendance upon them. Her experience and judgment on all such occasions are superior to those of most men, and in the absence of her son she will give orders what work the horses are to perform, and direct the pace with unequivocal propriety. In cases of illness she is particularly clever, and she compounds all the medicines. The mares and foals come especially under her care, and her treatment of strangles is said to be particularly successful. Such an assistant is invaluable; for although servants may be employed, they cannot be expected to evince the same interest as so near a relative; neither are there many to be found who possess her judgment. The respect which her meritorious conduct ensures adds vastly to her authority, and she is one of the most entertaining companions that can be met with."* [82]

81 The New Sporting Magazine, May 1831, p. 206)
82 *American Turf Register And Sporting Magazine*, (1840 Vol 11, p.321)

And if all that wasn't enough, if women were allowed in the Royal Veterinary College then people of the time would have regarded her as its ablest member. *"Grandfather Day used to train at Houghton Down, where he was right ably assisted by his fine old Saxon Dame, who knew as much about condition and farriery (strangles was her great subject) put together, as the ablest member of the Royal Veterinary College."* [83] She must have been pretty good as they were still talking about veterinary skills 50 years after she had died in 1892. *"Grandmother Day mother to Old John Barham Day the rider of Crucifix in all her engagements was a better "vet" than any of the southern counties of England or the Metropolis could supply."* [84]

It goes some way to demonstrate her position within the racing world. Evidence shows that they were probably the first man and wife to form the first professional training stables. The combination of veterinary surgeon with professional trainer as man and wife under one roof was a bench mark of things to come and perhaps this was the first time this had been achieved in the racing world. Further testament to her ability can be seen below.

'I remember the late George Bentinck buying Defender of Mr. Isaac Sadler for 200 Guineas. On his arrival at Danebury his Lordship asked my Grandmother (Mrs. A Day to look at him; and she said he had a thorough pin, adding that he would never stand a preparation. On this startling and unwelcome announcement his Lordship immediately sent for that eminent veterinary surgeon the late Mr. Field who after examining the horse said he apprehended no danger, and that he thought the defect would yield to mild treatment; if not, that a section would effect a cure. This and many other remedies were tried but to no purpose and the horse never ran and was put to stud.' [85]

There are many other published sources of the time which cite Anne, written by respected authors of the time, I feel inclined to share one more as those writers from history are able to provide a more accurate account of her than me and providing further clarification of both the skills and the ability of the early Houghton Down stables, helping move the early Day family away from the realms of the amateur image they have been given and perhaps reframing them as the first professional in-house race horse training establishment in England. *"Grandmother Day too was well-known in the racing world as Crucifix herself, who's racing triumphs she was spared to see. She was equal to be Lady President of the Royal Veterinary College, and, in fact, I doubt whether the great Field himself would have cared to encounter her in an argument on ringbone. In*

---

83 H.H.Dixon, *Post and Paddock*, (1856, p.24-25)

84 Baileys Brothers Baileys Magazine Of Sports And Past Times, (vol.57 1892)

85 Day, A. D. W., *Racehorse in Training.* (1925, p.117.)

short she trained the horses and went regularly round to see if they were properly done up, so we cannot wonder that the children and grandchildren of such a rare old Saxon dame both train and ride so well." [86]

THE DAY FAMILY OF HOUGHTON DOWN FARM

John and Anne had eight sons and one daughter, most of whom would become successful in the horse racing business as stated by James Rice in 1879. *"The name of Day has been for many years been one of the best known on the turf, old Grandfather Day's numerous descendants having kept the family name well before the public. Alfred Day was the son of John Day who trained for the Dukes of Grafton and Portland; his uncle was that excellent horseman Sam Day: and the other uncles Charles and William were well known riders. Their mother old Mrs. Day had on one occasion seen four of her sons riding in one race. The next generation contained a Sam Day of great promise, who met with an accident; John Day who was as savage as if he was screwed on' and our William whose fame as a trainer eclipses his fame in the saddle."* [87]

John Barham Day (1793-1860) was the eldest and went on to become the successful trainer who we shall pick up on later. James Day, named after Anne's father (b. 1795), was apprenticed as a jockey to the Earl of Thanet and was to go on to ride exercise for Jem Robinson in Newmarket. He was also trained as a veterinary surgeon like his mother. He moved to Kenford in Devon and set up his own training establishment there in 1817 and placed an advert in the paper informing the public of the same *"James Day son of Mr. John Day of Stockbridge Hants begs leave to inform the Noblemen of Devon and the west of England that he has taken the extensive and convenient stables at Kenford near Exeter Racecourse upon Haldon that belonged to Henry Davis."* [88]

Ann Day the only daughter of John and Anne married Henry Scott, becoming Ann Scott Day, and moved to Ascot where Henry's father raced horses. Later the duo had a son Sam Scott who also became a trainer, first at Ascot and later at Danebury.

---

86 H.H.Dixon, *Post and the Paddock with recollections of George IV Sam Chifney and other Turf Celebrities,* (Rogerson and Tuxford, London 1862, p.24-25)

87 James Rice, *A History Of the British Turf,* (Sampson , Low Marston, Rivington London Vol 1 1879, p.271-272)

88 "Exeter Flying Post (20 March 1817)

Figure 15 Priam, Sam Day Up by Benjamin Marshall winner 1830Epsom Derby

Henry Day (1799-1861) became a solicitor as did Frederick Day (1813-1861). They both moved to Hertfordshire near to their uncle, Henry Gould Day, who was an Attorney at Wickham Market. Henry Day went on to succeed his uncle's practice in Wickham Market after his uncle's death in 1826 caused by a fall from a horse.[89]

Charles Day, John and Anne's fourth son, was also a jockey, and in 1831 moved to Russia to train the horses of Count Messeloff a famous and powerful Russian noble. The Russians had sent a Russian nobleman to England to purchase 100 horses there with the purpose of returning them to Russia to form the Russian Racing Stud some of the horses were *"the winner of the St Ledger 1829 Granby, bought for 355 Guineas, Red Rover winner Derby Stakes same year; Miss Chance winner of the Oaks 1830 and other good horses. The value of the 15 horses is not much less than 5,000 Guineas."* [90] Red Rover was indecently purchased by Sam's brother John Barham Day for Mr Etwell for more than 1000 Guineas Charles stayed in Russia for many years where he was married in St Petersburg 1854 to the Czarina of Russia's governess.

---

89 Bury and Norwich Post (20th September 1826)"We are requested to state that the business of the late Henry Gould Day of Wickham market Attorney at Law will be carried out at his offices as usual by his nephew and successor Mr. Henry Thomas Day"
90 *Fashionable World the Majesty's and Windsor* Emperor of Russia's racing Stud 1st June 1831

William Day 1803-1836 went to Ascot in 1830 to train horses at Sunningdale, and trained the first classic for the family in 1834 called Pussy (Pollio-Valve by Bob Booty) for Thomas Crosby. William died two years later in 1836 and Thomas 1809-1818 John and Anne's final son unfortunately died aged nine years old after drowning in Houghton Lake.

Samuel J Day or Sam Day (1801-1866) was trained as a jockey, and became quite a famous one at that. He started off riding for the Duke of St Albans in Barnett and then went to ride for Cooper for six years, trainer for the Duke of York at Newmarket.[91] Samuel also won the first recorded classic for the family in 1821 when he won the Derby on Gustavus, for John Hunter, and by all accounts beat the favourite by half a length named Reginald. Sam Day was considered a beautiful rider, with immense strength. Sam later went on to win the Derby again in 1830 for William Chifney on the famous horse Priam, Figure 15 bred by Sir John Shelly and won the Chifney's £12,000. I bet the Chifneys absolutely loved him. *"Sam Day took his pull, and waited with them to the Grand Stand, where the "narrow blue stripes" declined, and all Templeman's efforts on his chestnut could do nothing against Priam when he came in earnest." Two lengths " was the fiat, and the Chifneys won about £12,000, including the stakes."* [92] Priam was sent to Sam Day for schooling before being trained and sent out by the Chifneys[93].

Shortly after that win Sam Day retired to be a farmer it was reportedly his passion, but modern historians say that at the time he wasn't very good at farming so he returned to racing. He returned to racing in 1846 at the Danebury Stables because the Stewards of the Jockey Club had stopped John Day Junior from riding, due to the Crommelin affair which we shall cover in depth later, and the stables needed a jockey they could trust to honour their mounts.

So Sam was brought out of retirement and had to lose weight fast. He picked up the reins and had not lost his skill in the saddle, as he instantly returned to racing with his win at the 1846 Epsom Oaks with Mendicant-(Touch stone-Lady Moore Carew by Tramp) trained by his brother John Barham Day and owned by John Gully, beating 24 other horses in the race. Then he won for the Danebury stables the 1,000 Guineas with Mendicant. He did not stop there he brought a triple that year with another famous

---

91 H.H.Dixon, *Scott And Seabright*, 1862)
92 H.H.Dixon, Post and Paddock, (1856, p.160)
93 www.tbheritage.com/Portraits/Lottery.html accessed 9th October 2009 "Priam, who eventually reached 15.2 hands, was sent to Sam Day for schooling. He was immature at age two, and was not started in races until age three. "

Figure 16 Gustavus Epsom Derby 1821 Sam Day Jockey by Jean Louis Theodore Gericault

horse Pyrrhus the 1st-(Epirus-Fortress) who was also trained by his brother John Barham Day. He won the 1846 Derby, where there were 193 subscribers and 27 horses turned up to the start of the race, it ended between Sir Tatton Sykes, losing by a short distance, the stake money was £5,250[94] quite amazing winning 3 classics in one year and three Derbys during his lifetime. Samuel retired from horse racing that year for good. He went on to live until he was 65 and died in 1866.

I have a funny encounter to share regarding the early riding of Sam and his older brother John Barham Day 1793-1860 and an incident involving his younger brother Sam, in which they tried to turn up at a race and win all the money. Sneakily, it also shows how easy it was to be fooled in racing, and I bet the young lads learnt a lesson from it *"John had a wonderful little Brown Pony that he expected to clear out the Hampshire yokels, and he was so haunted by the fear of being got at, that he persuaded his brother Sam to get into a crate in the stable and watch her all the afternoon, the brothers preceded to the course, but it got buzzed about who they were and how high they had tried their pony. A country lad came out in an apron, "I run my old pony out of a cart there against you" "Who are you sir may I ask? "Said john drawing himself up with native dignity; "Put down your Ten Pounds and then I'll see about it" the money came out and John began to smell a rat but there was no*

---

94 George Tattersall *The Pictorial Gallery Of The English Racehorse*, (Henry G Bohn, London 1850)

Figure 17 Chapeau d Espinage Winner 1000 Guineas 1837 Venison and the Day Family 1838 by Abraham Cooper The race horse in Training Page 53

retreating. When the Danebury Pony had been beaten by some twenty yards, John learnt he had been matching her against Gulliver, whose fame was in all the West Country." [95]

There exists an oil painting produced by Abraham Cooper in 1838 showing the Day Family on Danebury Downs Figure 17 Chapeau d Espinage Winner 1000 Guineas 1837 **Venison and the Day Family 1838 by Abraham Cooper The race horse in Training Page 53**It is considered to be the finest work of Abraham Cooper, and goes someway to demonstrate the success and power of the Day family in racing at this time. Cavendish Bentinck ordered the painting as a gift with the wish that it was passed on to the next eldest son. *"The most successful picture was one of a family picture painted by order of Lord George Bentinck who presented it to the late John Day with the understanding that it was to descend to his eldest son, in this group John stands in his Great Coat by the side of the mule Phaeton by which are seated his wife and his mother, while his son Sam is mounted on the game Venison and his son William on Chapeau d Espinage" by Abraham Cooper 1838, Exhibited in the Great Exhibition of 185.* [96]

The jockeys and trainers produced by John and Anne Day won 32 English Classic races. The stables created by Grandfather Day and Anne Barham at Houghton Down were now booming; they had attracted many notable patrons of the turf and were winning a lot of great races. On 20th March 1828 John Day died from a heart attack aged 61 years. I have captured an announcement from the time *"At Houghton Down near Stockbridge Hants John*

95 H.H.Dixon, *Scott And Seabright*, (1862, p.40)
96 The Sporting review edition ed by Craven Rogerson and Tuxford 1869 p.139

Day the Celebrated Trainer In a few hours after his attack his son observing he had seen him much worse, John immediately said I bet you 50 to 1 I don't last 24 hours he died in 19 hours after his taking ill."[97] He left the family in an excellent condition and his will was drawn up and signed on the 2nd of April 1825. He left his estate in its entirety to his wife Anne Day, in trust that she should invest the estate and effects in Government stock with the dividends and interest being paid to her annually until her children turn 21. Anne took an advertisement out in the papers requesting all debts to be paid to her and any claims on the estate to be settled. [98]They left a poem in the paper of the time to his memory, *"Oh day and night, but this is wondrous strange......Shakespeare, What two Days gone at once, Why Thirsty Death, and so Scottish Grown to drink up old Johns Breath."*[99] The poem goes on; it is interesting and funny that even in his death they sing about his drinking.

John Day and Anne Barham had established their own race-course and race meeting. Also, their partnership had established one of, if not the first professional racing stables in the South of England. The combination of the veterinary surgeon's skills of Grandmother Day and the horsemanship and connections of Grandfather Day, along with the business sense of them both, is what allowed the racing establishment at Stockbridge to flourish. They were involved in the breeding and training of some of the very early English pedigree horses, that would go on to make up the British Thoroughbred Horse Bloodstock we see today, and nothing could stand up to them. They were the first, family of professional trainers, which combined both husband and wife.

Prior to the Day family's arrival in Stockbridge there was minimal attendance by the aristocracy or landed gentry. The prize money was also very low at the Stockbridge races, partly due to the lack of attendance. The Day Family had brought the party to town and made the races at Stockbridge explode into life. The most noted of John and Anne's sons and the person who really took the horse racing at Stockbridge to the next level was their eldest son John Barham Day, inheriting the name of his mother when he turned 21 as part of a will endowment. We will look at the life and times of John Barham Day quite heavily in the next chapter.

---

97 The Newcastle Magazine 1828
98 Hampshire Chronicle 19th May 1828
99 Berkshire Chronicle 4th October 1828

John Barham Day (Honest John)

Figure 18 John Barham Day 1848 (from a miniature)

1793-1860

Won 16 Classics as a Jockey
Won 7 Classics as a Trainer
Own Colours Black Jacket Orange Cap

CLASSICS WON AS JOCKEY AND TRAINER

TABLE 1 CLASSIC RACES WON AS A JOCKEY

John Barham	Horse	Year	Owner
2,000 guineas	Grey Monmus	1838	Lord George Bentinck
	Dervise	1826	4th Duke Of Grafton
	Crucifix	1840	Lord George Bentinck
	Ralph	1841	Lord Albemarle
1,000 guineas	Problem	1826	4th Duke Of Grafton
	May-Day	1834	9th Baron Berners
	Destiny	1836	T Houldsworth
	Chapeau D Espagne	1837	Lord George Bentinck
	Crucifix	1840	Lord George Bentinck
Epsom Oaks	Turquoise	1828	4th Duke Of Grafton
	Oxygen	1831	4th Duke Of Grafton
	Pussy	1834	Thomas Cosby
	Deception	1839	Fulwar Craven
	Crucifix	1840	Lord George Bentinck
Epsom Derby			
St Ledger Stakes	Chorister	1831	Duke Of Cleveland
	Elis	1836	Lord George Bentinck

TABLE 2 CLASSIC RACES WON AS A TRAINER

John Barham	Horse	Year	Owner
2,000 guineas	Grey Monmus	1838	Lord George Bentinck
	Crucifix	1840	Lord George Bentinck
	Ugly Buck	1844	John Braham Day
1,000 guineas	Destiny	1836	T Houldsworth
	Chapeau D Espagne	1837	Lord George Bentinck
	Crucifix	1840	Lord George Bentinck
	Mendicant	1846	John Gully
	Virago	1854	Henry Padwick
Epsom Oaks	Crucifix	1840	Lord George Bentinck
	Pussy	1834	Thomas Cosby
	Mendicant	1846	John Gully
Epsom Derby	Pyrrhus The 1st	1846	John Gully
St Ledger Stakes			

EARLY LIFE

JOHN BARHAM DAY WAS CHRISTENED AT Stockbridge on 27th October 1793 and was first son to John and Anne Day and my great-great – great-grandfather. Horsemanship was in his blood and his father had already set a predetermined course for this eldest son, he was to continue the work of his father in building a reputable stable at Houghton. Immediately after his father's death he had formed a partnership with his brother, William. They would work together as trainers and stable keepers at Houghton Down Stables.[100] However, the partnership did not last long and from all accounts they had a falling out as William went to Ascot and John went on his own at Danebury.

John Barham Day served his apprenticeship with Frank Smallman, trainer to the Prince of Wales (later King George IV) and grandfather to the most famous of jockeys of the time Sam Chifney. Whilst there John Barham Day earnt 10 guineas a year as salary complete with two suits of livery[101].

One of John Barham Day's first mounts was for the Prince of Wales to which his father was racing advisor. *"One of his first engagements "out" was encouraging enough. It was with no less a personage than His Majesty King George the Fourth, at that time Prince of Wales, for whom he rode light weights. The King, indeed, never forgot him, and only two years before the Royal George's decease that is in 1828, John had the honour of riding his favourite mare, Maria, for the Somersetshire, at Bath."* [102] By all accounts John rode lightweights for the Prince then.

John Barham Day was a strict Protestant like his father and mother, with the latter more so. One time he was recorded as having sent a letter to Lord Palmerston the then Prime Minister about the Prime Minister's duty regarding religion, *"With the upper classes he was always an immense favourite, Lord Derby being as fond of him as Lord Palmerstone, and the former was not little amused at the receipt of a message from him, "with his duty he hoped he would not give the Catholics any more privileges", for John was a true Protestant."*[103]Palmerston was not amused but John managed to get away with these comments with everyone.

---

100 The Law Advertiser, Vol VIII, (J. W. Paget, 1830)
101 H.H.Dixon *Scott And Seabright*, 1862, p. 40
102 Henry Corbett, *Tails and Traits of a Sporting Life*, (Rogerson and Tuxford London 1864, p.58)
103 Baileys Brothers *Baileys Magazine Of Sports And Past Times*, (1860, p.232)

Figure 19 Three Cups Inn Held by Michael Goddard by thethreecups.co.uk

By all accounts John was educated privately like some of the children were by their uncle Henry Thomas Day LL.D who was rector of Mendlesham along with their cousin the Reverend Russel Day who was a master at Eton.

On 23rd April 1814 John Barham Day, aged 21, married his sweetheart Harriet Goddard (1794-1846) who was the daughter of Michael Goddard an attorney of Stockbridge and he owned the Three Cups Inn at Stockbridge it had been in the Goddard's family since the 18th century with Hugh Goddard. The Goddard family were also involved in the local race scene at Stockbridge and bred race horses from the rear of the Three Cups where they held an acre or two. Mr. Goddard raced many horses at Stockbridge and, according to the Racing Calendars, Sam Day[104] Johns brother was his jockey, so I think it could be fair to say the Goddard family were patrons of Houghton Down Stable. Harriet's family was also connected to Woodyates in Dorset where John Barham Day later in life would set up son William at Alverdistan. Harriet was 20 years old when she married at St Peter's Church in Stockbridge her father Michael was witness, as recalled by one writer the groom was married in a stable jacket, *"He had one boast- a very proud one for a man who has reached his double eminence- that he was married in a stable jacket, and that for two years after he did not treat himself to a bottle of wine or sturtout."* [105]

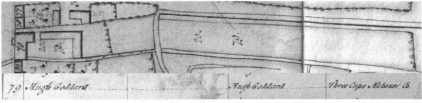

Figure 20 Three Cups Inn Borough of Stockbridge Plan 1790 kind permission of the Hampshire Record Office

104 E. J. Weatherby, *The Racing Calendar* 1823 vol.51 page 81
105 H.H.Dixon, *Silk And Scarlett*, (Frederick Warne And Co, London, 1859, p.117)

John's father was very much against the union of John Barham and Harriet, for what reason we shall probably never know. However, some old sources indicate it was because his father didn't want to lose his son's services from the Houghton Down stable where he was champion jockey. At one point his father even offered him £500.00 pounds to break off the engagement, a fantastic sum of money in 1814, but all of this was to no avail as he married Harriet anyway. *' Never was there a better,' was his remark to us one day, when speaking of her; ' in fact she was the very best I ' ever knew in my life,' although to her successor's virtues he paid every credit. His father knowing he should lose the value of his services resolutely opposed the match, as a Lincoln's Inn solicitor would do that of a ward with an Irish adventurer. But all to no purpose ; and although five hundred pounds—a perfectly fabulous sum to him in those times—was offered him to break off the engagement, he would run it off, and with a ten-pound note of his own earning, and in a stable jacket, he began the battle of life, which he fought as long and earnestly as Lord Eldon did, when he brought his wife to a garret in Chancery Lane, and could afford her no better meal than a mutton-chop."* [106] Good for him, sounds like a bit of a romantic.

So John Barham Day had left the comfort of his family home in Stockbridge, aged 22 years, for his wife Harriet. He had next to nothing to support her with apart from a ten pound note, he then goes on to say, *"For two years I never had a coat to my back or a glass of wine in my house."* [106] This never seemed to stop him, and this early story of their union goes on to lament. *"with a wife on his hand and the prospect of a family to support, he was not the man to let the grass grow under his feet, he wasted hard, worked hard, saved all he could, and within twelve months had the satisfaction of putting beyond all doubt that he was able to maintain his position and keep himself independent."* [106] He had managed to obtain the best credentials for his future career from his father who was racing advisor to George IV and by also being apprenticed to George IV's trainer.

John Barham Day and Harriet had their first child on 18th January 1815 and called him John, a tradition of the Days to call the first born by this name which has not done me any favours in the researching of this book. This child John Day Junior later in life inherited the stables and Danebury, as you will see. John and Harriet had a further 7 children making 8 in total, John 1815-1882 who became the famous trainer at Danebury, Harriet 1816-1893, Elizabeth, 1821-1862, Henry,1826-1883 who went on to become Coroner for Hertfordshire, Hope, 1828-1894, Edward, 1831-1884, Anne,1835-1929, Emma, 1836. Poor Harriet must have been so tired, like many of the wives of big families in those days.

---

106 Bailey Brothers, *Baileys Magazine of Sports and Past Times*, (Vol 1 1860, p.229)

Figure 21: Mango, Sam Day Up Won St Ledger 1837 by Frederick Herring Senior

John Barham had 4 sons who would be jockeys and all of them brought home Classic race wins. One of these was Samuel Goddard Day, who won the St Leger in 1836 on Mango-(Emilius-Mustard by Merlin), who was bred by Mr. Thornhill and purchased by C.C.Greville, trained by William Chifney & Montgomery Dilly. Samuel Goddard Day was the youngest jockey at 18 years to ever win this race. He had such a promising career ahead of him but died two years later, on 14th March 1838, when he was out hunting with hounds with Sir John Barker Mills and fell with the horse then coming down on him, he died shortly after. *"The celebrated young jockey, Sam Day, second son of Mr. John Day of Danebury, whilst riding with Sir John Mill's hounds (March 14th) had a very severe fall, his horse falling on his chest. He was removed to the house of his brother in law Mr. William Sadler, near Stockbridge, where he lingered till he died. By his conduct and skill he had acquired the respect of all gentlemen connected with the turf. He was the youngest jockey that ever won the Leger. Mr. Charles A.day Bevois Hill Southampton Hambleton races may 5th 1829 was a noted member and supporter of the Hambleton Hunt from 1829 to 1849. On his grave stone can be read the following "Till Pity Wept over his untimely grave, whose gentle manners sorrow never gave, whose life was love and G sincere, a youth of much simplicity lies here."*[107]

---

107 AESOP, Sporting reminiscences Of Hampshire 1745-1862, (Chapman and Hall, London 1864,p.221-222)

Figure 22 Jockeys by Anson Ambrose 1830 Guinness Book Great Jockeys of the Flat

Alfred Day, 1830-1868 was amazing, just like the rest of them, and stayed as a jockey throughout. He won first in 1847 the 2,000 Guineas on Conyngham-(Slaine-daughter of whisker) for Sir R Piggott. He then won, in 1849 the 1,000 Guineas on Flea-(Coronation-Puce) for Mr. F.Clarke. Next, in 1850, he won the 2,000 Guineas on Pittsford-(Epirus-Miss Horwood) for Harry Hill the bookie. Again in 1852, won the 1,000 Guineas on Kate-(Auckland-Gypsy Queen) for Mr. J Sergeant. His next classic, trained by John Day Junior, won a double in 1854 the 2,000 Guineas on that famous horse Hermit-(Bay Middleton-Jenny Lind). Continuing on to then win the 1854 Derby on Andover (Bay Middleton-Daughter of Defence) winning both races for John Gully. In 1856 Alfred won the Epsom Oaks on Mince Pie-(Sweet Meat-Foinnuallia by Birdcatcher) for Harry Hill, and finally took his last classic, the 2,000 Guineas in 1859 on the Promised Land-(Jericho-Glee) trained by William Day, his brother, and owned by James Merry. Alfred retired after that and died in 1868. William Henry Day 1823-1908, was never meant for the saddle "due to weight," as his father said. Therefore he answered to the trainers' calling and his father John Barham Day set William up as a trainer at a stable called Woodyates in Wiltshire. We will see later on in the story why William left Danebury and split up from his family as there is much more to the story than has been told. William won first as a trainer in 1855: the 2,000 Guineas with Lord of the Isle-(Touchstone-Fair Helen) for Mr. James Merry. Next he won in 1859 with the Promised Land-(Jericho-Glee) the 2,000 Guineas, and his final classic

Figure 23 John Barham Day Black Cotton Umbrella Cartoon

victory as trainer came in the Epsom Oaks of 1869 with Brigantine-(Buccaneer-Lady McDonald by Touchstone) for Sir Frederick Johnstone.

It is worth pausing for breath at this point to reflect that this is the third generation of jockeys and trainers to carry the name of Day. This generation, born to John Barham Day and Harriet, won a combined total of 26 English Classics as jockeys and trainers, an amazing number of wins. Between the years of 1820-1869 the Day family of Stockbridge won a combined record of 58 English Classics. They truly dominated this sport. This includes all the family that won classics and also helps to build a sort of chronology, as I know many other writers have had trouble placing the jockeys and trainers of the Day family and which generation they belong to due to the repetition of names.

John Barham Day's life as a jockey must have been extremely difficult, and according to history *"His early life was one of no common toil, and he had often to ride from racecourse to racecourse on his ponies, with his saddle bags in front, nearly 100 miles a day."*[108] He would ride on his father's horses for small fees, this was an amazing feat, I find it difficult to travel 100 miles a day in a car but cannot imagine traveling the same distance on a horse.

John Barham Day was reputed to have always dressed in black and carried a small black cotton umbrella regardless of the weather **Figure 23 John Barham Day Black Cotton Umbrella Cartoon**It was said he looked more like someone from the clergy than a jockey.[109] He was a member of the Protestant Church with a strong belief, and installed the same discipline in all the stable lads and the jockeys too. *"Whatever the nefarious activities in which he might have been engaged in the week, he attended church every Sunday, making his presence felt by beginning the response in his deep sepulchral voice long after the rest of the congregation had finished."* [110]

---

108 H.H.Dixon, Silk and Scarlett, (1859, p.116)

109 James Rice, History Of The British Turf, (1879, p.277) He married young, and much against his father's wishes, whose opposition appears to have been based solely on the knowledge that if his son got married his services would be lost to the stable. The son, however, was resolute. In his stable suit, and with ten pounds and a wife, he began the world for himself'

110 Roger Mortimer, Richard Onslow, Peter Willet, *Biographical Encyclopaedia of British Flat*

He was quite famously known on every Sunday to compel the stable lads attend church not once but twice in a day. *"After this they were assembled in John's dining room at Danebury, where he read to them Blair's Sermons, and holding a menacing silver handled horse whip. With his round hat scarlet coat and massive silver handled whip (Which John Day rigidly preserves as his staff of office) He made up admirably as Clerk of the course at the Stockbridge meeting."* [111]He would use the whip for any that would fall asleep. Like his father and his great uncle, John was the Clerk of the Stockbridge course and Bibury Club, a position his son would go on to undertake as well.[112]

He was known to exclaim "Beggar my Limbs" when surprised, and it was also said that he wore a serious look on his face without the hint of any well doing, even after winning a race. This was a trend also renowned in the Cannon family; even to this day we can see this in Lester Piggott and a natural trend amongst all the other jockeys from this family to wear a poker face and never to give anything away. Also unfortunately for me and history, they never wrote anything down.

John Barham Day managed to acquire the nickname of Honest John *"A good name is as a precious ointment," and by uniform correct conduct in the saddle, as well as in the stable, John Day — a very celebrated jockey — has acquired that of "honest John." The endowments of nature are not always hereditary, and well for our hero that they are not, for he is the son of a man who weighed twenty stone, whereas he himself can ride seven!"*[113], we have already addressed the spin that modern historians have placed on his name in the start of the book it was clearly given for his good conduct.by Lord George Cavendish Bentinck, in the early part of their relationship. *"John Porter Began his career at Danebury under the rule of John Day or as Lord George Bentinck named him "Honest John"* [114] We will pick up on this later in the story. By 1820 John Day was riding the Prince Regent's horses, to which his father was racing advisor. By this time the family were attracting some powerful patrons, and building on their good name as we have already seen in the previous chapter.

Racing, (MacDonald and James 1978)

111 H.H.Dixon, *Scott And Seabright*, (1862, p.43)

112 Newmarket(pseud), *Chapters From Turf History*,(The National Review Office 1922, p.62)

113 Nimrod (pseud), *the Chace the Turf and the Road*, (John Murray London 1850, p.151)

114 Thormamby(Pseud), Kings of the Turf Members Owners and Distinguished Backers, Owners, Trainers And Jockeys, Hutchinson London, 1898)

John Barham Day had a very good weight at seven stone that he managed to keep until the end of his riding career of 25 years. He was also reputed to have ridden with an arch in his back which stopped him from being a great jockey, because it prevented him from exerting a strong finish. He is recorded in the racing calendar of 1823 as a jockey, and we can find him riding in local papers from as early as 1804 for his father John Day Senior. One such local event was in 1809, the Hunt Cup at Winchester the celebrating of these events were really quite important and fashionable. *"Some of the first jockeys were up on the occasion, including John and Sam Day, Dockery, &c. In the evening there was a splendid ball at the White Hart, attended by all the fashion of the neighbourhood."* [115]

John Day managed to acquire the patronage of the 4th Duke of Grafton and was riding against rivals such as the very famous Frank Buckle and all the other great jockeys at Newmarket. One minute Day was a small unknown jockey and the next he was winning the major races. Samuel Day, John's brother, had already won the Derby on Gustavus in 1821, and again in 1830 on Priam. John Barham Day was soon to follow by winning a double Classic on Dervise – (Merlin - Pawn Junior-Pawn by Waxy) in the 2,000 Guineas see pic and Problem-(Merlin Pawn-Prunella by Trumpeter) in the One Thousand Guineas in 1826 for his new Patron the Duke of Grafton, who paid him £20.00, *"After john had won the Two Thousand and One Thousand Guineas for the Duke of Grafton, his grace sent for him. In John's own words, "I came to the door with my hat in my hand. "Come in, John Day" So I did, and stood on the mat. "John Day I'm going to make you a present for the manner in which you have ridden my horses this week. I am about to give you £20 in bank notes of Messrs.......bank at Bury St Edmunds-most highly respectable bankers." "Thank you my Lord, for your great kindness." It was a great present in those times. After that I got £500 for winning one race."* [116] And this created quite a storm in the racing profession. That is a very nice sum of money to be earned by a new jockey, and especially against such accomplished jockeys as Frank Buckle who is described by John in the following quote. *"If you threw him up in the air in any part of the country he would be certain to fall on a horse at the post."* [117]

Day succeeded Frank Buckle as main jockey to the Dukes of Grafton and then started to earn good money. It was noted that at the time jockeys were accustomed to receiving small presents from the trainers or even the owners of the horses when they did well, but this did not always happen.

---

115 AESOP, Sporting reminiscences Of Hampshire 1745-1862, (1864 p.108-109)
116 Mortimer, Onslow, Willet, Biographical Encyclopaedia of British Flat Racing, 1978
117 H.H.Dixon, *Scott and Sebright*, p.26

Figure: Houghton Down Farm

However, Day was one of the first people, if not the very first, to set the precedent for all jockeys to receive money for winning on horses. Tom Cannon, John's granddaughter's husband, would up the ante at Danebury in later years in the same way, for a wage. Early in his career John was shown to be making twenty pounds on some races, given by the Duke of Grafton. However, as his success grew with the Duke so did his wages, before long he was receiving wages of £500 per race, [116] a considerable amount in those days. We have records within the family and at Winchester for riding and training receipts from Sir John Barker Mills dated 1835 which illustrates his charge for riding and training fees was £182.6shillings 4d and by 1856 there is a record of £221.10shillings 4d.[118]

So far the Houghton Down stables were on an ever increasing climb with more money coming in from wins for rich aristocrats and patrons. At this point the stables patrons included such members as Lord Palmerston, Dukes of Grafton, Sir lewyn Glen, Lord Sligo, Lord Glenlyon, Mr. Pyrse of Aberystwyth, Ralph Etwell MP, Sir John Barker Mills for which the family hold some training receipts. It might be beneficial to remind the reader that the patrons of the stables at this point were also the members of the Bibury Club, which we will cover later in more detail.

As already stated, John Barham Day's break up with his father was due to him marrying against his father's wishes but love seemed the stronger

---

118 Hampshire Record Office Race Horse Training Bill for Sir John Barker Mills from John Day Danebury 1856 4M92/N4/18

John Barham Day by Harry Hill Detail

course. Also maybe he was tired of riding all the way just to be a jockey, because at this time it looks like his father had given up racing horses, as from the Deeds of Houghton Down Stables. It can be seen in 1824 Joseph Foster Barham, MP and member of the Bibury Club, purchased the lease on Houghton Down Farm[119,] John Day had already held the lease for 21 years from 1809, and he was still running his stables.

By 1828 John Barham Day was Royal Jockey to King George IV who the family were already acquainted with and his father was a close associate of in the days when the King was Prince of Wales and Regent. John won on Maria-(Gibside Fairy-by Whisker) in the Somersetshire Stakes, the same year that the King died. Day went on to win The Oaks the same year of 1828 and his third win on Turquoise-(Selim-Pope Joan-Prunella by Trumpeter) for the 4th Duke Of Grafton, and win by two lengths.

---

119 Hampshire Record Office Lease on Houghton Down Farm 18th November 1824 by Joseph Foster Barham 85M2/5

After his father's death in 1828 the Houghton Down estate was divided equally between his eight children and Anne Day was responsible for the distribution. John Barham Day being the oldest received the running of the stables and estate, which additionally had Houghton Down Farm and significant stabling built up by his father. Day must have had a busy life as he was responsible for his mounts as a jockey and as a trainer, and would prove an even better trainer than he was a jockey. John Barham Day and his brother William Day were running the stable jointly. *"Shortly afterwards, Grandfather Day, who posted with the horses on their various journeys, as he was unable to ride from his weight, died ; and the Houghton Down establishment was taken by his sons John and William Day. The latter soon quitted his brother, and went to reside at Ascot; and Honest John getting a lease of Danebury, which was more adapted for his increasing business, took his son into partnership, and the horses of Lord Palmerston followed with the other employers of the stable."*[120]

The death of his father seemed to have opened up new avenues for John Barham Day as he started at this point to concentrate on the Stables and therefore on the training of horses. He now had his eldest son, John Day Junior, to provide some of the leg work. A move which would later prove very beneficial and he became thought of as the first professional trainer in the south of Britain with John Scott in the North. [121] So the Dukes of Grafton were readily added as patrons of the Houghton Down stables along with Lord Palmerston and many others. John Barham Day still continued to ride for the Dukes of Grafton and Lord Palmerston throughout the 1830s, and he was competing for business with the top trainers in the country attracting all the noted Lords of the turf by this time. *"Other employers, in the shape of the Duke of Grafton, Lord Berners, Mr. Batson, and Mr. Biggs were booked in his list, which put him on a par with the cracks of the age"*[122]

A Momentous event was about to happen, if winning The Oaks with Oxygen in the St Leger was not enough in 1831, the Bibury Club was moving from Cheltenham to the Danebury Downs. The Bibury Club based their headquarters at the Star and Garter Hotel in Andover and after The Market Room in the Grosvenor Hotel Stockbridge which adjoins the main hotel and was originally called the Marky Room built by Lord Grosvenor of the Bibury Club as captured from 1835 *"The market, on Thursday, is well attended and a large and handsome market-room, adjoining the Grosvenor Arms, has been built, at the expense of the Marquis of Westminster."*[123]

---

120 Bailey Brothers, Baileys Magazine of Sporting Pastimes (Vol II 1861, p.231)
121 Mortimer, Onslow, Willet, Biographical Encyclopaedia of British Flat Racing, 1978 "Indeed he was the first Southern trainer of his era to match the skill of John Scott"
122 Bailey Brothers, *Baileys Magazine of Sporting Pastimes* (Vol I 1860, p.230
123 Samuel Lewis *A Topographical Dictionary Of England*, S. Lewis Co London ,1835, p.195)

DANEBURY

Figure 24 Landscape of Danebury viewed from Chattershill by Abraham Cooper R.A 1848

AFTER 1828 AND THE DEATH OF his father, and shortly after his marriage to Harriet, John Barham Day moved to London and then to Newmarket. Eventually he came back to Stockbridge and started up a stable of his own. Located a few miles from Stockbridge he had moved to where Danebury is now. I wish to note at this point that historians have John Barham Day arriving at Danebury after or at the date of 1831 and have attributed the building of the Danebury House and even the Bibury Club moving there to Lord George Cavendish Bentinck. I wish to correct this here and now, we will deal with the Bibury Club claim later. Danebury was set up and established by John Barham Day prior to 1831 and when he moved there he took his mother with him as the lease states, *"and also all that cottage and garden near to the said premises and late in the occupation of Mr. Robert Plank. But now of Mrs. Day mother of the said John Barham Day."* [124]

There exist three leases in the Hampshire Record Office for Danebury. The leases were drawn up and prepared by John Barham Day's brother, Frederick Day, Attorney of Hemel Hempstead for the years of 1831, 1837,

---

124 Hampshire Record Office "Danebury Leases Bolton estates Ref: (M57/T63: leases for 1831 for 20 years, 1837 for 37 years, 1841 for 32 years of newly erected messuage, tenement and garden with racing stables on Danebury Down later called Upper Farm, Nether Wallop - built on part of Place Farm - with land and cottage attached James Blunt of Nether Wallop Esq.(ii) Anthony Mist Lewis of Place Farm, Nether Wallop, farmer(iii) John Barham Day of Danebury, Nether Wallop, jockey and trainer 1831-1841

1841. The 1831 lease is dated 11th October for a period of 20 years with rent payable at £150 per year consisting of two payments due on the 6th April and the 11th October. The lease lists the House or Message as being built by the then land owner James Blunt *'to let both demise and to lease and to*

Figure 25 Danebury or Trainers Cottage as in 1831

farm let unto the said John Barham Day, all that newly erected messuage, or Tenement Offices and Outbuildings with the Yard, Garden and several Stables belonging and occupied therewith as the same are now in the occupation of the said John Barham Day and recently erected and built by the same James Blunt, on the part of his land belonging to Place Farm." [124]

So we can conclude that Lord George did not build Danebury Establishment as previously claimed by so many. He just added to the paddocks and stables for the benefit of his own horses, which are mentioned on the 1837 lease as being added. Danebury was built by the land owner James Blunt for John Barham Day to set up the Stockbridge Races on, it is also worthy of note and further correction that John Day moved back to Danebury and commenced his position as Clerk of the Stockbridge Races in 1829 as his father had been before him. *'To start a two o'clock precisely W. Sloane Stanley Esq Steward John Day Clerk of the Course Stockbridge Races 1830."* [125]

John Barham day built the Racing Stand and other buildings there prior to October as included in the lease *"that it shall and maybe lawful for the said John Barham Day his executors administrators assigns to pull down and remove the racing stand and buildings lately erected and built by him and at his expense on the said down to take carry or sell or dispose of the materials for the first fourteen years thereof but not afterwards, or during the said term convert the said race stand into a dwelling house but allow the same dwelling house to be occupied by his servants".* [124] At this point John Barham Day would have been very busy making alterations to Danebury and the new stables to form a brand new racing establishment

---

125 Salisbury and Winchester Journal 14th June 1830

that was completed by 1831. Prior to 1831 Danebury was no more than a cottage the cottage is still there today and is called Trainers Cottage and was incorporated by my Great Grandfather Tom Cannon when he rebuilt the Danebury establishment in 1883. But 17 years after the lease was taken out in 1831 we can see what Danebury looked like as there exists an Oil Painting by Abraham Cooper titled "Landscape of Danebury from Chattershill" Dated 1848 **Figure 24 Landscape of Danebury viewed from Chattershill by Abraham Cooper R.A 1848**. The stabling and the paddocks are extensive.

John Barham Day, like his ancestors before him, had now set up his new racing establishment and like his father had enticed the Maddington Club from Winchester 30 years before. He was about to play host and had enticed the most prestigious racing club of the turf, the Bibury Club, to move to Stockbridge. This was a fantastic opportunity for John Barham Day and his family and a business explosion for the town of Stockbridge putting it firmly on the map in the racing world. We will now explore the Bibury club in a bit more detail in order to understand the absolute financial and political power of its patrons and members, and also the opportunity that had been presented to John Barham Day and the Danebury Stable.

THE BIBURY CLUB

THE BIBURY CLUB WAS THE MOST exclusive racing club of the day, being formed from the wealthiest patrons and owners within horse racing. The membership was very select and by invitation only. Members included the most powerful and influential aristocrats and statesmen of the time including Lord Palmerston, Prince of Wales, Duke of Wellington to name but a few. In the 18th Century there were only a few racing clubs in existence and the Bibury Club was distinguished by only allowing Gentlemen riders who were members of the Club to ride their horses the races were run annually on Burford Downs. *"Tuesday was the annual meeting of the Bibury Club which was followed by two days racing. This meeting is the only one of the kind in the kingdom; none but gentlemen members of the club being permitted to ride."* [126]

The weights for the race were never under 10 stone no professional jockeys allowed. The prizes and events varied consisting of 3 days eventing *"Racing Stakes of 25 sovs with 50 added by the club over a mile and half, 25 sovs each with 100 added by the club if three horses start last for mile and half."* [127]

---

126 Bath Chronicle and weekly Gazette Monday May 9th 1791
127 James Christy White *History of the British Turf* 1840 p.244

The Bibury Club is said to be one of the country's longest running horse racing clubs, it is believed that it was formed in 1681 in Bibury, and from the Clubs website we can see they believe so too. *"The Bibury Club, established in 1681, is the world's oldest racing club and the Bibury Club Meeting is one of Britain's longest-running meetings. Originally this meeting was held at the now-defunct courses of Bibury and Stockbridge before moving to Salisbury in 1899."* [128] There is however a dilemma as according to historic sources the Bibury Club was more of a renewal of the Burford Races and it was the Burford Races that were one of the oldest in the country not the Bibury Club[129].

I have however found one paper of the time referring to a Bibury Club pre dating Lord William Pitt Lennox in 1791 but the reference is just due to local races and the money for the races and the members were nothing as lavish in 1791. The racing was held over three days for a mixed purse *"The 1st Day the 50 l. three mile heats, the subscription sweepstakes for one three mile heat. Second day was the hunter's plate was won at three two mile heats, the handicap was won at three excellent heats."* [126]

The Bibury Club according to Lord William Pitt Lennox fourth son of Charles Lennox the 4th Duke of Richmond and a member of the Bibury Club, was formed in 1798 by General Grosvenor. *"The bibury club was formed in 1798 by General Grosvenor and other fashionable sporting men of that day, among the members were the Duke of Dorset (then lord Sackville), Lord Jersey, Sir John Shelly, General Grosvenor, Mr. Pryse Pryse M.P, and Colonel Melish."*[130] Additionally, this has been voiced by the Sporting Review of 1869 and Baileys magazine in 1899 [131] and further by the Illustrated Sporting and Dramatic News of 1874 who wrote *"The Bibury Club were established as far back as 1796 and the races were at first celebrated on the Burford Course in Glostershire and a few years subsequently in the Cheltenham Course."* [132]

So we can conclude that 1798 was the likely formation date for the actual Bibury Club. The club moved from Burford, after 1801, to Cheltenham. *"In 1801 the Bibury club races were run over the Burford Course, from this they were removed from Cheltenham and in 1831 to Stockbridge."* [133] Some racing historians have Lord George Cavendish Bentinck as being the person responsible for

---

128 www.racenewsonline.co.uk (accessed 18th July 2013)

129 Gifford *The Quarterly Review* (1833 Vol. xlix April and July, p.435) "Stockbridge is now in repute, owing to the Bibury Club being held there-a renewal of the Burford Races one of the oldest in the country"

130 Lord William Pitt Lenox, *Celebrities I Have Known, With Episodes, Political, Social, Sporting And Theatrical,* (Hurst and Blackett 1876, p.23)

131 Bailey Brothers, *Baileys Magazine Of Sports and Pastimes* (Vol 72 1899, p.105-106)"this ancient and memorable traditions of the course, must have been the reason for its selection when the Bibury Club, was proper established there in 1798"

132 Illustrated Sporting and Dramatic News July 4th 1874 p.443

133 James Christy Whyte., *History of the British Turf,* (1840, p.244)

the Bibury Club's move to Stockbridge and the reason why the races became so popular this is simply not true and I would like to explore this claim now. Lord George Cavendish Bentinck wanted to join the Bibury Club and was worried about his acceptance as a member as he feared he would be "Black Balled" by the Squire who he had a duel with in 1836. *"Then there came a time when Lord George, whose horses were trained at Danebury, wished to be- come a member of the Bibury Club, and old John Day tried his diplomacy upon the Squire to ascertain whether he would interfere with his former antagonist's election. All animosity, however, had long died away in the Squire's breast; and after Lord George's admission to the club, he invited the Squire to come and see the Danebury horses, and treated him with marked politeness."* [134] So we can see that given the fact the duel between the Squire and Lord George happened in 1836 and George after 1836 was applying for membership it would be silly to suggest that George moved the club in 1831.

In the Bibury Club the owners of the horses had jockeys that were only gentlemen and lords riding for them for pre-agreed monies and wagers, *"It is beyond a doubt that there were gentlemen-jockeys at that time, almost, if not quite, equal to the professional artists, and a few of them nearly in as high practice in the saddle. Amongst these first-rate hands were, the present Duke of Dorset, and George Germaine, his brother; Lords Charles Somerset, Milsington, and Delamere, (then Mr. Cholmondeley); Sir Tatton Sykes; Messrs. Delme Radcliffe, Hawkes, Bullock, Worrall, George Picot, Lowth, Musters, Douglas, Probyn."* [135] Perhaps the aristocrats would not mix with the normal class of people, this was especially apparent within the Bibury Club which was considered the most exclusive of clubs. This rule was abolished sometime around 1830 [136] which allowed for professional jockeys to then be hired. John Barham Day was Clerk to the Club and, in 1825 he rode the winner for Mr. Pryse at the Bibury Club meeting run on the Burford course June 18th 1825. [137]

Being the most secret of clubs some of the members still remain elusive. There are references made to them over time by some of the club's more prominent members in autobiographies and the club did publish some of the names of its new members on 29th November 1831. [138] So I have pieced

134 John Kent, *The Racing Life Of Lord George Cavendish Bentinck MP*, 1892, p.408
135 Quarterly Review, (April and July 1833, p.436)
136 Sporting Magazine or Monthly Transactions of the Turf, The Chase, etc., (1832, p.114)
"The Bibury Races Originally the horses were all the property of, and rode by members of the club, no others being allowed, but latterly jockeys have been permitted to ride"

137 E. A. Weatherby *Racing Calendar*, 1825 "J-Day won on Mr. Eady-Rubens for Mr. Pryse at Burford in the Bibury Club Stakes Burford Course 18th June 1825"
138 London Morning Post 29th November 1831

Figure 26 Prince of Wales by John Hopner

a story together using those references, as we mentioned before, the Day family seem to have a connection with the Bibury Club dating back to its formation in 1798 with Charles Day, John Barham Day's great uncle who was clerk of the Burford Course where the races were run then. The Days can also be seen riding in the Bibury Club races at Cheltenham right up until its move to Stockbridge[17].

It is important for the reader that the noble figures of this exclusive and secretive club are known, so that the reader can understand who they were and what sort of monetary, political, and influential power made up the Bibury Club Members 1798-1832. I have compiled a list of members Appendix 4: List of Members of the Bibury Club 1798-1832. But for our story, I have taken a snapshot biography of some of the more prominent, and founder members of the club to provide an understanding of its central power house.

The Prince of Wales turned 21 years of age at which time he in 1783 obtained a grant of £60,000 from Parliament with an annual income of £50,000 from his father King George III. He then established his residence in Carlton House, where he lived a profligate life. Animosity developed between the Prince and his father, a monarch who desired more frugal behaviour on the part of the heir-apparent. The King, a political conservative, was also alienated by the Prince of Wales's adherence to Charles James Fox and other radically-inclined politicians.

Arthur Wellesley the Duke of Wellington, derived from Wellington in Somerset, is a hereditary title and the senior rank in the peerage of the United Kingdom. The first holder of the title was Arthur Wellesley, 1st Duke of Wellington (1769–1852). The noted Irish-born British career officer and statesman, and unqualified references to the Duke of Wellington almost always refer to this particular man. He is together with Bulcher most famous for defeating Napoleon at Waterloo. The Wellesley families are, in origin, an Anglo-Irish aristocratic dynasty. (Steward)The titles of Duke of Wellington and Marquis Douro were bestowed upon Arthur Wellesley, 1st Duke of Wellington, on 11 May, 1814.

Henry John Temple, 3rd Viscount Palmerston, KG, GCB, PC (20 October 1784 – 18 October 1865) was a British statesman who served twice as Prime Minister of the United Kingdom in the mid-19th century. He was in government office almost continuously from 1807 until his death in 1865, beginning his parliamentary career as a Tory and concluding it as a Liberal. He is best remembered for his direction of British foreign policy through a period when the United Kingdom was at the height of its power, serving terms as both Foreign Secretary and Prime Minister and became closely associated with the phrase, "gunboat diplomacy"

Earl Robert Grosvenor, 1st Marquis of Westminster, KG, PC (22 March 1767 – 17 February 1845) was the son of the 1st Earl Grosvenor, who he succeeded in 1802 as 2nd Earl Grosvenor. He was created Marquis of Westminster in 1831. The Hon. Robert Grosvenor was educated at Westminster School, Harrow School and Trinity College, Cambridge. He was responsible for the development of Belgravia. The 2nd Earl also purchased the Stockbridge estate in 1822.

Major General Thomas Grosvenor (30 May 1764 – 20 January 1851) was the third son of Thomas Grosvenor he was commissioned into the First Foot Guards in October 1779 and promoted to full General in 1819. He succeeded his father as Whig member for Parliament in 1795. He was member for Stockbridge Parliament in 1826 and cousin of the 2nd Earl Grosvenor and reported Founder of the Bibury Club in 1798.

Joseph Foster Barham was from a family of sugar plantation owners that lived in Jamaica and whose father became stepson to an English surgeon in the West Indies, that by 1798 from inheritance and both marriage he held vast estates of land and possessed large amounts of money that came to him from this inheritance, both from land in England obtained through marriage in Wales to Lady Vaughn of Trecom, and income from the use of sugar estates in Jamaica willed to him through his grandfather Thomas Foster His father's name was originally Joseph Foster but he changed it in pursuit of a will of the then Dr. Henry Barham of Jamaica whom his mother married[139]. He became involved in politics and built the Town Hall in Stockbridge in 1790, and then went on to buy the manorial rights and the parish of Stockbridge from the Luterell family, who subsequently purchased it from James Fox when he was in desperate need of money.

Charles Lennox, 4th Duke of Richmond and Lennox, KG (9 December

---

139 Sir Edward Hyde East ESQ, *Reports of Cases Argued And Determined In The Court Of The Kings Bench,* (Edition II London Lea and Blanchard 1845)

1764 – 28 August 1819) was a British soldier and politician and Governor General of British North America.

George John Frederick Sackville, 4th Duke of Dorset (15 November 1793 – 14 February 1815), styled Earl of Middlesex until 1799, was a British nobleman. The only son of John Sackville, 3rd Duke of Dorset and his wife Arabella, he was educated at Harrow and Christ Church, Oxford, receiving a MA from the latter on 30 June 1813. He was appointed High Steward of Stratford-on-Avon, and was commissioned a captain of the local militia on 27 April 1813.

George Child Villiers, 5th Earl of Jersey GCH PC (August 19 1773 – October 3 1859) was a British Conservative politician. The son of George Villiers, 4th Earl of Jersey and Frances Twysden, Lord Jersey took his seat in the House of Lords on the death of his father in 1805. He later served as Lord Chamberlain of the Household under the Duke of Wellington in 1830 and under Sir Robert Peel from 1834 to 1835, as Master of the Horse under from 1841 to 1846, and briefly under Lord Aberdeen in 1852.

George William Frederick Villiers 4th Earl of Clarendon (12th January 1800-12th June 1870) British foreign secretary under four Prime Ministers at various times from 1853, including the Crimean War period; he was known as "the great Lord Clarendon." After serving as a customs commissioner in Dublin and Paris, Villiers was British ambassador to Spain in 1833. Inheriting the earldom of Clarendon in 1838, he returned to England the next year and served as lord privy seal (1839–41) and then as president of the Board of Trade (1846–47). As lord lieutenant (viceroy) of Ireland (1847–52) during the disastrous Irish famine.

William Henry Cavendish Cavendish-Scott-Bentinck, 4th Duke of Portland PC (24 June 1768 – 27 March 1854) was a British politician who served in various positions in the governments of George Canning and Lord Goderich. He was the eldest son of William Cavendish-Bentinck, 3rd Duke of Portland and Dorothy Cavendish. His maternal grandparents were William Cavendish, 4th Duke of Devonshire and Charlotte Boyle. Bentinck was Member of Parliament for Petersfield between 1790 and 1791.

Henry Charles Somerset, 6th Duke of Beaufort, KG (22 December 1766 – 2 December 1835) was a British peer, the son of Henry Somerset, 5th Duke of Beaufort. He was styled Marquis of Worcester until 1803. He was educated at Westminster School, London and graduated from Trinity College, Oxford, on 28 June 1786 with a Master of Arts. Somerset was a Tory Member of Parliament for Monmouth between 1788 and1790, for Bristol between1790 and1796, and for Gloucestershire between 1796 and 1803. He held the office of Lord Lieutenant of Monmouthshire between 1803 and 1835, Lord Lieutenant of Brecknockshire between 1803 and 1835 and Lord Lieutenant of Gloucestershire between 1810 and 1826. He was invested as a Knight of the Garter on 17 January 1805.

Lord Charles Henry Somerset (2 December 1767 – 18 February 1831) was a British governor of the Cape Colony, South Africa, from 1814 to 1826. He was the second son of the 5th Duke of Beaufort and became a Privy Counsellor on 26 April 1797. In June 1788, he married Lady Elizabeth Courtenay (died 1815), daughter of the 8th Earl of Devon, and had six children. After the death of Lady Elizabeth, he married Lady Mary Paulet, daughter of the 4th Earl Paulet, on August 9, 1821.

Charles James Fox (24 January 1749 – 13 September 1806) was a prominent British Whig statesman whose parliamentary career spanned thirty-eight years of the late eighteenth and early nineteenth centuries and who was particularly noted for being the arch-rival of William Pitt the Younger. The son of an old, indulgent Whig father, Fox rose to prominence in the House of Commons as a forceful and eloquent speaker with a notorious and colourful private life, though his opinions were rather conservative and conventional.

Not all of the members have emerged from the shadows, these early members would have attended the Cheltenham meetings, and later at Stockbridge. We are talking about one of the most powerful and exclusive clubs within the British Empire in the Regency period made up of the country's richest men, the most influential politicians and the summit of the aristocracy hidden away for a meeting in a simple, remote country town. No records of the club were written, only references, but the club existed.

The most important early Patron of the Bibury Club was his majesty George IV,[140] so for one week of the year all the cream of the aristocracy would descend on Burford, Cheltenham and later to Stockbridge to race their horses for three days. Perhaps even the story of John Day going to see Lord Palmerston, the then Prime Minister of Great Britain and being able to extract him from the great debate of the century that was raging in the House of Commons, the Irish Question to request a job for his son. A

---

[140]Sporting Magazine or Monthly Calendar of the Transactions of the Turf the chase etc., (1822, p.110) "He particularly distinguished himself as the patron of the old Bibury Club, which he regularly attended for some years"

request that you would have thought could have waited until the debates conclusion. The fact that the Prime Minister left the debate to hear John Days request was at the time unheard of, was this due to the influence of the Bibury Club?

The Bibury Club races were a very strict and private affair, to the point that no one could talk of them. We have one example, captured from the Sporting review in 1869. *"George the fourth when Prince of Wales often honoured the course with his presence it was in riding a horse for the Prince called Ploughator a very hard puller that the Duke of Dorset broke a blood vessel, and was for a time in a great danger though it, not being allowed to speak of for twelve months after the accident occurred."* [141]

At some point the Jockey Club was calling for the disclosure of the Bibury Club's rules, and in 1831 the Bibury Club published them, or at least a draft of them that was going to be voted on by all the members. It also for the first time ever published a list of some of its members. I have placed of copy of these rules in Appendix 3: Bibury Club Rules First the Days, then the Cannons; my ancestors were the clerks and secretaries of this club from 1798 the start to 1898 when it moved to Salisbury 100 years later. Newmarket had its own clubs but the Bibury Club was far more exclusive, where membership was obtained by invitation only, and then it was put to the vote of those members. *'The Bibury Club is immensely popular amongst the Patrician Contingent of racehorse owners and election there to be eagerly sought. The club maintains its character for exclusiveness and heart burnings are occasionally caused after the deadly blackball has been at work."* [142]

141 John William Carleton, *Sporting Review ed* Craven (1869, p.340)
142 Charles Richardson, *The English Turf A Record Of Horses And Courses*, (Dodd Mead London 1901, p.153)

THE MARQUIS, BIBURY CLUB & THE ROTTEN BOROUGH

IN 1831, THE BIBURY CLUB moved from Cheltenham to Stockbridge, we find General Grosvenor is still head of the Bibury Club Committee, and it was in that year that the club first published its Committee. This Committee consisted of General Grosvenor, Lord Jersey, Mr. Dundas, Mr. Pryse, Mr. Rawlinson and Mr. Thornhill[143].

General Grosvenor by 1831 owned substantial property in Stockbridge including the Manor which he purchased in 1822 from Forster Barham and large amounts of land the Stockbridge racecourse was built on. Some may ask why did the club move what was the point? Was it for financial or monetary gain or maybe both?

Figure 27 Earl Grosvenor 1st Marquis of Westminster by John Jackson

The Bibury Club races, now a public event, had declined. The Club when in Cheltenham was not making much money due to lack of public support as stated in the sporting calendar of 1831 *"Cheltenham has certainly not advanced of late years, and the intended defection of the Bibury Club next year (which is to be removed to Stockbridge) the truth is the public money is wanting."* [144]The Bibury Club was suffering in Cheltenham where it was based then due mainly to no public purse, the racecourse itself was dwindling as there was no public interest as stated by the Sporting Magazine of 1831 *"Cheltenham, like all*

---

143 Sporting Magazine or Monthly Calendar of the Transactions of the Turf the Chase and every other diversion interesting to the man pleasure enterprise of spirit (M. A. Pitman London Vol 4 Second Series, 1832, p.115) "That General Grosvenor, Lord Jersey, Mr. Dundas, Mr. Pryse, Mr. Rawlinson, Mr. Thornhill, and the steward for the time being be a committee for managing the affairs of the club"
144 Sporting Calendar Or Monthly Transactions Of The Turf, The Chase etc., (Vol II 1831,p.66)

other places which give no public money to be run for, has been gradually dwindling away. The Glostershire Stakes in every view is but a shadow of what it used to be, and the withdrawal this season of the Bibury Club to Stockbridge reduced the meeting to two poor days sport; and if it was not for the locality which is just convenient to Messrs. Day, Sadler they would have no racing at all." [145] The Bibury Club first gave a year's notice of its move from Cheltenham to Stockbridge in 1830 *"at a meeting held lately at Cheltenham it is resolved to move the Bibury Club from Cheltenham where accordingly the races will take place next year a clear week after the Bath Races."* [146] There is a record that the Bibury Club was shifted to Stockbridge due to the vote or the motion of the Marquis of Worcester. [147]So in 1831 the Bibury Club moved to Stockbridge, where it would stay and flourish.

The Manor of Stockbridge, which at this time and for many years previously was a Rotten Borough involved in a large scale scandal. The MP's of the borough were involved in bribing the members of the Stockbridge electorate with houses and money the going rate up to 1820 was 60 guineas per vote a huge sum in those days the records show this bribing had happened before in Stockbridge. In 1754 the borough of Stockbridge was under the charge of the Attorney General Robert Henley, who it was said had a personal interest in the ownership of the Manor rather than an official government interest. Control of the Borough was given to his colleague Henry Fox, or the rights of control were leased to him for a set number of years. Control of the borough was then passed at some point to Henry's son, Charles James Fox who was also an MP and member of the Bibury Club, and leader of the Whig party. In pursuit of securing the seats for the election he admitted that bribery was necessary, and 96 voters had already been bribed in order to secure one seat but he was doubtful he could secure the second seat. The bribes had been paid to the voters in the second seat as well as to the returning officer appointed by the court leet around 1767. But he was worried if the election came to a close vote further bribery of the voters, and the returning officer, could bring the cost to secure the seat to £2,500.

Later, in need of money Fox sold the manor to the Lutterells in 1774, an act that was seen as not to oppose the Lutterel candidates and bid up the price of votes, as in the end it would cost him more than the going rate of 50 guineas per head. The Borough then passed to Joseph Foster Barham 1759-

---

145 Sporting Calendar or Monthly Transactions of the Turf, etc. Vol 79 (1832, p.67)
146 Berkshire Chronicle and Bucks and Windsor Herald October 1st 1830
147 A.H.Bailey *Baileys Magazine Of Sports And Past Times*, 1899,(Vol 72 p.86)

1832 a member of the Bibury Club, who became MP. Barham was buying up as much land as he could around Stockbridge using the money from his sugar estates in Jamaica to secure as much land and as many votes as possible, even building a lavish town hall in the centre of Stockbridge. Eventually Barham had achieved 2 seats, one of which he kept for his son John Foster Barham, also member of the Bibury Club and Lord of Houghton Manor.

Joseph Forster Barham now Lord of the Manor of Stockbridge from around 1780-1832 held also the manorial rights of the Manor. Lord of the Manor also meant that the Court Leet served him; the Court Leet was the legal administration for the Manor.[148] Such was the corruption that there was a case argued in the Courts of Chancery in 1825, regarding the unlawful exercise of a non-appointed Bailiff James McKay in Stockbridge. The case was that James McKay had been collecting rents and taxes on behalf of the Courts Leet and acting as a bailiff, but the appointment of the bailiff was supposed to be made through the Lord of the Manor, and the tax collected was supposed to be returned by the Lords Steward. *"The Parliament Burgesses of Stockbridge in Hampshire were chosen by the free Burgesses in the Court-Leet, and the Return made by the Lord's Steward."* [148]Lord of the Manor was Barham and Lord of the Court Leet, and he had never appointed McKay to that position.[148]

Around 1822 Barham sold his Stockbridge Estate to 2nd Earl Grosvenor founder member of the Bibury Club. Lord Grosvenor had appointed a nominee as MP Edward Stanley, a future Prime Minister. Grosvenor had also been accused of bribery by trying to find new jobs for voters and the unemployed with the surveyor of roads. Arguments erupted between Earl Grosvenor and Barham and much political competition over seats ensued. By 1831 Earl Grosvenor had enough of the arguments and sparing with Barham and the accusations of bribery over the seat for Stockbridge, he relinquished his claim.[149] Earl Grosvenor was saved from further claims of corruption and investigation as the Borough of Stockbridge was abolished as a borough in 1832. Under the Great Reform Act it was returned to a Manor, at the time the inhabitants numbered 663 with 188 dwellings.

---

148 Sir Edward Hyde East ESQ, *Reports of cases argued and determined in the court of kings (Reports of Cases Argued And Determined In The Court Of The Kings Bench* (1826, p.354)

149 Historyofparlimentonline.org "At the 1831 general election Grosvenor appears to have decided that the borough was no longer worth the trouble and on the morning of the election his voters were reportedly told by his steward that they 'could do no better' than to vote for John Barham and Stratford Canning, a diplomat and cousin of the former prime minister"

Scandal and corruption was very much a part of political life. Votes were famously being secured by the voters being paid and also given houses this can be seen by the voters' returns and that between the years of 1821 and 1831 the number of houses had risen from 128 to 188 that's an increase of a staggering 60 houses this did not include the 13 houses that were under construction, was this was down to Foster Barham's endeavours or Grosvenor's?

John Forster Barham (Bibury Club) had inherited Houghton Down estate and other lands in Stockbridge from his father and had then married Lady Katherine Grimston in 1834. By 1836 he was under medical superintendence and in March of 1837 he was certified by a commission of lunacy as of 'unsound mind'. He died in March 1838. After his death his widow married the 4th Earl of Clarendon George Villiers (Bibury Club) on the 4th June 1839 and all the land that was in the hands of Forster Barham was now in the hands of John Barham's widow and being administered by 4th Earl of Clarendon of the Bibury Club.

By 1851 the Manor of Stockbridge belonged to the Earl and Countess of Clarendon. On the 27th June 1870 the 4th Earl of Clarendon died and his Houghton Down estate came up for sale as early as the 7th July and consisted of *"999 acres of land 22 lots including racing stables training grounds and breeding paddocks occupied by John Day also the Grosvenor Arms Hotel the Manor of Stockbridge and fair tolls the Cossack pub and 2 beer houses."* [150]

Within the Houghton Down Estate sale it refers to the *"Houghton Down Estate 389 acres the training grounds of Houghton Down 130 acres are leased to John Day, the Paddocks Stabling and residence of Houghton Down are let to Mr. Day for 14 years from 25th December 1866 for 210 per anum, shooting on Houghton Down is also letting to John Day for £25 per annum"* [150] The Stockbridge Racecourse was also on much of this land which was owned and rented by John Day for the exclusive use by the Racecourse. It appears that many of the MP's were members of the Bibury Club and also, Lords of the Manor. Barham and General Grosvenor stood to gain the most from its enterprise. They would have access to money from the clubs members but more importantly they would gain the most important of all things that MPs need popular, public votes. But for now the Bibury Club had succeeded in moving to Stockbridge, and my ancestors the Days were set up ready to make the racing scene explode.

---

150 Hampshire Record Office Sale Particulars of 990 acres of freehold estate 7th July 1870 4m92/n122/4

RISE OF THE DANEBURY STABLES

THE FIRST RACE ON THE NEW Stockbridge course was on the 8th and 9th of June 1831. It would have been a magnificent sight and what an event for the local population. The most fashionable London patrons would have infused that country scene with glamour and opulence and generated a crackle of excitement. The races would have brought much needed work and wealth into Stockbridge, and provided a massive boost to the existing race scene there, the press of the day gave the following account. *"Honest John Stands Sober with all ranks; he is a sober, steady and pains-taking body, and goes to church on a Sun-Day. He has done wonders towards bringing Stockbridge "to the fore" and deserves very great praise; the dear boy as he is termed by the jockeys has not only made rich stakes and erected a new stand but has seduced many of the principal horses and their masters from Newmarket-but let the sport speak for itself. the first race was between Rough Robin, Jocko and Rigmarole for a sweepstakes of 10 sovereigns each 10 subs the former rode by Lord Wilton rode cleverly won by half a length" A Sweepstakes of 100 Sovs each twelve subs followed it was won by delight rode by Chapple. Then followed a Sweepstakes of 50 Sovs each for two year olds seven subs was won by Mr. Wrefords Margrave. On the second day a plate of 50 was given by Lord Grosvenor who won it with Metheglen. The Hunter Stakes were won by Jocko rode by Mr. H Peyton, the 5 Sovs stakes (twenty subs and 25 added) were won by Little Red Rover rode by John Day the races finished with a handicap of 20 sovs each won by Lord Chesterfields Splendour"* [329]Shortly following on Tuesday 28th June 1831, was the Bibury Stakes, 25 sovereigns each horse 30 added by the club.[151]

The Bibury Club was "the" racing club". It consisted of the most powerful members on the turf, and also in politics, and everyone wanted a seat. The party had come to town and John Barham Day had been involved in enticing it here.

Prior to 1832 and the Great Reform Act the Borough of Stockbridge had now returned to being a village. But the glamour of horse racing circles provided all the residents of the town with the opportunity to earn enough money in three days to feed their families for most of the year, the villagers would even rent out their houses during race week.

One of the first roles of the Bibury Club was to extend the existing race track at Danebury to 24 furlongs 3 miles, making the course more professional, and enabling the races to have a straight mile, because to have a nationally competitive course under the Jockey Club rules you had to offer a straight mile *"Stockbridge Course Is nearly a round course somewhat hilly the*

---

151 London Morning Post 2nd June 1831

last three quarters of a mile straight for the run in, there is also a straight mile." [152]The lease of some of the land enabling the straight mile was over part of the Barker Mills estate, which would later prove to be a catastrophic mistake.

Danebury was fast becoming a very popular event with the racing elite, and John Barham Day was becoming one of the finest trainers in England by 1833 two years after he had opened his Danebury Stables the racing press were holding him in high regard as the New Sporting Magazine a respected journal of the day records *"Stockbridge race course is one of the prettiest in the kingdom. A spectator can stand on almost any part, and see the horses all around; the turf is inferior to none, and the regulations superior to most meetings (I mean of course racing ones), how indeed can it be otherwise when such a man as John Day is at the head of affairs?" it is also supported by downright good men, who are willing to give honest John a turn by taking a ticket to his elegant little stand. John Day has become very popular as a trainer and can boast of as good a lot of horses as any trainer in the west of England."* [153]

John Barham Day's popularity was growing and so was his large chain of the country's best Patrons. Records show that John Barham Day even stole the best Patrons and Horses from Newmarket *"dear boy" (as he is termed by the jockeys), has not only made rich stakes, and erected a new stand, but has seduced many of the principal horses and their masters from Newmarket."* [81]

This growth of the new business required, like any other business would, as his father's before him in Houghton Down, bigger stables and a larger house. Day had already started enlarging the Danebury House and buying up more property in the town. To illustrate the greatness of the Danebury Stables and the ability of John Barham Day as trainer I have included a few years' worth of wins. John won altogether 16 Classic races as a jockey and 12 as a trainer but the below I have included an out-take of some of the others that did not make the eternal Classics hall of fame. *"In 1836, he won with Chapeau-d'Espagne the Criterion Stakes, value £750, and £175 at the Houghton Meeting:—with a Brother to Mar- pessa, a Match at the Bibury Club Meeting :—with a Sister to Waresti, £195 at Brighton :—with Westonian, £290 at Winchester, £450 at Goodwood, and £50 in the Second October Meeting."*

In 1837, he was still more successful, as we find him the winner of the following important races:—Clara, £150 at the Bibury Club, and £90 at Salisbury :—Cuirass, £250 at Bath Spring Meeting, and £140 at the Bath July Meeting :—D'Egville, the

---

152 E. J. Weatherby, *Racing Calendar*, 1832,p.Li
153 The New Sporting Magazine, M. A. Pittman, London Vol 5, 1833, p.265

Prendergast Stakes of £900 at the Second October Meeting, the Criterion Stakes of £850 and the Gunton Stakes of £500 at the Houghton Meeting :—a filly by Camel, dam by Rubens, £100 at Salisbury :—Grey Momus, the Lavant Stakes of £860 and the Molecomb Stakes of £750 at Goodwood ; also a Sweepstakes of £450 at the Newmarket Houghton Meeting :—Volunteer, £170 at the Bibury Club Meeting, £250 at Stockbridge, and £160 at Winchester."

In 1838, John Day was in great force with his two-year-olds, as the names of the following good runners can testify:—Arrian, Bulwark (winner of the July Stakes), Wapiti, and Westonian. I cannot pass over the capital exploits of Wapiti. At Goodwood, she won the Lavant Stakes of £730, beating Deception and several others; at the same place, she received £100, also won £350, and finished by winning the Molecomb Stakes of. £575, again beating Deception: in the subsequent year, ran second for the Derby (she ought to have won), and won the Oaks in famous style from a large and good Field. Wapiti was naturally infirm on the legs, and the wonder is how John Day managed to keep her on her legs so long as he did. She did not go for any of her three- year-olds engagements."

In 1839, John Day carried everything before him with the flying Crucifix, whose deed» are so well known to the? Pieldert, man of whom that superfluous: suffice it to say, that after winning all her two-year-olds engagements—save one, in which she, giving nine pounds, ran a " dead heat" with Gibraltar—she came out at three years old, and won in glorious style the Two Thousand Guineas and the One Thousand Guineas Stakes in the First Spring Meeting, and the Oaks at Epsom. In 1889 the following other two-year-olds did credit to "honest John:"— Wardan, Grey Milton, and Capote."

In 1840, Thistle whipper and Wahab picked up some valuable Stakes:—the former, unfortunately for Mr. Etwell, met with an accident which prevented his running at three yean old. £500. In 1841, Wiseacre proved himself a very good performer, by picking up for Mr. Wreford £2450 at Goodwood, and the Prendergast Stakes in the Second October Meeting, value." [154]

At the new Danebury Stables the patrons were galloping in, wanting their horses trained by Day. The next Classic wins came for Day in 1831 and the fourth Classic for the Dukes of Grafton; he won The Oaks with Oxygen-(Emilius Whizgig-Penelop by Rubens) for the Duke to which Grafton called him a thief, joking of course. "John Day, you're a thief." "My Lord," cried out the astonished jockey, "what have I done to displease you?" "What have you done," answered the Duke, still looking stern, "you stole

---

154 Sporting Calendar Or Monthly Transactions Of The Turf, The Chase etc., (Vol XXV1842, p.328)

Figure 28Choiroster with John Day Up 1831by John Frederick Herring Snr

that race!" Day was known as a "good rough jockey". [155] I have included a closing account from the history of this race, written by an eyewitness, *'The struggle however lay between Lord Exeter's Sultan Filly (Marmora) and Oxygen the latter winning by a neck. John Day rode like a prince and at once ought to have been raised to the peerage; indeed after the race several of the surprised at once exclaimed "Lord John Day".*[156]

Day did not stop there he won another Classic the St Leger with Chorister[157] at Doncaster the same year for the 1st Duke of Cleveland, where it was said he beat 23 other good horses in a race where 83 showed at the starting post. The betting opened at 5-2 on Chorister and finished on 6-4, Lord Cleveland was said to have won £8,000 in winnings.[158] *"On 20 September, Chorister was one of twenty-four colts and fillies to contest the Great St Leger*

155 Mortimer, Onslow, Willet, *Biographical Encyclopaedia of British Flat Racing*, 1978
156 George Tattersall *The Pictorial Gallery Of The English Racehorse*, 1850, p.15
157 www.tbheritage.com/Portraits/Lottery.html accessed 9th October 2009 "He next went to Doncaster, where he won the St. Leger, beating twenty-three other horses in an exciting driving finish from the outside to best The Saddler by half a length. The field included Liverpool, Colwick, and other good horses, including three other youngsters by Lottery, La-Fille-Mal-Gardee (later named Hope, from Morgiana and so sister to Sheet Anchor), Lady Elizabeth, and Tetotum, who finished third, fourth, and sixth respectively "
158 George Tattersall The Pictorial Gallery Of The English Racehorse, 1850, p.20

Stakes at Doncaster. The Saddler started 3/1 favourite ahead of Lord Cleveland's more fancied runner Marcus on 7/2, while Chorister, ridden by the southern jockey John Barham Day and started a 20/1 outsider. In a strongly run race, Day restrained Chorister just behind the leaders before producing the colt with a strong run on the outside in the straight. Well inside the final furlong, Chorister made a "tremendous rush" to catch and overtake The Saddler and win by a short head. The New Sporting Magazine expressed the view that The Saddler was by far the best horse in the race, and that Chorister's victory had been almost entirely due to Day's superior jockeyship." [159] Chorister ran one more race and then retired, having generated valuable publicity for the stables and the Day family.

John Barham Day was not just a famous jockey but also a famous trainer and as a multi-talented master he trained for many famous names of the turf: Lord George Bentinck, John Gully, Henry Padwick, the Duke of Grafton, Lord Berners and Mr. Batson who were all very powerful men at the time to have in your stables. Just to provide some idea of the population present to run this establishment, of which he was head, by 1844 there were over 100 people working for him at the stable, this figure was taken as accurate from an account he gave to the courts as a witness in 1844 over gaming.[160] He then goes on to say there are 35 servants that sit down to dinner every day, a significant number of people to oversee on a daily basis and must have acquired all his strength and vigour, even the people in the court exclaimed that was a large number. He clearly presided over one of the largest and most powerful stables and training establishments in the country, and he was certainly starting to draw money, business and interest away from Newmarket.

History records John Barham Day as starting training as a career in 1835, but he was in fact doing this earlier when his father died in 1828, with his brother William[100]. As a trainer he was referred to as over working the racehorses in his care *"A firm believer in keeping his horses light and wiry, he never spared them in the work he gave them on his famous gallop up Danebury Hill. Consequently they went to the post absolutely fit, with a great advantage over most of their rivals, provided they could stand up to their preparations."* [161] But as you can see from his extensive winning numbers John obviously trained for success, and it was his rival trainers who were accusing him of this overworking of the horses, so there may have been jealousy at play between the stables.

---

159 The New Sporting Magazine, (M. A. Pittman, London May-Oct , 1831, p.413)
160 House of Lords, *The sessional papers (reports on gaming evidence for the select committee of the House of Lords).* (Volume XIX 1844, p.155). "I have known as many as 100 labourers to be employed at Danebury"
161 Mortimer, Onslow, Willet, *Biographical Encyclopaedia of British Flat Racing,* 1978

John Barham Day had waltzed in and danced off with the prizes along with the leading share of the training business. When John Barham Day was criticized for the over working of his horses Day would reply that he liked to know the worst of a horse as well as the best. It was also reported that he would cover the horses in heavy woollen blankets and run them up Danebury hill in order to sweat them more, "the Sweats" as it was known. His mother assisted him in the practice she was famous for it within racing circles. Sounds a bit barbaric if judged through our modern eyes as does strapping a plough to horses and running them up and down a farm all day or running them at full speed into a cavalry charge of heavy cannon with cutting sabres and musket fire but that was then.

At this point we shall now concentrate on some of the larger patrons of the Danebury Stables, and look at the relationships with the family, there were many patrons, but history only records the larger and more famous ones. Like any successful establishment where we find powerful and famous people, there is always scandal, and the Danebury establishment was about to have more than its fair share.

LORD WILLIAM GEORGE HENRY CAVENDISH BENTINCK

Figure 29 Lord George Bentinck by Sir Thomas Lawrence PRA

Lord William George Henry Cavendish Bentinck second son to the honourable 4th Duke of Portland, born 22nd February 1802 came from a very old and noble family and a sporting one of high repute, with his father winning the Derby in 1819. He was closely involved with the Jockey Club in Newmarket some may say intimately regarding that his family, well his father owned much of the Newmarket Heath and the land the gallops were set up on and had loaned the Jockey Club money to buy the freehold of their rooms. [162]

Lord George in 1820 was 18 years old he started a career in the army entering the 9th Lancers as a Coronet. Not long

---

162 Thormamby, Kings of the Turf *Members Owners and Distinguished Backers, Owners, Trainers And Jockeys*, 1898

into his army career he had a disagreement with a higher ranking officer a Captain Ker the Captain had written to Bentinck directly stating his dissatisfaction with his conduct. Bentinck took the letter and sent it to his superior who through a court of enquiry forced the captain to apologise to Bentinck. After this Bentinck had become dissatisfied enough to run back to the family and obtain a position as private secretary to his uncle George Canning, the leader of the House of Commons, a very powerful and influential man.

Bentinck who was by all accounts addicted to gambling, he managed to lose £26,000, around £3 million in todays value by the age of 26 at Doncaster, that is one thousand pounds for every year of his age. His father in order to prevent him from further public embarrassment provided him with an estate in Ayrshire to keep him busy, but this did not distract him from his love of horse racing. As far as can be recanted Lord George had started racing as a 22 year old jockey when in 1824 he rode in the Cocked Hat Stakes at Goodwood Racecourse. In 1833 Lord George had started racing seriously after seeing his cousin Charles Greville's horses, he had his eyes on bigger races like the Classics. Lord George was established at Danebury by 1836 *"My first recollection of racing, dates back from 1836, when Bay Middleton won the Derby, and was soon afterwards transferred from Newmarket to Danebury. Lord Jersey having sold him to Lord George Bentinck for 4,000, this will serve as a fit introduction to the latter's connection with the Danebury Stables"*[163], referred by William Day who was there.

Danebury was considered one of the finest and most powerful stables in the South if not the whole of England it had some of the most extensive stabling of the time and was revered as recorded by a reporter prior to 1840 *"Mr. John Day ranks in such high estimation in the racing world, that I have been for a long time anxious to see his training-stables and exercise-ground. The accommodation for horses far exceeds anything that I have ever met with at one establishment, both as regards comfort and convenience, and also extent. There are upwards of fifty stalls and loose boxes, and there did not appear to be a great many unoccupied. There are two distinct yards, adjoining one of which the dwelling-house is situated: over the stables are granaries, hay-lofts, and sleeping-rooms for the boys, for whom every accommodation is provided."* [164] There are many myths and untruths that have been created by historians surrounding the formation of the Danebury Establishment and Lord George Cavendish Bentinck, I wish to review them here.

---

163 William Day, *Reminiscences Of The Turf, with Anecdotes And Recollections of its Principal Celebrities,* Richard Bentley and Son, London 1891, p.82-83
164 John Stuart Skinner, *American Turf Register and Sporting Magazine,* Vol 11, 1840, p.320).

Lord George funded the whole of the Danebury Establishment, and was responsible for moving John Barham Day and his family to Danebury. The early Danebury House was built by the landowner James Blunt prior to 1831 and before Bentinck's arrival in 1836. Lord George was responsible for the payment on his own stable that he insisted on having and on the setting up of Gallops [165], The establishment of the Gallops is further referenced from the lease of 1837 [124] and he also made additions to the existing paddocks for his own stud [166], so the truth is Lord George made additions to Danebury for the purpose of his own horses, and, in particular, the expense on the Paddocks was for his own use, £1,500 of which was just for the laying of bone dust, a project which took over three years to complete. *"Lord George whose heart was at one time never far from the Danebury Paddocks, he spent no less than fifteen hundred on them over three years in bone dust alone."* [167].

There is also popular belief that Bentinck pulled all the business to Danebury and that he was responsible for the Bibury Club move from Cheltenham to Stockbridge. This again is just not true due to the fact that Lord George Bentinck was not a member of the Bibury Club until 1836, sometime shortly after his arrival at Danebury which was in 1835-36, and. the Bibury Club, as I have shown, was already there and very well established.

In 1836, Lord George was involved in a famous duel [168] with the Squire Osbaldeston, a noted man of honour of the day, in the end, like many people who are spoilt or are considered a bully as Lord George appears to be, they meet somebody who will not stand for it. On one occasion this is exactly what happened for our dear Lord George Bentinck. Bentinck had been accused by a well renowned honourable man of the time of being a

165 John Stuart Skinner, *American Turf Register and Sporting Magazine*, 1840, p.321 "John Day's principal employer is Lord George Bentinck, who has several extensive paddocks adjoining the training-stables, which, by a liberal outlay of capital, are in a way to become very complete. His Lordship spares no expense to render everything as perfect as the art of man can make it. Under his directions the exercise ground has in several places been newly laid down and improved, and fresh gallops have been made, so that there is plenty of change"

166 John Kent, The Racing Life of Lord George Cavendish Bentinck MP, (William Balkavood and Sons London 1892) "Lord George made considerable additions to these Paddocks when he went to Danebury"

167 H.H.Dixon, Silk and Scarlett, 1859, p.188

168 John Kent, *The Racing Life Of Lord George Cavendish Bentinck MP*, 1892, p.401"Touching the famous duel between squire Osbaldeston and Lord George in 1836"

cheat and swindler, his name was Squire Osbaldeston (Bibury Club). Lord George had lost £400.00 to him previously in a bet at Heaton Park and Lord George when asked by the Squire to settle the bet said that the Squire had swindled it from him. Well this insulted the Squire to which he immediately challenged Bentinck to a duel, which at first Bentinck declined but was advised to accept in order to avoid looking like a charlatan.

The duel was fought at Wormwood Scrubs with pistols in 1836.[169] Lord George fired into the air, and then the squire fired and shot him through the hat apparently just a little bit above his head. But there is another account given by Pitt Lennox that says Lord George first fired at the Squire and missed, and then upon the Squires turn announced that it was two to one in the Squire's favour. Upon hearing this Squire, a recounted excellent shot, fired his pistol into the air and declared the bet was off and the "twelve paces on the daisies"[170] came to a peaceful end.

After the duel was finished, Lord George wanted to join the Bibury Club and was worried about his acceptance as a member as he feared he would be "Black Balled" by the Squire who was already a member. *"Then there came a time when Lord George, whose horses were trained at Danebury, wished to be- come a member of the Bibury Club, and old John Day tried his diplomacy upon the Squire to ascertain whether he would interfere with his former antagonist's election. All animosity, however, had long died away in the Squire's breast; and after Lord George's admission to the club, he invited the Squire to come and see the Danebury horses, and treated him with marked politeness."*[134]

Bentinck would arrive at Danebury in his yellow carriage by night and was reputed to stay at the Star Hotel, close by in Andover. He would then proceed to Danebury to watch the early work at 5am. By this time John Barham Day had taken his son John Day Junior into the business with him as father and son. The relationship between Lord George Bentinck and John Barham Day was reported as one of constant distrust, and later proved to be the ruin of their relationship. This distrust can be seen in letters held at Nottingham University. Somehow in spite of this John Barham Day and Lord George Bentinck together managed to dominate the turf in the early days of their partnership.

---

169 Thormamby, (Pseud) *"Wilmott Dixon" Kings of the Turf Members Owners and Distinguished Backers, Owners, Trainers and Jockeys*, 1898)
170 Lord William Pitt Lenox, *Celebrities I Have Known, With Episodes, Political, Social, Sporting And Theatrical*, 1877

Lord George on one occasion was so happy with John Day after consecutive wins that he commissioned Abraham Cooper of the Royal Academy in 1838 to paint a picture of John Barham Day with all his family. That painting now hangs in the Tate in London and a second picture was painted by the same artist of John Day upon the famous horse Ellis, the pictures were exhibited as some of Cooper's finest work at the Royal Academy in 1838. *"When we called the other day on Mr. Cooper to make some arrangements for our future embellishments, we found him busy superintending the packing of those beautiful pictures " the Day Family," and " Elis with John Day on him," intended as presents to John Day; and likewise a duplicate copy of Elis presented to John Day the trainer. These are the liberal gifts of that munificent patron of the Fine Arts, Lord George Bentinck, who has commissioned Mr. Cooper to make him another copy of the whole of the picture of" Elis, and The Drummer, with the caravan," which was exhibited this season at the Royal Academy."* [171] Figure 53Ellis John Barham Day Up with Van by Abraham Cooper 1836.

Abraham Cooper painted more pictures of John Barham Day than of any other jockey, including him up on the famous Ellis, Deception and Crucifix, *"Abraham Cooper were indeed fast friends as it was written the Royal Academia had more sittings at John than any other artist and painted him in turn on Ellis, Deception, and Crucifix. The most successful picture was one of a family picture painted by order of Lord George Bentinck who presented it to the late John Day with the understanding that it was to descend to his eldest son, in this group John stands in his Great Coat by the side of the mule Phaeton by which are seated his wife and his mother, while his son Sam is mounted on the game Venison and his son William on Chapeau d Espinage."* [172] **Figure 5** Day Family by Abraham Cooper R.A.1838 Day 1925.

With John Day Senior now totally busy conducting both roles as a trainer and jockey and with his first son John Junior and sons, Alfred and William in the saddle, there was no stopping the Day Family and the Danebury Stables dominating the turf. *"The record of the Day family as Jockeys and Trainers in Classic Races is unsurpassed over two generations they rode 30 winners and trained 22."* [173]

John Barham Day won another classic in 1834 with Pussy-(Pollio-Valve by Bob Booty) [174] who was bred by Lechmere Carlton of Ludlow Park

171 The New Sporting Magazine, (Walter Speirs, London Vol 16, 1839, p.87)

172 The Sporting review (edited John William Carlton by Craven London, Rogerson and Tuxford, Jan 1869, p.139)

173 Ray Vamplew and Joyce Kay, *Encyclopaedia of British Horse Racing*, (Routledge, Oxford 2005, p.91)

174 www.tbheritage.com/Portraits/Lottery.html (accessed 9th October 2009) "Pussy (1831,

THE CARAVAN.

Ellis (winner of the St. Leger of 1830) was thus conveyed to Doncaster.

Figure 30 Ellis in the (Caravan) Horse Box 1826 by

Shropshire, and raced by Thomas Crosby and owned and trained by his brother William Day at Ascot[175]. William Day had trained this horse and wanted to ensure success so, instead of letting one of his regular jockeys ride her he gave it to his brother John Barham Day to ride and he won. That same year 1834 he won the 1000 Guineas with Mayday-(Lamplighter-Mare-by Rubens) for Baron Berners his second Classic for the Baron, but after-wards Mayday was shot, due to breaking down during the running of the Oaks.[176]

In 1836, John Barham won the 1000 Guineas with Destiny-(by Sultan) for Mr. T. Houldsworth, this was a horse both trained and ridden by John Barham. He then went on in the same year to win the St Leger with Ellis and this event became quite famous as this was apparently the first time a

---

Pollio - Valve) was a dark brown filly bred by Lechmere Charlton of Shropshire, and later owned and raced by Thomas Crosby. She won ten races between 1833 and 1837, including the Oaks in 1834 and the Ascot Derby. She is depicted here with her trainer, John Day, and her jockey, Day's brother, William."

175 George Tattersall, *The Pictorial Gallery Of The English Racehorse*, 1850"Mr William Days Pussy"

176 www.tbheritage.com/Portraits/Lottery.html (accessed 9th October 2009 "May-day later broke down in the running of the Oaks, and was shot.

cart or horse box had been used to take a race horse to a meeting, and the crowd were quite surprised at Doncaster. Maybe this was the first time a cart was used in such a public event but we will pick up on this story later. Lord George Bentinck, took 12-1 odds and was reported as winning a packet on the race, the Classics were flying in for John, and the Danebury Stables.

The next year 1837 saw him snatch the 1,000 Guineas on Chapeau De Espinga-(Doctor Syntax-Chapeau De Paille) for Lord George Bentinck, It was a horse John Barham Day trained and rode. Following in 1838 he won the 2,000 Guineas with another victory for Lord George on Grey Monmus to which he again trained as well as rode[177]. In 1839 John Barham, now forty-six years old, stole the Epsom Oaks on board Deception-(Defence-Lady Stumps) for Mr. Fulwar Craven. The list seems endless, and as he progressed in his career the winning list became longer, as we shall see for the next year.

Bentinck had a reputation as a turf reformer and wanted to become known as the most successful patron the turf had ever seen. In 1840, his horse Crucifix-(Priam-Octaviana by Octavia who was bred by Lord Chesterfield, trained by John Barham Day and ridden by John Day won for him the 2,000 Guineas, the 1,000 Guineas, and The Oaks. It was an amazing feat for John Barham and the Danebury Stables and Lord George Bentinck was revelling in the glory.

Lord George Bentinck in modern and times past has been credited with the invention and creation of many things as we have already seen. This deceitfulness knew no bounds, he even tried to claim the honour of inventing a new form of bridle, but according to William Day this was not the case and it was not Bentinck. *"As for the original bridle, I am afraid that its use as well as invention is lost to posterity, for even the maker's name is unknown, so far as I have been able to discover."* [178]

He also announced to the public that he was the first to invent the horse box. Even the modern day writers claim that it was Lord George's idea and by his design in 1836 the first horse box carried Ellis and the horse Drummer to the Doncaster races. The van as it was known was pulled by

---

177 www.tbheritage.com/Portraits/Lottery.html accessed 9th October 2009 "GREY MOMUS was conceived and born in 1835, at the other end of ' long career as a sire, at the Sledmere stud of Sir Tatton Sykes"
178 William Day, Reminiscences Of The Turf, with Anecdotes And Recollections of its Principal Celebrities, (1891, p.82)

four horses and this enabled the horses to arrive fresh, instead of the old way which was to walk or ride a pony and trot the horses alongside. Lord George was credited by William Day with the *"Fashion of the Van"* [179] but that is all, the builder of the van and the first horse box was *"Herring of New Road London."* [179] So any Herring descendants out there you can be proud of your ancestor.

According to Mr. Tatton Sykes, a very famous and reliable name of the turf the first recorded horse pulling caravan or horse box was invented by a Mr. Territ where in 1816 he transported his horse Sovereign to Newmarket from Worcestershire for the 2,000 Guineas *"Mr. Territt was the first person who used a caravan fort the conveyance of race-horses. This was in 1816, when his horse Sovereign was thus transported from Red Marley, in Worcestershire, to Newmarket, where he was engaged in the Two Thousand Guineas Stakes."* [180]

Lord George has also been recorded as a breeder of horses, which he was, but history has him breeding such animals as Hermit, Aphrodite and Vanderdecken. However according to William Day in his book says he never bred them at all.[181] I could be considered biased when quoting from John Barham Day's son William, but William Days work was published in the 1880's and could have been contested by anyone of the day but it was not.

Lord George was not, the most generous or fair of patrons as some historians have portrayed him to be. He once made a present of a Silver Cup to my great-great-grandmother Harriet Day this cup was reputed to have been a thing of beauty. However after a few years of it being in her possession Lord George asked for it back, saying that he had never offered it as a present but offered it to be admired only how can you offer an item to be admired only? This is a story remembered in our family incidentally she returned the cup immediately.

---

179 William Day, Reminiscences Of The Turf, with Anecdotes And Recollections of its Principal Celebrities, (1891, p118) "The Drummer and Elis had, in 1836, the honour of being taken to Doncaster in a van, drawn by four horses, made for the express purpose by Herring, of the new Road, London, though the fashion of it was due to his lordship's inventive faculty."
180 George Tattersall, The Pictorial Gallery of The English Racehorse, (1850, p.133)
181 William Day, Reminiscences Of The Turf, with Anecdotes And Recollections of its Principal Celebrities, (1891, p.83) "Nor were Hermit Aphrodite or Vanderdeck bred by Lord George"

THE DOWNFALL OF THE DANEBURY STABLES

THE BEGINNING OF THE DOWNFALL OF the Danebury Stables began sometime from 1840. The stables had started to take on patrons of ill repute and different to those they were used to dealing with. Unfortunately for the stables, the publicity from these affairs and the court cases that followed left their most prized possession in tatters, their reputation. Unfortunately, this is what they have been remembered for most, so I feel it is very important in the next section to look at a few of these affairs and investigate what happened and who was really to blame.

One such affair was known as *the Spider and the Fly letters* according to James Rice who was writing in 1879 it started when John Day wrote two letters, one was to Bentinck, instructing him as the owner to bet what he liked on one of the horses because it would win. The other letter was to Lord George's bookmaker, telling him to lay against Lord George what he liked on the horse because it was not fit and would not win. So what was John Days motive? Was it to make money from the bookie, or was it to warn the bookie that the horse was lame and to take no notice of Lord George Bentinck's ravings that the horse was fine as he had done so many times before. According to Rice John Day made a huge mistake and he put the letters in the wrong envelopes. [182]So Bentinck received the letter stating his horse was in no fit state and the bookie received the letter proclaiming the horse would be sure to win. Modern Historians claim this was the Catalyst leading to the severance of Day and Bentinck.

This story was first claimed to have happened many years after both John Barham Day and Lord George had passed away, and was told by James Rice in the History of the Turf written in 1879. This story was told again in the History of the Jockey Club Rooms by David Oldrey who surprisingly did not mention William Day's version of the story but he did however state that maybe there was some doubt attached to its authenticity.

According to William Day the story told by Rice was a fabrication, totally made up by Mr. Rice in his book "History of the Turf" which was written

---

182 James Rice, History Of The British Turf, (1879, p.274 "John Day sat down to his desk to write two letters — one to his lordship, and the other to a celebrated bookmaker at Tattersall's. The letter to his lordship ran thus: — "My Lord — the colt is quite fit, and has done a rattling gallop. I fancy he is bound to win. Pray back him for all you can on Monday next, if you can only get a fair price." The other letter was as follows: — "Dear Joe — the long-legged lord will be at Tattersalls on Monday. Lay him all you can, the horse is a dead one," Unfortunately, Mr. Day put the letters in the wrong envelopes. The result is obvious."

in 1879 many years after the Days and Lord George had parted company and William Day, who was present at Danebury when Lord George left. William would have known better than Rice or Oldrey what had happened and he mentions this story in his book Reminiscences of the turf published in 1891, *"Now, as I lived at Danebury at the time, if such a thing had occurred, I should most likely have heard something of it; but I must confess I never did, until reading it many years after in Mr. Rice's misleading book."* [183.]

I have also checked this story in many other books and magazines of the time, prior to James Rice's writing to validate his claim and found absolutely no mention of the event or the said letters they were never recorded in 1841 or after. There is no record of it happening whatsoever, I should imagine if there ever was a letter written of such importance it would have been kept along with Bentinck's letters in Nottingham. Additionally having proof of Day cheating him Bentinck would have sought legal counsel against the Days and sued for Liable without hesitation. I wonder if he, or maybe the Jockey Club, had a copy of the letter that Lord George was referring to, I bet they don't.

William Day alluded to Lord George's hatred of his brother John Day Junior which he told in a story, John Day Junior discovered Lord George's horse Lecturer was not running very well, and invented a shoe that the horse Lecturer could wear to stop its knees knocking together. With this Lord George was really pleased and wrote to John Barham Day saying *"For his skill in detecting the injury he John ought to have a crown of Gold as a fitting tribute for such eminent services"* William then goes on to say, *"but how did he show his gratitude, by within a very short space of time persecuting him with all the most bitter Malignity, until his Lordship left Danebury and even after."* [184]

To further illustrate Lord George's dislike of Day I shall recall one more source from history regarding the removal of Lord George's horses from Danebury *"but he was no doubt offensively arrogant, and the truth lies rather between the extravagant hero worship of John Kent, and deliberate belittlement of John Day, the removal of his horses from Danebury is sufficient reason for the latter"* [185]

Further events contributed to Lord George leaving the Danebury stables, he requested to have my great-great-grandfather John Day Junior, John

---

183, William Day, Reminiscences Of The Turf, with Anecdotes And Recollections of its Principal Celebrities, (1891, p.125)

[184] William Day *Reminiscences of the turf* 1886 p.82

185 Theodore Andrea Cook, *A History of The English Turf*, H. Virtue & Company, London, 1901-1904,Vol II p.460

Barham's son, removed from Danebury for his alleged involvement in the Crommelin Affair that had given the Danebury stables a bad name[186]. John Barham Day, his father, would obviously not comply with Lord George Bentinck's wishes and kept John Day Junior on. In the next chapter we shall cover the Crommelin case, in a bit more detail, but it does appear that Lord George was using and abusing his position and power in the Jockey Club to influence the downfall of the Days. After all, the Jockey Club was not about to be blamed for the behaviour of their highest profile member.

CRUCIFIX

CRUCIFIX IN HER DAY WAS A famous racehorse that had won The Oaks and was purchased for 65 guineas with her dam by John Barham Day for Lord George Bentinck. When she was fully grown she was described as a very powerful wiry horse at 16 hands high, she was trained by John Barham Day at Danebury and ridden by John Day Junior and in 1840 won the 1,000 Guineas, 2,000 Guineas and the Epsom Oaks. Amazing achievement but The Oaks would prove to be her last race due to in numerous false starts which extended over an hour, 15 false starts before the race began. These false starts took the toll on Crucifix as shortly after winning The Oaks she was pulled up with a lame leg. Was it the false starts that took their toll or was there something else?

When Crucifix ran in the Criterion Stakes at Newmarket prior to The Oaks she had sustained an injury to her leg. When the race was over the horse's leg was considerably swollen. Lord George sent for the vet a Mr. Barrow who after examination suggested Crucifix should never run again as she would not be able to withstand the training and that the horse should be rested. Lord George on hearing this was very concerned as he had backed Crucifix very heavily to win in The Oaks of 1840. His only choice was to hedge or bet against her.[187]

Upon Crucifix's return to Danebury John Day Junior who was a veterinary surgeon schooled at Cambridge University inspected the horse himself and diagnosed that the injury was not that bad and would be healed in ten days.

---

186 Nottingham University1845 "Exercise book written in by Lord George Bentinck, "Provides an account, under the title 'Delicate, Investigation', of the enquiry by the Jockey Club into the affairs of Mr. Crommwelin and John Day in relation to the 1840 Derby; an account entitled 'Another Rattan Affair. Extraordinary Disclosures Snakes in the Grass' is also included and is dated 1 June 1845"
187 Tony Byles *In Search of Running Rein The Amazing Fraud of the 1844 Derby* Apex Publishing LTD Essex 2011 p.200

After hearing this Lord George hatched a deceitful plan to recover all the money that he had bet against Crucifix and win even more on top of that. He was planning to convince the public that Crucifix was lame and would never run again. He requested the favourable opinion of the vet Mr. Barrow and requested him to put his diagnosis into writing.

When Lord George had obtained the favourable diagnosis he immediately copied the letter and sent it to John Day at Danebury instructing him to show it to as many people as possible. At the same time Lord George would take the original letter and show it to all who he came in contact with around the betting ring moaning about his bad luck and advising all those people to hedge their bets as well in order to create himself more favourable odds. Crucifix ran the race for The Oaks and won for Lord George Bentinck honourable member of the Jockey Club whose deceitful plan had worked to perfection, he had deceived everyone.

Bentinck was reported as having won a fortune over Crucifix's Oaks wins, a gamble which was said to have left the betting ring 'crippled.' This was one of his dreams and aims. The report was that he won £20,000 but others including William Day estimated the figure was nearer to £100,000, *"If we double the sum and add £60,000 for his winnings on her in other races, we should not be over- shooting it."* [188] That is a fantastic sum of money to win even by today's standards, but this was nearly 170 years ago.

The deceitfulness of Bentinck had gone too far and John Barham Day had enough. Prior to the race Crucifix was out on the Gallops at Danebury, and William Saddler who was a relative of the family married to Day's daughter and also a trainer of high repute was coming to see her run, Bentinck also wanted Saddler and the betting men to see Crucifix. The only problem was that Crucifix was in bad shape due to the swollen leg, or as Day said, if she ran she would be lame, so Lord George Bentinck requested the horse be sent back to the yard and be made look in good shape for the purpose of deceiving them. In reply to this John Barham Day said, *"if your lordship insists upon this being done, you may take your horses to Goodwood or wherever you please."* [189]

With that Lord George did, he removed them to John Kent at Goodwood but had little success there the argument was even recorded by the press of the day *"Lord George Bentinck's lot then being there; but from some misunderstanding, on which probably both parties were a little to blame, the horses of Lord George were*

---

188 William Day, *Reminiscences of the Turf,* (1891)p.66-67
189 William Day, Reminiscences Of The Turf, with Anecdotes And Recollections of its Principal Celebrities, (1891, p.96)

removed in the autumn of last year to Goodwood, where they now stand under the management of Mr. Kent." [190] Remember Bentinck was also the top member of the Jockey Club so wielded great power and influence, in and around the turf in those days.

Even though Crucifix had sustained the leg injury after The Oaks, Bentinck still wanted the horse to go on. The injury meant Crucifix could not run in the St Leger, another classic race of the same year. Although Bentinck knew this, he maintained an elaborate pretence that she would run, all the time laying her to substantial sums. Bentinck, when called to account after the race, completely blamed the trainer John Barham Day as he couldn't accept the blame for himself.

Nicholas Foulkes in his book Gentleman and Blackguards writes that "*In his memoirs William Day records how his father succumbed to a nasty and rare attack of scruples when Bentinck asked him to deceive the touts.*" No! Mr Foulkes William Day didn't write that and it wasn't the touts to be deceived it was his Son in law William Sadler!

Lord George kept the training of his horses very close to his chest, and would not often race them. Instead he saved them for the big racing events. On the occasions he did race his horses he would wish to create the illusion that they were unprepared or untrained as he had done with Crucifix, to make them look to the public like they were not very good. This was done in order for Lord George to enter them in big races and deceive the public and even his friends, enabling him to bet heavily on them and receive odds disproportionately to their abilities[191]. Was this corruption?

We find Bentinck at it again with odds for his horse were put in at 7-2, a trainer named William Scott backed his horse for £2,000 in the race, and Lord George backed his horse that previously he had raced unprepared for £7,000. It was even said in his time, who would put seven thousand on a horse that previously had not shown any promise? This is what Lord George appeared to do, time and time again, in this instance the man that lost the money paid him but gave him the money in a dressing room with the court disgust saying "*that he can have his money, and what price is it but a few dirty acres of land'.* [192] That was the price the nobleman had on his own

190 John Stuart Skinner, *American Turf Register and Sporting Magazine,*1840, Vol 13, p.558
191 William Day, *Reminiscences of the Turf,* (1891, p.72) "There is no doubt that many of his lordship's horses, with his knowledge, ran unprepared, for the purpose of deceiving, not only the world at large, but his friends also"
192 William Day, Reminiscences of the Turf, (1891, p.83)

honour. It seems from reading the history that Lord George only betted with trainers that he could control in some way.

Lord George's deceitfulness on the Turf was well known, I will provide a funny account of one here to show the lengths he would go, to achieve favourable odds on his horses in that way even painting the horses nostrils to make the horse appear to have the flu to deceive the public to achieve better odds as penned Clarence Levey a writer in the late 19th Century *"This had the effect of making a healthy horse appear with the effect of a severe cold her nostrils were painted inside and out with starch flour and a colouring matter resembling mucus."*[193]

It is clear to see Lord George would go to extraordinary lengths to achieve his goals, After Lord George had been thrown out of Danebury John Barham Day then waited ages for the Lord to settle his training bill, which was £8,000 a year for his horses[194], the payment from the Honourable Lord still did not arrive so Day eventually took Lord George Cavendish Bentinck to court and sued him successfully. Bentinck had to pay the money and the cost of what was considered a heavy law suit. It is very important to remember the reason Lord George Cavendish Bentinck left Danebury was because John Barham Day refused to cheat on the Napoleon of the Turf the Honourable Lord Bentinck's behalf. This is all taken from accounts of the time, such as the Bailey Brothers in 1860 *"their final grand quarrel when he refused to comply with a request which not even the Napoleon of the Turf" could expect him to acquiesce in ."*[195]

Summed up by Lord George Bentinck's own cousin and member of the Jockey Club Mr. Charles Greville when writing in his diary *"He cannot but know that if all of the circumstances relating to Crucifix, by which he won so much money, were revealed, they would be considered disgraceful and dishonest, but no doubt he justifies them to himself. Then about betting against horses, nobody has ever been more unscrupulous than he in making money in this way. In short while he is thundering away*

---

193 Clarence D Levey, *The Torrance-Clendennin Episode and the Melville Letters: On Racing, Hunting, Steeplechasing, Clubs and Club Life,* 1892, p.139
194 Henry Corbett, *Tails and Traits of a Sporting Life,* (1864, p.61)"My racing establishment costs me eight thousand a year, and I can't win a fifty." Ill fortune, as usual, led on to disputes and dissensions, and my Lord and John Day parted anything but the friends they should have done.
195 A.H.Bailey *Baileys Magazine Of Sports And Past Times,* (1860, p.231) "His engagement with Lord George Bentinck; his successes for him and his friend Lord Litchfield, for whom he won the St. Leger on Elis, after having suggested the idea of running him to Doncaster; and lastly, their final grand quarrel, when he refused to comply with a request which not even the Napoleon of the Turf could expect him to acquiesce in."

against the poor low lived rogues for the villainies they have committed, he has himself been doing the same." [196] I wonder if that story about Lord George Bentinck was recorded in the book "The Jockey Club Rooms?"

In 1846 Lord George Cavendish Bentinck lover of the turf, top member of the Jockey Club mysteriously sold all of his horses for £10,000 when it was worth and had been valued at £100,000. The whole of the racing world was shocked. *The lot Payne said he to George Payne at Goodwood from Bay Middleton to little Kitchener, for 10,000 yes or no, Payne replied I will give 300 till breakfast time tomorrow"* replied George Payne, *"give me till then I will say yes or no. With pleasure my Dear fellow."* [197] The next morning Payne arrived with the bank cheque for £300, to which Lord George refused the offer on the spot, however someone over-heard the conversation and said *"I'll take the lot Bentinck for 10,000 and I will give you a cheque for 10,000 before you go to the course"* [197]Lord George replied *"if you please"* and the deal was done there and then.

Lord George after winning the 1845 Goodwood Gold Cup with Miss Elis exclaimed *"I think I have at last got the better of Danebury"*[198] In 1846 Bentinck, sold all his horses, and entered the House of Commons maybe the change of profession would have calmed him? No he still managed to harbour such a hatred and bitterness to anyone who would disagree with him, as written by his cousin Charles Greville *"G.Bentinck made another exhibition in H. of Commons the night before last in the shape of an attack on Labouchere more violent and disgusting than any of his previous ones. He seems to have lost all control over his temper and indiscretion and his arrogance has excited bitterness against him to be described "*[199]

THE DANEBURY CONFEDERACY

IN THIS CHAPTER I DEFINE THE passing over of the Danebury stables from John Barham Day to his son John Junior and endeavour to cover the handover providing an insight in to some now revealed events that could have influenced the premature handover of the Stables that John Barham Day had built.

The Day family featured in many stories as well as being involved in many

196 Charles Greville *The Greville Memoirs A journal of the Reigns of King George IV, King William IV and Queen Victoria* 1814-1860 Vol 5 Jan 1845-Dec 1847, p.185
197 Thormamby, (Pseud) "Wilmott Dixon *Kings of the Turf,* (1898, p.68)
198 John Kent, *The Racing Life Of Lord George Cavendish Bentinck MP,* 1892, p.179
199 Charles Greville *The Greville Memoirs second part a journal of the reign of Queen Victoria*1837-1852, p.71

scandals. Horse trainers of the time would of course be attracted to the owners who had the biggest pots of gold, which would provide for a larger and more stable racing stud. Horse racing costs exceptional amounts of money to procure and sustain today as it did then, and as seen with Lord George, his training bill for his vast stud was 8,000 pounds a year, and he was driven to obtain that money from somewhere.[194] This is called the sport of Kings, and Kings are expensive. From a horse trainer's point of view, it would be better to deal with as few owners as possible and the ones that you did procure, make sure they had enough money as your bills would need to be paid.

At this time the Danebury Stables were one of the most powerful and famous in the land and attracted all the good patrons of the turf, but as with any business that is booming, it attracts the good clients and unfortunately the bad Clients, and along with them are the money lenders crooks cheats swindlers etc. I can imagine once you were caught up in their net it would be difficult to get out and even worse if your patrons had become reliant on borrowing and lending money. Maybe they didn't have a choice any more over whether they stayed or left. With this in mind the Days became involved with a group of people who would become known as the Danebury Confederacy, which was for a while excellent news for the stables and its patrons and they sent out many winners, but eventually it became their downfall.

Danebury as we have seen in the previous chapters was the home of the Bibury Club, a club comprised of the richest men of the turf. Stockbridge was where they would meet for one week of the year and it was where the money and influence in Britain came together. So where ever there is a swill of money there can always be found some unsavoury swine, and the swine of the turf would run to the trough and that is exactly what happened here with the Danebury Confederacy.

The Confederacy set up shop and eventually from all accounts became the Bibury Clubs bank, and here they could have all the business they wanted on tap. Most of the patrons of the club lived in London where the ring leader of the Danebury Confederacy had his headquarters, and where the borrowing would have taken place. It was never the horses the Danebury Confederacy were interested in, that was the front for their business, the Confederacy were only ever interested in the owners of those horses.

The Confederacy knew that by keeping horses at Danebury it provided them with exclusive access allowing them to circulate and make introductions with the Bibury Club and other rich people whose circles they could now infiltrate. Once established the Danebury Confederacy would be difficult to remove.

There has in recent years been much attributed to the Danebury Confederacy with many local historians, writing passages here and there, but never quite exposing what was beneath the surface of it all. The formation of the Danebury Confederacy is quite interesting, we shall examine it as it helps place my family at the time and show what involvement they had with this group. Many good but also bad things arose out of this period and I think ultimately the Confederacy were responsible for a huge argument within my family that later led to a rift that would be catastrophic, and lead to the downfall of the stables. We have already put one era of accusations to rest regarding the Days and Lord George Cavendish Bentinck, let's see if we can do the same with the Danebury Confederacy. Lord George Cavendish Bentinck was responsible for introducing the Confederacy to Danebury in the first place, and Harry Hill, a member, was his "Chief Ring Commisioner"[216]. We shall now look at some of the members of the Danebury Confederacy in more detail, in a bid to throw some light into the shadows.

HENRY PADWICK

HENRY PADWICK ALTHOUGH NOT MENTIONED BY William Day as part or member of the Confederacy, from all historic accounts that I have read I believe he was. The nature of his business was the same as theirs, and William Day probably out of fear, didn't mention him as part of that group in 1880 but he does allude to Gully, Hill and Padwick being in the Confederacy.[200]

Henry Padwick was regarded in his day as one of the most successful men on the turf, he came from humble beginnings, as did many of the successes in that time. Padwick's father, by all accounts, was a butcher in Sussex, and this was the place where he was raised. This claim of his father being a butcher's son in Horsham made by William Day, from my research seems very far from the truth, and his powerful connections that he made later with the aristocracy, and also his ability to cover the largest of debts was enterprising and his son also Henry Padwick went on to marry on the 24th

---

200 William Day, Reminiscences Of The Turf, with Anecdotes And Recollections of its Principal Celebrities, (1891, p.33) "He was undoubtable a confederate with John Gully with Andover and other horses, and was even reputed to have been connected in the same way with the redoubtable Harry Hill, although Gully and Hill were too clever to accompany Padwick"

September 1861 Jane Eleanor Cheval Tooke, niece to Thomas Cheval Tooke born 1810, who was at one time Director of the Bank of England, and Lieutenant of London. [201] It is interesting that a connection from the son of a butcher could marry the niece of the Director of the Bank of England.

Padwick was well educated particularly in the law, and went on to become a Magistrate, and Deputy Lieutenant. So it was fair to say he had a very good grasp of all matters legal and all matters contractual, it had also been said that

Figure 31 Henry Padwick (photo-history-sussex.co.uk)

his study of the law was specifically to benefit his own future needs. In 1851 Padwick attended the Great Exhibition, and in his official position, was in attendance to Prince Albert Sax De Coburg husband of Queen Victoria.[202] So you can see he mixed in the circles of power. At some point he entered into money lending which he developed into the largest player of this business in his day. Padwick attracted patrons by taking securities that a bank would find too risky from a potential borrower and lend against them. So in gambling on the turf we can imagine his client base would have been extensive, and his clients came from all walks of life, aristocrats, politicians, and the general public, he did not refuse an opportunity to turn a profit.

He made all the comforts of rich living and employed a gourmet chef at his house and kept a wine cellar stocked with vintage wines. This was all part of the front, to attract and maintain rich clients.

Henry Padwick commenced racing under the Name of Mr. Howard, and first sent his horses to Danebury, to be trained under John Day Junior, and according to William Day the horses were about 40 in number, which was an impressive collection. But great success did not appear to happen for him at the Danebury stables, but as will be seen I think the whole reason for the transfer is shadowed in mystery.

---

201 Sir Bernard Burke, *Genealogical and Dictionary of the Landed Gentry of Great Britain and Northern Ireland*, (Harrison Pall Mall, London, 1863, p.1519)
202 William Day, *Reminiscences Of The Turf*, 1891, p.3 "At the opening of the Great Exhibition of 1851, which in his official position he was in attendance of Prince Albert"

JOHN GULLY

Figure 32 John Gully engraving by Joseph Brown 1860 (Wikipedia.org)

JOHN GULLY WAS AN acceptable sort of everyday man, who rose from nothing and made everything that he acquired. He was born 25th August 1785 in the Crown Inn Wick and Abbson near Bath. After a short time his father moved to Bristol and set up as a butcher a profession to which Gulley was schooled. After getting into debt he ended up in prison in Fleet Street, at the age of 21 years, but he was bailed by a fellow boxer, this boxer was a reputed champion of England who seems to have cut a deal with Gully in return for his release. Gully had to appear in a fight and get beaten, which was readily accepted and the fight took place on the 8th October 1805 at Hailsham Sussex in front of high regarded English aristocrats, where he was fighting a man called Pearce. After 70 minutes Gulley lost, but Pearce approached him after and said he was the best he had ever fought When Pearce retired Gully was offered the title of Champion which at that moment he refused. [203]

In his time of fighting Gully had made such a name for himself that he decided to retire and returned to his father's old trade of a publican and took a public house called The Plough at Lincolns Inn Field in London. After a while he saw his future was not in keeping a pub, as there was little money to be made.

Gully next went into bookmaking and became a bookie for the turf, and within four years of doing this he had made enough money to procure his own racing stud. He had performed very well and in 1827 bought a horse called Mameluke, for 4,000 guineas. But luck did not hold out for Gully for in the same year he was recorded as having lost amounts near to 45,000 guineas with his horse Mameluke against a horse called Matilda owned by Edward Petrie, but Gully paid up.

---

203 Thormamby, (Pseud) *Wilmott Dixon "Kings of the Turf*, 1898)

We next find Gully in a joint partnership or a Confederacy as it was called then with a man named Robert Risdale, they are recorded as having won bets of £60,000, and £45,000 on two horses in the St Leger and the Derby, that is a fantastic sum of money to win on a horse race even by today's standards, near to £7million in today's value. However the business partnership did not last and ended with Gully horsewhipping his partner. Risdale took Gully to court and won £500 damages, this left Gully's reputation in the gutter. There are many other incidents of Gully publicly losing his temper, but eventually he started to settle his matters in private, this together with his prize fighting career, made people wary of him, a person not to be crossed.

Gully's main love was the turf and he can first be seen attempting to launch a turf career in 1834 when he vested his first throw of the dice with the Chifneys and tried without success to win the Derby that year with a horse called Shillelagh. After a while he gave up on the Chifneys in Newmarket and transferred his horses to the powerful stables at Danebury under the care of John Barham Day and the riding skill of John Day Junior and Sam Day, John Barham's brother.[204]

The Danebury stables started to return some amazing results, firstly for Harry Hill with Ugly Buck, who they won the 2,000 Guineas with in 1844 and then in 1845 came Pyrrhus the 1st and Mendicant with which they pulled of The Oaks and the Derby, and if that wasn't enough they went on to win with Hermit the 2,000 Guineas and Andover they won the Derby. That is an amazing stock of wins for one owner, considering that previously the Chifneys and Newmarket could not do anything for him.[204]

HARRY HILL

HARRY HILL LIKE GULLY, and Padwick was a bookie, and also like Gully and Padwick had started in life at the bottom, and worked his way up. From the accounts I have been able to find, Harry Hill began his working life in hotel, as an "under boot", which appears to have been a porter, but by the 1850's he owned Marwell Hall in Winchester an aristocratic palace, and like Gully and Padwick had made a packet out of racing.

---

204 Henry Corbett, *Tails and Traits of a Sporting Life*, (1864)

HARRY HILL

Hill did as Gully and Padwick did, always mixed with the people of influence, which was a requirement in their business. People with position and influence loved gambling on the turf, and some would bet very large amounts. So the gambling fraternity would rely on the bookie for loans, the loans would be kept quiet, and in return for this discretion the bookies received not only business from these rich and powerful people, but they also gained access to their friends and acquaintances thereby elevating their stations or positions in life and enabling them to mix freely amongst the rich and powerful of the day. For example, "*Harry Hill would always come to Danebury*

Figure 33 Harry Hill (New York Public

and was frequently accompanied by Baron Martin." [205]who was a judge, and they were described as being good friends.

DANEBURY CONFEDERACY FORMATION

THE DANEBURY CONFEDERACY WAS IN ESSENCE a betting group of men who would lend out money in the return for securities. This group had the same idea in mind, to make as much money as they could by using a similar method to a bank, lending vast sums of money against a security. What made them stand out from all the other gamblers of the day are the huge amounts of money they would bet, the extortionate rate they would lend at and the clientele they served.

The Danebury Confederacy consisted of the following people, John Gully, Harry Hill, Pedley, Arnold, and Turner. This was the famous Danebury Confederacy.[206] The membership list came from William Day, one of my ancestors who named them as the group in 1880. But from my own research there is one more person. I think William Day left out Mr. Henry Padwick from this group, through fear of repercussions. But I, unlike my ancestor am not in racing, so I am free from those fears.

---

205 A.H.Bailey, *Baileys Magazine of Sports and Past Times*, (1883, p.70)
206 William Day, *Reminiscences Of The Turf*, (1891, p.43)

Mr. Henry Padwick, I believe was the brains behind the operation of the Danebury Confederacy, he had the education, he had the contacts the legal know how, and the background, he also had joint shares in some of the horses, notably Andover who he shared with John Gully[207].

Many people have stated that it was John Gully, who was the mastermind, but from what I have read I believe it was Padwick, and I believe Padwick has not been included in historic accounts to distance the aristocracy from any involvement with the Danebury Confederacy and his clandestine operation.

It seems that Padwick would obtain money from all areas of business including banks and private investors to money lenders, and in addition to this *"he worked other capital besides his own from Messrs. Hill and Gully."* [208]

He would obtain this money at a charge to himself of 10% the banks and others were eager to lend, when the normal interest rate of the day was 1-1.5%[208]. Padwick would borrow the money by using securities deposited by his clients, and then lend out the money to his gambling aristocratic clients at a much higher rate; 100%-300% had been seen but unverified. The securities ranged from stocks to mortgage deeds that were in the names of the borrowers, usually the aristocracy, who wished to have quick access to the money for betting.

So he was a middle man with access to an endless supply of money, which to the gambling aristocrats was a necessity. This was not the only benefit of the Danebury Confederacy, the aristocrats requiring money for gambling were assured the utmost secrecy *"whatever the adventurer may do is little noticed and certainly not canvassed."* [209] Discretion was key.

STARKEY OF SPYE PARK

This can be clearly seen in the case of John Bayton Starkey of Spye Park who became involved with borrowing money from Henry Padwick and within 6 years had lost his entire fortune which was estimated at 300,000 pounds and his ancestral estate of Spye Park, in Wiltshire, which had one time been considered the preferred option over Sandringham by the Prince of Wales, who had offered 300,000 pounds for it previously, but was

207 William Day, *Reminiscences of the Turf,* (1891, p.43). "Writing on John Gully, he was only part owner of the horse Andover when it won the Derby in"
208 William Day, *Reminiscences of the Turf,* (1891, p.4)
209 William Day, *Reminiscences Of The Turf,*(1891, p.37)

Figure 34 Spye Park Bayntum-history.com

declined by Starkey.
[210] In 1864 the estate
was sold and Padwick
became short time
owner and sat in the
ancestral seat of the
Starkey's of Spye
Park, however the
crown purchased the
estate apparently for
275,000 pounds and
the aristocracy were
not having that. Starkey was only 27 and it must have been all too much for
him because after this affair he ran away to Australia. John Bayton Starkey
prior to being ruined requested my ancestor William Day to be guarantor
against a debt of 300 pounds which William Day did cover but John Starkey
never paid the debt, which was then sold to a debt collector, and eventually
William Day had to honour this bill, when a writ was issued against it in
court.

Padwicks business HQ was located in Berkley Square in London, and when
he accumulated too many customers, which he regularly did, he would pass
them on to Gully and Hill. So you can imagine that Padwick was the top of
the chain and Hill, Gully and the rest did the leg work and were the touts,
that pulled the clients in, making the money revolve in a circle back to its
source namely Padwick, relieving or greasing the ancestral estates from the
aristocrats in the process. The British landed gentry was fast losing its land.

The way in which Hill and Gully and the Confederacy made their money
was not just in the lending but also in the betting. *"For with Hill offering to lay
and Gully offering to back, and Joshua Arnold willing to do either, the public was
completely mystified by the adroit art of these professors."* [211] This practice would
manipulate the betting price of the horse making it look like it was a dead
cert, so then the public would see this and hand over their hard earned
cash, with the false prospect of winning. Of course the problem was, the
horse that the bookmakers had laid against and backed was more dead than
a dead cert, for a lot of the horses never even made the start of the race,

---

210 William Day, *Reminiscences Of The Turf*,(1891, p.29) "I believe at one time, 300,000 was
offered and refused for the estate, the offer I am correct in saying was made on behalf of the
Prince Of Wales, before the purchase of Sandringham was decided upon"
211 William Day, *Reminiscences Of The Turf*, (1891, p.69)

and if they did, they finished far down the field. The group would travel the country to appear at the big racing events to conduct this business.

The men on the ground were the bookies or the touts at the stalls, who took the public's money. They would be in the know that the horse was out of condition and would not run or perform well, and it would be in their interest as well to make sure that the horse was laid against, so they could then make a killing from it. [212]

The private and big money bets, by all accounts were taken by people such as Gully or Hill, and backed by the Chief Padwick, and as already said, they laid against dead horses to make a packet, but in some instances if the horse won, and the backer came to collect his winnings, the bookies would pretend that they never put the money on in the first place, or had simply forgot. On one occasion according to William Day, Harry Hill was caught cheating like this and publicly disclosed for it. *"Mr. Rayner asked Hill to put him a pony on a certain horse, the horse won and the next day Hill was asked for the money"* to which he replied *"I did not put it on and forgot to declare so before the race."* [213]

The Confederacy were extremely clever, they had started off as a small operation and eventually built themselves into a power group and disguised their dealings behind all sorts of people and businesses jockeys included. *"Moreover to carry the system to success it became necessary to bring into the services of stable boys jockeys and others, as a result of these nefarious practices rightly or wrongly imputed to well-known jockeys who have suffered the severest penalties."* [214]. Hill and Gully were not the only ones using this system but it was said they had perfected it.[215]

They had involved all sorts of people from noble men to peasants, mugs whose egos were bigger than their wallets. If they could not pay what they had borrowed the noble men could be in fear of losing their securities, which were deeds to land or estates, and in some cases, as already seen, their debt was even sold to other money lenders, or maybe favours were

212 William Day, Reminiscences Of The Turf,(1891, p.68) "Be considered other than dishonest, in the case where laying commissions are accepted, for the agents who receive them know that the horse so laid against will not run, and it is their interest to see that they do not, thus the backers have no chance of winning"
213 William Day, *Reminiscences Of The Turf,* (1891, p.73)
214 William Day, Reminiscences Of The Turf, (1891, p.69)
215 William Day, Reminiscences Of The Turf,(1891,p.52-53) "To messes Gully Hill and their confederates may be attributed if not the initiation at least the perfecting of this pernicious system"

exchanged in payment such as introductions to new prospective rich friends, which would leave the nobility indebted to the Confederacy allowing them to bank later favours.

This system had been seen before and on one such occasion had been publicly disclosed by one of those noble men, the Duke of Cleveland, and Gully was there as well. They were apparently all at a party in 1832 awaiting the St Leger races of that year, and the Duke of Cleveland started denouncing, the Confederacy, and it ended with one of the party members *"mounting the table and denounced the gang as a crew of robbers and miscreants for whom the gallows would be too good."* [206] after this was said, the room erupted into applause, followed by a fight that brought the party to a rough conclusion.

The Confederacy had become established at Danebury and Stockbridge, as said, before the home of the then richest racing club in England the Bibury Club, which contained most of the prominent and famous members of the turf. The noblemen of the Bibury Club would have developed a dependency on them, and by this method the Confederacy would have attached itself to the Bibury Club, and also to Danebury, feeding of its host.

When looking at history we must ask the question was it the Day family that wanted the Confederacy to be formed at Danebury, or was it down to a clandestine requirement of the aristocratic heavy gambling patrons and members of the exclusive and elite Bibury Club that the Danebury Confederacy set up shop, and were retained there for so long, as in history it is the Day family and the Danebury Establishment that have taken the blame and the aristocrats some of whom were also members of the Jockey Club have as usual, have walked away with clean hands.

Clientele of the Danebury Confederacy:-

THE BIG MONEY CUSTOMERS OF THE Danebury Confederacy were from the nobility many were members of the Bibury Club and in some instances also the Jockey Club and some found ruin at the hands of the Danebury Confederacy. John Bayton Starkey of Spye Park, who we looked at before, the Marquis of Hastings member of the Jockey Club, who we shall look at later Lord Francis Villiers, a Jockey Club Steward, who had to leave the country in 1855 due to his apparent debt of 100,000 pounds. So you can imagine the influence they had, you can almost imagine what protection they were afforded on the turf how many favours were owed, the Danebury Confederacy probably considered themselves untouchable.

Another unaccounted client of the Danebury Confederacy and of Hill and Gully's, and Padwick's friends and very close associates, was our dear old friend Lord George Cavendish Bentinck, also a top member of the Jockey Club, renowned turf reformer, this relationship does not appear in modern records, and by all means has been removed as has the Confederacy, but was very much a customer in their time.

I thought we were finished with him but modern history has done its utmost to hide him from scandal and as always he keeps popping up. Harry Hill was described as being Lord George's "Chief Ring Commissioner" *Writing on Lord George "Mr. Harry Hill was his chief ring commissioner, in truth high betting was the only source he could find and meet such a stud and stable outlay ."*[216] It was said Lord George needed to bet and win lots of money as that was the only way he could afford a stud the size that he had. Also, Hill had been his Chief Ring Commissioner and maintained the cost of Bentinck's stud for years as seen from a different source *"Lord George for years kept up his magnificent stud by his book and Mr. Harry Hill his chief ring commissioner."* [217]

Lord George's involvement with the Danebury Confederacy has been kept firmly out of the horseracing history records the large sums of money he was winning and betting however has kept him in, for example in 1845 he won £20,000 on Miss Mary, £23,000 on Miss Ellis and in the Derby with his horse Gaper he stood to win upwards of £120,000 but that was foiled and we shall see why later. Another source says *"Hill like Gully used to bet for his Lord Ship, and I presume for or against his own horses."* [218] So we can see where Lord George had the idea of trying to run dead horses, which he had tried to do by deceiving Mr. Saddler, in 1841 which we covered previously, and John Barham Day told him to take his horses elsewhere.

There is another account I wish to recant of Lord George who owned a horse called Grey Momus, William Day was riding it in the Ascot Gold Cup, of 1838 and the Jockey on the leading horse in the race Epirus rode up beside William and told him to *"go on or you will be beat"* [219], and Epirus the winning horse disappeared from the front, William won easily and so did Lord George he won 20,000 pounds.

William Day further goes on to say and this was all in the public print of 1890, that *"There is no doubt that many of his Lordships horses with his knowledge,*

---

216 The Gentleman's Magazine, (Bradbury Evans, Vol 1 June-November, 1868, p.73)
217 The Gentleman's Magazine, (Bradbury Evans London, Vol 235, 1873, p.45)
218 William Day, *Reminiscences Of The Turf,* (1891, p.72)
219 William Day, *Reminiscences Of The Turf* (1891, p.93)

ran unprepared for the purpose of deceiving, not only the world at large, but his friends also, in order that on future and fixed occasions he might reap the full reward of this policy."[219] It ties him quite nicely into the Danebury Confederacy. William Day could be accused of just writing bad things about our Lord George as he was a member of the Day family, but please remember William wrote his book in 1886, and he mentions that all of this evidence was in public print by then.

There is one more piece of astounding evidence that was written a few years after time of the Qui Tam cases which we will cover in a moment, and involved a bet that was made between those arch enemies John Barham Day and Lord George Bentinck, and a horse called Gaper, and I will show, using historic accounts how much aligned and involved, Lord George Cavendish Bentinck was with the Danebury Confederacy, and his good old "Chief Ring Commissioner" Mr. Harry Hill how far their relationship went, and to have even influenced the decisions made in a court of law.

GAPER AFFAIR

GAPER WAS LORD GEORGE BENTINCK'S HORSE running for the 1843 Derby. It was placed as favourite to win against Cotherstone. John Barham Day knew Bentinck was up to his old tricks of running what appeared to be a (dead) horse in front of the public for the Derby, so John Barham Day laid £20,000 against Gaper to win the Derby, against £250, this would raise Gaper to the position of favourite and in one hand reduce the betting odds substantially in the ring, therefore making Lord George unable to win a vast sum of money. In the end John Barham lost £2750 as just before the opening of the race Lord George induced the bookmaker to increase the bet from £20,000-£350 to £20,000-£3,000, so when Gaper lost John Barham Day lost £2,750 to Lord George. John Gully took the bet for John Barham Day, Harry Hill took Lord George's bet, and upon losing John Barham Day was said to have paid the money and thus settled the bill. But on the 8th August 1844, the bill had apparently not been settled, and a writ was issued against Lord George for its recovery, in a strange action called Qui Tam another illustration of how bitter the feud was between the two men. Later on John Barham Day admitted he was wrong in the whole Gaper Affair and his regret was recorded in a magazine of the day *"The Gaper business he admitted was wrong, and the fault of temper, which he would never allow to get the better of him again."*[220]

---

220 A.H.Bailey, *Baileys Magazine Of Sports And Past Times*, (1860, p.231)

QUI TAM

QUEEN ANNE ACT:

QUI TAM IS AN ABBREVIATION OF the Latin phrase *"tam pro domino rege quam pro se ipso in hac parte sequitur"*, meaning "he who sues in this matter for the king as well as for himself." Which consisted of, *"The ninth Act of Parliament for Queen Anne's Reign the Qui Tam act menaced racing for nearly 150 years because of its aim to confine betting to very small amounts of money it laid down that any amount in excess of £10.00 won in betting could be sued for and recovered, together with treble that amount."* [221]

In laymen's terms this act allows a private individual, or "whistle-blower," with knowledge of fraud i.e. amounts betted privately over £10 committed in the past or present against the government or king to bring a law suit on its behalf and recover the amount betted plus treble the amount. However this mainly concerned bets that were taken on commission and by non-owners if the money was bet between say two individual owners or laid down, then the Qui Tam Action or Law could not be applied.

This was however a not well known or practiced law and in 1844 found itself under question by the house of commons select committee as this law could have reigned havoc on the practice of betting which was not actually legal anyway. Qui Tam could be applied to all sorts of sports it was allowing many gamblers to default on their bets if they lost as stated Richard Tattersall when being questioned over Qui Tam *"there are many men living at their country houses who owe thousands which if they were honest men they could pay; but no law can make them and they laugh at you."* [222] The Government were worried and were looking to repeal it the Duke of Richmond for the select committee on 30th April 1844 asked Mr Charles Weatherby keeper of the Jockey Club Match Book "Do you know of any law that would prevent two race horse owners making a match for £10,000" Weatherby replied "No if they make a match for £10,000 and pay the money down, I have never heard a law which would prevent that" however it was not the case to non-owners, *"If two men of middle class society bet ten guineas on that race they will be liable to a Qui Tam action"* Weatherby replied *"I believe that is the effect of the law under which the actions have been lately bought."* [223]

---

221 Gerald Hammond *The Language of Horse Racing* Fitzroy Dearborn Chicago 1992 p. 169
222 *House of Lords, The sessional papers* Volume XIX 1844, p.102
223 *House of Lords, The sessional papers* Volume XIX 1844, p.269

This all started when between the 1st July and December 31st 1843, 34 writs using the Qui Tam Act for the recovery of moneys won or lost in the Sport of Kings was taken out at the Court of Exchequer. All the writs were taken out by a Mr. J.T.Russell who was an attorney; most of the defendants in this case were noble men. 30 of those writs belonged to a Mr. Charles Henry Russell, who was the plaintiff, in the case, and amazingly our Jockey Club stewards appeared in the dock as the defendants. The following six writs were issued against Lord George Cavendish Bentinck, George Anson had one, and Colonel Peel had two.

The record shows that when the plaintiffs received these writs they were astounded that such a law existed and thought it un-gentlemanly, but never the less it was a law, and it was served on them. The amount that was to be recovered in total was said to be £500,000 from the 34 writs that were issued. An amazing sum of money and the majority of that sum were owed by a few noblemen but it does not mention who but writing of the case at the time it was thought that. *"The penalty would be something considerable"* *"One nobleman was sued for 68,000 another for 102,000, and a Member of Parliament for 120,000 pounds."* [224]

But on assumption Lord George had 6 of those 34 writs, and he was the only one who appeared in court so it is fair to assume that the lion's share could have been owed by him. I have found by reviewing the minutes for the select committee on gaming of 1844 Mr. J.T.Russell was in the dock and was asked the question *"what have you sued Lord George Bentinck for, upwards of 100,000 pounds."* [225] But of course the establishment didn't like this one bit, as the Solicitor J.T.Russell of 37 Percy Street Bedford square when pushed to divulge who is Client is firstly prior to the suit being brought for trial claimed he did not know him and that he had been engaged anonymously, but during the second round of questioning and after the case had been brought divulged his identity as his brother.

So it looks like these highborn powerful members of the Jockey Club had been called to account under the law by sons of the owner of a betting house man, imagine that could it be possible that they were going to feel the weight of the law? Only one of the Qui Tam suits was actually brought to court, meaning the others must have been dismissed or settled. Russell vs Lord George Cavendish Bentinck appeared before Guilford Assizes on

224 Saunders Otley and Co, *Horse Racing Its History and Early Records of the Principal and Other Race Meetings* Saunders Otley and Co, London, 1863, p.404)
225 House of Lords, *The sessional papers reports on gaming evidence for the select committee and the House of Lords*, (1844, p.155)

Thursday 8th August 1844. And strangely enough it was concerning John Day and his bet made at the 1843 Derby over Cotherstone and his horse Gaper. The case outline was," *that on May 31, 1843, one John Day did, by betting on a horserace, contrary to the law, lose the sum of £3,000 to the defendant, and that the said sum of £3,000 was paid by the said John Day to the said defendant, and that he did not, within a period of three months, sue the said defendant for recovery of the amount which he had so lost, and therefore that the plaintiff was entitled to sue for and recover of and from the said defendant, the said sum of £3,000 so won and paid, and treble the value thereof, making together the sum of £12,000."*[224]

So John Day bet with Lord George for amounts exceeding £10, the bet should have been null and void as it was contrary to the 9th act of Queen Anne. John Day had paid the bet and didn't sue for its recovery within 3 months, so this then enabled Russell as a whistle-blower to sue under Qui Tam, under the act of Queen Anne, for the recovery of the three thousand on behalf of the King and treble the amount thereof. We can see that all of the noblemen and politicians were betting illegally, Peel, Anson and Bentinck, who were also top members of the Jockey Club, and who were stewards at John Day Junior's dismissal. Under the Qui Tam (Queen Anne Act) it meant that Lord George was now being sued.

Russell having been in front of the select committee of the House of Lords respecting gaming twice now for questioning under the Duke of Richmond. He had gleaned lots of information prior to the Qui Tam action being brought to a trial and did leak the same to the defendant Lord George Cavendish Bentinck it was never going to be accepted that a middle class person would ever dream of taking a high born aristocrat and member of the Jockey Club to court how dare they!! Bentinck by all accounts used his position and influences to lobby all the other members of the court to the point that when the case reached trial Mr Russell the Solicitor was laughed out of court!

Russell lost the case as he had failed to prove that the bet had actually taken place. But 20 years later in 1863 and published in a very respectable magazine of the day the Gentleman's magazine the following was written, *"He gave Mr. Hill a bill for the balance, and that gentleman had it in his pocket when he was examined on the Qui Tam action against Lord George at Guildford; but the jury did not love informers, and gave a verdict for the defendant without its being produced to show that no money had passed."* [226] So there was evidence to prove that the bet had in fact taken place and it was known and submitted to the court, but

---

226 The Gentleman's Magazine, (Bradbury Evans Vol 1, June-November 1868, p.73)

they dismissed the evidence and stated there was none. A court of law had bent the knee to the power and influence of the Jockey Club not surprising really when its members were also the members of the House of Lords, Parliament etc.

Not long after the House of Lords abolished the penalties of the Qui Tam and other penalties that had been in place for years, I wonder if the boot had been on the other foot if it was not the gentry being sued if the Qui Tam actions were taken against the lower classes, I wonder if the outcome would have been the same, of course not no House of Lords select committee to gather advance information for them. By the look of it Lord George and his group of friends at the Jockey Club were abusing their positions of power for their own gains whilst being proclaimed heroes by the Club, at the expense and blame of the innocent.

If that wasn't enough for the Jockey Club, some of their members, were denounced for secrecy in 1844 by the press and the public, it concerned the famous scandal of the 1844 Derby, and turned into a very public affair.

The Practice of Hedging a bet

"Hedging a bet" was a practice whereby a person had laid a bet say for instance of 100 on the nose of a horse to win, then the horse damages himself or doesn't look in good shape prior to the race, so in order for the person that laid the bet to recover some of the 100 he will lose he places a second bet on another horse. People will never win more money but they will lose less This practice was perfectly allowed in Horse Racing it only fell under question if the jockeys or trainers were doing this as they had direct influence on the outcome of a race and it may be considered fraud if a jockey had placed large sums of money on other horses in his race and little amounts on his own and then failed to win if he had a chance the Commissioners or bookies were supposed to report or pick this kind of action up but they were only after their commissions.

This practice was legal and many racehorse owners adopted it as stated in the select committee on gaming of 1844 when the Duke of Richmond was questioning Vincent George Dowling editor of the Sporting paper Bells Life the Duke asked the following question "*are there not many instances of Race Horse owners Hedging Stakes betting 25 or 100 against their own horse for the purpose of if they lose of losing nothing and if they win winning that which satisfies them*" Dowling replied as "*It is a very common turf Axiom that a bet has never been properly laid until it is well hedged, nothing is more common than for a racehorse owner to come to Tattersalls and bet against his own horse"[227]?*

RUNNING REIN 1844 DERBY FRAUD

FOR THIS STORY I HAVE READ many books and articles on the subject in particular a book called *"In Search of Running Rein the Amazing Fraud of the 1844 Derby"* written by Tony Byles and *"Gentlemen and Blackguards"* by Nicholas Foulkes. The Day family was running two horses in the Derby, of 1844 Ugly Buck and Voltri owned by John Barham Day these horses were not involved directly in the scandal but this story helps give a good account of fraud going on at the time and more importantly some of figures that were involved with it.

The Derby of 1844 turned out to be riddled with fraud, the winner of the Derby a horse called Running Rein was found to not be Running Rein at all but an entirely different horse, and in other words the horse known as Running Rein had been replaced with another sometime prior to the start of the race. Suspicion had been reported to the Stewards at Epsom racecourse prior to the Derby by a number of people including Lord George Bentinck, but the Stewards of Epsom had failed to act on those suspicions so the race had gone ahead unhindered. *"We the undersigned (G.Bentinck and John Bowes) owners of horses engaged in and intended to run for the approaching derby having strong reasons for believing the horse meant to be started as Mr. Goodman's Running Rein is not the b.c by the Saddler, out of Mab by which the Running Rein is described etc.to the Stewards of Epsom Races John Scott."* [228]

Another objection was made against a different horse called Leander in the same manner this objection was made to the Jockey Club stating that the horse was a four year old *"Gentlemen Sinister reports have been prevalent with regard to the identity of Leander and Running Rein. I therefor think it highly important to give the respective owners an opportunity of proving their pedigrees and their ages etc. Lord Maidstone"* If it was left like that everyone involved would have been satisfied that the Stewards at Ascot would inspect the matters prior to the race if they thought there were grounds for suspicion.

The race started with Leander leading followed by Voltri, then close by Akbar, with the Ugly Buck third, Orlando behind right with Rattan behind left. Most of the horses retained their positions throughout the race with

---

[227] House of Lords, The sessional papers (Volume XIX 1844, p.269
[228] Tony Byles *In Search of Running Rein The Amazing Fraud of the 1844 Derby* Apex Publishing LTD Essex 2011 p.98

exception to Leander who had received an injury to the leg struck by Running Rein. As the horses turned for Tattenham Corner, Akbar started to wain followed by Ugly Buck. Colonel Peel's two horses Orlando and Ionian made up the running to catch the leader Running Reign and the field stayed like that to the finish post, with Running Reign winning followed by Orlando and Ionian.

So Running Reign and his owner Mr. Wood had won, but this was not the case because the Stewards dispatched a letter to Weatherbys instructing them to not pay the winnings to Running Reign but to pay it to Colonel Peel as owner of Orlando until further notice. With that Mr. Goodman, Running Reign's owner filed an action in the court. Colonel Peel also claimed the stakes but had no confidence in any action from the Jockey Club as it was suspected its members may have backed Running Reign and therefore they would have no interest in an investigation.

Lord George Bentinck had already amassed a large amount of information against Goodman and Running Reign. Bentinck had backed Colonel Peel's horse heavily, as had Bentinck's commissioner Harry Hill (Danebury Confederacy). Hill had underhandedly received a letter with information regarding Running Reign; Hill took the letter immediately to Lord George Bentinck who realized that the information in the letter would award the Derby to Orlando, Peel's horse.

The long and short of it was that an investigation was eventually conducted by the Jockey Club with certain members including Lord George Bentinck being at the thick of it. The public who had backed the winner Running Reign were desperate to receive their winnings. Maybe the Jockey Club should not have become involved in the case but left it to a proper investigation by the Stewards at Epsom, as the Stewards had already made it clear that should either horse Running Rein or Leander win the Derby the Stakes would not be awarded immediately pending an investigation. Colonel Peel, stood to lose thousands in bets and Bentinck and Hill who had secretly backed the same horse so had vested interests in Orlando being declared winner. After quite some deliberation in court between both parties Colonel Peel, and Mr. Cockburn defending for Mr. Goodman bringing witnesses and neither party getting anywhere, I will not go into detail here as others have already examined it far better than I .In the end the defendant and owner of Running Reign Mr. Goodman instructed his solicitor Mr. Cockburn to withdraw the case stating that he himself had been deceived and that he was not prepared to go on with it. Strange, had Mr Goodman been got at?

Surprisingly Mr. Cockburn the defendants solicitor then turned and addressed the court stating that *"My Lord I have received a communication from my Lord George Bentinck, couched I must say in terms of perfect courtesy to myself, and perfectly unexceptionable in every point of view, in which my Lordship complains of my having made a charge against him yesterday, with respect to his conduct in the matters connected with the case, and that I have not put him into the witness box, or called a witness to prove that charge. My lord, I will just explain in a moment the position in which I stand; my instructions were clear, specific, positive and unqualified as to this- that my Lord George Bentinck had for I can use no milder term tampered with the plaintiffs witness; that he had held out threats to them, and where threats had failed, had held out promises to them to induce them to withhold their evidence. That he had procured by the greatest exertions, and by the use of his personal influence, witnesses to appear for the defendant; that he had a certain degree associated with those witnesses; that he had them at Harcourt House his new place of residence, that he had fed them, that he had clothed them, that his valet had been seen to take one of them to a tailors to fit them out with clothes, and that his lordship had helped out to another pecuniary promise. I was instructed; my lord that from his lordship, if he was called as a witness for the defendant, I should be enabled to extract these matters, instructed that from the defendants witness when called. Under these circumstances, my lord, it being a fact in the cause, if Lord George Bentinck was not a party in the cause still he had been the great mover in it, which is not denied by my learned friend the Solicitor General."* [229]

Amazing really that Lord George never made it into the witness box to answer any of the charges that would have been levied against him. The defence withdrew the case before that could happen as the solicitor for the defendant stated *"I had no opportunity of doing that which his lordship complains I have not done —put him in the box as a witness, or examined any one witness as to the matters I have charged against Lord George."* [229] It smells very bad of corruption perhaps given the defending lawyer, had suspicion and intention of putting Lord George in the box and publicly levying those charges against him, but it appears the Noble Lord had got at the defence and either threatened or influenced them to withdraw their case, either way we will never know. But what is certain is that Bentinck and Peel were very close in horse racing and a few things were true, that Peel had bet heavily on his horse to win and it didn't, prior to the race Lord George Bentinck lodged a complaint based on the identity of the winner Running Reign, and after the race he encouraged Peel to do the same. So that was it, Running Rein was disqualified and Colonel Peel's horse was declared the winner.

---

[229] Tony Byles *In Search of Running Rein The Amazing Fraud of the 1844 Derby* Apex Publishing LTD Essex 2011 p.181-182

RATTAN AFFAIR

Rattan was owned by Lord George Bentinck and was one of the favourites to win the 1844 Derby. It had been seen prior to the start of the Derby that there was something wrong with Rattan, or that she may have been got at. The jockey Sam Rogers was also in question for betting against his horse Rattan the bet was for the sum of *"£2,000 to £10,000, in today's terms would be around £200,000 to win £1 million."* [230] The jockey had been persuaded to bet against Rattan. So Rogers the jockey informed the owner Mr. Crockford's son that he had been offered a large amount to make Rattan Safe. The son immediately told Lord George Bentinck and Lord George requested the jockeys betting book. Was anyone bribing Sam Rogers to make Rattan safe an investigation ensued?

Lord George as recalled by Sylvanus announced at the Spreadeagle Hotel in Epsom *"Gentlemen I am going to call over my jockey, Samuel Rogers's book and I will thank you to answer your names and bets, 'Mr. Gully! shouted he in his best manner from the Rostrum! Here Growled old Gully from the crowd, removing the cigar from his lips to give place to a sardonic, catch me if you can implied smile. "You have bet Samuel Rogers 350/25 against Ratan, I perceive why this is all right he seems to be backing his horse. Ah but he stands a Pony with you on Ugly Buck, it seems overleaf (Gullys Horse) This has an ugly look. Are those all the bets you have with him, Mr Gully?" "If you have any more in my name and will specify, my Lord I may then be better able to answer you replied the cautious old gladiator" And so Lord George proceeded through the harmless little volume (Sam Rogers betting book) ticking off Master Crommelin, Jerry Ives, the Dollar and a whole heap of worthy betting men."* [231]

So Sam Rodgers the jockey had made plenty of bets, bets also made with a Mr Crommelin as well who was a respected commissioner of the Jockey Club and who I would like to highlight here as he appears later and forms part of an investigation by the Jockey Club Stewards brought about by Lord George Tony Byles asks this question on Sam Rogers the Jockey. *"was Sam a party to the Robbery? He seemed to have convinced Lord George of his innocence. There was a plot no doubt, and he knew well of it he told Lord George that he intended if possible, to drop his seducers into a hole, by winning if he could, also he did not intend to pocket a single guinea of the shamefully offered money. It did not appear that he was true to his word especially in respect of not receiving any money, for it turned out he had*

---

[230] Tony Byles *In Search of Running Rein The Amazing Fraud of the 1844 Derby* Apex Publishing LTD Essex 2011 p.14

[231] Charles Dickens William Harriet Ainsworth Albert Smith *Bentleys Miscellany volume* Richard Bentley London 1849 Vol 26 p. 414

received £1,660. This fact induced Lord George and Captain Rous to request the Jockey Club to investigate the matter." [232]

On 20th October the Jockey Club met in secret, and refused the attendance of a public reporter:-On 20th October 1844, there were letters published in the Times newspaper, one letter requesting a reporter to be present, to satisfy the public that there was nothing underhand going on, I have included these letters below:-

"To the right Hon. the / Stewards of the Jockey Club.

"October 14, 1844.
"MY LORDS—Understanding that it is your lordships' intention to inquire into the truth of certain charges made respecting the treatment which the late Mr. Crockford's horse Rattan experienced prior to his race for the last Derby, I have to call your lordships 'attention to the fact that the public will anxiously look for a correct report of the evidence given before you. I therefore respectfully request your lordships will allow a reporter from ' The Sunday Times' to attend the investigation. Waiting your lordships' reply," I have the honour to be, &c. (Signed) "JOHN K. CHAPMAN."[224]

"October 14, 1844.
"Sir—I am requested by the Stewards of the Jockey Club to acquaint you, in reply to your letter, that it is not intended to admit any reporters for the public press during the investigation into the Rattan affair, and that they are, therefore, unable to comply with your request.

"I am, Sir, &c.
(Signed) "C. WEATHERBY.".J. K. Chapman, Esq.[224]

As can be seen, there was no way the establishment were disclosing this one to the public, the doors were shut and the ranks had been closed. After quite some deliberation the Jockey Club announced its decision in a report *"the Stewards of the Jockey Club assisted by the Duke of Beaufort and Colonel Peel having investigated the charges bought forward against S. Rogers (Rattans Jockey) and J. Braham and heard their statements as well as the evidence of various witnesses , and the account given by Mr Crommelin and Mr Ives of their share in the transaction og betting for Rogers and Braham against Ratan for the late Derby Race are of the opinion that the transaction originated in an agreement between S. Rogers and J. Braham to bet both ways about Ratan, under the impression that the parties whom they might commission to*

---

[232] Tony Byles *In Search of Running Rein The Amazing Fraud of the 1844 Derby* Apex Publishing LTD Essex 2011 p.194

bet for them against the horse would be influenced , by the representations of the impossibility of his winning, to lay such sums of money against him as to prevent their appearing on the selling day. S Rogers and J. Braham confess they had received a large portion of the money won by laying against Ratan although it was not their intention to pay if the horse had won. Their conduct during the whole proceeding was of such a nature as to merit the severest punishment in the power of the Jockey Club to inflict.[233]

So that was that Sam Rogers was barred from racing due to the fact that he had commissioned a bet against the horse he was riding Ratan. He had claimed that Mr Crommelin the Jockey Club Commissioner had tried to bribe him to stop Rattan from winning the race but the Jockey Club Committee were of course not accepting that, I mean how could they? They are the Jockey Club, Purveyors of Standards! But the club knowing Crommelins hands were stained did however concede. *"The committee has further to observe, that although the conspiracy to bet large sums against Rattan originated with Rogers and Braham and that no inducement (*bribe*) was held out to them by any party to prevent the horse from winning yet it would have been difficult for them to have carried their plan into execution unless persons of influence (Crommelin and Ives) had been found to execute their commissions, the committee cannot express too strongly their opinions of the impropriety of Gentlemen betting large sums of money for jockeys or for parties intrusted with the charge of race-horses."* [233]

Tony Byles the author of "In Search of Running Reign" refuses to believe that the Jockey Club commissioners could do such a thing as he writes in his book *"Sam had maliciously insinuated that Mr Crommelin and Mr Ives-both respected commissioners- had gone to him to "offer a bribe to induce him to prevent the horse from winning. Nothing could be further from the truth."* [234] Tony Byles goes on further to defend the accusation against Mr Crommelin the Jockey Club commissioner *"The accusation Rogers and Bream had concocted against Crommelin and Ives that these gentlemen were connected with the robbery had left them under an implied cloud of distrust for having executed the commissions, and what had been for aeons a recognised practice."* [235]

I wonder if Sam Rogers had won the Race on Rattan no one would have said a thing as he would have not profited from his losses. From all accounts Sam had made several bets through Crommelin hedging some of

---

[233] Sporting Magazine, patronized by H. R. H Prince Albert (Vol 4, 3rd Series, London 1844, p.355

[234] Tony Byles *In Search of Running Rein The Amazing Fraud of the 1844 Derby* Apex Publishing Ltd Essex 2011 p.196

[235] Tony Byles *Running Rein* 2011 p.197

his bets this practice was normal but if they lost could be disastrous as their integrity could be called into question. If they won the race and lost their bets it was ok as had been seen on an occasion before back in 1833 with John Barham Day *"John Day in 1833 when he trained and rode Little Red Rover for the valuable Goodwood Stakes stood to lose £1,500 by his winning, with nearly every other animal in the race a winner to his book! Most people know that John Day goes by the name of "Honest John," and in this instance, and we believe every other, he is deserving of that epithet. Little Red Rover won in a canter while John Day the Trainer and rider, lost a large sum!!"* [236]

Sam Rogers had however apparently stated to lord George he had lost his money, and according to Lord George this was not the case hence the investigation so Sam had his licence as a jockey removed for betting against his horse. The Jockey Club were outright refusing to believe that their commissioners Mr Crommelin or Ives could have bribed the jockeys or trainers to fix the race in their favour we shall pick up on this later as this is not an isolated event the same Jockey Club commissioner Mr Crommelin it will be seen was potentially doing this same scam for years.

We have now reached 1844, many things have started to go wrong for John Barham Day and the Danebury Stables, this year was not as happy as it should have been as John Barham Day's mother Anne Day died on 3rd July 1844. She had been a great support to the stables and the Day family all her life and of course, was responsible for the start of it all. If her passing was not enough, two years later in 1846 his wife Harriet of 31 years also passed away peacefully at Danebury, and to add insult to injury William and John Day Junior had been removed from riding by the Jockey Club. There was much trouble and stress between the years of 1840-1846.

But in testament to his character John Barham Day appears to have held it together as that same year in 1846, after everything that had happened we can still find him bringing home the Classics, first in 1844 the father and son team were to bring home the 2,000 Guineas, with Ugly Buck-(Monstrosity-Plenipotentiary by Venison), owned by John Barham Day, trained by John Barham Day and ridden by John Day then for John Gully with Mendicant-(Touch stone-Lady Moore Carew by Tramp), the 1846 Epsom Oaks. The same year he pulled off the 1,000 Guineas with Mendicant, and again for Gully to train the 1846 Derby Winner Pyrrhus the 1st-(Epirus-Fortress). Even after all that he was still winning races.

---

[236] Sporting Magazine, (Vol 4, 3rd Series, London 1844, p.356

In 1846-47 John Barham Day had a large argument with his son John Day Junior and handed over Danebury to John Day the third perhaps the preceding two years and the loss of his family members was just too much for him sounds like he was sick of it, according to William Day *"Before leaving Danebury of his temporary retirement from business my father sold all his horses, in training mares and foals."*[237] The retirement didn't last too long and we next find John, in 1849, when he went to set his second son William up in Woodyates, another training yard in Wiltshire which perhaps he purchased from his wife Harriet Goddard's family as they held Woodyates first and other land there. He later moved on to Michaelgrove for a short time and eventually to Findon to train for Mr. Howard (Henry Padwick). John Barham trained and won with such horses as Virago, Rataplan, Oulston, Little Harry for Padwick. *"He also trained a horse named Scythian, who won the Chester Cup. For reasons best known to himself, Day did not intend that Scythian should win the Chester Cup; and for other reasons, best known to themselves, his two sons J. and W. Day, were determined that Scythian should, if he could, win the race. About four days before the contest Mr. Padwick received a letter from J. Day, junior, imploring him to come to Stockbridge, and accordingly Mr. Padwick went. On his arrival the state of affairs was fully explained to him by the sons, and the resolution was formed to exclude the old John from the stables, and to entrust the horse to the care of the two brothers. John Day does not appear to have been at all hurt by this slight upon his honesty, but to have been very much hurt at the prospect of losing all the money he had laid against Scythian."*[238] Unfortunately the relationship was not to last as in 1854 William Day also went on to set up house as private trainer to Henry Padwick. William had an argument caused by Hill and Gully over that horse Scythian.

VIRAGO

VIRAGO-(PYRRHUS THE FIRST) WAS PURCHASED when she was one year old by John Barham Day at Doncaster for £300.00, on behalf of Mr. Padwick. John thought she was *"the finest yearling in the world"*[239]. Virago was a foal of that famous horse Pyrrhus The First, and in her early days raced once at Shrewsbury, where she was unplaced, the winner was sold for £80, but apparently the owners at the time knew Virago was worth much more money so they didn't let her show what she was capable of.

---

237 William Day, *Reminiscences Of The Turf,* (1891, p.46-47)
238 James Rice, *History of the British Turf,* (1879, p.275
239 John Porter, Edward Moorhouse, *John Porter of Kingsclere an Autobiography,* (Grant Richards London, 1919, p.10)

VIRAGO

After being purchased by Padwick and trained by Day they entered her into the City and Suburban Races at Epsom and then the Metropolitan and Suburban races there as well and she won both on the same day. Mr. Greville, a former patron of John Barham Day, told him before the trial that no three year old could possibly beat Muscovite his horse. John Barham Day assured Mr. Greville to have a five hundred pound bet on his horse Virago.[240]

I wonder if he placed the five hundred Pounds. John Barham Day at one point heard a report that Virago was to be poisoned so wrote to John Porter the famous trainer of Kingsclere who recollects *"When she reached York that week we heard a rumour that an attempt was to be made to poison Virago, Day was taking no chances. He and Goater sat up all night in a room near her box and I myself slept in the box."*[240] Nothing came of the rumour, so wrote Porter but this shows how difficult it must have been in those days to protect your horses. Virago went on to win 11 races in three seasons, the most noted of which was a Classic she won, the 1,000 Guineas at Newmarket altogether in prize money she collected Mr. Padwick £10,420, which is not a bad return when the outlay was £300. They carried on racing Virago until 1855, by then she had already started to decline, and was sold to Lord Stradbroke for £500, and died in 1869.

One last story of John Barham Day and I will borrow heavily from that old legendary trainer John Porter of Kingsclere. In 1854 at Michel Grove were two horses, St Hubert and Oulston. Mr. Padwick had purchased Scythian as a three year old and won four good races in 1855 he won the Chester Cup which was a very good win. Oulston triumphed in three of the four races he ran for Mr. Padwick as a two year old, and as a three year old also won races, one of them the Vase at Ascot in which he beat the famous horse Rataplan. St Hubert, a colt, was not considered very good as he had never won a race and not been run as a two year old. Porter was the jockey who used to ride him for exercise and even he didn't think he was very good, Porter goes on to say that he did not know when St Hubert became a good horse, but he did say there was another jockey who used to give him sharp gallops on the way back to the stable out of the eye of John Barham Day the trainer. In April of that year they tried St Hubert against a good horse called Little Harry and both the owner Padwick and the trainer John Barham Day were surprised at how well St Hubert performed, Porter says John Barham Day was more surprised than Padwick.

240 John Porter, Edward Moorhouse, *John Porter of Kingsclere an Autobiography* (1919, p.17)

Figure 35 Virago, John Barham Day Trainer by Barrett of Stockbridge 1851(Day, 1925)

At Woodyates John Barham Day's son William was training a horse called Lord of the Isles, this horse was the son of a very famous horse called Touchstone and had already won the Biennial at Goodwood and the Lavant Stakes and developed a reputation as a clever and good runner.

As usual, gossip started to fly around the racing circles that the Day family had come to a private arrangement that William's horse Lord of the Isles was going to be allowed a clear run in the 2000 Guineas of that year, and in return St Hubert, John Barham Day's horse, was to be similarly favoured in the Derby. Mr. Padwick was soon to hear of this gossip about his trainer. Porter says that this allegation was not founded on fact but alludes to there being circumstantial evidence to support Mr. Padwick's attitude.

Porter then goes on to say that some time prior to the 2000 Guineas Padwick had sent to Findon, where John Barham Day was, a Mr. Gannon who was a celebrated pigeon shot with instructions to keep an eye on St Hubert. Day soon became aware of the spy arriving in the village and regarded this as an outrage against his dignity. That was to prove too much for John Barham Day and he left immediately to join his son William in Woodyates. John Barham Day was heard to say *"you will be glad to know that I have taken care of myself. If I had not I should like to know who would have done so."*

[241] Perhaps he was alluding to Mr. Gannon being sent by Mr. Padwick as not just a spy but also as a potential assassin, that would have been more than enough for anybody.

In his life John Barham Day revolutionised racing, the stories have been told by the people that both knew him, and the public that loved him, John Porter said *"It has been said that he did more than any of his contemporaries to raise the trainer's calling to a higher plane than it occupied in the early years of the nineteenth century."*[241] John Porter was one of the most respected trainers in horse racing history he was apprenticed to John Barham Day in 1853, so he knew him well. Following the trouble with Lord George Bentinck, and then the Danebury Confederacy and finally with Padwick must have made John Barham Day very tired of it all.

John Barham Day died at Woodyates on 21st March 1860, from softening of the brain his son William was with him for his final days. The press and aristocracy at the time nicknamed him Honest John, and some modern day writers say it was "ironic" and that he was a crook, but when you read the tribute from people like John Porter of Kingsclere one of the leading trainers of the Nineteenth Century who personally knew him they have a different picture, *"The name Honest John so often applied to him was indicative of his reputation in the racing world. The most prominent men on the turf were among his greatest admirers."* [6]

John Barham Day was not a crook or a thief as historians eager to please the Jockey Club have written, the only credible reference in all the writings to him being a thief made in his lifetime was by the Duke of Grafton, and that was done in jest. *"Grafton said to Day, "John Day, you're a thief." "My Lord," cried out the astonished jockey, "what have I done to displease you?" "What have you done," answered the Duke, still looking stern, "you stole that race!"*[242]. He survived, as I am sure all the trainers had too, as the world they lived in was much different to ours and he was considered as being a man that could talk to everybody with courtesy at every level as again stated by John Porter. *"It has been well said that he was as simple as a child in his tastes and pursuits, but, in his intercourse with society, a perfect man of the world, as respectful to the Peer as courteous to the peasant."* [243]

---

241 John Porter, Edward Moorhouse, *John Porter of Kingsclere an Autobiography* (1919, p.6)
242 Bernard Falk, *The Royal Fitzroy's; Dukes of Grafton through Four Centuries* (London, 1950, p.233)
243 John Porter, Edward Moorhouse, *John Porter of Kingsclere an Autobiography* (1919, p.7)

John Barham Day was considered most trust worthy in his pursuit of his business, as he was remembered by Lord William Pitt Lenox who referred to John Barham Day as *"one of those in which the public placed entire confidence"* [244]

A further example of this rests with a story regarding his betting against a horse he was riding called Red Rover, if he won the race he stood to lose thousands, but win the race he did and it was reported he lost thousands *"John Day in 1833 when he trained and rode Little Red Rover for the valuable Goodwood Stakes stood to lose £1,500 by his winning, with nearly every other animal in the race a winner to his book! Most people know that John Day goes by the name of "Honest John," and in this instance, and we believe every other, he is deserving of that epithet. Little Red Rover won in a canter while John Day the Trainer and rider, lost a large sum!"* [236], now if that isn't a demonstration of honesty then I don't know what is.

He was at the top of his profession as can be seen when in 1844 Day was called before the House of Commons to provide evidence to a committee on gaming and horse racing. *"Let us hear what Mr. John Day, one of the most celebrated and experienced trainers of the present period, has to say with respect to the effects of horse- racing, in connection with the improvement of the horse, in his evidence as given before a Committee of the House of Commons, in 1844."* [245]

There is a quote I wish to include from the time after his death where a valid point is made, and this was how he should have been remembered, and not how the modern writers have penned and I hope I have gone some way to dignify his memory, *"John Day's life as a jockey and trainer, his connection with Lord George Bentinck. When that grand meteor gradually shone forth upon the hemisphere, John Day was his attendant satellite. It was John who advised who trained, who rode, who bought, and who betted. It was John Day who vanned Elis into Doncaster, and courted Fortune with a bold stroke for success that was fate"* [246]

I feel it fitting to finish with a poem that was dedicated to him after he died, written seven years after his death.

"A LAY OF MODERN EPSOM
Made about the Year, 1867. A LONG WAY) AFTER MACAULAY
The stout John Day, of Danebury, by the nine gods he swore,

---

244 Lord William Pitt Lenox, Celebrities I Have Known, 1877, p.
245 Saunders, Otley and Co, *Horse Racing Its History and Early Records of the Principal and Other Race Meetings*, (1863, p.8)
246 Henry Corbett, *Tails and Traits of a Sporting Life*, (Rogerson and Tuxford London 1864, p.60)

Crucifix 1840 The Oaks, 1000 and 2,000 Guineas Winner by John Frederick Herring

That the great house of Beaufort should suffer wrong no more;
By the nine gods he swore it, and called to Mrs. Day, and bade his jockeys all ride
forth, exercising south and north,
For the Epsom race of May. South and north in exercise, the jockeys onwards ride, and
Vauban, champion of the stud, is with Lord Ronald tried.
Shame on the tout obtrusive, who lingers on the course, when our stout John of
Danebury Roughs ups a Derby horse."[247]

---

247 A.H.Bailey, *Baileys Magazine Of Sports And Past Times*, (1867, Vol 13, p.169)

John Day III 1815-1882

Figure 36 John Day Illustrated Sporting Dramatic News Dec 18th 1882

Won 1 Classic as a Jockey
Won 13 Classics as a Trainer
Own Colours Black Jacket Orange Cap

Classic's won as Jockey and Trainer

Table 3 Classics Won As Jockey

John Day Jnr	Horse	Year	Owner
2,000 guineas	Ugly Buck	1844	John Barham Day

Table 4 Classics Won As Trainer

John Day Jnr	Horse	Year	Owner
2,000 guineas	Conyngham	1847	Sir R Pigot
	Pittsford	1850	Harry Hill
	The Hermit	1854	John Gully
	Vauban	1867	8th Duke Of Beaufort
1,000 guineas	The Flea	1849	F Clarke
	Siberia	1865	8th Duke Of Beaufort
	Repulse	1866	Marquise Of Hastings
	Scottish Queen	1869	8th Duke Of Beaufort
Epsom Oaks	Cymba	1848	Harry Hill
	Mince Pie	1856	Harry Hill
Epsom Derby	Cossack	1847	T.H.Pedley
	Andover	1854	John Gully
St Ledger Stakes			
Grand Prix Paris	Ceylon	1866	Duke Of Beaufort

EARLY LIFE

JOHN DAY JUNIOR OF DANEBURY WAS born on 19th January 1815 the same year as the Battle of Waterloo; he was the first son of John Barham Day and Harriet Goddard and was my great-great-grandfather. His life was already set-out for him; he was called John and would become a jockey. Just as his father had groomed his pedigree horses to race, so his children were groomed in the same way, a tradition that carried on to my grandfather's day.

As a child he was known to want to win, particularly in competition with his brothers, John additionally possessed great physical strength. This natural competitiveness would in later years turn into a feud with his brother William which would divide the Day family. John was apprenticed to his father we find him riding for his father at Danebury he soon progressed to head jockey as would have been expected. His father had certainly set the bar high for him. By the time he was ready to ride professionally he found himself standing in his father's very big shadow, created ironically by a very small man, the Classic challenge awaited and from all accounts he met the challenge with determination and vigour.

John Day Junior was schooled in Winchester, and then on to Oxford to study to be a veterinary surgeon, [248] he spent three years under the eminent Mr Wild[249] which would stand him in good stead later when he would be forced to turn to training. The family had been so long in racing that they had moved the Danebury stables up a gear; they were ensuring that the children of the Day family empire would have the complete knowledge of the horse, not just the skills of a jockey, but also the skills of a trainer. Racing was a cut throat business, one day you could be the greatest jockey in the country the next you may not be able to ride.

As a jockey John Day Junior was said to have had a very graceful seat his style of riding[250] was considered much more beautiful than his father John Barham Day, who was said to look like "*he was screwed onto a horse*". Unlike most other jockeys of the time who were coming from various backgrounds to try their luck, John like his father and his grandfather before him, had racing and the training of the thoroughbred horse very much in his blood.

---

248 H.H.Dixon, *Silk and Scarlett*, (1859, p.119) "John Day started off as a veterinary surgeon "Young John Day, who was then with a veterinary surgeon in Oxford,
249 House of Lords, *The sessional papers* (Volume XIX 1844, p.137
250 Sporting Magazine, or monthly Calendar of the Turf and Chase, (Vol 25 1842, p.329)

From his first breath and some of the first things John Junior would have seen with his eyes as a child would have been the finest thoroughbred racehorses in the world at that time in his back garden, all the years through growing up and into his teens he would have been exposed to and involved with all the finest patrons of the turf from the highest nobility in the land, to the most powerful of politicians coming in and out of his house at Danebury. Imagine around the breakfast table would have been discussed horses, dinner and tea, would have been horses, I bet he even dreamt of them in his sleep no counting sheep for John.

John Day Junior's upbringing was strict as his father John Barham was a determined Protestant, who demanded church for his family twice on Sundays and this was also the case for all the jockeys at Houghton Down and later Danebury. He would almost certainly not have had much time for pleasure, and much would have been expected of him when he was at home.

In 1837 John married Miss Mary Wilkins Tarver on 14th November in North Baddesley near Southampton, he was 22 years old and she was 30, Mary came from an old land owning family in Hampshire, and together they had seven children, the first two died in the first year, Francis Mary Tarver, and Mary. The first boy, as dictated by tradition, was called John 1841-1881, who also became a veterinary surgeon, then Sam 1843-1856 named after his uncle, was born, then Catherine or Kate my great-grandmother 1844-1892 who was to go onto marry Tom Cannon, and who we shall pick up on later, then Leonard 1846-1936 and finally Harry 1850-1914.

After John had finished his studies at Oxford to be a vet, he returned to Danebury, where a massive stud had been created by his father, which was at the time considered one of the largest in the country, the stable as we have already seen had all the most powerful turf patrons in England, Lord George Cavendish Bentinck, Lord Palmerston, Dukes of Grafton. Danebury had been enlarged to meet the demand, and Stockbridge, this small village in Hampshire, had grown to become one of the most popular and fashionable race meetings in the country, backed by the Bibury Club, which we have already seen was considered the most powerful racing club in the land. The Day Family and Danebury Stables were at the top of the game. John could on one hand be considered extremely lucky to sit in the saddle at this time, but the pressure to perform must have been immense, for winning was not down to luck or chance for him, he would not have that leisure, for him winning would be expected.

I will attempt at this point to call forth some old voices who were very well respected in their time as turf consultants and take from them a character description of John Day, I think this is important before we delve into his life, like I have said before, we did not know him but the people whose accounts I have taken both knew him and lived in his time, so in order to see his character it is to them we must turn. *"John Day, his manners were quiet and unobtrusive, he was closely associated in business matters with the late Marquis of Hastings, and so great was his success at one period of that exciting era, that the cry was "John Day will break the ring" within a short period of time he had a great number of good horses under his charge. It says much for John Days business ability, tact and integrity that at one time he had in his stables horses belonging to, The Duke Of Beaufort, Lord Hastings Colonel Baillie, Colonel Berkeley and others all who were entirely satisfied with his management of their interests. John Day was a man of genial disposition kindly and hospitable, and a companion full of amusing anecdote."* [251]

Another story that illustrates the high regard John was held in by his aristocratic patrons. A training invoice was long overdue to John Day and the Danebury stables and needed paying, the invoice was to a Colonel Bailey, whose father was I think the Earl of Shaftesbury, John Day, was in need of money so he reminded the Earl for payment, at which point the Colonel paid John Day, but he overpaid him by it was said a large amount, when John inquired to the large amount, the Colonel replied *"I would not give a fig for a man that would not give his trainer £2,000 when he was in need of money."* [252]

We will cover two large affairs that would change the career of John Day Junior significantly and these episodes were known as The Crommelin Affair and Old England. It is worth noting that these events date from when Lord George Bentinck left the Danebury stables in 1841, harbouring a complete hatred for John Day Junior that would persist until the time of his death. Upon examination we will see that there was malice afoot, to bring ruin to the Danebury Stables.

OLD ENGLAND AFFAIR

OLD ENGLAND WAS A HORSE OWNED JOINTLY BY John Gully and John Barham Day and had been placed as the first favourite to win the Derby of 1845. Day had purchased the horse in 1843 from Colonel

251 George James Cawthorne, Richard S.Heron, *Royal Ascot Its History And Its Associations,* (A.Treherne, London, 1902, p.325)
252 A.H.Bailey, *Baileys Sporting Magazine And Past Times,* (December 1883 Vol 40, p.69)

Bouverie of Delepre Abbey Northamptonshire for £150.00.[253] He had also purchased Pyrrhus the First's colt and the mother Fortress for £250 the same year. He took both the horses straight to Danebury, and at some point Gully obtained a 50% share in the horse Old England.

In 1844 The Day family had raced Old England in The New Stakes of Ascot a two year old race of that year where Old England took second place to a horse called Bloodstone, however something was wrong with the winner and after the race *"Mr Gully, Mr John Day and Mr John Day Junior objected to the stakes being given to Bloodstone and on the following day after hearing evidence and having the colt examined the Stewards decided in John Days favour that the colt was three years old."*[254] Hence she was disqualified and the Days won the stakes.

In 1845 There had as usual been rumours circulating in racing circles about how John Day Junior, had been apparently involved in some plot to disable Gully's horse Old England that was at the Danebury stables. Having heard this rumour Gully boarded the train straight to Danebury Stockbridge, on the Sunday before the meeting, and on arrival confronted John Barham Day. Day couldn't believe something like that would happen in his stables, but Gully persisted and managed to get the information out of William Day, John Barham's second son. [255]

On the following Monday afternoon, Gully appeared at Tattersalls and climbed the rostrum to make a speech in front of the whole sales ring, he blamed a Mr. Hargreaves for trying to "seduce young Billy Day", he then went on to say that temptations had been held out to William's brother John Day Junior, but John had refused according to Gully, who stated that *"John Day Junior was above price or could not be bought."*[256]

On 2nd June 1845, Gully brought a charge against a Mr. Stebbings; Mr. Bloodsworth chaired and it was heard by the Jockey Club at Messrs. Weatherbys, for the intention to plan and conspire to injure Gully's horse, and to bet against the horse after doing so. The charge also included William Day, as being a spy at John Day's stable and feeding them secret information about the horse, having secret meetings with Stebbings and

---

253 William Day Reminiscences Of The Turf, 1891
254 The New Sporting Magazine, July 1844, p.6
255 Thormamby, (Pseud) "Wilmott Dixon "Kings of the Turf,1898)
256 The New Sporting Magazine, July 1845, p.3 "He also said that temptations had been held out to his brother, "young John Day, "which failed; that young man being— according to Mr. G.'s expression, "above price," which I suppose means not to be bought."

Bloodsworth. *"The Stewards of the Jockey Club having attended at Messrs. Weatherby's office, in Burlington-street, on Saturday the 31st of May, and by adjournment on Monday the 2nd of June, to hear a charge brought by Mr. Gully against Mr. J. F. Bloodsworth and William Stebbings, of having conspired to bet against Old England for the Derby, in connection with William Day, and through information clandestinely derived from him, and subsequently to lame, or, by other means, to prevent the said horse running for that race ; having heard the confession of William Day, and the evidence of William Barrett, Jan., and of John Day, Sen., are satisfied that Messrs., Bloodsworth and Stebbings did conspire to bet against Old England. That communication was kept up by Stebbings writing letters through Bloodsworth to William Day, which letters were sent under cover to William Barrett, jun., of Stockbridge, for several months. It appeared that William Day and William Barrett, Jan., did, on different occasions, meet Stebbings at Bloodworth's house in London, and at other places, to carry out their plans. It was also positively stated by William Day and William Barrett, that Stebbings did, at Bloodworth's house, recommend that the horse's foot should be bruised by striking it with a hard stone, or by tying a handkerchief round the leg and striking the sinew with a stick, and if that was not sufficient, that he, Stebbings, could easily get a powder which, being mixed with the corn, would stop him. They added that Bloodsworth was averse to the last part of this proposal, saying it was a lagging affair. Messrs. Bloodsworth and Stebbings dented the whole story of having desired William Day to maim the horse, but admitted that they had betted largely against Old England in consequence of the information they had obtained from William Day; and Stebbings acknowledged that he had received full information from William Day for several years as to the qualities and condition of horses in John Day's stables, and had betted largely for himself and for William Day in consequence of such information."* [257]

Nicholas Foulkes refers to this case in his book Gentlemen and Blackguards just simply states that *"The Days who trained old England were found guilty."* [258] Yes guilty, but guilty of what for Mr Foulkes "everything?"

After the hearing of William Day and John Barham Day's accounts, and other peoples it turns out that Stebbings and Bloodsworth were responsible for trying to lame the horse Old England by recommending to William Day that he strike the foot or the sinew with a rock, Stebbings and Bloodsworth even went as far as to suggest if that did not work then they had some special powder that could stop the horse. Obviously the two denied the story but did admit to trying to bet heavily against Old England in the Derby.[259]

---

257 The New Sporting Magazine, (July 1845, p.63)
258 Nicholas Foulkes *Gentlemen and Blackguards* Orion 2010 p.263
259 Charles and Edward Weatherby, *The Racing Calendar,* (1847)

Figure 37 John Day Jnr by (Harry Hall) 1840 National Horse Racing Museum

Stebbings also confessed that William Day had been sending him information on the horses in John Day Junior's stable for years, and after the findings the Jockey Club ruled that Stebbings and Bloodsworth and William Day not be allowed on the course at Newmarket, or any other course that carries Jockey Club rules, and additionally William was not allowed to ride as a jockey in any race there or where there were Jockey Club rules. The steward's findings were:- *'The Stewards therefore order—That J. F. Bloodsworth, William Stebbings, and William Day be warned off the course at Newmarket, and out of the Coffee-room Yard there; and that William Day be not permitted to ride in any race at Newmarket. They also recommend the proprietors and stewards of all race courses where the rules of the Jockey Club are in force, to prevent them from appearing on such courses.*

Signed, Stradbroke Rosslyn (for the Marquis of Exeter). Geo Anson." [257]

So John Day's own brother William was selling him out and perhaps that is why their father John Barham Day set William up in a stable of his own. It appears that William was a bit jealous of John. That story explains a lot to me, you see it is heartening to find the truth, instead of just believing what you hear. The dispute must have endured because in our family it was tradition to hand down names of the brothers or fathers but John Day Junior never called any of his children William, and in William's writings he does not really provide any kind references to John his brother, so maybe John never forgave him and this caused a rift in the family. What it looks like is somebody initiated rumours against John Day Junior, blaming him for trying to nobble a horse prior to the Derby. But it turns out that there was no infliction on the animal and all that happened was information was being bought and sold from John's brother, William, regarding the horses and their performance within the stables, no evidence was found against John Day Junior for cheating quite the opposite. He had actually refused the offer from Bloodsworth and Stebbings and was regarded as, *"John was above price and could not be bought."*[256]

Someone was definitely out to get John Day Junior, and the next case that came before the Jockey Club was very similar, that case came just 2 weeks later, it was originally to be tried on 2nd June, the same day as the previous case was adjourned, but was eventually tried on 18th June 1845, not giving the Day family time to recover from the previous barrage this case was called the Crommelin affair.

CROMMELIN AFFAIR

THE EVENTS SURROUNDING THIS CASE HAPPENED around 1840; it was regarding a Bribe offered to John Day Junior to pull the Horse "Melody Colt" that he was riding in the 1840 Derby. But the case was not brought before the Jockey Club until 18th June 1845 5 years after the event, and caused a major stir both on and off the turf. It involved John Day Junior, and a very odd looking man called Mr. Crommelin, who was by all accounts dressed in a cloak had a big moustache and wore glasses, and whilst in a Pub in Winchester, approached John Day Junior, with a scheme, and should like to discuss it with the jockey in private, the scheme involved a horse called the Melody Colt who was owned by the MP for Andover at that time a Mr. Etwell.

The case came to the attention of the Jockey Club as after the Old England affair in 1845 John Day Junior approached the Jockey Club regarding a Mr Crommelin he had felt aggrieved against the clubs attempt to frame him in the Old England case and probably wanted retribution.

Bentinck was as usual all over everything even manipulating and influencing the press as can be seen in the collection of Bentinck's Letters held in the Nottingham University there exists an exercise book with an Article written by hand titled "Delicate Investigation Conclusion of the inquiry by the Jockey Club, and sentence pronounced."[260] This story dated 22nd June 1845 found handwritten in Bentinck's personal exercise book was either authored or co-authored by him. In other words he was manipulating the press. Bells Life dated 22nd June 1845 a sporting paper of the time ran the story as did the Sporting magazine of the

---

260 Provides an account, under the title 'Delicate Investigation', of the enquiry by the Jockey Club into the affairs of Mr. Crommwelin and John Day in relation to the 1840 Derby; an account entitled 'Another Rattan Affair. Extraordinary Disclosures - Snakes in the Grass' is also included and is dated 1 June 1845; it describes an altercation which took place between Mr. Gully, the owner of 'Old England' and Mr. Hargreaves, a constant frequenter of betting circles, concerning the odds against the horse and treachery in his stable."

same date. Bentinck was making sure the Jockey Club's version of events was the only one that was getting printed.

John Day Junior expressed his intention to request the Jockey Club after his brother's case had been disposed of to hear a charge which he had to make concerning the Melody Colt, as well as some other matters. This intention having reached the ears of Lord George Bentinck his lordship had an interview with Mr Etwall touching the circumstance which had come to his knowledge. So John Day Junior was about to hold the Jockey Club's Bookie Mr Crommelin to account for Bribery the second time he had been accused and Lord George had been made aware of this, you can imagine the frantic behaviour of the Stewards. Mr Etwall after knowing that Lord George was involved summoned all concerned John Day Junior, Senior. *"He then stated to John Day Junior that he had kept his promise and not divulged to any person the statements that he had made to him in 1840 respecting Mr Crommelin that having been now called upon to corroborate that Statement all secrecy was at an end. John Day thanked him and repeated his intention of bringing that matter before the Jockey Club."* Another paper of the day stated that John Day had informed Mr Etwall back in 1840 who had said *"to take the Bribe and win anyway"* Not the same as the club's revised version.

John Day Junior said that he received an anonymous letter, a week before the Derby of 1840 the letter said a friend would meet him in the pub in Winchester one week before the 1840 Derby was to be run, and have something to tell him that was to his interest.[261] The week passed and John went to the pub and asked after a Mr. Webb. All this was fine, the man took of his cloak and spectacles and it was a Mr. Crommelin, hence the case was called the Crommelin affair, unbeknown to John Day Crommelin was a member of the Jockey Club and the Jockey Club's commissioner or "bookie",

Mr. Crommelin propositioned young John asking if he could lose the Derby on the horse he was riding Melody Colt, as the bookmaker was up to his neck in debts and if the horse John was riding was to win he was worried that he would be unable to cover the debts. He offered John Day a five hundred pound note, and said after the deed was done he could have another thousand. Immediately John Day declined this offer, and apparently told his father John Barham Day and the owner of the horse Mr Etwall who said why not take the bribe and win anyway, and that was the end of it, or so you would think.

---

261 James Rice, History Of The British Turf, (1879)

The problem was that Day lost the race, but everybody could see that he tried his best to win it. There was no case brought against John Day or questions asked about his character at the time of 1840. Five long years later a case was brought against Day by the Jockey Club a week after they had tried to frame John in the Old England affair of which he was found innocent. It was initially tried on the 2nd June 1845, but was adjourned until 18th June, when it was tried by Lord Normamby Stradbroke, and Lords Exeter or Colonel Peel, George Anson and with two other members of the Jockey Club, who were not named. This band of brothers found John Day Guilty and charged him with *"endeavour to support a criminal charge by wilful falsehood"* and for the second time completely exonerated their own Commissioner Mr Crommelin of the charge of Bribery.

John Day Junior had instigated reporting Mr Crommelin to Mr Etwall who had informed Lord Stradbroke a Steward of the Jockey Club who had instead of holding their own Serial offending Bookie to account on bribery charges tried their upmost to frame John Day Junior instead. Crommelin had according to Bells life produced letters showing John Day Junior and Senior had sent him tips a practice that was normal and a tradition of the turf amongst trainers and jockeys. With these letters the Jockey Club had dismissed John Days charges and accusations as being untrustworthy and went on to state that why once the bribe had been turned down, did he John Day Junior and the Day family continue the association with Mr. Crommelin. The Jockey Club found John Day Junior guilty 5 years after the event took place for doing the right thing for turning down the bribe and then for reporting the offender. Something was not right. The ruling by the Jockey Club completely ruined his career as a jockey by removing his ability to ride. The same as with Sam Rogers and Gaper, no action was taken against Mr. Crommelin who was the instigator. Was this a setup to punish the Day family and stop John Day Junior from riding horses by destroying his career as a jockey?

Many members of the Jockey Club and the public thought so Mr Gully defended the Day family, and the press had this to say of that defence *"He spoke of a rumour afloat that it was the intention of the Club to warn John Day Junior of all the racecourses in the Kingdom where the Newmarket rules were applied. He protested against such a mode of proceeding as being unjust and unconstitutional in as much as John Day Junior had merely attended as a witness and could not be liable unless such distant charge was bought against him"*[262] I have included the findings of this

---

[262] Sporting Magazine, patronized by H. R. H Prince Albert (Vol 6, 3rd Series, London 1845, p.57)

case by the noble lords that passed the sentence and as you will see later it was connivance and everyone knew it:-

"John Day Junior, reads their written award", "having before us endeavoured to support a criminal charge by wilful falsehood, we direct that he be turned off the course at Newmarket, and out of the coffee-room there, and be not per- mitted to ride in any race at Newmarket." And, in addition to this, the Stewards of the Jockey Club recommended all other proprietors and stewards prevent him from appearing on their courses." [263]

This was not received well by the whole of the racing world as afterwards there was an uproar from all the other members of the Jockey Club who knew it was a construction, and in response a while later a petition or memorial was drawn by the remaining Influential members of the Jockey Club and headed by the Prime Minister Lord Palmerston himself, because he knew it emitted a foul smell. The Sporting magazine who published it wrote a little while after the event *"From the first we considered and spoke of the sentence of this young man as unnecessarily severe an opinion in which we believe we were supported by all the sporting world an attempt however has been unfavourably met by the Stewards of the Jockey Club. The Marquis of Exeter, Honourable Colonel Anson and Lord George Bentinck to whom in the first place it was submitted."*

"CASE OF JOHN DAY, JUNIOR. A Very strong memorial, signed by a large and influential body of Gentlemen, including Members of the Jockey Club and Owners and Breeders of race-horses—at the head of whom was Lord Palmerston— was presented to the Stewards of the Jockey Club at the late Craven Meeting. The object of the memorial was to obtain a remission of the severe sentence passed on John Day jun. for certain offences imputed to him, by virtue of which he has been interdicted from since appearing on the Turf, or within any space over which the Jockey Club exercises jurisdiction. The effect has been to deprive John Day jun. of the means of earning his daily bread. He has been declared an outlaw from the Turf. The Stewards, after a short deliberation, returned an answer, stating, in substance, that they must decline submitting the case to the General Body; but adding, they had "no objection" to Gentlemen allowing John Day jun. to assist in the training of their horses at Danebury! Here is significance indeed! No objection to allow—what? that which they have no power to prevent, that with respect to which they have no manner of control! We may ask whether it is consistent on the part of the Stewards of the Jockey Club to inflict such ruinous penalties upon a jockey lad, for delinquencies we admit, and at the same time dismiss Members of their own body who were the very instruments of causing those delinquencies with a few words of gentle reproof." [264]

---

263 James Rice, History Of The British Turf, (1879, p.238)
264 Sporting Magazine, or monthly Calendar of the Turf and Chase, (Vol 7, 1846, p.330)

So what happened next? The Jockey Club Stewards consisting of The Marquis of Exeter, Hon Colonel Anson, and the honourable Lord George Bentinck who the case was submitted to in the first place, received the " Strong memorial" from Palmerston and the other members and Mr Weatherby was directed by the Jockey Club Stewards to respond to them as per below:-

"The Stewards of the Jockey Club beg to acknowledge the receipt of the memorial which has been presented to them on behalf of John Day, jun. They regret extremely that a sense of duty prevents them from advising the members of the Jockey Club to rescind the sentence which has unavoidably been inflicted upon that individual, by which he is prevented from riding or from appearing upon any race course where the rules of the "Jockey Club are in force ; but having taken into consideration the anxiety which the gentlemen who have signed the memorial express upon the subject, as well as the unfortunate circumstances in which the Day family are at the present moment placed by the severe illness of John Day, Sen., they beg to state that they do not wish to prevent any of the gentlemen who have signed the memorial, if they shall ɓO think fit, from employing John Day, Jun., in assisting to train their horses at Danebury, although they cannot consent to a remission of his punishment, until he shall have had an opportunity of proving, by his future behaviour, and by honest and upright conduct towards his employers, that he is heartily sorry for having betrayed the confidence of his former masters, and for having given wilful false evidence before the Stewards of the Jockey Club." [265]

So there you have it the Days did not commit a heinous crime but John Day Junior lost his ability to earn a living because he turned down a bribe 5 years before, a bribe that was offered by a Jockey Club member and commissioner. The memorial that the Jockey Club members raised was turned down flat the other Jockey Club members even asked for the case to be seen and tried under the main body of the Jockey Club, in other words they didn't trust the Jockey Club Stewards that had found John Day Junior guilty, but again the Stewards of the Jockey Club led by Bentinck refused as they knew if the case would have been heard by the general body of the Jockey Club, the charge would have been revoked, then the main body of the club would have had to conduct a formal and thorough investigation revealing the set up and farce that it so clearly was. What a difficulty when the person who has set you up is also the judge and the jury and they had once again closed ranks.

---

265 Sporting Magazine, or monthly Calendar of the Turf and Chase, (Vol 7, 1846, p.349)

The public and press reaction was uproar they knew that John Day was a victim of those Jockey Club Stewards and this is reflected in the press cuttings of the time *"The effect has been to deprive John Day jun. of the means of earning his daily bread. He has been declared an outlaw from the Turf. The Stewards, after a short deliberation, returned an answer, stating, in substance, that they must decline submitting the case to the General Body; but adding, they had "no objection" to Gentlemen allowing John Day jun. to assist in the training of their horses at Danebury! Here is significance indeed! No objection to allow—what? That which they have no power to prevent, that with respect to which they have no manner of control! We may ask whether it is consistent on the part of the Stewards of the Jockey Club to inflict such ruinous penalties upon a jockey lad, for delinquencies we admit, and at the same time dismiss Members of their own body who were the very instruments of causing those delinquencies with a few words of gentle reproof."* [264]

To sum up the mood of the public I have extracted from a magazine of the time that was covering the story The Sporting Magazine had this to say of Bentinck and his Stewards *"As before stated the sentence is deemed by thousands of too harsh a nature, but having given a full report of the "merits of the case" we will leave the public to draw their individual opinions"* [266] Even the Bells Life article co-authored by Lord George thought the charge was harsh *"It does seem harsh that the severest punishment within the power of the club to inflict should have followed the mere betrayal of the secrets of his stable."*

Why would the country's most professional family of jockeys and trainers at the height of their success, risk their reputations and careers and the whole family business, fabricating a lie about Mr Crommelin who was no threat to them at all. John Gully member of the Jockey Club spoke of a rumour. *"He spoke of a rumour afloat that it was the intention of the Club to warn John Day Junior of all the racecourses in the Kingdom where the Newmarket rules were applied. He protested against such a mode of proceeding as being unjust and unconstitutional in as much as John Day Junior had merely attended as a witness and could not be liable unless such distant charge was bought against him."* [262]

Why were the Jockey Club Stewards so protective over Mr Crommelin the Clubs Bookie? Perhaps John Day Junior was trying to disclose something else, something that concerned all those Stewards?

---

[266] Sporting Magazine, patronized by H. R. H Prince Albert (Vol 6, 3rd Series, London 1845, p.58

THE JOCKEY CLUB CONFEDERACY

CHEATING IN SPORT WAS AN ACCEPTED practice in the early 19th Century so wrote a visitor to England of that time. *"Cheating in every kind of sport is as completely in the common order of things amongst the highest classes as well as the lowest it is no uncommon thing to hear gentlemen boast of it*

Figure 38 the Jockey Club Meeting 1775 Thomas Rowlandson

almost openly. Some of the members of the Aristocracy are quite notorious for their achievements of this description." [267] The ruling class or the aristocracy were the Lords and Masters and everyone else served that's how it was then, but times were changing the balance of power had started to shift, the aristocracy were starting to be challenged, maybe the public had had enough of blind eyes being turned when the ruling class were caught cheating.

In 1841 John Barham Day had kicked Lord George Cavendish Bentinck out of Danebury and told him to take his horses elsewhere, then successfully sued him because the trainer would not cheat for the honourable Lord in the Crucifix affair, ever since Bentinck had harboured a terrible hatred for the Day family, he was out for his revenge, and what better chance than orchestrating the Day family's dismissal from racing.

There was an all-out attack on the Danebury Stables by a splinter group of members of the Jockey Club, it was known and alluded to by members of the turf *"He spoke of a rumour afloat that it was the intention of the Club to warn John Day Junior of all the racecourses in the Kingdom."* [262] That splinter group would succeed in bringing the Danebury Stables to its knees. I would like to hereby propose a fitting name for those members of the Jockey Club, The Jockey Club Confederacy. The horse racing establishment would prefer that these confederates remain hidden, below is a summary of the cases they were involved with.

---

[267] Tour of a German Prince in England Ireland and France Blacklegs in the years 1829 London Effingham Wilson, Royal Exchange1832, p.236

CRUCIFIX Lord George Chief reformer of the Jockey Club upon hearing his horse Crucifix was injured but not that badly immediately advertised this injury to the public and the betting ring so that they would think it was a bad bet and hedge their bets that were already on making the odds more favourable for Lord George, then he could lay large amounts of money on the horse knowing full well it would recover so committing fraud and netting thousands of pounds in fraudulent winnings, kicked out of Danebury by the Day family after they refused to cheat on his behalf, Lord George was publicly embarrassed.

QUI TAM Bentinck and Colonel Anson and Colonel Peel were answering a charge brought against them regarding illegal betting by a Solicitor J. Russell. Only Bentinck's case made it to court and although the law that upheld it Qui Tam was considered outdated it was still the law. There was even a select Committee hearing in the House of Lords presided over by Duke of Richmond, where he used his position to gain information from the Solicitor J Russell that he then leaked to the defending solicitor and they managed to get the case laughed out of court. Bentinck and the Jockey Club members had succeeded in getting a court of law in England to bend its knee to them when passing its verdict and dismissing the case against Lord George Cavendish Bentinck, even though there was evidence to convict him is beyond belief.

RUNNING REIGN although Lord George was never examined in the Box by the defendants solicitor Lord George was accused by him of *"Lord George Bentinck had for I can use no milder term tampered with the plaintiffs witness; that he had held out threats to them, and where threats had failed, had held out promises to them to induce them to withhold their evidence. That he had procured by the greatest exertions, and by the use of his personal influence, witnesses to appear for the defendant,"*[229] it is strange how the defendant himself decided to withdraw his claim had the club got to him as well? I think a modern day jury would find Lord Georges involvement in all the cases an absolute conflict of interest and a farce the Stewards of Epsom should have been left to deal with it, given the fact that Lord George, and Peel the Prime Minister's brother had bet heavy sums of money on Peel's Horse Orlando it was in their interest to have him declared the winner.

THE RATTAN AFFAIR, Something was found to be wrong with the horse Rattan a contender of the 1844 Derby. Sam Rogers the jockey of the horse was hunted and singled out by Lord George Bentinck for trial by the Jockey Club for betting against his own horse something that was frowned upon as it may be considered the jockey would be less inclined to win the race if it meant he would lose a lot of money. Sam Rogers's bets were taken and accepted by Jockey Club commissioners Mr John Crommelin and Ives without an eyebrow raised. Sam was rightly dismissed from riding as a jockey and trainer for three years by the Jockey Club Stewards, the interesting part of this case was that Mr Crommelin a Jockey Club Commissioner or bookie had taken the bets in the first place knowing full well it was not allowed. An act that he had his wrists lightly tapped for by the Club also the jockey Sam Rogers had accused Mr Crommelin of bribing him to lose the race which was of course dismissed.

OLD ENGLAND rumours were initiated against John Day Junior, blaming him for trying to nobble (damage) a horse prior to the Derby, but it turns out that there was no infliction on the animal and all that happened was information was being brought and sold from John's brother, William regarding the horses and their performance within the stables no evidence was found against John Day Junior for cheating quite the opposite he had actually refused a bribe from Bloodsworth and Stebbings and was regarded as, *"John was above price and could not be bought."*[256]

CROMMELIN AFFAIR John Day Junior was offered £500 from a Jockey Club member Mr. Crommelin in 1840 as a bribe to pull the horse he was riding in the Derby the Melody Colt and make sure he did not win. John Day Junior refused this bribe and informed his father and the owner of the deceitful act by the Jockey Club member. No more was said until five years later when it was reborn from the books of Lord George and the club when they needed something to pin on John Day. Even though he had done the right thing and refused the bribe the Jockey Club confederacy blamed him for continuing to do business with Mr. Crommelin a member of the Jockey Club coffee rooms and a chief Jockey Club Commissioner he was found guilty on the charge of *"endeavour to support a criminal charge by will full falsehood"* and stopped from riding as a jockey. They did nothing to the Jockey Club bookie and member Mr. Crommelin and this is the second time Crommelin had been accused of Bribery.

Ironically Lord George the Turf Reformer had committed a similar offence with a Lord March in 1845. March had tried to bribe Bentinck's trainer to throw him over in a race, as wrote Bentinck in a letter to John Kent, *"bribe of £500 to my trainer to throw me over in a £1000 match;"* refers to the behaviour of Lord March in this matter after Bentinck's constant efforts to treat him fairly."The letter goes on to say *"I forbore from making any complaint, I willingly drew a veil over the whole proceeding and instead of doing by Lord March as he did by me.*" [268] outside of this letter I have never found any record of Lord March being brought before the Jockey Club by Bentinck for reprimand. As he said he drew a veil over the whole proceeding of course you did, Lord March was a Jockey Club member and one of the establishment.

Let us look at some of the stewards who made up the Jockey Club Confederacy for the same stewards were present in Old England, Crommelin, Gaper and Running Reign cases these cases were tried before Lord George Cavendish Bentinck, Lords Exeter, Colonel Jonathan Peel MP and younger brother of Sir Robert Peel Prime Minister, Major General George Anson and Lords Stradbroke John Rous who was the elder brother of Admiral Rous also of the Jockey Club who John Day junior twenty years later in 1868 would bring a libel suit in court over fabrication and lies which he would win making Admiral Rous commit a public apology.

The Jockey Club Confederacy led by Lord George Cavendish Bentinck, Paladin arch enemy and punisher of the Day family, who had harboured a burning grudge since he was kicked out of Danebury by the Days, after their refusal to cheat their brother in law William Sadler and the public with the horse Crucifix. Bentinck absolutely hated the whole of the Day family. [269] After Crucifix Bentinck became a stalker of the Day family using his network of spies and touts he gathered information on their activities at Danebury and reported those activities to John Kent his trainer at Goodwood as seen in letters held at Nottingham University.[270]

Colonel Johnathon Peel, brother of the Prime Minister Sir Robert Peel and his group of friends were hammered by the House of Lords when

---

268 Nottingham University Pw L 346
269 Henry Corbett, *Tails and Traits of a Sporting Life* (1864, p.61) "my Lord and John Day parted anything but the friends they should have done. There was to be no integration to the amantium irae. On the contrary, the feud raged with all the proverbial acerbity of a civil war. Lord George declared himself not so much at variance with John as against the whole of the Day family"
270 Nottingham University associated letters of Lord George Pw L 356," discusses the success of John Day's training, achieving both galloping and sweating", Pw L 355/1-2," comments on Day's training progress19th March 1845," Pw L 354/1-2, comments on John Day's training successes, having got the horses out galloping on the Downs and sweated a fortnight ago," Pw L 354/1- however Kent has still spent six more days training than Day in the last fortnight; 'Ugly Buck' and the Monimia colt have still not had a sweat 17th March 1845, asks after 'Ugly Buck' whose joint gave out about three weeks ago; discusses the condition of the Monimia colt and 'Ratafia'; Day has achieved a sweat with several of his animals including, 'Wasp' and 'Benyghlo' but is now confined due to a cold; hopes that will give him an advantage at Northampton, Pw L 351/1-2 10th March 1845, Pw L 350/1-2discusses John Day's activities with a new horse called 'Wasp 17th March 1845

complaining about getting cheated on the turf *"He connects himself with a system in which he knows all sorts of swindling and cheating go on, and attends the same meetings that swindlers and sharpers come to; and when he and his friends find them bit and stung, they fly to their kind nurses apron strings, and take refuge behind the honourable house."*[271]

Having tried once and failed to ruin John Day Junior, in the Old England case when it was decided that *"John was above price and could not be bought"*[241] the same collaborators whip a second time two weeks later, in the Crommelin case. These confederates were Instigator Judge and Jury the same group that were involved in Running Reign fraud of the 1844 Derby and the Rattan Affair.

Mr Crommelin serial offender, chief commissioner and member to the Jockey Club accused of bribery not once but twice by jockeys in separate occasions spanning over 5 years, found not guilty by the Jockey Club Stewards on both occasions, was summed up best by the public and papers of the day when speaking of the Jockey Club Confederacy judgment against John Day Junior. *"We may ask whether it is consistent on the part of the Stewards of the Jockey Club to inflict such ruinous penalties upon a jockey lad, for delinquencies we admit, and at the same time dismiss Members of their own body who were the very instruments of causing those delinquencies with a few words of gentle reproof."* [264]

There was no way in the world the Jockey Club were going to let John Day Junior's charge of Bribery stand against their bookie. They quickly locked the doors and denied the press entry the same procedure as the Rattan affair they then started their witch hunt. If John Day's statement was proven correct then all of the honourable members who betted with Crommelin would be under suspicion and the Club would come tumbling down. Like the Mob they had closed ranks to protect Crommelin their bookie.

Bentinck, Chief Orchestrator and his gang were feverously manipulating and influencing the press who had no story, apart from the one that he, Bentinck, had handed them. The Jockey Club Confederates were writing and authoring their own version of events to suit their devious requirements, a 19th Century version of damage control titled "Delicate Investigation Conclusion of the inquiry by the Jockey Club, and sentence

---

[271] Thomas Curzon Hansard, William Cobbett, *The Parliamentary Debates* London 1844 Vol.74, p.794

pronounced."[272] 22nd June 1845 authored and polished by Bentinck it found its way everywhere. Bells life a sporting paper of the time ran the story as did the Sporting magazine both stories contained an exact copy of the words found handwritten in Bentincks exercise book at Nottingham University. The Club like a modern day version of Watergate were making sure their version of events was the only version being told.

The public knew it was a set up by the Club to protect their own. The deceit was so great that Lord Palmerston himself drew up a memorial and mounted an unsuccessful challenge in trying to get the case reheard by the general body of the Jockey Club who responded as. *"The Stewards, after a short deliberation, returned an answer, stating, in substance, that they must decline submitting the case to the General Body."* [264] Of course they refused as the general body of the Jockey Club would have examined the case closely and professionally and whatever else the Jockey Club Confederacy were hiding would have come out perhaps John Day had only reported the tip of the ice berg?

The Jockey Club Confederacy powerful and protected, ever ready to punish the powerless and vulnerable but always forgiving for its own members the untouchables of the Turf. Those untouchables had Mr Russell the Solicitor in the Qui Tam actions put in front of a select committee from the House of Lords to extract information on the case prior to Lord George agreeing to appear in court. That same select committee that John Day Junior was subjected too whose purpose was to gather information under the guise of reform on the laws of gaming, once they had the information they required they then leaked that information to Lord George giving him a head start with the preparation of his defence in the case of Qui Tam then got the case laughed out of court. That corrupt powerful group had managed to get a court of law to bend its knee.

Summed up by the Solicitor Mr Russell *"Why are immoral practices to be condemned in one class and allowed in another. I ask again Gentlemen why should a man in a higher station of life be allowed to do anything, when those of a lower rank are thus to be punished for doing the same thing can that difference be reasonable, can it be honest, can it be just?"*[273]

---

[272] Provides an account, under the title 'Delicate Investigation', of the enquiry by the Jockey Club into the affairs of Mr. Crommwelin and John Day in relation to the 1840 Derby; an account entitled 'Another Rattan Affair. Extraordinary Disclosures - Snakes in the Grass' is also included and is dated 1 June 1845; it describes an altercation which took place between Mr. Gully, the owner of 'Old England' and Mr. Hargreaves, a constant frequenter of betting circles, concerning the odds against the horse and treachery in his stable."

[273] James Rice, *A History Of the British Turf,* (Sampson , Low Marston, Rivington London Vol

Charles Greville Bentinck's cousin speaking of Bentinck, *"In short while he is thundering away against the poor low lived rogues for the villainies they have committed, he has himself been doing the same."* [196]

The Sporting Magazine Crommelin Affair *"We may ask whether it is consistent on the part of the Stewards of the Jockey Club to inflict such ruinous penalties upon a jockey lad, for delinquencies we admit, and at the same time dismiss Members of their own body who were the very instruments of causing those delinquencies with a few words of gentle reproof."* [264]

Mr Cockburn Running Rein *"Lord George Bentinck had for I can use no milder term tampered with the plaintiffs witness; that he had held out threats to them, and where threats had failed, had held out promises to them to induce them to withhold their evidence. That he had procured by the greatest exertions, and by the use of his personal influence, witnesses to appear for the defendant; that he had a certain degree associated with those witnesses; that he had them at Harcourt House his new place of residence, that he had fed them, that he had clothed them, that his valet had been seen to take one of them to a tailors to fit them out with clothes."*

John Gully Crommelin Affair *"He spoke of a rumour afloat that it was the intention of the Club to warn John Day Junior of all the racecourses in the Kingdom where the Newmarket rules were applied. He protested against such a mode of proceeding as being unjust and unconstitutional in as much as John Day Junior had merely attended as a witness and could not be liable unless a distant charge was bought against him."* [262]

Charles Greville Bentinck's cousin receives damming letters about Lord George from the Day Family themselves, as recorded in 1937 by Chester Kirby in his book "the English Country Gentleman" *"It was only when the Days put Charles Greville in possession of their past correspondence with Lord George that they were able to check the Ardour of their persecutor disclosed is a systematic course of treachery, falsehood and fraud which would have been far more than sufficient to destroy any reputation."* [275]

Nicholas Foulkes appears to frame my ancestors as crooks and cheats and misleadingly writes in his book "Gentlemen and Blackguards" *"His cousin Greville was approached by someone once connected with the Days who had kept hundreds of letters written by Lord George during the time his horses were at Danebury"*

---

1 1879, p.227)

[274] Mr Foulkes Ignored Chester Kirby writing in 1937 altogether and just wrote, *"disclosed is a systematic course of treachery, falsehood and fraud which would have been far more than sufficient to destroy any reputation."*[275] Mr Foulkes it was not *"someone connected with the Days"* that passed Charles Greville those letters, it was the Days themselves in order to vindicate themselves, but we understand writers need to sell books!

Bentinck and the Day Family once shared a close and warm relationship which later combusted into a bitter hatred that drove Lord George to wield the power and influence of the Jockey Club to exact his revenge and destroy the Day Family and the Danebury Stable crushing the Danebury Confederacy with it. The Confederacy he had introduced to Danebury through his relationship with Harry Hill in the first place. After the demise of the Danebury Confederacy perhaps Lord George Cavendish Bentinck was left without a source of disposable income for his horses and no longer a "Chief Ring Commissioner" in Harry Hill to back and pay for his racing stud. Perhaps that went some way towards explaining his decision to sell every horse he had, his entire stud. In a letter written by Bentinck referred to by Nicholas Foulkes Bentinck states "I must be ruined if I went on with the racing establishment without time to look after it and attend to it myself that I felt quite a load off my mind as soon as they were sold for 10,000 gns, I owed Drummonds (Bank) £17,000 I have paid them off £7,000 and mean to pay them off the remaining £10,000 at Christmas when Mostyn is to pay me for the stud."[276] Maybe the Danebury Confederacy members or someone else considered retribution? Maybe the stress of it all was too much for the Lord. He was found strangely dead in a field close to his home in 1848, apparently a heart-attack; he was only 46 years old.

After all has been said over Lord George I must include Tim Cox's assessment of Lord George extracted from his review of this book when writing on Lord George he said "I don't think he did anything against his own moral code, In the main I would judge him to be a force for good in racing."

---

[274] Nicholas Foulkes *Gentlemen and Blackguards Orion* 2010 p.44

[275] Chester Kirby *The English Country Gentleman; A Study of 19th Century Types* J. Clarke and Company Ltd London1937, p.50

[276] Nicholas Foulkes *Gentlemen and Blackguards Orion* 2010 p.327

AGAINST ALL ODDS

THESE WERE A FEW BAD YEARS for the Danebury establishment and John Day Junior after the departure of John Barham Day the falling out and betrayal of William. His grandmother Anne died in 1844 and his mother Harriet died two years later in 1846, he had been accused twice by the Jockey Club in 1845 of taking bribes to which they revoked his ability to ride professionally. In 1846 a significant argument erupted concerning Gully, Hill and Padwick, William Day in his book accounts for Gully and Hill's involvement but does not attribute anything to Padwick. John Barham Day had an argument with John Gully after the Old England Affair, and the end result according to William Day was that *"Of his quarrel with my father, I may perhaps say a word needless though an explanation is, he contrived to set his son John against him, making a small rift end in an open rupture, which would have been peacefully concluded but for his "blowing the coal" aided and abetted in this disgusting business by his faithful ally, Harry Hill. I must admit with sorrow, not all together mingled with shame, that the machinations of this worthy pair, the Downfall of the once Glorious Danebury must be attributed."* [277] Gully and Padwick set John Day Junior against his father John Barham Day, which resulted in a catastrophic rupture. John Barham Day and William left Danebury with Henry Padwick as their Patron, Gully and Hill stayed at Danebury with John Day Junior, who set up as trainer.

Sounds like an uphill struggle I want to see how John Day Junior managed and how he turned it around. These were punishing events and he was on his own now, but as we shall see his resolve and will was demonstrated by going on to train the largest number of winning horses to be sent out in one season in 1867, and that record lasted until 1987, until it was broken by Henry Cecil 120 years later. That alone is testament to his character.

So we pick him and the story up in 1846 he is 31 and the Stewards of the Jockey Club have just dismissed him from riding as a jockey, his father has gone with William, he is alone and has control of the Danebury Stables, as owner/trainer. His brother Alfred has stayed with him as jockey and he has a powerful and loyal group of patrons, he is emerging from the worst six years of his life.

John Junior, remarkably starts the year of 1847 with a Classic win as trainer, he sends out Conyngham-(Slaine-daughter of whisker) for Sir R Piggott, to win the 2,000 Guinea's, his first Classic. His brother Alfred Day was jockey,

---

277 William Day, *Reminiscences Of The Turf,* (1891, p.64)

also a first Classic for him. The same year John Day Junior and the Danebury stables sent out that famous horse Cossack-(Joannina-Priam by Hetman Platoff) bred by R.C.Elwes to win the Derby for T.H.Pedley, collecting stakes of £5,250, not a bad comeback after being dismissed from the saddle. He seemed to have inherited his ability to train horses like his father and didn't have to wait long to send out another winner, 1848 he had trained the winner Cymba-(Skiff by Melbourne) bred by H.S.Thompson, for Harry Hill, which was sent out to win the Epsom Oaks.

1849 came another Classic win for John Day Junior with Alfred his brother back in the saddle they stole the 1,000 Guineas with Flea-(Coronation-Puce) for F.Clarke. Like his father before him he had kept Danebury firmly in the spotlight and in 1850, sent out Pittsford-(Epirus-Miss Horwood), trained by John Day Junior, again with Alfred in the saddle, they took the 2,000 Guineas for Harry Hill. He had overcome all of the obstacles, and managed to keep the Danebury Stables alive and winning.

By 1854 John Day had the patronage of 15 good owners at Danebury, his brother William had 11 good owners at Woodyates, and his father John Barham Day had a few as well, they were controlling the market as can be seen in the classics table. They also saddled some good Derby horses that year as well. John Day Junior had Andover, Changarnier, Hermit, St Stephen, Stonehenge and The First Lord in his stables at Danebury. William had Cheshire Marquis, Ecclestone, Grimalkin-(Valentina by John O Gaunt). Their father had Belgrave, Glenstrae and The Star of Surrey, and that was just Derby horses, leading a collection of high quality equine racers. [278]

For 1854 was a good year and was to see the Stables and John Junior and Alfred pull off a double classic win when they sent out Hermit –(Bay Middleton-Jenny Lind by Touchstone), and took the Epsom Derby with Andover -(Bay Middleton-Daughter of Defence) for John Gully.

In 1855 there was a large dinner in honour of John Day at the Grosvenor Arms in Stockbridge and I have rescued the event from history because it provided a great account of the support he was receiving and how much esteem he was held in as a fine trainer of racehorses and a good man to both the rich and the poor". *R Etwell Esq. took the chair and on his right and left were the guests Walter Blunt Messer's Gully W Etwell, Grem Low Padwick, Hill, Sadler John Day Senior, and about seventy other friends who had assembled to certify their approval of Mr. John Days Character as a neighbour in both his relation to both*

---

278 W. H. Langley, *Ruffs Guide To The Turf Pocket Racing Companion*, Piper Stevenson and Spence (1854, p.viii)

the rich and the poor ... Mr. Gully who was twice complemented for twice bringing of the Blue Ribbon of the Turf." [279]

1856 saw the next Classic win for John Junior when he trained the horse Mince Pie-(Sweet Meat-Foinnuallia by Birdcatcher) for Harry Hill to win the Epsom Oaks once again ridden by Alfred Day.

1860 saw the death of his father John Barham Day at Woodyates of softening of the brain, this must have been a blow for John Day Junior, and I wonder if he ever settled the dispute that he had with his father that caused the family breakup. I would like to think he did.

1861 continued the success as seen in the press of the day *"In John Days Garden might be described every grade of the Peerage, with intellect enough for a cabinet council, Art Journalism and Finance were also well represented."* [280]

1862 was considered a low year for the stables, and nearly reached breaking point, and the stables nearly closed, but one horse saved the day. That horse was Canary and the race was the Royal Hunt Cup. After this, the business at Danebury started to pick up; John is on his feet, and on his way up. In 1866 a new stand was erected on the Danebury course by the Bibury Club and a fund started by Sir John Astley, exclusively for members of the Club. *"Stands there are, one for the use of the general public, and one (built by private subscription from a fund started in 1866 by Sir John, then Colonel, Astley) the property of the Bibury Club."* [281]

In late 1866 John Day had purchased the entire east window of the new St Peters Church Stockbridge at a substantial cost of 120 Guineas, three large stained glass windows installed ready for the Christmas season *"The East Window is a new and perfect development of the style with three long lancet arches, it is of rich stained glass a gift of John Day ESQ of Danebury and cost 120 guineas, the scenes represent the agony in the garden, the crucifixion and the resurrection."* [282] I have been in the church many times and I am sure I have never seen any commemorative plaque for John Day perhaps there never was one, or perhaps there was and Vaudrey Barker Mill heiress to Sir John Mill and some of the land the course was placed on had it removed.

---

279 Salisbury and Winchester Journal 17th March 1855
280 A.H.Bailey, *Baileys Magazine Of Sports And Past Times*, (1861, Vol 3, p.211)
281 Henry Charles Howard Earl of Suffolk and Berkshire, William George Craven, Arthur George Coventry Arthur Alfred Thomas Watson, *Racing And Steeple Chasing*, (Longmans Green London 1893, p.97),
282 Hampshire Chronicle 5th January 1867

Marquis of Hastings 1842-1868

So business was booming and in that year John Day achieved the impossible by sending out a record 167 winners, a record that was not equalled or beaten for another 120 years until 1987, when Henry Cecil managed it. The main jockeys of the stable were George Fordham and Thomas Cannon my great grandfather. George Fordham rode for the Duke of Beaufort, and Thomas Cannon was riding frequently for the Marquis of Hastings.

The unbroken record of 1867

1867 proved to be a remarkable year for John Day Junior and the Danebury stables. *"Such a wonderful season at Danebury enjoyed in 1867 may never be experienced again by any training establishment 16 horses went from there to Goodwood it that season and they captured 14 races between them"* [283] John was to make history and set a record that would remain unbroken by any Horse Trainer for 120 years by sending out 146 winning horse's in one season from a single stable. The record was attempted to be broken in 1979 with 128 winners by Sir Henry Cecil but remained unbroken until 1987 when Cecil topped it by 34 horses sending out 180 winners quite remarkable to have stood for such a time I wonder how many trainers had tried to beat that record in 120 years? The next few years were to provide both amazing results in the Danbury Stables and at the same time potentially huge scandals

Marquis of Hastings 1842-1868

Born on 22ND of July 1842,
Henry Weyford Charles Plantagenet, by all accounts was only two years of age when his father died in 1844, his mother the Marchioness had already passed away. He became Marquis in 1851 aged nine after his oldest brother died, He was schooled and then went to Oxford as an undergraduate, but this did not last long. Aged 21 the Marquis of Hastings joined the Jockey Club.

Figure 39 Marquis Hastings 1866 Baileys Monthly Magazine Vol XII

283 Sydenham Dixon, *From Gladiator to Persimmon, Turf Memories of Thirty Years.* (Grant Richards, London, Volume 1, 1901, p.82)

It was not long before he made, through a mutual acquaintance, the friendship of an old friend Mr. Henry Padwick, the money lender who in racing circles went by the name of Mr. Howard who you will remember was a member of the Danebury Confederacy. The Marquis was top prey of the Danebury Confederacy like John Bayton Starkey 26 years of age, and like John Bayton Starkey, extremely rich.

Henry Padwick introduced him to John Day at Danebury, who he went on to have 50 horses with. Two horses out of those fifty named the Earl and Lady Elizabeth were supposed the best of the bunch, the Marquis was recorded as having won in 1864 £10,000 in racing stakes in 1866 £12,837, and in 1867 £30,000, in that time was an incredible sum of money. But as the history books confirm the Marquis was more renowned for gambling heavy sums on other people's horses. It was said he won £75,000 on Lecturer at the Ceasarwitch, a huge sum, and it was also said his judgement in gambling on horses was so good that he could have made £30,000 a year in betting had he kept his head.[284]

In 1864, the Marquis developed a liking for a certain lady who was due to be married in the same week, and he made the big mistake of running away with her. She was Lady Florence Paget, the daughter of the Marquis of Anglesey, and was due to marry Mr. Henry Chaplin a good friend of the Prince of Wales. This must have caused major public embarrassment to Mr. Chaplin but by all accounts he did not respond publicly to the insult but ignored it.

The Marquis registered his racing colours of scarlet and white hoops in 1868, and these colours were later to be owned and registered by my great grandfather Tom Cannon, an act no doubt in honour of the Marquis's memory.

It was true to say that the Marquis of Hastings was a substantial gambler, and like with any gambler you will always hear of what is won but they never will tell of what is lost, but the amounts were such large sums of money that they could not be kept quiet.

One example of this was when the Marquis of Hastings had laid heavily against Hermit owned by Henry Chaplin his enemy and the father of the daughter he ran off with. It was in the Derby that he managed to lose £120,000 a colossal sum and he only managed to pay that bill by selling his Scottish Estate in London for £300,000, and paid all his other bills that

---

284 Thormamby, (Pseud) "Wilmott Dixon "*Kings of the Turf*, (1898, p.8)

Figure 25 Danebury or Trainers Cottage as in 1831 *Trainers*

amounted to £103,000, probably conducted by the Confederacy. For anyone else that would have been a lesson not ever to have been repeated, but not for the Marquis of Hastings, because in 1864 at the October meeting at Newmarket for the Middle Park Plate he entered Lady Elizabeth and had all his hopes set on her winning and backed her heavily, but she came in fourth and he managed to lose £50,000, but he did not stop there, and later you will see that gambling eventually became the ruin of him.

I will recall in a quote made at the time about the Marquis *"The ring that had cheered him in 1867, hooted him as a defaulter of the Derby in 1868, for he was £40,000 in their debt."* [285]

To conclude this chapter I include the following quote that was both acknowledged and accepted at the time of racing and recorded by a well-respected author and turf member, many historians have acknowledged that it was the turf that was the ruin of the Marquis of Hastings. The turf was introduced to the Marquis by Padwick and the Danebury Confederacy and it bled him until it hurt. *"The idea that the Marquis was ruined by his connection with the Turf is altogether untenable, his income was a small one yet he lived at a rate that could only be attained by a man of almost unlimited wealth, and he looked to the turf to enable him to do this. His idea that of breaking the ring was a chimera. But when a man is spending five or six times his income every year is not adverse to dice or cards."* [286]

I do not like to end on a sad note so we won't, there is a cottage near to Danebury that I think is called Trainers Cottage, John Day Junior stayed there sometimes, when John Barham Day was living at Danebury. The Marquis of Hastings did stay there as did many other famous turf patrons.

285 Thormamby, (Pseud) "Wilmott Dixon" Kings of the Turf Members Owners and Distinguished Backers, Owners, Trainers And Jockeys, (1898, p.282)
286 Sydenham Dixon, *From Gladiateur to Persimmon, Turf Memories of Thirty Years.* 1901, p.93)

"Just outside of Stockbridge and on the road from Danebury stands a Cottage that belongs to the Day family. It used to be the pride of the Day family for this cottage to be inhabited by the young John Day whilst the senior lived at Danebury. During a particular race meeting, Lord Hastings hired the cottage for the use of himself and friends. In this cottage was an oil lamp, with a large glass globe. One evening whilst the lamp was burning on the table, Mr. Wilkinson stood at the far end of the room with one of the old "Broad Wheeled" penny pieces in his hand, and cried out that he would make a bet on the double event. Namely that he would send the coin at a throw clean through the glass globe and the window. Away flew the Penny smash went the globe and crash went the window, the double event came off." [287]

LADY ELIZABETH AND THE 1868 DERBY

THE DERBY OF 1868 GAVE RISE to John Day Junior having yet another black mark against his name, by again a few members of the Jockey Club, who threw accusations both privately unprompted and publicly at the Day family over the training of the horse Lady Elizabeth. As will be seen later the accusations were quickly dismissed as rubbish, by both trainer and owner and then a law suit for liable was prepared by the Day family Solicitors to instigate to the accuser who was Admiral Rous a top member of the Jockey Club, the liable suit brought by the Days would only be dropped after a public apology by the Admiral. The Jockey Club was desperate to lay blame for this affair upon the Day Family, as they could not possibly accept it was down to the reckless gambling and behaviour of the Marquis of Hastings who was a member of the Jockey Club. Again the Club tried to appropriate blame against the Day family as we shall see.

The horse Lady Elizabeth belonged to the Marquis of Hastings, and was considered by the people of the day to be amazing, in fact in her first two years racing she had never known defeat, and in 1867 she had managed in one year to win £9,665 in stake or prize money, so she was considered an amazing horse or a sure bet if there was such a thing. Prior to the Derby of 1868, she was entered for an important race The Middle Park Plate, which she lost, it has been said that if she had won the Middle Park Plate held in October of that year at Newmarket her winnings as a two year old would have amounted to over £14,000 for the Marquis of Hastings, who as we have seen was a noted gambler within the betting ring, and who had at the time of the Derby had been up to his neck in debt, to the betting ring. If Lady Elizabeth would win the race all his debts would be cleared. The Marquis ran Lady Elizabeth ragged prior to the Derby of 1868, trying to

---

287 A.H.Bailey, Baileys Sporting Magazine And Past Times, (Vol 40 December 1882, p.69)

Figure 40Admiral Rous (History of the English Turf Vol1) 1879

alleviate some of the debt he owed to the Danebury Confederacy and this is probably what added to her breakdown. John Day Junior would have known she was not up to it, but what could he say? It was the Marquis of Hasting's horse, and ultimately his decision. [288]

Lady Elizabeth started the Derby of 1868 as the favourite, with odds of 7-4 bet against her, from this we can see that a large number of people had backed her to win, including her owner the Marquis of Hastings, who stood to win £35,000, this would have cleared all debt to the betting ring, everything he owned in the world was on the horse, and on the run of that horse everything was all about to change. Lady Elizabeth was nowhere to be seen in the group of finishers, and lost so much money that sore punters were looking for someone to blame, and the Jockey Club in particular were looking for heads for the guillotine and you can imagine the first port of call had to be the Danebury Stables. Once again John Day Junior would find himself in the thick of it. [289]

SPIDER AND THE FLY LETTERS

WE PICK UP THIS STORY NOW in the aftermath of the Derby of 1868, and that old tried and tested favourite method of the Jockey Club, of starting rumours as we have seen before, for now John Day Junior had been accused of plying Lady Elizabeth with Laudanum. Admiral Rous top member of the Jockey Club who astonishingly was the younger brother of John Rous or Lord Stradbroke who was one of the Jockey Club Confederacy stewards in the Old England and Crommelin case responsible for revoking his license twenty years before, had started this rumour but he of course denied it. Yet again in John's career a mandarin of the Jockey Club or the Dictator as he was known, had written a letter to the editor of the Times in London this time on the 15th June 1868, to which in the

288 James Rice, *History Of The British Turf,* (1879)
289 Louis Henry Curzon, *A Mirror Of The Turf, Or the Machinery of Horse Racing Revealed: Showing the Sport of Kings As It Is Today* (Chapman and Hall, London 1892)

pursuit of truth I include it below:-

"Sir — Observing in your paper of to-day the following paragraph quoted from the Pail Mall Gazette:—" The Sporting Life, with more audacity, mentions what Admiral Rous said on the course- that if he had taken as much laudanum as had been given to the mare, he would have been a dead man." Permit me to state that it is perfectly untrue. My belief is that Lady Elizabeth had a rough spin with Athena in March, when the Days discovered she had lost her form — b. very common occurrence with fillies which have been severely trained at two years old; that when the discovery was made they reversed a commission to back her for the One Thousand Guineas Stakes at Newmarket; and they declared that Lord Hastings would not bring her out before the Derby, on which he stood to win a great stake. I am informed that when Lord Hastings went to Danebury to see her gallop, they made excuses for her not to appear. If he had seen her move, the bubble would have burst. But the touts reported " she was going like a bird." Ten pounds will make any horse fly if the trainer wishes it to rise in the market. She has never been able to gallop the whole year. Lord Hastings has been shamefully deceived; and with respect to the scratching of The Earl, Lord Westmoreland came up to town early on Tuesday from Epsom to beseech Lord Hastings not to commit such an act On his arrival in Grosvenor-square, he met Mr. Hill going to Weatherby's, with the order in his pocket to scratch The Earl, and Mr. Padwick closeted with Lord Hastings. In justice to the Marquis of Hastings, I state that he stood to win thirty-five thousand pounds by The Earl, and did not hedge his stake money. Then you will ask, "Why did he scratch him?" **What can the poor fly demand from the spider in whose web he is enveloped?**

I am. Sir,
Your obedient servant,
H. J. Rous.
13, Berkeley-square" [290]

So as you can see, the last few sentences of the letter provided this event with its name, and there are many insinuations in that letter and all of them unfounded. Without so much of an investigation by the Jockey Club, how one of their top members could unchecked publish to the public such slanderous accusations against the trainer John Day. Well the response was, I bet, far from what the Admiral had expected. Firstly by the owner of the horse the Marquis and secondly by John Day Junior the trainer, who had been here before with the Dictators elder brother, and wasn't going to let it happen again.

---

290 James Rice, *History Of The British Turf*, (1879, p.371)

Just as before when Day was unfairly accused by the Jockey Club, which ended in them removing his ability to ride, they were now trying to remove him as a trainer. As before when the owner of the horse had tried with many others to protect him from the unfair rule of the Jockey Club, the owner of the horse this time, the Marquis of Hastings publicly replied to Admiral Rous of the Jockey Club:-

Sir — I have read with the greatest astonishment a letter in The Times of to-day bearing the signature of Admiral Rous. I can only characterize this letter as a tissue of misrepresentation from first to last There is no one single circumstance mentioned as regards my two horses — ^Lady Elizabeth and The Earl — correctly stated. I wish also to add that, so far from being '^ shamefully deceived," as stated in Admiral Rous's letter, The Earl was scratched by my express desire and authority, and that I myself wrote to Messrs. Weatherby to scratch him, and that no one either prompted me or suggested to me to adopt that course. I trust that this distinct contradiction will induce Admiral Rous to ab- stain in future from publishing statements which he could find to be unfounded if he had previously taken the trouble or sought the opportunity of verifying them. Your obedient servant, 34, Grosvenor-square. Hastings. [291]

Well, it didn't stop there John Day was more experienced this time and quickly instigated a liable suit in the courts against Admiral Rous top member of the Jockey Club for suggesting he and his stables at Danebury had deceived their employer:-

"Sir— We have been consulted by Mr. John Day, of Danebury, in reference to a letter which appeared in The Times of the 16th instant, signed by the Hon. Admiral Rous. We have been instructed by Mr. Day to institute legal proceedings against Admiral Rous, with a view of vindicating Mr. Day and his family against the imputations which have been cast upon them, and we have, by to-day's post, written to Admiral Rous, requesting to be furnished with the name of his solicitor. In the meantime, we rely on your sense of justice to permit us to give, on behalf of Mr. Day, in your columns, the most unqualified and un- conditional contradiction to the aspersions which Admiral Rous has thought proper to cast upon Mr. Day.

We are. Sir,
Your obedient servants,
Vallance and Vallance.
20, Essex-street, Strand, June 17." [291]

---

291 James Rice, *History Of The British Turf,* (1879, p.374)

The letter concluded with the Day's vindicating themselves when a certificate shown by a vet demonstrating to the Earl that the other horse that was removed from the Derby had in fact been lame and that was really that. It did however cost John Day £800 to defend himself against the Admiral's constructions. The Day family in the end dropped their case in the courts against the Admiral when he provided a public apology, and the whole affair was forgotten, but as you can see, the slight against the Days name had publicly had been made, yet again putting their livelihood in danger by members of the Jockey Club.

SHORT STORIES AND RACING RECOLLECTIONS

HOW DIFFICULT IS THE LIFE OF a racehorse trainer, when they reach the top of the profession. One more historic case put to bed against the Danebury Stables and the good name of John Day Junior, I wish these modern writers would do their own homework as in the stroke of a pen they remove 100 years of good racing history, the information is there you just have to look for it. The Danebury Stables were the best at what they did that is why they attracted all the business they could.

Another occasion demonstrates John Day Junior's shrewdness, and thorough knowledge of the horse, and can illustrate the difficult position he could sometimes find himself placed in by his employers where he may have little

Figure 41 John Day Jnr by (Nat Flatman)

control over the outcome which could have devastating effects. This incident was caused by the Marquis of Hastings, who had purchased a horse called Glendusk, from a Mr. Tom Parr; the horse had won a "sprint race" at Newmarket previously. The Marquis paid between £2,000 and £3,000 for the horse without the consultation of his trainer John Day, the transaction happened quickly and the first that John Day knew of the horse was when he saw it in his stable. His suspicions aroused John approached the horse and struck it with his walking stick, to which Glendusk gave a sharp cough, and John knew immediately the horse was "broken winded" and was unfit for racing. First thing the next morning John Day raced to the Marquis of Hastings house, to inform him of this discovery, the servants of the Marquis would not disturb him, but John persisted and demanded an Interview with the Marquis. In the end the Marquis saw John and explained what had happened with the horse, and this was just in time, as Tom Parr who had sold the horse was on his way to collect the money from the Marquis, but John's information, and prompt action allowed the Marquis to cancel the transaction, and not be cheated.[292]

Another incident occurred involving the Duke of Beaufort and John Day, at Danebury. The Duke of Beaufort possessed a bad temper and was well known for it. The Duke the Marquis of Hastings and Colonel Baille, were all together at Danebury one day, and a debate was in full swing about the pedigree of a horse belonging to the Duke, who was saying one thing and everyone else saying another, and from the sound of it John Day was keeping quiet. And then John was asked what he thought, to which he replied against the Duke and agreed with the others. The Duke then grabbed John Day by the shoulders and shook him, saying "you know John I hate to be contradicted", and the account goes on to say that quiet came across the room of people and they thought that worse would come. But then they all started laughing, even the Duke who was deadly serious at one point was laughing as well. [292]

A Horse called Birdhill was considered by all accounts to be good but not the most reliable of horses that the Duke owned. In 1863 she was entered for the Cambridgeshire Cup at Newmarket, and the Duke of Beaufort had on her £500. The Duke liked her, but John Day knew she was unreliable, so this was presented to the Duke a few days before the race started, and the Duke took her for a gallop an hour before, and Birdhill broke down and was scratched saving the Duke's embarrassment and his money.[292]

One more story and then back to the horse business, there was a ball or party thrown by the Marquis of Hastings at Donnington, John Day was also invited as a guest, to which he attended, but left early as it was said it not really to be his forte. But he was missed and sent for to return, which he did. On re-entering the ball John trod on the skirt of a very well-known lady, to which apologized she bowed in acceptance and then he recognized her to be the Countess of Winchelsea.[292]

---

292 A.H.Bailey, *Baileys Sporting Magazine And Past Times*, (December 1882, p.68-69)

THE FINAL YEARS & THE HANDOVER OF THE STABLES

Figure 42 Danebury Handover 1882, Left to right back row Tom Junior and, Tom Cannon Senior front row Thomas Hopkins Cannon Harriet Cannon Kate Cannon (nee Day) at her knee Mornington Cannon John Day Junior and Henry Day

THERE IS MUCH DEBATE ABOUT THE time of the handover of the Danebury Stables to Tom Cannon, the stables were handed over in 1877, the reason they were handed over was John Day Junior found himself like many trainers in the profession of horse racing did, with insufficient funds and also without his sight as he was ageing.

There was at that time a bankruptcy proceeding being issued against him by the Beaufort Family of Badminton and the Berkley family of Stoke Gifford, as can be seen from the record below[293].It seems that John's eldest son the veterinary surgeon was also caught up in the bankruptcy, as in 1875 he was living in a country house Eastrop House addressed New Road Eastrop Basingstoke, and was declared bankrupt in 1875 and subsequently discharged on 17th January 1877. He was moved from the house to 6 Church Square, Basingstoke, perhaps the whole of the Day Family were in financial trouble. John's eldest son, the Basingstoke vet, died in 1881 aged 41.

---

293 Gloucestershire Record Office D2700/QG4/11Bankruptcy proceedings relating to John Day snr., Nether Wallop, Hants, race-horse trainer 16.1.1877

Tom Cannon who was his son-in-law and my great-grandfather had no choice but to take over the Danebury Stables due to the illness of his father-in-law and the financial status of the Day family, but Tom publicly waited until 1882 to announce the handover, in honour of his father in law he also waited until his death to alter the stables and Danebury, to how it looks today, he removed nearly all the old dwelling house, and left only the kitchens, and the turret, more of which I have captured from family records below, and in 1883 from paper cuttings. *"Already the repairs and general overhauling of the stabling are going to assume a somewhat dilapidated aspect it has been nearly completed. And it will not now be long before the large racing stud under the care of Tom Cannon will be sheltered under one roof at Danebury. Though of course considerable time must necessarily elapse before the Dwelling house is ready for Habitation. The shrubbery in the front is to be all together remodelled and by the way it may here be noted that the old paddock on the race course is to be converted into a promenade lawn, tastefully laid out with flower beads, and the saddling enclosure will in future be on the other side, so it will be seen."* [294]

I find it amusing just that Tom Cannon completely removed Lord George Cavendish Bentinck's Paddocks, and turned them in to a *"promenade lawn"*. Shortly after his death there was an auction of John Day's belongings and effects as dictated by his will, I have included this auction as it helps, to give an insight at what was going on at the Danebury Stables at the time, and

---

294 Tom Cannon, Garlogs, 1898

also provides an account of the revolutionising of the Danebury Establishment, to what it was then as seen in Abraham Cooper's Picture in 1848 **Figure 24 Landscape of Danebury viewed from Chattershill by Abraham Cooper R.A 1848** to what it would become after Tom Cannon had finished. Tucked away in the family book titled "Tom Cannon Garlogs 1882 **Appendix 2:** Tom Cannon Garlogs (Family Book)was also found a list of some very famous paintings which were sold at auction after John Day's death. I sent the list to the British Sporting Arts Trust, many years ago but never received a reply. John Day Junior had only two horses in his ownership at the time of his death, Confessor and Prince Edward, and they were purchased by a Mr. Jacobbs, I have included full list of the pictures in Appendix 11 List of Sporting Pictures Sold from John Day's Estate 1883 *"It might have been expected on Wednesday that the highest priced picture was that by, A. Cooper of Andover (A.Day Hermit Wells) a portrait of the then "Leviathan, Gully and sundry members of the Day family". Cannon was a purchaser, and to his final nod was also knocked down "Harry Halls painting of Crucifix and junior Portraits of Auburn Vaun with Fordham up by the same band now still in death, and decisive with portraits of Tollard and the late Master of Danebury were likewise amongst the paintings secured by Tom Cannon. Mr. Toovey was a conspicuous bidder and bought Coopers picture winner of the Oaks and virtually the foundation of the Late Sir Josephs Hawleys great success on the turf. As after the Kentish Baronet had purchased her from Mr.' Gulley daughter of Touchstone had turned out a veritable goldmine at the stud amongst her produce, being beadsmen in addition to winning the derby, was the Sire of many other good horses that carried the cherry black cap to victory at important races."* [295]

THE DEATH OF THE LAST JOHN DAY OF DANEBURY

NOW WITH EVERYTHING TIED UP AND Tom Cannon at the helm, John Day, my great-great-grandfather could relax, I am sure he still carried on working or giving help to Tom Cannon in the years towards his death, but for now he could relax.

John Day III died on 3rd of December 1882 at his home in Danebury he was 67 years old and master of the turf, in his time, he had won 1 Classic as a jockey, and succeeded to win 12

Figure 43John Day William his brother 1883 Danebury (Family Collection)

295 Tom Cannon, Garlogs, 1898

English Classics as a trainer, he had sent out the largest number of winning pedigree horses in one season a record to last for 120 years. He had been at the top of his profession most of his life, his knowledge and ability was unsurpassed, he was involved in some of the largest scandals the turf and the racing world had ever seen and survived those scandals and no doubt avoided some that the history books failed to record.

Prior to his death John Day's eyes also started to fail him, there is a record that the Duke of Beaufort tried to restore his sight, *"Duke of Beaufort paid 100 guineas to a noted physician for operating on John Days eyes, but it was too late for all the skill in the world to restore the sight."*[296] Perhaps a horse trainer without any sight would be about as good as a fisherman without a fishing rod, so all of these things together would have required him to hand over the stables and there was no one left within the family that could do the job, as his son John had died in 1881, his brother Alfred had died in 1868, and he was embroiled in a feud with William who had his own training establishment at Woodyates in Dorset. For the Danebury Stables to continue and all John Day's commitments to his patrons to be met, Tom Cannon head jockey and son-in-law aged 31 had to step in to the breach, it is not known if he did this willingly, but in 1877 that is exactly what he did he picked up the reins and went on to completely revolutionise Danebury.

He picked Danebury up from the floor where it lay battered and bruised and instigated new methods with a new generation of master horse men for this was now the time of the Cannons and with each breath that John took the Days were slowly getting darker as they had served their time on the turf and served it well and a new sun was rising on Danebury. We shall see in the next chapter the Cannons and the Danebury Stables went on to completely dominate the turf.

---

296 A.H.Bailey, *Baileys Sporting Magazine And Past Times*, (December 1882, p.70)

OIL PAINTINGS

GUSTAVUS WINNER 1821 DERBY

Figure 44 Gustavus Winner 1821 Epsom Derby Sam Day up by Jean Louis Theodore Gericault oil on Canvas

MARIA WINNER SOMERSETSHIRE STAKES 1828

Figure 3 Maria Owner George IV John Barham Day Jockey by R. B. Davis 1828

Figure 46Priam Sam Day Up 1830 winner Goodwood Cup by Benjamin Marshall

PRIAM:-Winner of the 1830 Goodwood Cup

Figure 45Priam Sam Day up by John E Fernley 1830

Figure 48Chorister John Barham Day up Winner 1831 St Ledger by John E Fernley

CHORISTER: -Winner 1831 St Ledger

Figure 47Chorister John Barham Day Up by John Frederick Herring 1831

GREY MONMUS: WINNER 2,000 GUINEAS 1838

Figure 49Grey Monmus John Barham Day 1838 Artist Unknown

PUSSY:-WINNER EPSOM OAKS AND DERBY 1834

Figure 50Pussy John Barham Day up William Day Trainer at Newmarket 1834 by John E Fernley

Figure 52Mango Sam Day up Winner 1837 St Ledger by John Frederick Herring

MANGO WINNER 1837 ST LEDGER

Figure 51 Mango Sam Day up 1837 Winner St Ledger by Abraham Cooper The Racehorse in Training p103

Figure 54Ellis John Barham Day Up by Charles Hunt 1836

ELLIS: Winner 1836 St Ledger

Figure 53Ellis John Barham Day Up with Van by Abraham Cooper 1836

TOUCHSTONE:-WINNER OF THE 1836 ASCOT GOLD CUP

Figure 55 Touchstone Winner 1836 Ascot Gold Cup John Barham Day Jockey John Scott Trainer by John Frederick Herring Senior

CHAPEAU D ESPINAGE AND VENISON WITH THE DAY FAMILY:-

Figure 17 Chapeau d Espinage Winner 1000 Guineas 1837 Venison and the Day Family 1838 by Abraham Cooper The race horse in Training Page 53

VIRAGO: - Winner City Suburban and Metropolitan 1854

Figure 56Virago John Barham Day Trainer John Wells Up by Thomas Baratt Stockbridge Racecourse Racehorse in Training p.93

CARAVEN: John Day Junior Up by John Frederick Herring

Figure 57CaravenJohn Day Jnr Up by John Frederick Herring

Figure 59 Wisdom Sam Day Up by Abraham Cooper 1838

WISDOM: - SAM DAY UP 1838 BY ABRAHAM COOPER

Figure 58Wisdom Sam Day Up by John E Fernley 1838

Figure 60 Crucifix Winner of the 1840 Oaks John Day up by John Frederick Herring The Racehorse in Training p.40

CRUCIFIX: WINNER OF THE 1840 OAKS

Figure 61Crucifix John Barham Day Up 1840 by Harry Hall

VULCAN: Winner Tradesman Cup Liverpool 1843

Figure 62 Vulcan John Day Jnr Up by William Tasker 1843

SPUME: - John Day Junior Up by Abraham Cooper 1837

Figure 63 Spume John Day Jnr Up by Abraham Cooper dated 1837

DECEPTION: WINNER OF THE OAKS 1839

Figure 64 Deception John Day Up. Winner of the Oaks 1839 by James Loder of Bath

DECISIVE:- JOHN DAY JUNIOR UP BY GEORGE COLE

Figure 65 Decisive John Day Jnr Up 1843 by George Cole Stockbridge Racecourse

PHYRRUS The First WINNER OF THE 1846 EPSOM DERBY

Figure 67 Pyrrhus the First winner 1846 Epsom Derby Sam Day Up by Thomas Alken

OLD SAM: - OLD SAM DAY UP ON UNKNOWN HORSE 1842

Figure 66 Old Sam Day Up unknown horse 1842 by Harry Hall

THE HERO: - WINNER ASCOT GOLD CUP 1847 AND 1848

Figure 68 the Hero Winner Ascot Gold Cup 1847 and 1848 Alfred Day Jockey John Barham Day Trainer

ANDOVER:-1854 DERBY WINNER

Figure 69 Andover Winner Epsom Derby 1854 Alfred Day up Aquatint after Harry Hall

Figure 70 John Day Junior by Harry Hall (National Horseracing Museum)

Figure 71 A Reminiscence of Danebury, by Sextie, Tom with sons Tom Morny Kempton and Charles.

THOMAS CANNON 1846-1917

Figure 72 Thomas Cannon Danebury (Racing Illustrated 1895)

Classic Wins as a Jockey and Trainer

Table 5 Classic Races Won As a Jockey

Tom Cannon	Horse	Year	Owner
2,000 guineas	Pilgrimage	1878	4th Earl Of Lonsdale
	Shotover	1882	Duke Of Westminster
	Enterprise	1887	Douglas Baird
	Enthusiast	1889	Douglas Baird
1,000 guineas	Repulse	1866	Marquise Of Hastings
	Pilgrimage	1878	4th Earl Of Lonsdale
	Busy Body	1884	George Baird
Epsom Oaks	Brigantine	1869	Sir Frederick Johnstone
	Marie Stuart	1873	James Merry
	Geheimniss	1879	7th Earl Of Stamford
	Busy Body	1884	George Baird
Epsom Derby	Shotover	1882	Duke Of Westminster
	St Blaise	1883	Sir Frederick Johnstone
St Ledger Stakes	Robert The Devil	1880	Frederick De lagrange
Grand Prix De Paris	Ceylon	1866	Duke Of Beaufort
	Trent	1874	W.R.Marshal
	Thurlow	1878	Prince Soltycoff
	Frontin	1883	Duc De Castrie
	Little Duck	1884	Duc De Castrie

Table 5 Classic Races Won As a Trainer

Tom Cannon	Horse	Year	Owner
2,000 guineas	Busy Body	1884	George Baird
1,000 guineas	Busy Body	1884	George Baird

THE MASTER

BEFORE WE START ON TOM CANNON the *"Prince of Trainers"* [297] long career in the saddle 32 years as a jockey, and later trainer and breeder, the rider of 1,544 winners, let us open it with a few passages from history written by the men that knew him. The first from George Lambton who rode for Tom Cannon at Danebury, he said *"A slight, delicate-looking man, good-looking, a bit of a dandy, and a beautiful jockey. I can think of no other word that describes his style so well. In finesse, and the fine art of jockeyship, he had no superior, and in the handling of a two year old I should say no equal."* [298] Charles Morton the leading trainer in 1930 spoke of Tom Cannon *"there is no doubt he could outride anyone of his time and during the years that he, Archer and Fordham were in evidence we saw what I consider to be the three greatest jockeys the English Turf has ever seen."* [299] Fred Archer the leading jockey of that time spoke of Cannon as *"the most beautiful, too pretty at times and most finished of Jockeys."*

Tom Cannon was born to Thomas Hopkins Cannon and Harriet Townsend 23rd April 1846 at nine o'clock in the evening he was born in the George hotel in Eton which is over the footbridge from Windsor Castle. In those days the George hotel was a livery stable to which his father was a horse dealer and took the hotel on the 5th March 1842 as can be seen from the occupation advertisement in the local paper *"George INN livery Stables Yard Eton THOMAS CANNON in announcing that he has succeeded to the business of Mr. G DELL at the above yard respectfully solicits a continuance of the patronage which has so long been bestowed on him and previously on his Uncle Mr. Robert Davis T.C. assures the public that they can be accommodated by him with good hunters ladies horses, gigs fly's and etc. March 4th 1842."* [300]

The Hopkins in Tom Cannons fathers name came from his mother's maiden name, Caroline Hopkins who was born 25th December 1787, his father Joseph Cannon born 13th March 1778 was also a horse trainer and probably knew the Days in Danebury, We find Thomas Hopkins Cannon

297 Parke Buckley, *The Harmsworth London Magazine, the Amalgamated Press*, 1902-1903. IX August, p.75

298 Hon George Lambton, *Men And Horses I Have Known*, (Butterworth London, 1930, p.156

299 Michael Tanner, *Guinness Book Of Great Jockeys Of The Flat*, Guinness Publishing London April 1992, p.95

300 George Inn Yard Livery Stables Eton, *Windsor and Eton Express* (R. Hoxley, Windsor, Vol XXXI Saturday Evening March 5th 1842

Winning a race in Eton on the 3rd September 1842, the race was Steeple-chase in Slough. An excellent advertisement for his horses. [301]

By 15th January 1853, disaster had struck and Thomas Hopkins was now in debt and required to appear in court to answer for those debts *"Whereas a petition of Thomas Hopkins Cannon of*

Figure 73 George Hotel Eton

Brochas Street in the Parish of Eton, livery stable keeper and insolvent debtor, Thomas Hopkins Cannon is required to appear to the said court on the 15th Day of February." [302]By all accounts Thomas Hopkins Cannon was in business with his uncle. He was the proprietor of the George Inn until 15th November 1862 as his business was growing he moved establishment to a more convenient location by the railway station and also gave tuition on horse riding to the local Lords at Eton School and was also a painter. *"Thomas H Cannon Livery Stable Keeper begs most respectfully to acquaint the Nobility Clergy and Gentry of Winsor that he has removed from the George Inn Eton to the Stables of the Swan Inn Eton opposite the South Western Railway the latter situation being contiguous to both Railways."* [303]

Before Tom Cannon was ten years old he was already well known by Etonians as a fierce rider in the Queen's Staghounds as was his younger brother Joseph.[304]Tom was born the eldest of two sons and three sisters, his younger brother Joseph Cannon the steeplechase jockey was born three years later on 10th December 1849 at 12:20 they were educated first at Eton

---

301 Windsor and Eton Express Saturday, (R. Hoxley, Windsor, 1842) the ground selected for the event was altered from where we mentioned last week, to near the Dolphin; and as Mr. Sharpe declined to start his mare, Mr. Skivens's mare was ridden over the ground by Mr. Cannon of Eton, and the stake claimed.

302 Windsor and Eton Express Saturday, (R. Hoxley, Windsor, Vol XLII January 15th 1853)

303 Windsor and Eton Express Saturday (R. Hoxley, Windsor, Vol LL November 15th 1862)

304 Tom Cannon The Sportsman, The Press, (Volume XLVI, Issue 7238, 19 February 1889, Page 6)

Figure 74 Tom Cannon 1865

by Dr. Hawtrys School the Provost of Eton College then by Dr. Powney also at Eton. These brothers were to go on to dominate the turf, for they like the Day family of Danebury had grown up in the saddle not just started at 14 like most boys of that time. The Cannon brothers first memories would have been about horses, and sport would have been their life.

Unlike the Day family Tom Cannon had to leave home early in life at the age of 13 and in October 1859 [304]went to live with Mr. William Sextie a painter and friend of Tom's father in Newmarket where he was apprenticed to Sextie, Sextie then owned horses with Tom's Father[305] and Sextie used to paint portraits of the Queens horses at Winsor.

Tom Cannon's first recorded race was in 1860 when he was thirteen years old and riding in the Saltram Handicap at Plymouth in which he was registered at 4 Stone 7Ib's. He was riding a horse called Mauvoreen, owned by Mr. Williams. This first race was a very unfortunate one, "*as coming round the turn Mauvoreen struck into one of the leaders coming down heavily throwing her diminutive pilot who weighed little over 4 stone, although severely shaken the boy was not severely injured by his fall and later in the afternoon by his own particular request that he was allowed to ride the mare again and obtained second place in the Tradesmen's plate*" [304] The fall would certainly have put doubt in the mind of a young apprentice, and left him wary, but not Cannon, he was not to be beat and the next day young Cannon at 54lbs in weight scaled his first winner in the Chelson Meadow Stakes, for Lord Portsmouth on "My Uncle." Cannon also had an engagement with Mr. E Brayley where he remained under his tutelage wearing his red jacket and yellow cap.

The race was run in three heats each heat was run over three quarters of a mile. His main opponent in the race was a horse called Lisp. Cannon won the first of the three heats by a head, second heat they could not separate them so they had to run a third heat, to which Cannon took My Uncle past the post to win by half a length.[304] The way Cannon had ridden My Uncle

---

305 John William Carleton, Sporting Review ed Craven, Rogerson and Tuxford, London 1869

led to an immediate engagement with Lord Portsmouth, who Cannon rode many races for and Lord Portsmouth held a retainer for Cannon until he retired from racing. [306]

Before the Close of the year 1860 racing season Cannon moved to Marlborough with William Sextie the painter *"At the close of this year 1860 Cannon removed to Marlborough where he remained until 1865 with on his marriage with one of John Day's Daughters he settles himself on Houghton Down in a Cottage called the Elms."* [307] The racing was quiet for Tom over the next few years and in 1863 Cannon rode Isoline-(Bassishaw by Prime warden) which was owned by Mr. Tom Parr for which he won the Manchester Tradesmen's Cup beating Caller Out by half a length, in a race of 38 which is quite a considerable number of horses to race against.

THE MARQUIS AND THE SCARLET AND WHITE HOOPS

IN THE YEAR 1864 CANNON WAS 18 years old and had won a total of 15 races. A noted race was on Pearl Diver for Mr. Bayley for the Nottingham Handicap. In the Ceasarwitch of that year Cannon rode for Harry Hill of the Danebury Confederacy. Cannon rode the horse Ackworth and came third in the race due to a post train upsetting the race. Ackworth was purchased afterwards by the Marquis of Hastings for 2000 Guineas, and Cannon was engaged as the jockey to ride him in the Cambridgeshire, which he won, *"as in the scarlet and white hoops he rode what has been considered to be one the very finest races ever seen and bringing his horse with one final rush got the better of an intensely exciting struggle by a head, beating Maidment on Tomato, it led to him being retained by his Lordship to ride second to Fordham."*[304] That event is what gave Tom Cannon the introduction to John Day Junior and the Danebury Stables which was a great step in the young jockey's career, and probably the most steering one. Tom was to move to the powerful Danebury stables near Stockbridge and change his life forever.

The Marquis of Hasting's racing colours were Scarlet and White Hoops. These colours were first carried in 1863 in the Althorpe Park Stakes and from all accounts the first time the colours won was with Gatroter in the Spring Meeting of 1862 for the Marquis, and Tom Cannon was riding her. [308]Tom Cannon would in later year make these colours his own perhaps due to the memory and out of respect to the Marquis of Hastings for the opportunity the noble lord had given to Cannon by engaging him to ride

306 Theodore Andrea Cook, *A History of The English Turf*, 1901-1904
307 John William Carleton, *Sporting Review ed Craven* (1869, p.340)
308 Argus Eye, Observer , Tom Cannon, 25th December 1885

Figure 76 Tom Cannon 1874 (Family Collection)

Ackworth in the 1864 Cambridgeshire and as recalled in The Press of the time *"his lordship had been advised by his friends not to put young Cannon up but the result proved that he had made no mistake as he rode perhaps one of his finest races, bringing his horse up with a fine rush beating Maidment on Tomato."* [309]

Tom Cannon, now second jockey to the formidable George Fordham who referred to Cannon as "My Boy"[309] or the Devil as he was known, riding under the trainer John Day III was invited to move to the powerful Danebury Stables he later suffered *"a starters suspension of two months was not thrown away he found his way to Danebury where he became enamoured to the charms of Kate the only daughter of John Day."* [304] So as the story goes they had arranged to meet whilst Tom Cannon was in Stockbridge, probably secretly, Tom had rented a small open top carriage pulled by two ponies. On the way to Kate one of the ponies had hurt his leg and wouldn't go any further, Tom was becoming late for his rendezvous with his sweetheart. Tom unhitched

Figure 75 Kate Day (Family Collection)

the pony and jumped on its back and rode the rest of the way to meet Kate.

His charm must have worked as they were married on 13th December 1865 at Nether Wallop Church *"on the 13th Inst.. at the parish Church of Nether Wallop, by the Rev Walter Blunt, M.A Thomas Cannon of Marlborough to Kate only daughter of John Day of Danebury Hants."* [310] Tom was 19 years old, Kate was 21. He should be considered quite brave because some people would think it dangerous to be involved with your boss's daughter, not Tom though. They

---

309 The Press Tom Cannon the Sportsman, Volume XLVI, Issue 7238, 19 February 1889, Page 6
310 Reading Mercury 23rd December 1865

Figure 77 Tom Cannon by Harry Hill 1867 Private Collection

were married by Walter Blunt who was the proprietor of some of the land at Danebury.

The newlyweds first moved to a property known as the Elms or Snails Creep Pictures which is situated in Houghton and quite an established property too, he is recorded as living there in 1865 [307] and in 1867 [311] as the resident jockey. The property was perhaps given to Kate and Tom as a wedding present from Kate's father John Day Junior. But Cannon was earning very well at this time and he is recorded as living there prior to being married so probably purchased it on his own. Cannon and his employer John Day would walk the grounds of Danebury everyday around the Danebury Rings, probably discussing tactics.

Danebury by this time was already a very powerful and well established stables that had boasted some of the turf's finest patrons and most successful thoroughbreds, so I would imagine to Cannon it was a dream come true for at that time the Danebury Stables were packed with horses and eager young jockeys, and competition for the best mounts was high between the jockeys. The most noted, and head jockey, at the stables was George Fordham, nicknamed The Devil, and his trick was to make a late challenge on the other jockeys near the end of a race, a tactic that was most definitely passed on to the Cannons. Tom Cannon's racing career flourished and under the tutelage of John Day and George Fordham he achieved many successes and the all-important Classic wins, mainly on

---

311 Piggott's directory , 1867)

fillies, and on two year olds is where he excelled. To ride a two year old would require the lightest of touches and the slightest movements from the jockey, and it was this that he was to go on to become the master of. In a time when many other jockeys were used to heavy handling the horses, this is where Cannon brought his excellence, and was admired for his lightweight hands.

To give you some idea of his ability as a jockey at this time we can see from the races won in these years as taken from 1869 sporting review,[307]

1860 he won............	1 race
1861 "	3 "
1862 "	5 "
1863 "	16 "
1864 "	15 "
1865 "	31 "
1866 "	76 "
1867 "	60 "
1868 "	40 "

Tom Cannon's first great win, the Cambridgeshire Cup was now in the bag. This race was an important step in Tom's career, because for winning with Ackworth he received a large sum of £500, from the Marquis of Hastings, who had purchased the horse for £2,000, and won £30,000. Cannon and the Danebury Stables were at it again, as his predecessor his wife's grandfather John Barham Day had done, with the Dukes of Grafton he had raised the stakes in earnings for a jockey *"With her he had won almost £30,000, he gave Tom Cannon the unprecedented sum of £500.00 for riding her, and this commenced the fashion of giving jockeys large presents after being successful in a large event.*[312]

1866 was a great year for Cannon he won his first Classic success, the 1,000 Guineas on Repulse-(Stockwell-Sortee), the Marquis of Hastings's horse that was trained by John Day at Danebury. It was now his time as the same year he won the Grand Prix de Paris in France on Ceylon-(Idle Boy-Pearl by Alarm) owned by the Duke of Beaufort trained by John Day. At this point he was only 20 years old, and winning these Classic races enabled the Danebury Stables to come out of the rough patch it had been suffering, and obtain an injection of new life. They were rising again and Tom more than doubled the number of races won in 1866, totalling 71 compared to the previous year's 31 wins, Cannon was on fire.

---

312 Argus Eye, The Plunging Marquis, The Observer, (Volume 7, Issue 346, 25 July 1885, Page 11)

Figure 78 Tom Cannon 1875 Wearing His Own Colours (Family Collection)

1867 proved a good year for Cannon, a quiet year on the Classics but he still managed to win 60 races. Celebration was in the air for the young family as his wife gave birth to their first child Miss Alyce Mary Cannon who was born in Winchester, middle name Mary after Kate's sister who died at birth in 1839, she would go on in later years to create the poker work or Pyrography of Tom Cannon currently hanging in the Grosvenor Hotel in Stockbridge.

In 1868, George Fordham (the Devil), Tom Cannon's mentor at Danebury for the past three years, retired from racing, which meant Cannon was now number one jockey to the Danebury Stables and that all the mounts now went to him. Cannon was at this time also training his own horses, these were cast-offs from other stables and to which he was applying great skill.[313]

Tom and Danebury did not have to wait long to receive another Classic, this time in 1869 Tom won the Oaks on Brigantine-(Buccaneer-Lady McDonald by Touchstone, owned by Sir. Frederick Johnstone, this proved good for the stable as it was making publicity all the time Cannon brought 40 winners home that year. It seemed that year the young couple celebrated the Classic win as another child was born to Kate, another girl who was named Florence, tragically she died at only fourteen days old.

There is a good story from 1870 that goes some way to show Cannon's shrewd style of riding. He was engaged to ride a famous horse called Paganini, owned by Mr. T. Smith at a Weymouth meeting. Paganini had frightened all the competition, Mr. Smith had perhaps considered Cannon's racing fee to be too high and had second thoughts about putting him up and put a stable boy on instead. Let us pick the story up as recalled from The Press *"Cannon determined to teach this Gentleman a lesson and he managed to get the leg up on the Boy Paganini's only opponent, Mr. Smith's Horse lobbed along home*

---

313 The Press Tom Cannon the Sportsman, Volume XLVI, Issue 7238, 19 February 1889, Page 6

followed by the Boy who looked hopelessly beaten, when the two got to the distance post the lad who was riding Mr. Smith dropped his hands thinking the race was won stopping his horse. A few strides from Home Cannon came with a rush and beat him by the best part of a length" [309]

In 1871 Letitia Maude Cannon was born to Tom and Kate, and went on to marry Mr. Henry Wood who also rode and trained horses, and they went later in life to India and South Africa to live where Henry became an established trainer.

Figure 79 Tom Cannon own colours Oil on Canvas Unsigned

1872 put an end to the wait, a son was born and it is tradition in our family for the eldest son to be named Thomas. The Day family kept a similar tradition of calling the first son John. He was named Thomas Leonard Gilbert Cannon, or as he was to be later known Tom (junior) I named my first born Charles after my grandad. Tom Cannon became champion jockey in 1872 with a total of 87 winners and it must have done wonders for the Danebury Stables.

In 1873 Tom Cannon registered as an owner trainer, the colours were red with yellow sleeves and cap, but in 1874 changed them to scarlet with white hoops which were the colours of the unfortunate Marquis of Hastings and the background to this book. This registration was a sign of what was to come, as John Day, his boss and father-in-Law was becoming ill and his eye sight was fading fast.

But business still had to continue as many people depended on it, and the stable triumphed with another Classic for Tom in 1873 when he won the Oaks on Marie Stuart-(Scottish Chief-Morgan La Faye by Cowe) owned by Mr. Merry.

Apart from the Classic win the best thing that year was the birth of Herbert Mornington Cannon on 23rd March 1873, and would in later years exceed the ability of his father in some respects, this was another name that has started to find its way through our family and all who possess the name ask where does it come from?

Figure 80 Tom Cannon Brighton 1876

The same day that Morny was born Tom was riding in Bath and the baby was born early, to which Kate Toms wife had not prepared a name as this was the father's honour. Kate sent a telegraph to Tom requesting a name for the new son, while this was happening Tom was sending a telegraph to the stables informing them of his win on the horse called Mornington, well the two telegraphs were mixed up and the maid handed Kate the winning horse's name to which she thought was the baby's intended name, I mean no offence to my great uncle Herbert but you can see why Mornington was favoured.

In the following year 1874 it was back to France and a win for Tom in the Grand Prix de Paris on Trent-(Broomielaw-The Mersey by Newminster) which was owned by Mr. W.R.Marshall. Tom must have celebrated with Kate by having another child called Agnes Mable who later went on to marry a Mr. Paul McAlister, a Cambridge Architect.

Cannon's career in the saddle was progressing nicely and he was recorded as driving a hard bargain but being a very honest man, a trait that reflected well in all the Cannons. On one occasion he even sacrificed his own money to win the race *"Cannon was scrupulously honest, never hesitated to beat his own money. As he considered Lady Atholstone, whom he rode for Sir George Chetwynd* at Windsor in the spring of 1875, had no chance of giving 39lb to Chester, he had £20 on the latter and then forced Lady Atholstone up to beat Chester by a head in the last stride."* [314]

Another child was born in 1877 a girl named Margret Kate Cannon, Kate after her mother, would Marry Ernest Piggott and they would create a racing dynasty of their own, becoming the grandmother of the famous jockey Lester Piggott. *"Marriage of Mr. E Piggott and Miss Cannon, The Marriage of Mr. Ernest Piggott of Stockbridge and Miss Margaret Cannon daughter of Mr. T Cannon of Springfield was solemnized at the parish church on Monday afternoon, the bride who was given away by her father was attended by Misses Cannon, Piggott and Reynolds as bridesmaids and Miss Martin and Master Cannon as train bearers Mr. C*

---

[314] Michael Tanner, *Guinness Book Of Great Jockeys Of The Flat*, 1992 p.

Piggott was best man a reception was subsequently held at the Grosvenor Hotel and later in the day the Bride and Bridegroom left for East Bourne where the honey moon is being spent." [315]

Figure 81 Tom Cannon Tristan 1884 Hardwick Stakes Cook History of the English Turf

Margaret and Ernie Lester's grandparents lived in Stockbridge for a while Lester's father Keith Piggott was born there in 1904. Cannon had been carrying the weight of being a jockey and now a behind the scenes trainer as John Day Junior was aging and could no longer see, additionally John Day and the Danebury Stables were facing bankruptcy by the Duke of Beaufort so now was the time Tom had to take over the reigns as there was no one else capable.

He shouldered it well and it was business as usual. In 1878 Cannon had won two English Classics that year and the one in France resulted in a family effort, as he achieved it with his brother Joseph Cannon. The first was in the 1,000 Guineas on Pilgrimage-(The Palmer by Lady Audrey) and again he won on Pilgrimage claiming the 2,000 Guineas.

Pilgrimage was owned by Lord Lonsdale, and trained by his brother Joseph Cannon, if that wasn't enough, he took another win that year with the Grand Prix de Paris on Thurio-(Tibthorpe-Orlando by Cremo) owned by Prince Soltykoff. Could it get any better? Well history shows us that it did. The same year Tom had another child it was a girl she was named Blanche Harriet after Tom's mother, very sad story of Blanche, who unfortunately drowned in the lake at Garlogs many years later.

In 1879 Cannon took the lease on Danebury training stables, but out of respect did not take possession of them until 1882 when his father-in-law John Day died. His world was getting very busy and he had no time to enjoy his family or wins and the next decade would prove even more so. His position meant that he would have to conduct his engagements as a jockey, step up his life as a trainer and also look after the breeding stud as

---

Figure 82 Robert the Devil Oil on Canvas 1881 by Alfred F. Deprades

well. It was a massive operation, but as John Day had done so would he, the only difference was that Cannon had kept up his riding engagements as well, and would take on many more in the next ten years.

Some trainers were in the habit of burning their secret books, and it seems to have been the case in the stables at Danebury when the management passed to Tom Cannon, the books for Danebury that recorded the horse trials in John Days' time do not appear to have been passed on, they were thought to be in existence but could not be found and this was still the case in 1893 *"Many who do keep them destroy them every two or three years ; and in other cases these records are for some reason or another inaccessible — e.g. the books of the late John of Danebury, which we believe to be in existence, but in whose hands we are not aware, though Thomas Cannon would probably pay a hand- some price to the present possessor."* [316]

Towards the end of that year John Day's wife Mary died, on 29th October, she had been with him for 42 years, and died at Danebury aged 72 years. However it was not all doom and gloom as Tom and Kate had yet another child, their ninth, Walter Kempton Cannon, who was also destined to carry the silks to victory.

---

316 Henry Charles Howard Earl of Suffolk and Berkshire, William George Craven, Arthur George Coventry Arthur Alfred Thomas Watson, *Racing And Steeple Chasing*, (1893, p.169)

Figure 83Stockbridge Race Cup June 4th 1868Illustrated London News

1880 brought again more trying times, but under pressure Tom seemed to excel he brought home his only ever St Leger win on Robert the Devil-(Bertram-Castoff) for Frederick De Lagrange, and a big picture painted to commemorate the race. Figure 82 **Robert the Devil Oil on Canvas 1881 by Alfred F. Deprades**

Tom was now riding heavily for that famous trainer John Porter of Kingsclere who was one of the top trainers in the country. Porter, as we already know, was apprenticed to John Barham Day so there for a familiar person with the Day family, and John Porter had all the good horses. Soon Cannon would be publicly seen to be at the reigns of the Danebury Stables a great responsibility he was 36 years old.

In 1882, John was in a bad condition he could no longer see and no longer walk he was restricted to his bed, and it seems Cannon would not let his father-in-law board the boat to the Isle of Sticks without a few more winners to take with him, so he won the Epsom Oaks on Ghemisis-(Rosicrucion-Nameless by Blinhoolie) for the 7th Earl of Stamford.

He then went on to win on Shotover-(Hermit-Stray Shot) in the 2,000 Guineas, for the Duke of Westminster. If that was not enough he brought home the Derby on Shotover as well for the Duke, amazing. It must have put a smile on old John Day's face, and then near the end of the year John Day passed away to that great stable in the sky on the 3rd December 1882. And control of the Stables publicly passed to Tom Cannon; he was also appointed Clerk of the Stockbridge course and the Bibury Club at the same time.[317] They had another child in that same year and called her Ethel Louisa she was to go on in later life to marry Dr. Adolf Dan Tennison, and move to Devon.

---

317 Argus Eye, The Observer, (23rd December 1883) "Tom Cannon has gone to Danebury; great alterations are being made, in the old place. I wish him every luck in his new undertaking as Clerk of the races"

DANEBURY AND THE FORMIDABLE YEARS

The first thing Tom Cannon was to do on acquiring Danebury was to pull down the Danebury house, as it was then see **Figure 24** Landscape of Danebury viewed from Chattershill by Abraham Cooper R.A 1848. All he left standing was the turret and the kitchen. Everything else was replaced as seen. I was told that even the exterior of Danebury was scarlet and white hoops with vines and flowers in Cannon's colours. Tom Cannon ensured the Day family memories were kept very much intact at Danebury as he decorated the walls with all the great oil paintings of John Day and the Day family that were sold by private auction, of which he purchased many. **Appendix 13** List of Sporting Pictures Sold from John Days Estate 1883

This renewal signalled his time now a new beginning a fresh start Cannon continued to ride for John Porter and win many races. In 1883 aged 37 years old, Cannon took home his second Derby on St Blaise-(Hermit-Fusee) for Sir Frederick Johnstone, and boarded the ship to France to also claim, his 4th Grand Prix De Paris on Frontin-(George Frederick-Frolicsome by Weatherbit) for the Duke De Castrie, there was no stopping him, and he did all of this as well as manage the training and breeding stud of Danebury, to which he already had a long string of horses under his care.

Tom was renowned for his expertise and knowledge of the racetracks and this was shown in 1883 when he was asked to design the new track at Leicester after the previous track at Victoria Park had to close despite having 11,000 signatures presented to the keeper the Duke of Rutland. Tom designed and laid out the new track at Oadby which is the present site. Cannon put in a straight mile which enabled the course to be unique among other courses of the time as most had inherited the curves and corners which is not quite the ideal for trainers and produces a bias in the draw for stalls.

Figure 84 Busybody Tom Cannon up 1884 illustrated London News 1884

Danebury was starting to flourish under Cannon's care and knowledge, and there were many horses in the boxes at Danebury by 1883, and many of them belonged to Tom Cannon whose Danebury it was said had more horses than anyone else. *'In 1883 when Tom Cannon took possession of Danebury, where during his reign I was a frequent visitor. Tom*

Cannon was the most hospitable of men and the most interesting of hosts to an enthusiast like myself, keen to learn what he could about the horse and how to train him. In the days of which I am writing there were several different gallops on the spacious Downs I think there were more horses in training at Danebury then than in any other stable, the majority of them being Tom Cannon's own property."[318] He was extremely busy at this time, he had a huge breeding stud and many engagements for the top patrons on the turf, and he was also hard at work as a trainer as well, he had now reached his peak for riding for Porter the Kingsclere trainer.

By 1884 the refurbishment and building work to Danebury was completed and on the second of July 1884 Tom threw a party for three days and invited everybody to tea.[435] There is an excerpt from the Press that I wish to include as it gives an idea of his home life and a tour round Danebury.

"Just inside the door of the Mansion is the Telegraphic Apparatus which has become a necessity in such a large establishment, the vast hall displays some part of the occupation of the inmates of the house, a Piano is in one corner and by it a Harp and on it a Violin Case and a Banjo, a fireman's Helmet is on the pillar of the staircase and the walls are hung with the pictures of the horses which may be noticed Tom Cannon on Robert the Devil, the dining room whereas on the sideboard stands an admirable Silver Model of the flight between Sir Guy of Warwick and Colbran the Giant, this was the Stockbridge Cup of 1882 other cups stand on brackets in the corners of the room. On the wall are portraits of the Master of Danebury on Shotover in Duke of Westminster's yellow jacket, Ghemises in Lord Stamford's blue and black belt, playfair George Mawson up all these pictures being by Sextie, the panels of the doors are also to be noted for a Miss Alice Cannon paints very tastefully indeed as does Miss Lettie the latter lady is an accomplished violinist and her elder sister plays the Harp with Mrs. Cannon at the Piano."[313]

The same year in 1884 Tom Cannon purchased the horse Busy Body for Mr. Abingdon for £8,800 a good sum of money, Busy Body was to be trained by Tom Cannon and ridden by Tom Cannon this was a rare thing to achieve to become a trainer rider, like John Barham Day.[313]

Cannon pulled off the double, he first won the Epsom Oaks on Busy Body-(Petrarch-Spineaway by Macaroni), and then went on to win the 1,000 Guineas as well, with Busy Body, all for the Scottish millionaire George Baird, this was fantastic, and great publicity for the stables, and for him as he had proved he could train classic winning horses and win on them as well. If that was not enough he also took his fifth Grand Prix De Paris, on

---

318 Alfred E. T. Watson, *A Great Year, Lord Glanleys Horses*, (Longman Green and Co London, 1921, p.204)

Figure 85 Danebury Stables 1882 Family Collection

Little Duck-(See Saw-Light Drum by Rataplan) for the Duke De Castrie, what a year.

As they always celebrated and luckily for me they did for my grandfather was born the fourth son to Tom and Kate, and the eleventh child, they called him Charles Edward Cannon, and I named my son Charles after him. Charles Edward was born on 26th March 1884, and would be the last child they would have together, and he would be the last jockey to receive tuition from the great Tom Cannon. Tom seems to have taken a backseat from the classics at this stage he did however seem to be concentrating on breeding. Cannon as a breeder was also making his mark, one of his lifelong dreams and greatest ambitions was to breed, own, train, a horse, and he nearly achieved this in the 1895 Derby, the horse was Curzon-(Ocean Wave-Tib) [319]and she came in second place being beaten by Sir Visto.

Curzon did however win total stake money of £3,489, which was excellent, and won 12 races, not bad for a half bred gelding. Cannon had another horse out that same year that he bred at Danebury called Reminder, who won the 1895 City and Suburban Plate[320.] Playfair which was owned and bred by Cannon won the 1888, Grand National. He achieved his wish however with Ilfra – (Wren by Touchet) the winner of the last race to be run at Winchester in 1887. It was a great success. Tom Junior went on to win on Ilfra at Leicester on the course that had been designed by his father.

---

319 www.tbheritage.com/Portraits/Lottery.html accessed 9th October 2009 "Curzon, bred by Cannon at Danebury, won the Great Surrey Foals plate and eleven other races, with total winnings of £3,489. He ran second to Sir Visto in the 1895 Derby, beating the 2,000 Guineas winner Kirkconnel and twelve others. His sire, Ocean Wave, was a son of See-Saw His dam, Tib, bred by Newmarket trainer John Dawson, won five of her nine races as a juvenile, and was picked up by Tom Cannon in a selling race for 320 guineas. For Cannon she won the Chatsworth Plate at age three, dead-heated for Newmarket's September Stakes at age four, and won Goodwood's Stewards' Cup, beating twenty others, at age six. She was retired after her season when six years old, having placed third in one of her three races that year."
320 Tom Cannon Garlogs 1898

Figure 86 Tom Cannon from a pencil sketch by Jane E. Cook.

1886 was a good year; Cannon won the Eclipse Stakes at Sandown Park with Bendigo, a horse who he would be immortalized with. Also worthy of note for this year was Cannon achieving his sixth Ascot Cup[313]. Postscript was another good horse bred by Tom at Danebury Postscript won the Metropolitan stakes in 1886. There really are too many horses that he bred to list here; it gives an indication that he was an all-round horseman. The same year his friend, also rival in the saddle, and reputed to have been the greatest jockey of all time Fred Archer committed suicide with a revolver. Cannon attended the funeral of this great jockey. They were always in the top finishers, Archer Cannon and Fordham, and between Archer and Cannon there seems to have existed a great variance in style, as pulled from an account of the time by a credible author who had penned many books on the subject, and provides an instinctive full view of Cannon's style of riding, compared to that of Archer's, but Archer did win more races in his time.

"Born with a jockey's highest instincts, Tom Cannon became notorious chiefly on account of his deliciously persuasive hands. Light, yet very decided, they have never been excelled, more especially upon a two-year-old. They quieted down the most fractious mounts, or inspired faint-hearted race-horses with a sense of victory. When riding a cur, Tom Cannon was artistically insinuating. Stealing almost imperceptibly to the front, he had the knack of landing the odds, without touching his horse with the whip, unless absolutely necessary.

To illustrate the head-strong riding of the late Frederick Archer, let us imagine a steamer, vibrating from stem to stern under the impact of too powerful engines, driven along at the highest pressure. And granted these comparisons are correct, we may surmise that Cannon's more sympathetic style injured fewer horses than his formidable rival, who was cruel to two-year-olds in the early part of his racing career; but he was more considerate to them towards the close of his life. "Cannon's genius lay in his insinuating hands, and Archer depended chiefly on the use he made of his whip and sharp spurs. Perhaps the strongest resemblance lay in their constitutions, for, though muscular, Tom Cannon was delicate, whilst poor Archer's health was ruined several years before he committed suicide; yet he performed wonders, with an impetuous, dare- devil genius. Cannon, on the other hand, was patience personified." [321]

What I found interesting in this period is that two disciplines of rider sprang up, one that followed Archer's method, and one that followed Cannon's method, there was a further method that developed later known as the Third School of Riding, brought in by Tod Sloan, he was to change the style of English riding forever, and was responsible for the modern crouch position seen in today's jockeys.

Apart from being a great jockey, breeder and trainer Cannon is also remembered as an astute businessman and he sold one of his Danebury bred horses in 1887, as recalled by *George Lambton. "With all his suave manner and geniality, Tom did not wear his heart on his sleeve, knew how to take care of himself, and was a good business man. In 1887, "he sold Humewood to Lord Rodney, as everyone thought very cheaply". When Lambton asked Cannon why had he done this Cannon replied "Yes the horse was cheap, but look at the advertisement; everyone who wants a horse will now come and buy another cheap one from me.* [322] Pretty clever an early form of marketing, and must have been a tactic inherited from his father who was a horse trader in Windsor.

After Archer's death, John Porter was short of a top jockey so he approached Cannon to ride for him, he was considered the best jockey of the time, and there was obvious rivalry and jealousy from the other jockeys as illustrated by an account of Cannon losing his temper in public a very unique occurrence I draw this information from old accounts of a race that Cannon was riding in, and I shall let the person who saw it tell the story, Lord Arthur Grosvenor.

"I have never seen such excitement on a course before or since, the most splendid finish ever seen on a racecourse".[323] The race was the titanic contest for the 1887 Hardwicke Stakes, Tom Cannon was up on Ormonde trained by John Porter of Kingsclere, and owned by the Duke of Westminster due to Fred Archer's death who was John Porter's usual jockey. John Porter had approached Cannon to ride his horse Ormonde who won the race with Cannon up but the race was not easily won as told by Grosvenor, *"Ormonde defeated Minting and Bendigo, the latter pair led into the straight but the real battle was taking place behind them. George Barrett, the rider of the fourth competitor, Phil, was incensed that he had not inherited the ride on Ormonde and coming round the bend he*

321 Godfrey Bosville, *Horses, Horsemen and Stable management,* (Routledge and Sons London 1908, p.74)
322 Hon George Lambton, *Men And Horses I Have Known,* (1930, p.158)

Figure 87 the Winning Post 1888 by Vanity Fair (Family Collection)

bored his horse into the favourite, causing four inch flaps of skin to be torn from Ormonde's near hind. Cannon and Ormonde managed to regain their poise, got to minting at the distance and after a ding dong tussle won by a neck." [323] After the race Cannon was enraged with Barrett and had harsh words with him and I think he even reported him to the stewards.

His fame was peaking now both on and off the turf, he was now being known as the Master, through his brilliance in the art of jockeyship in the training of horses as well as now in breeding. This meant as stated by Charles Morton a leading trainer of the time, "Nearly everybody in England wanted him." [323] In 1887 Cannon took home another Classic on Enterprise-(Sterling-Daughter of King Tom) for George Baird in the 2,000 Guineas, and this caught Baird's attention, he wanted Cannon to ride for him exclusively.

In 1888 the Scottish millionaire George Baird approached Cannon requesting his services. Cannon now 42 years old renowned for being shrewd and a good businessman, and knowing horse racing to be a cut throat business, thought he might not have long left in the saddle and Baird was known to be eccentric, and a bad payer. *"Aware he might suffer instant dismissal with little or no salary, Cannon refused a one year contract and instead*

---

323 Michael Tanner, The Guinness Book Of Great Jockeys Of The Flat, 1992, p.97)

Figure 88 Garlogs Estate Tom Cannon on Horseback

demanded one for three seasons at £3,000 each, with the full £9,000 to be paid in a Lump sum at the outset." [323]

The London Magazine 1902 writing at the time of Cannon's life put the amount at £15,000[297] so we will go with that amount. The figure of £15,000 was not just for jockeyship alone and did include full consultation and everything, and in comparison to other top jockeys of the day we can well see his worth. He managed to acquire £15,000 paid in advance for his services for three years, Fordham another great jockey received £1,000 a year and this was considered a fine sum but Cannon was earning 5 times that amount.[325] In 2003 I applied and was invited to visit the Rothschild family archive and found a bill from Danebury in which Fordham was paid £767.20 for riding fees by Leopold De Rothschild which is a substantial difference when compared to Cannon.[324]

Cannon started earning what was considered fine amounts back in 1867 and 1868 £500 per year from the Marquis of Hastings in 1869 and 1870 he had earnt the same amount from Sir Frederick Johnstone for the first call on his services, 1871, 1872, 1873 a similar amount was paid by the Marquis of

---

324 The Rothschild Family Archive, Payment Receipt for Riding Fees from Danebury George Fordham London 2003

Anglesey 1874 but never had any jockey earnt the amount Baird was paying of 15,000 pounds in advance for three years. He had achieved the same as John Barham Day in raising the jockeys earnings.

Cannon had ridden three Classics for Baird in his time and trained two, and in 1888, under contract with Baird he rode home his fourth Classic win for him on Enthusiast-(Sterling-Cherry Duchess) which again was in the 2,000 Guineas, this was also his 4th 2,000 Guineas success and the end of his Classics as a jockey. In total he had ridden and won on 13 English Classics 5 Grand Prix De-Paris, and trained 2 Classic winners, and bred so many others, he truly was the master of the art of horsemanship.

In 1888 he purchased the Garlogs estate, perhaps with the £15,000 paid by Baird, and he and his wife Kate moved there with some of the children, as I think by this time Kate was ill. In closing on his career on the turf I found a quote that describes his achievements well, It was said *"that if you were to combine race riding, horse training and jockey making, then Tom Cannon knew more about it than any man alive."* [325]

In 1892 aged 56 years Tom publicly retired from racing and training *"His race-riding career extended over 32 seasons (and 1544 winners),"* [326] coupled with the success of winning himself 13 Classic races.

By this time the Cannon family's success had earnt them a formidable name in racing, some of the finest horses in the game had continued to be trained at Danebury, they had also entertained some of the most famous and distinguished guests and friends at their houses the most famous of those friends being King Edward VII.

Tom Cannon like the Day family before him held prestigious house parties after the races had finished always entertaining all the dignitaries and the Prince of Wales was frequently a guest *"There was always huge house parties and after the races King Edward VII when he was Prince of Wales used to come in for tea. The most brilliant men in their respective professions used to gather in Tom Cannons house, Cannon said to the Prince one day "I don't know what you would say Sir if you knew that in the next room there was a prize fighter", the late Prince Edward said "I have heard he is a very game man if I had my own way I should like to shake hands with him."* [327] Tom Cannon's hard work would afford him a very nice retirement, but he was only to retire from public racing, as at that time his wife Kate

---

325 Theodore Andrea Cook, *A History of The English Turf*, (Vol III 1901-1904, p.543)
326 Michael Tanner, *The Guinness Book Of Great Jockeys Of The Flat*, 1992, p.97)
327 Yorkshire Post and Leeds Intelligencer Tom Cannons House 24th May 1912

Figure 89 Charles Compton Martin 1893 (Family Collection)

was seriously ill, she was what kept the family together again as her mother and grandmother before her, she had played the unsung role of wife and mother.

Tom Cannon handed the reigns of Danebury over to his 20 year old son Tom Junior who was, in truth, too young for the responsibility and on 14th December 1892 Kate died at Garlogs surrounded by her family. After Kate's death Tom still had 5 children under 16 to care for, although they had a governess and many servants around the estates the ultimate responsibility would fall to Tom and the next move he made would prove extremely decisive in his family's future, one which would bring grave consequences to the family as a whole. In 1893 he married what appears to have been the governess, Miss Jessie Catherine Cameron.

The same year his eldest daughter Alice was married to Mr. Charles Compton Martin who was the eldest son of Mr. W. B. Martin of Paulsgrove Hampshire. The date was set for 8th December 1893 in Nether Wallop Church with a fully choral choir and a great deal of guests (*see wedding present list*) some of the guests to name but a few, Leopold de Rothschild who gave a gold bracelet, Baron De Hirsh Dick Marsh. The wedding style was a hunt wedding considered rare even then. I have included a picture of Alice's eldest brother in his hunt dress, Tom Cannon Junior Figure 124 **Tom Cannon Jnr in Hunt dress 1883 (Family Collection)**

Figure 90 Great Auntie Alice

"A charming hunt wedding took place yesterday at Nether Wallop Church where Miss Alice Cannon daughter of Mr. Tom Cannon of Danebury was married to Mr. Charles Compton Martin eldest son of Mr. W.B.Martin of Paulsgrove Hants. The Bride wore a green habit with gold hunt buttons, a black hat and brown top boots and a hunting tie fastened by a diamond pin. Instead of the orthodox bouquet Miss Cannon carried a Gold Hunting Crop,

Figure 91 String of Horses exercising 1898

surmounted by a bunch of Orange Blossoms. The bridesmaids were attired in covert shirts, with scarlet waistcoats and hunt buttons, brown boots and Spats, and soft felt hats with trim black toke feathers. The bridegroom presented them with Gold Horn and Fox Head Rings and Horseshoes of Scarlet and white flowers. The Bridegroom and the father and the brothers of the bride also wore hunt dress." Not long after that Morny Cannon also tied the knot with a Miss Dennett in Kensington, so this was a busy year for the family, I feel sorry for my great grandmother Kate, if she could have lived a few more years she would have seen everything that she worked so hard for and this reminds me of what happened to my own mother.

In 1894 Tom's reputedly greatest horse Reminder, bred owned and trained by Cannon came third in the 1894 Derby. This year was also quite profitable for the Cannon family as they won 29 races and netted nearly £10,000 in prize money alone between them.

Figure 93 Tom Cannon Racing Illustrated 1895

After retiring from racing Tom put most of his energy into gardening, he seemed to be into everything, a workaholic, and among other things he was the Chairman of the Horticultural Society in Houghton and was praised for his gardening abilities, and he was also very much into the breeding of sheep. Among other things he purchased a yacht and took up sailing as it was in fashion then. Tom Senior was busy overseeing his young son Tom

Figure 92 Cannon Girls Watching the String of Horses 1898 Stockbridge Racecourse

Figure 94 Tom Cannon overseeing Tom Junior at Stockbridge 1895 Racing Illustrated

Junior who was installed at Danebury as trainer and was very busy attending to the Stockbridge course as seen above and a lot of his energy was put into the training of jockeys.

The Stockbridge race course by 1898 was booming having been built up under the expertise of one successful family of owners over a period of 100 years, it was considered one of the finest sporting venues and most beautiful racing meetings of the day. Its reputation handed carefully from father to son since John Day had arrived in the 1780's, where hundreds of the finest thoroughbred racehorses had been bred, trained and thundered to the post. boasting the home of the powerful and successful training establishment of Danebury. In the next chapter we will explore the Stockbridge Racecourse for the first time in over 120 years bringing to light that course and some of its races.

THE STOCKBRIDGE RACECOURSE

Figure 95 Stockbridge Course 1898 Richardson, 1901; p, 155

BY THE 1890'S THE STOCKBRIDGE RACECOURSE was booming the Danebury Stables were packed with some of the finest racehorses racing had to offer. Tom Cannon was now one of the leading names in horseracing and so were his sons. The town of Stockbridge and its races since 1831 under the Days had been turned into a rival of Newmarket for one week in July all the glamour and fashion of London would descend on this town it was the place to be. Stockbridge Racecourse was the last racecourse in Hampshire

The course was an oval with a straight mile a condition in those days set by the Jockey Club for a national course. The Danebury Stables adjoined the course and had been laid out by John Barham Day in 1831 a clever move as he did not have to transport his horses anywhere to race them as the track

Figure 96 Stockbridge Racecourse 1896 O/S Map

was on his doorstep. In 1883-1884 Tom Cannon totally re-built Danebury and the stables to what it is today. Writers of the time referred to the Stockbridge Course as one of the best in its day, I have revived some of those accounts here

The first racing to be run on the new Stockbridge course was on the 8th and 9th June 1831 and as recalled by the New Sporting Magazine of 1831 *"Honest John Stands Sober with all ranks; he is a sober, steady and pains-taking body, and goes to church on a Sun-Day. He has done wonders towards bringing Stockbridge "to the fore" and deserves very great praise; the dear boy as he is termed by the jockeys has not only made rich stakes and erected a new stand but has seduced many of the principal horses and their masters from Newmarket-but let the sport speak for itself. the first race was between Rough Robin, Jocko and Rigmarole for a sweepstakes of 10 sovereigns each 10 subs the former rode by Lord Wilton rode cleverly won by half a length" A Sweepstakes of 100 Sovs each twelve subs followed it was won by delight rode by Chapple. Then followed a Sweepstakes of 50 Sovs each for two year olds seven subs was won by Mr. Wrefords Margrave. On the second day a plate of 50 was given by Lord Grosvenor who won it with Metheglin. The Hunter Stakes were won by Jocko rode by Mr. H Peyton, the 5 Sovs stakes (twenty subs and 25 added) were won by Little Red Rover rode by John Day the races finished with a handicap of 20 sovs each won by Lord Chesterfields Splendour"*[328]

A few years later in 1833 a writer had this to say about the Stockbridge Racecourse *"Stockbridge race course is one of the prettiest in the kingdom. A spectator can stand on almost any part, and see the horses all around; the turf is inferior to none, and the regulations superior to most meetings (I mean of course racing ones), how indeed can it be otherwise when such a man as John Day is at the head of affairs?" it is also supported by downright good men, who are willing to give honest John a turn by taking a ticket to his elegant little stand*[135]

Many races have since followed and it is outside of my area of interest to try and collect them all here, what is interesting is how the sums of money for the winning stakes had increased so much from 1831 to 1898. I have in the interest of history captured the first day of three days racing of the Bibury Club race week at Stockbridge which for the year of 1898 commenced on Tuesday 5th July. I have illustrated that racing with tables of some of the winners and photographs of the races, and show them here together for the first time in 118 years.

---

[328] The New Sporting Magazine, Baldwin and Craddock, London Vol 1, 1831, p.207

THE STOCKBRIDGE RACECOURSE

BIBURY CLUB RACES TUESDAY 5TH JULY

14:00 HAMPSHIRE STAKES 1 MILE £468.00 FOR 3 YEAR OLDS

Orpah	8-9	John Porter	Duke of Westminster	M.Cannon
Leisure Hour	8-12	Gibbons	Prince Soltykoff	Robinson
Petty France	8-12	John Powney	Mr. Creswell	Allsopp

Winning Horse Orpah at 7/4 Won. By half a length

Figure 97 Hampshire Stakes July 1897Silver Post at the Start (Family Collection)

15:00 FULLERTON HANDICAP 6F £195.00

Red Virgin	7-9	Alec Taylor	Mr. R.Walker	N Robinson
Queens Wake	7-4	Darling	Mr. J.Lewis	K.Cannon
Privado	7-1	H.Bates	Mr. F Hardy	H Luke junior

Winning Horse Red Virgin at 5/1 Won. by half a length

Figure 98 Fullerton Handicap at the Post 1898Family Collection

BIBURY CLUB STAKES (HANDICAP) 1 MILE 4F 15:30 £251.00

Civiger	11-10	Peace	Sir J Thursby	Mr. Thursby
Bouncing Lad	10-0	Chandler	Sir Ernst Paget	Mr. Paget
Nouveau Rich	12-4	George Lambton	Lord Farquhar	Mr. Owen

Figure 99 Bibury Club Stakes 1898 Family Collection
Winning Horse Civger 11/4 Won by ¾ of a length

CHAMPAGNE STAKES 5F 16:00 £340:00 FOR 2 YEAR OLDS

Quassia	8-9	John Porter	Mr. F Alexander	M Cannon
Boucan	8-12	Mr. R Pryor	Chandler	Allsop
North Britain	9-8	T Cannon Jnr	Mr. T Cannon	K Cannon

Winning Horse Quassia 9/4 Won by two lengths

Figure 100 Champagne Stakes at the post 1898 Family Collection

THE STOCKBRIDGE RACECOURSE

16:30 NATIONAL HUNT FLAT RACE (SELLING) 2 MILES £97.00

Miss Cristo	12-7	Swatton	Mr. A Yates	Mr. Hobson
Burnett	12-7	Lawless	Mr. R Walker	Mr. GS. Davis
Privado	7-1	H.Bates	Mr. F Hardy	H Luke junior

Winning Horse Miss Cristo sold for 120 gns to Mr. W Walker

Figure 101 Start of the National Hunt Flat Race 1898

17:00 BIBURY CLUB JUNIOR STAKES 5F £225 10s 2 YEAR OLDS

Loandal	8-1	T Leader	Mr. J Joicey	Madden
Forse	9-5	Harry Enoch	Captain Baird	J Watts
Torpilleur	8-9	J Dawson snr	Mr. W Johnstone	S Loates

Figure 102 Bibury Club Junior Stakes 1898

Figure 103 View of the Post at Stockbridge Racecourse 1898

We have covered one of the three days racing of 1898. Figure 99 and the above picture gives a wonderful look at the finishing post on the racecourse how it would have been in 1898, as can be seen down the long field it is packed with race goers all eager for their horse to win. The Cannons were dominating the running having 4 brothers all who were jockeys Tom Junior Mornington, Kempton and my grandfather Charles.

There were three stands on the Stockbridge Racecourse The Jockeys Stand, The Grand Stand and the Bibury Club Stand a wonderful view can be seen of the Bibury Club Stand **Figure 106 A view of the Bibury Club Stand on the lawn at Stockbridge Course 1898**as it was in 1898 boasting the cream of the racing world statesmen, aristocrats even royalty would have graced its seats. John Barham Day built one of the Stands prior to 1831

Figure 104 Stockbridge Cup 1870

when he moved the Bibury Club to Stockbridge. Shortly after, followed the construction of the Bibury Club Stand. The Stand was diagonally placed to the course to enable better viewing a new idea as noted and praised in the 1831 Sporting Magazine "Stockbridge Racecourse is situated close to Danebury and has a small but exceedingly well arranged stand, the front of which is placed diagonally instead of parallel with the course, by

Figure 106 A view of the Bibury Club Stand on the lawn at Stockbridge Course 1898

which arrangement the spectators obtain excellent view of the horses all the way up to the winning post. If this plan were adopted by the architects of all race-stands, they would afford much greater accommodation to the public."[329]

The Stewards of the course were members of the Bibury Club and my ancestors were always the Clerks of the course, starting first with John Day of Houghton Down from 1804-1828 clerk to the Houghton Down Course then his son John Barham Day Clerk to the Stockbridge Course at Danebury from 1829-1860, passed to his son John Day clerk from 1860-

Figure 105 A view across the Paddocks at the Stockbridge Racecourse 1898

[329] Sporting Calendar Monthly Transactions Of The Turf, The Chase, (Vol 95,1839, p.467)

1882, eventually passing to Tom Cannon 1882-1898.

There were many prizes on offer and the stakes were high, there were many trophies of the course to be had but only a few of these survive until today. One of these was the Stockbridge Cup of 1870-71 which was a piece of silver Plate tooled by C.F.Hancock and is housed in the Metropolitan Museum in America. Another cup is the lesser value but just as important Stockbridge Common Down Cup of 16th June 1866 presented by John Day Esq of Danebury.

The weighbridge for the course can be seen with my Grandfather Charles Cannon sat on it with Tom Cannons name etched to it, the weighbridge was located adjacent to the Jockey Stands and we can only but imagine the number of jockeys to have passed through its scales over the years. I wonder where it is now maybe it didn't survive or like everything else is missing.

There existed a horsebox that was kept at Garlogs and was still there in the early 1900's, the horse box had significance and historical value *"The horsebox illustrated in the photograph belonged to John Day the famous Danebury*

trainer, and is now a valued relic in the grounds of Garlogs, the palatial residence of his son in law the great jockey Tom Cannon. The father of Mornington, Kempton Charlie and Tom Cannon junior is standing by the box. This horsebox which is in an excellent state of preservation actually conveyed "Ceylon" to Paris when he won the Grand Prix de Paris in 1866;

Figure 107 Tom Cannon Horse Box 1898 Danebury Family Pictures

this was Tom Cannon's first winning ride in the important French race." [330]Ceylon was the last horse the box was used for and that was in 1866 so we can imagine what other famous horses had stood inside in the years that passed I wonder if when the box was destroyed if anyone knew its provenance.

There were dark clouds on the horizon over Danebury, and absolute disaster was about to strike the Stockbridge racecourse and the Cannon family.

THE DISASTROUS DAME

ON 14TH MARCH 1894 THERE WAS a case brought before the Supreme Court of Judicature by a Mr. Lancashire, against Mr. Hunt and Mr. F. Maynard to prevent the exercising of horses on the Stockbridge Down. **Figure 105 A view across the Paddocks at the Stockbridge Racecourse 1898** and would prove disastrous to the local training and horse racing community, the case was called Lancashire vs. Maynard and Hunt.[331]

There had always been a right for the local population of Stockbridge to exercise themselves and their horses on the Stockbridge Downs, a right that was granted by the lord of the manor and had included the exercising of horses, which the local racehorse trainers took full advantage of. But now the new lord of the manor was claiming the right to refuse this custom, and would prove to be a sign of problems to come. The case Lancashire vs. Maynard and Hunt argued that he the plaintiff was not the lord of the manor and that the down did not belong to the manor so therefore had no right to remove this tradition. The case was awarded in favour of the people.

To this shared and common right there were also private and exclusive rights for exercise of the race horses required by the trainers for reasons of secrecy in trials for their horses, but for these rights they had to pay and legal agreements were set up between the owners of the land and the trainers as can be seen by John Day and Dame Jane Barker Mill for the exclusive right on the Longstock Downs 28th February 1865[332] and then

---

[330] The Tattler No.58 August 6th 1902p.222

[331] The Times, Times Law Reports and Commercial Cases, (The Times London Vol 11 1895)

[332] Hampshire, Record Office11M70/B1/1/6/5,Lease and counterpart of the exclusive right of racing, exercising and training horses over Longstock Down in the parish of Longstock 28 Feb 1865 between Dame Jane Barker Mill and John Day,

THE DISASTROUS DAME

Thomas Cannon and Dame Jane Barker Mill on 3rd March 1882[333], for the same right, when he took over Danebury he purchased the right to the downs from John Day Junior with 500 pounds worth of South Western Railway Shares as shown in John Days Will codicil Appendix 12: The Will of John Day of Danebury 1815-1882

In 1898 disaster struck the race course, in a wholly unexpected way. The eastern end of the course, which included much of the straight mile, had been owned by Sir John Barker Mill. Sir John and his family before him had been great supporters of the Stockbridge races and Danebury Stables, and were owners of many racehorses trained there and on several occasions performed the office of Steward of the races. In 1860 Sir John died without issue; ownership of the land covering the eastern end of the course passed to his widow Jane who carried on the racing tradition as she enjoyed the races too, she understood how much it meant to the local population but she died in 1884. The strip of land then passed to a Mrs. Marianne Vaudrey a third cousin of Sir John Barker Mill who eventually in 1903 adopted the family name to become Dame Vaudrey Barker Mill. The story goes that Sir John left the inheritance to his next of kin and didn't even know their identity.

Marianne Vaudrey Barker Mills strongly disapproved of gambling, and when the lease expired on the strip of land in 1898 she refused to renew it. What a total disaster this must have been to Tom Cannon who had spent a fortune on rebuilding Danebury a few years before, and what a shock it must have been to the people of Stockbridge. She was about to deprive a whole town of its livelihood.

Tom Cannon was speaking to a reporter in Newmarket prior to the closure of the Stockbridge course and the reporter wrote the following post. *'It is not often that Tom Cannon pays a visit to Newmarket these days and I was fortunate in having a long talk with him about Danebury which he will vacate at Michelmas for his new home at Garlogs where the late master J.H.Brewer lived for so many years. The property is held in trust by Mrs. Bigwood and Miss Blount who are anxious to let it but owing to the difficulty caused by Mrs. Vaudrey who inherited Sir John Barker Mills property at Mottisfont Abbey and was a patron of Danebury for many years-refusing to*

---

trainer of racehorses of Danebury, near Stockbridge
333 Hampshire Record Office 11M70/B1/2/40 Agreement relative to the racing down, Longstock3 Mar 1882 Dame Jane Barker Mill and Hugh Jones Hughes of Longstock, yeoman and Tom Cannon of Houghton, trainer of racehorses

renew the lease of that portion of the downs, which includes the new straight miles and the familiar bush on the Longstock side of the course, the present regrettable necessity of abandoning the Stockbridge and Bibury Club meetings has arisen." [334]

In defiance the last race to be run at the Stockbridge Course was won by Mornington Cannon second son to Tom, *"Oddly enough the last race to be ridden over the Stockbridge course was ridden by Mornington Cannon member of a family intimately associated since the death of John Day with the famous training establishment at Danebury."* [335] That's the spirit, good for Morny, if you are going to go out then let it be like that.

The Racecourse was the life and soul of the town of Stockbridge and had been for a hundred years. It employed most of the population of the town at some point during the year and was how the majority of the people provided for their families. They would rent out their homes for three days when the racing was on, and earn enough money to live off for the rest of the year. On occasion six hundred loaves of bread would be baked over three days to accommodate the racing. Danebury employed in excess of 100 local people, and that's not taking into account the other two stables in the area.

The Jockey Club had insisted that all racecourses should include a straight mile; as Barker Mill was refusing to renew the lease it would no longer be possible to have one so the racecourse was forced to close bringing hardship and suffering to many families. It was also said that years later when Marianne Vaudrey Barker Mill had realised her mistake, and the loss of revenue she had caused to the people, she asked the course to return, to which they declined. She must have felt extremely alienated from the local population and racked with guilt every time she saw a hungry face in Stockbridge.

In our family it was remembered that my great grandfather Tom Cannon sent a cheque for a stated amount to her, she refused. Prince Edward later King Edward VII sent a blank cheque which was also refused, if Prince Edward could not persuade her to renew the lease then no one could and the law was the law, it is told better by an eyewitness a farmer on her estate *"She had to give notice to the club that she was going to sell it, and the Prince of Wales afterwards King Edward VII, sent an equerry down there, with an open cheque to buy Stockbridge racecourse. But she tore it up and threw it in the fire."* [336]

---

334 London Morning Post Sporting Intelligence A long talk with Tom Cannon (18th July 1898, p.2)
335 London Standard, Racing Notes Eclipse Stakes, 11th July 1898, p.10
336 Tessa Lecomber *The Barker Mill Story, A Hampshire Family Since the 16th Century* Trustees

So that was it the Danebury Stables slowed down and as you can imagine the families of Stockbridge had to find new avenues of work the whole town life as they had known it for a hundred years would stop. As the same witness goes on to lament *"But she said afterwards that had she known the harm it had done Stockbridge, she wouldn't have closed it. It brought a tremendous income into Stockbridge; a lot of people in those three days racing made enough to last a year."* [336]

She is still remembered in the year 2000 *"Victorian Matriarch Mrs. Marianne Vaudrey Barker Mill was the opposite of Pickwickian. In a bid to curtail Drinking and Gambling, she revoked the lease of several local pubs, and a race course on her land at Stockbridge."* [337] I wonder what she provided the local people to eat in return, or to house and clothe their families. You guessed it, absolutely nothing at all. I bet old Sir John Barker Mills was turning in his grave.

To give the reader some idea of the impact Danebury and the racecourse had on the village of Nether Wallop which is not far from Danebury Stables and Stockbridge. In 1831 at the creation of Danebury Stables the population of Nether Wallop was 663 people. By 1871 the population had grown to 954 people an increase of 291 in forty years. 100 years after that in 1971 the population was only 887, so in 100 years it had fallen by 37 people. Additionally I wonder if there was ever a commemorative plaque for John Day and his gift of the entire East Window in the Church, there usually is, maybe after all the Days and Cannons had disappeared from Stockbridge, Vaudrey Barker Mill asked the Church to remove it after she closed the racecourse down I wonder if the Church even know? I did inform the church last year but to date there has been no response. *"The East Window is a new and perfect development of the style with three long lancet arches, it is of rich stained glass a gift of John Day ESQ of Danebury and cost 120 guineas, the scenes represent the agony in the garden, the crucifixion and the resurrection."* [282] Such a shame it seems like they wish to remove every trace of my family.

In a paper a few years after closing the course, the paper recalls how the Bibury Club meetings had lost their following since moving to Salisbury and at the time there were rumours that Vaudrey Barker Mill had regretted her decision due to the effect it had on the town and was going to revoke her decision *"the great attraction of the meeting departed with removal of their old quarters at Stockbridge, and notwithstanding the rumours afloat to the contrary there is no chance*

---

of the Barker Mill Family 2000, p.53
337 Tessa Lecomber The Barker Mill Story, A Hampshire Family Since the 16th Century Trustees of the Barker Mill Family 2000, p.65

Figure 108 the Racing Stands 1922

of return as long as the present landlady survives but like always rumours are only ever rumours. [338]

Five years later after the Bibury Club had moved to Salisbury and the course at Stockbridge had closed its members appear to have stayed in Stockbridge and taken up fishing. Support for the Bibury Club like before when in Cheltenham was slowly dying away as related by a paper writing in 1903 *"It is pleasant to be able to record successes in connection with the Bibury Meeting. The fixture is now however very different to that of the old days at Stockbridge, when the Bibury meetings were regarded as being the most pleasant of the whole year and few who had paid it a and knew its charms missed attending it. The holiday Character and the unbounded hospitality of Tom Cannon at Danebury have departed, and in place of the big attendance of members of the club is the usual racing crowd."* [339]

Tom's sons were becoming the master horsemen that their father and all their ancestors had been. Tom, Mornington, Kempton and my grandfather Charles painted below by William Sextie, had all been lucky enough to serve their apprenticeships under their father the "Master."

THE TRAINING AND INSTRUCTION OF JOCKEYS

TOM CANNON AS WE HAVE SEEN was not only a superb Jockey and later a trainer and breeder of horses, but was also considered a superb tutor of jockeys as well. On one occasion the jockey and apprentice scenario was put to the test when Tom Senior was in the strange situation of riding against his eldest son Tom Junior as the Day family had done back in the 1820's. I am pretty sure that this was one race Tom Junior did not want to lose but that is exactly what happened the race was the 1888

Figure 109Tom Cannon 1902 London Magazine page 80

Eclipse Stakes, Tom Junior was on Ossory and his father beat him on Orbit.

Tom Cannon, reflecting on the difference of his day learning to be a jockey and at the time of the article 1902 " When I first commenced learning the profession of a jockey," said Mr. Tom Cannon, "there were no School Board regulations in force". The consequence was, that a boy could commence his equine education as soon as the young jockeys parents thought fit, almost growing up in the saddle, then riding and jockeyship became second nature to them.[297]

Tom Cannon Senior made sure that the new jockeys did not win in their first races, as seen with Tom Junior the same was told by Morny Cannon *"My father put me up on a crock to ride my first race it was Coralline, in a five furlong stretch at Kempton Park in 1886, I came in last and disappointed a good many backers who never suspected my father would start me on anything but the best, He knew better"* *he knew that there was more in a race than mere riding, and that I should have to see how others won before I could win myself."* [340]

The instruction of his jockeys under an apprenticeship would last for 5 years. It was thorough, and this instruction was intended for them only and considered a secret to be well guarded. Tom was a fine tutor to such jockeys as Mornington Cannon, Kempton Cannon. Arthur Coventry, Jack

---

340 C. B. Fry C. B. Fry's Magazine of Sports, Riding a racehorse by Mornington Cannon, (London 1904, p.62-70)

Figure 110 Danebury Apprentice Jockeys 1902-1903 Charlie Cannon far Left 1902 London Watts, Sam Loates, W.T.Robinson, George Lambton and many more[341] and this is summed up by Lambton *"He was a good trainer of horses, but I think even a better trainer of jockeys."* [342]

The Cannons were famous for coming on at the last minute in a rush to the post, and playing the waiting game, their style of racing seemed to revolve around not giving anything away for example in this race recalled by George Lambton when speaking on Tom Cannon he was also a pupil. *"He taught me what a mistake it was to tie a jockey down with many orders. He would tell you what the horse wanted, and the sort of race would suit him best, and left the rest to the rider. But it was very rare for him to tell his jockey to go along; he hated to see a horse of his in front, and this has always been a well-known characteristic of all the Cannons."* [342] These were the waiting game tactics of the Cannons for which Morny is particularly remembered.

Jack Watts, a top rider of his day, was tutored at the hands of Tom Cannon in the Danebury style of riding.[343] Jack in 1896 won the Epsom Derby on that famous horse Persimmon for his Royal Highness King Edward.

---

341 Theodore Andrea Cook, *A History of The English Turf*, H. Virtue & Company, London, 1901-1904,Vol III p.539 "Certainly that brilliant horseman now provides an admirable example of what may be done, by the intelligent assimilation of new principles, and by the careful training of his lads, for his skill has not only been transmitted to four sons, but to Sam Loates, W. Robinson, and the Late John Watts"
342 Hon George Lambton, *Men And Horses I Have Known*, (1930, p.159)
343 Henry Charles Howard, *Racing And Steeple Chasing*, (1893, p.169) "John Watts, formerly a pupil of Tom Cannon, is now deservedly rated with the leading horsemen of the day"

Figure 111 Tom Cannon 1877 Pencil Sketch Baileys Sports and Past times

Cannon hated, above other things the ill treatment of horses, even to the point of the use of the whip *"That unfortunate whip loses such a lot of races for the boys! he says, and more especially on young horses."* [344]

Tom Cannon's elegance as a rider was well known and it was in the finishing of a race that this gracefulness was best seen. *"Why, then, if the race is over, as surely it must be, does Cannon suddenly, and within a few lengths of the post, catch up his whip, and sit down to a finish which for polished elegance, combined with determined strength, few horsemen have ever equalled"* [345] In the scrap book of Tom Cannons that was saved from the fire of my grandfather's papers was pasted instructions. The Instructions are for the young apprentices at Danebury and I think are the only surviving copy as they were secret they are in the form of a draft or a proof, there are notes and additions inked into the side of the instructions, I will place them in this book for all to see and finally the secret of the successful Danebury school of jockeys can be enjoyed and studied by people far more adept than me in horse riding see Appendix 5 the Instruction of Jockeys Tom Cannon.

Tom Cannon was approached by Mr. Horace Hayes on the subject, of how to ride a horse and a similar account is published in Horace Hayes's book titled, "Riding and Hunting" by M.Horace Hays, the wording in his book differs from the draft extracts we have, but they are similar, Cannon was renowned for his secrecy, but the Duke of Beaufort used exactly the same drafts in his book titled "Racing and Steeple Chasing" in 1893, and acknowledged

---

344 Robert Weir, James Morray Brown, *Badminton Library of Sports and Past Times* (Edition 2 Longmans London 1891, p.156)
345 Henry Charles Howard, *Racing And Steeple Chasing*, (1893, p.86-87)

Figure 112 Arthur Coventry apprentice to Cannon, Cannons colours Stockbridge Course 1898 F/C

Cannon as the author *"For demonstration of this the authors have to thank Tom Cannon."* [346] Morny Cannon would publish his style of writing years later and can be seen in **Appendix 6** Instruction of How to Ride a Horse Morny Cannon.

SHORT STORIES AND RACING RECOLLECTIONS

I HAVE RESCUED A NUMBER OF STORIES FROM our family scrap book. I will include them below; they are short recollections of encounters that took place in the time of Danebury.

THE EFFECTS OF DRINK;

"When St Gatien beat Melton without an effort for the Jockey Club at Newmarket in the back end of 1886 the fact is beyond dispute that Melton was under the influence of Liquor. The race aroused a considerable amount of interest, for both ranked as derby winners, Melton having gained a head victory over Paradox at Epsom in the previous year, while St Gatien had run a dead heat with Harvester in 1884. It was thought in a race decided a little time previously Melton had shown a little lack of courage a not unnatural result of running a horse with over 10st on her back- and it was determined to give him some whiskey before the cup contest. When Tom was about to get up the whiskey bottle was produced and the remark made that it was well mixed with water. "The jockey wants some as well as the

346 Henry Charles Howard, *Racing And Steeple Chasing,* (1893, p.322)

horse Cannon said chaffingly but he took a sip and found it very strong. Before Melton had gone half a mile in the race his jockey and the horse was quite drunk, and a hack could have beaten him. It is entirely doubtful that under any circumstances Melton would have beaten St Giles over the Ceasarwitch course but the horse would have doubtless made some show if sober."[347]

A DANGEROUS LUXURY

"On the night of the Cambridgeshire four years ago Joe Cannon at supper time, placed a roast suckling pig before his brother Tom. To most people the dish is dangerous if partaken freely, but when a person possesses a digestion that resents any liberties taken with it, he should be doubly cautious how he tackles the savoury porker. Despite the fact that his digestive organs were delicate, the genial Danebury horseman resolutely attacked the goodly fare and put in a lot of work in a short time, heartily enjoying his supper. Nothing more did he think of his unusual repast until the following morning when he rode Amphion in a rousing gallop of two miles. The horse was a very free goer and consequently a very tiring animal to ride. After about a mile had been covered Cannon began to experience an uncomfortable sensation beneath his diaphragm and he soon realized that the defunct porker was putting in some strong work. Riding under such circumstances was, as may be imagined the reverse of comfortable, and-but subsequent proceedings interested the unfortunate epicure more than an unsympathetic outsider could understand, and we accordingly draw a friendly veil over the scene that followed. Tom Cannon does not eat sucking-pig before going a two-mile gallop now."[348]

A BELIEVER IN LUCK

"Some few minutes before the Derby of 1881 Fred Archer, Tom Cannon, and Jem Goater, and Fred Webb were together in the weighing room. "Let's get into the paddock suggested Webb; the back way is much easier. "Suiting the action to the word he strolled off, followed by Cannon and Goater. Not if I know it called out Archer who was putting the finishing touches to his toilet, as the trio moved off. "No back way for me on a Derby Day; I'm going through the saddling enclosure. "After he had won the big race on Iroquois Archer reminded his companions of this incident."[349]

---

347 Tom Cannon, The Drunk Horse Garlogs 1898
348 Tom Cannon, A dangerous Luxury Garlogs 1898
349 Tom Cannon, A believer in luck Garlogs 1898

HE WANTED INFORMATION

"Some time after reaching his majority, Mornington Cannon had a rather funny adventure. On a cold morning before the commencement of the flat season the popular horseman set out for a long walk his intention to being to reduce some of the "too solid flesh" with which the majority of Horsemen are troubled. In addition to his usual attire Morny was wearing an overcoat with a collar of unusual dimensions, and a muffler that almost concealed the lower portions of his face, while his face was still concealed by a cap well pulled down over his eyes."

"After strolling along for some distance the pedestrian not unusually began to feel thirsty. Eventually he sighted an inn on reaching which he determined to indulge in the luxury of a drink. His landlord regarded his customer with more than ordinary interest. "Suppose you come over from Danebury" was his first remark, "Yes" quietly answered Cannon, "and how are they all getting on" queried the Boniface evidently intent on forcing the conversation "family all right,? Why I know every one of them Old Tom, Young Tom, Morny; in fact the lot," he rattled on and after a necessary pause for breath he began again. "I expect you ride in trials me lad eh? Of course you do?" as the visitor modestly nodded his head. "well now look here" the proprietor continued in a much lower tone leaning across the bar in order than the listener should hear better "whenever you know of anything that is really good business, you might just let me know, I will make it worth your while believe me, before you go" interposed the landlord who could not help thinking that the lad was more reticent than the occasion demanded "you had better let me know your name so when the note comes I will know who it is from "With pleasure" replied the unknown quickly unbuttoning his coat and discarding the muffler "Mornington Cannon at your service!"[350]

A USEFUL CONTINGENT

The finish of the Stewards Cup in 1887 was extremely reminiscent of Danebury, Morny Cannon rode the winner Upset, Tom Cannon Junior was on the horse called Tib and came second, while S. Loates and J. Watts occupied third and fourth places, both these having served their apprenticeships at the Stockbridge training establishment."[351]

---

350 Tom Cannon, the story of Boniface Garlogs 1898
351 Tom Cannon, A useful Contingent Garlogs 1898

THE FINAL YEARS OF TOM CANNON

AFTER THE CLOSURE OF THE COURSE Tom Cannon would have had to remove all of his possessions to Garlogs and send his horses to Chattis Hill, as picked up in a paper of the time *"Mr. Tom Cannon maybe expected to vacate Danebury for his fine seat at Garlogs very shortly and the horses will forthwith be moved to the new premises at Chattis Hill."* 352

Tom Cannon Senior in 1898 was in control of 2-3,000 acres of land *"Danebury is one of the most comfortable and luxurious dwelling houses and the owner has on his hands between two thousand and three thousand acres of land."* 353 Most of the land was freehold it is what Cannon seemed to invest his winnings.

Figure 113Tom Cannon with Sons Tom Morny and Brother Joe

By 1901 Tom Cannon Senior had announced his retirement indefinitely. In the paper he had publicly stated he would transfer of all of his horses to his younger son Thomas Cannon Junior, who had really been running things since 1902. Tom Senior was still living in Garlogs where his breeding stud farm was stationed. Tom Junior worked as a trainer from Garlogs and from the Chattis Hill Stable with my grandfather Charles, *"In this connection it must be stated that Mr. Tom Cannon has earned entire immunity from the cares of Turf Life and has made up his mind to leave the Garlogs next year and transfer the whole of his responsibilities of the Stables at Chattis Hill to his eldest son who has for some time been nominally responsible for the management and is well qualified to take sole control."* 354

352 Yorkshire evening post Sporting Notes (28th November 1898, p.3)
353 Cheltenham Chronicle 28th May 1898, p.6
354 Yorkshire post Leeds intelligencer Sporting News (23rd October 1901, p.10)

Tom Cannon Junior had already taken over Garlogs from his father and in 1900 Tom Cannon Senior removed to live in Springfield House at the far end of Stockbridge with his wife Jessie Catherine and son Ronald. The boys had work to do at Garlogs. Many events had taken place after the closure of the Stockbridge course in 1898, we must now have a recap to understand the final years and the positioning of trainers in the aftermath of the

Figure 114 Left to Right Meggie, Jessie, Ronald, Lettie and Mable 1898 Family Collection outside Danebury

closure of the Stockbridge course as it becomes very confusing without the chronology intact everybody in such a large family were now being moved all over the place the closure of the course had really affected every life in Stockbridge families would now not know what the year would bring and how to plan their finances whereas previously they knew the three days racing would have covered it all.

1892 Tom Junior living and in charge of Danebury due to Kate dying.
1898 Stockbridge course closed by Vaudrey Barker Mill.
1898 Tom Senior vacated Danebury to Garlogs.
1898 Tom Junior Stayed on at Danebury.
1900 Tom Cannon removed all the horses from Danebury with his father to Chattis Hill House Stables.
1900 Tom Junior moved into Garlogs with Charles his younger brother as resident jockey.
1901 Tom senior publicly announces retirement at Garlogs handing responsibility to Tom Junior
1901 Tom Senior moved into Springfield with Madam and son Ronald.
1901 Danebury rented to Freddy Withington.
1902 Tom Cannon Senior puts Garlogs estate up for sale.
1902 Tom Junior moves to Chattis Hill House with Charlie

THE DEATH OF TOM CANNON OF DANEBURY

WE MUST RETURN TO THE "MASTER" my great grandfather Tom Cannon Senior had been suffering with heart trouble for many years, his wife or Madam as she was known had passed away on 23rd February 1912, and he was retired and lived in the Grosvenor Hotel Stockbridge. The year is 1917 the world as he and everybody else knew it had been changed dramatically by the First World War. Three of his sons were involved in that War, Kempton Cannon was a pilot in the Royal Flying Corp, Ronald Portman Cannon was a Captain in the Royal Naval Air Service

Figure 115 Tom Cannon 1907 Sphere 8th June 1907

(R.N.A.S) and engaged in active service in the Middle East, Charles Edward Cannon was Lieutenant in the 19th Hussars and has by now been through many battles in France including the Somme which he survived.

In 1904 Tom Cannon fell very ill suffering from double pneumonia he was restricted to bed by his Doctor Loveless the local MD.

In 1912 Madam passed away at Springfield, Tom buried Jessie in the cemetery at the foot of the hill opposite the White Hart and removed himself from Springfield where he was living to the Grosvenor Hotel at least he could be around people there.

By 1916 Tom Cannon had been suffering from dropsy and heart problems, perhaps due to his long life of wasting on 27th June 1916, as reported, Tom Cannon suffered a serious heart attack, he was 70 years old *"Sportsmen will regret to learn that the Veteran trainer and old time jockey Tom Cannon Sen is seriously ill, he is confined to his bed in Stockbridge suffering from a severe heart attack."* [355] After this heart attack a full time nurse was provided for him.

On13th July 1917 Tom Cannon the Master passed away at the Grosvenor Hotel Stockbridge attended by his family and Dr. Loveless. Internment of Tom Cannon was on 18th July 1917 in the Stockbridge Cemetery *"the service which was choral was attended by Messer's Joe Cannon, Tom Cannon Junior, Morny*

---

355 Aberdeen Journal, Sporting News 26th June 1917, p.6

*Cannon, Lieutenant Kempton Cannon RFC, Lieutenant Charles Cannon RFA, Mr.
and Mrs. Piggott, Dr. and Mrs. Tennyson, Mrs. A McAlister, Messer's C. Martin,
J.H smith, the wreaths were numerous and mostly in the colours of the deceased"*[356]

FUNERAL OF THE LATE MR. TOM CANNON

On Tuesday, all mortal, of the late Tom Cannon was laid to rest at
Stockbridge. And so is severed a link between the old and new style of
racing, but his exemplary career will be remembered for apart from having
been one of the greatest jockeys ever known, he was one of nature's
gentlemen and memory of the "natty" Hampshire horseman will survive
him for many a year although his retirement as far back as 1891, from the
profession which he so brilliantly adorned left him comparatively unknown
to the present generation of racegoers.

Well advanced in years his end was perfect peace and he has left behind
him lasting fame as a jockey of superb artistic merit and a character
absolutely devoid of blemish. Now he rests in peace in the picturesque little
cemetery at Stockbridge, and it may be mentioned as demonstrating the
high respect in which he was held that every blind was drawn the while his
coffin was borne to the final resting place.

A choral service conducted by the Revd. Chanden assisted by the Revd.
Watts was held at St. Peter's Church and among the mourners were his
sons Thomas, Mornington, Kempton and Charles Cannon, Mr. and Mrs.
Ernest Piggott (Son-in-Law and daughter), Mr. Paul Macalister (son-in-law),
Mr. Chartes Martin (son-in-law), Mr. Joseph Cannon (brother), Mr. J. H.
Smith (brother-in-law), Dr. Loveless, and Miss Reid, whose nursing of
deceased had been untiring and beyond all praise. Others who paid a last
tribute to his memory were Messrs., Arthur Coventry, W. F. Robinson, E.
Page, W. Waugh, C.W. Waller, F Pothecary (Wallop), Harry Redford,
(Winchester) Cole Russell, (Vearncombe), F, Withington, Wm. Sperring,
representing Mr., H.S. Persse, Mr., Ernest Bradfield, Commodore Benson,
R.N. , Mr., E Hayter, Lieut. M. B. Bletsoe, the veteran Jim Goodyear, nigh
on an octogenarian, practically all the tradesmen of the town, and many of
the lads from the Danebury and Chattis Hill Stables of which Tom Cannon
had in turn been master and last but not least his old-time servers, William
Olding, head lad for many years, and Ben Blondin.

---

356 Liverpool Daily Post Internment of Tom Cannon 18th July 1917

Messages of condolence were sent from Lord Rosebury, Mr., Leonard Day, Mr., Wood, Mr. Marsh, Mr. Sam Darling, Mr., H. Redford, Mr. A Welby, Mr., R.H, Russell, Mr., John Hart, Mr., H Jesse, Mr. John Powney, Quilhampton Mr. Frank Hartfgan, Sir Walter and Capt Guy Giibey, Brig-General E.W. Baird, Mr., A, Sadler, Senior., Mr. T. Simpson Jay, Dr., Edwards, Mr., F. Pothecary, Mr. P Webster, Mr. Frank Hill, Mr., John Watson, Mr., Arthur Meyrick, Mr. H.W. Trewby, Mr., B, S, Strauss, Mr., William Bertram and many others.

The wreaths were numerous and beautiful, the predominant flower colour being red and white, reminiscent of the scarlet and white hoops, Among the senders were Mr., and Mrs. T.Cannon, Mr. & Mrs., Mornington Cannon, Lieut, and Mrs., K. Cannon, Lieut and Mrs., Charles Cannon, Lieut Ronald Cannon, R.N.A.S, (unavoidably on foreign service), Mr., and Mrs. Martin, Mrs., Henry Wood, Mr., and Mrs. Paul Macalister, Mr., and Mrs. Ernest Piggott, Dr., and Mrs., Jenison, Mr. and Mrs. Joseph Cannon, Mr., Joseph Cannon Jun, Mr. and Mrs. James H, Smith, Dr. and Mrs., Loveless, Mr. C.W, Waller, Mr. F.V. Gooch, Mr., E.A, Wolfe, Mr. and Mrs. F. Withington, Mr., W.T. Robinson, Mr. Samuel Loates, Mr., S. Donoghue, Mr., J.H. Bradfieid, Mr., and Mrs., Ernest Bradfield, Mr., Richard Figes, Miss Reid, Mr., and Mrs., Stares, Mr., and Mrs., E, East, Mr. and Mrs., Barnond, Mr., M. Warren and employees of the Grosvenor Hotel, Dr., and Mrs., Inness, Nurse Davies, Mr., and Mrs., H. Smith and Mr., and Mrs., Blondin

When speaking of so many great horsemen in one family it is easy to get lost, and one of the purposes of this book was to bring all the strings together, because it was not just Tom that made the Cannon name great, he had a brother Joseph Cannon who was a trainer, and Tom Cannon's sons went on to carry the name and the scarlet and white hoops forward and it is to them we shall look next.

"Tom Cannon the famous jockey than whom no straighter horseman ever donned silk transmitted his remarkable skill in the saddle to his four sons, Tom, Mornington, Kempton, and Charles, and they, in their turn, are equally renowned for their honesty on the,turf."[297]

THE SONS OF THOMAS CANNON

Figure 116 Tom Cannon Junior Racing Illustrated 1895

Figure 117 Tom Jnr

THOMAS LEONARD GILBERT CANNON WAS THE first born son to Tom and Kate Cannon. He was born in 1872 and died in 1942. Like all first born boys within our family who carry the name Cannon it is tradition to name your child Thomas, I don't quite know where this idea came from but I do know it started a long time ago, with Thomas Hopkins.

Tom Junior was first educated at Bannisters Court in Southampton and then at the illustrious Queenwood College in Hampshire like his brothers Morny, Kempton and Charles[400] and following his father became a jockey, with his first success on Red Cross in 1887 at Liverpool he was only 15 years old. Tom also lost to his younger brother Mornington the same year when riding in the Stewards Cup, Tom was riding Tibb owned and trained by his father at Danebury, 14 year old Mornington beat him by three lengths. If the previous was not enough his father then went on to beat him in 1888 in the Eclipse Stakes on Orbit.

Tom Junior had to wait a further two years before his next win in 1889 it was on Goldseeker and the race was the City and Suburban. After this both Tom and his father realised a career in the saddle was not for him as he had increasing weight problems, his bones were too big as members of the family recalled in old tales, and his father used to say he rode like a sack of spuds. Tom gave up riding all together in 1889, by which time he had ridden 33 winners.

Tom being the first born son had helped his father with the training of the huge string of horses that Danebury had boasted for years, as can be seen below. It was to the training of racehorses that he found his true calling and in 1892, Tom Cannon Senior handed over the Danebury Stables to Thomas Junior and retired to look after and be with Kate his wife who was seriously ill and who died on 15th December 1892.

Tom was only 20 years old and much too young to be running Danebury, his father was still assisting but probably stricken with grief, it must have been a very tough and trying time for them all. The number of horses in training at Danebury at this was sizeable as we can see from this extract.

Figure 118Tom giving instructions on the horse Melanchon 1895 Racing Illustrated

"young Tom finds plenty to do in looking after the horses at home, Morny has wintered well and there are yet two younger Cannons to keep up the Danebury Artillery; (59 aged Horses 3-5 year olds and 30 2 year olds)." [357] The horses names can be seen in the press cutting but there are too many to list here. There were not just a huge number of horses in the stables but there was also a very strong group of owners. Tom was now training for "Mr. L Rothschild, Baron Rothschild, Mr. Abingdon, Mr. H Ransford, Mr. W Smith, Mr. H S Leon, Mr. T L Springfield, Mr. E Loder, Mr. T Robinson, Mr. T Cannon 1892. Tom Junior 20 years old and in charge of a huge string of horses.

Even more trying times were on the horizon the young trainer with all his future ahead of him surrounding by some of the most talented Jockeys at the time, sitting on top of a horse racing empire had the world at his feet, in 1898, as we have already seen, the racecourse at Stockbridge closed. The impact on the family would have been massive as their racing world had been grown around it.

By 1900 Tom Junior and my grandfather Charles, who was an apprentice jockey and 16 years old was by now also learning to be a trainer, he moved from Danebury and took up residence in Chattis Hill House not far from Danebury they carried on training from there together. Danebury was

---

357 Tom Cannon, Garlogs, 1898

Figure 119 Tom Cannon Jnr Evening Dress Wedding Family Collection 1908

leased to Mr. W.Moore as a training establishment. *"Danebury so long the home of the Cannon Family, and before them of the Days, has lately been vacated by Tom Cannon and his sons, and taken over by the trainer Mr. W.H.Moore."*[358] At Chattis Hill Tom Cannon Junior had 66 horses in training there with seven jockeys under license"[359] In 1901 Tom Cannon, Senior, joined the boys Tom and Charles at Chattis Hill. *"Tom Cannon decided to take things a little easier than hereto and relinquish the Garlogs establishment and give up his breeding Stud and amuse himself with his son Young Tom with his Horses in training at Chattis Hill.'*[360] They continued their work there for many years. In 1902 Tom Cannon Senior sold the Garlogs estate for what reasons remain a mystery but

By 1908 the Chattis Hill training establishment was also under the hammer to Mr. Henry Persse or Atty for £6,500 under mortgage and [465]the same year Tom Junior married a Miss Dorothy Crabtree of Burnage Hall Lancashire, they were married in Danebury House first, it was quite a society wedding very lavishly decorated in both the reception and the church, the main wedding on account of Dorothy being an aristocrat ensured she had to be married at St Martins in the field London.

"At St Martins Church Trafalgar Square London on Saturday afternoon, the marriage took place of Mr. Tom Cannon Junior the well-known trainer of racehorses Compton Newbury Berkshire and Miss Dorothy Crabtree daughter of the late W.H.Crabtree of Levenshulme Manchester. The ceremony was performed by Prebendory Shelford, and the service was fully choral. The bride was given away by her mother, and Mr. Kempton Cannon brother of the bridegroom acted as best man. There were three bridesmaids who were daintily dressed. The bride wore a robe of White Mouseline de soie trimmed with lace and a long court train from the shoulders. While beneath her vail she wore a spray of orange blossoms.

Charles Richardson, The English Turf A Record Of Horses And Courses (1901, p.237)

359 Birmingham Daily Post Sporting News (16th February 1900) "Tom Cannon Jnr has sixty six horses under his care at Chattis hill Stockbridge the stable has a claim on seven jockeys"

360 Lancashire Evening post (2nd December 1901, p.5)

Figure 120 Tom Cannon Junior Outside of Danebury 1895 Charlie Cannon up

Among those present at Church were Mr. and Mrs. Mornington Cannon, Mr. Frank Woodbridge, Mr. Alec Taylor, Mr. J.H.Cannon, Rev Charles Roper, Mr. and Mrs. O.G.Moseley, Mr. and Mrs. J.A.Forsyth, Mr. and Mrs. C.A.Mills, Mr. and Mrs. Charles Marx, Mr. and Mrs. Humphrey William, Mr. and Mrs. Willie Ford, Mr. Simpson Jay, Mr. and Mrs. Douglas Mavor, Mr. W.H.Gilbey and Miss Pollen. After a reception held at the hotel Victoria, the newly married couple left for Switzerland."[361]

Around 1908 Tom Junior left Chattis Hill and Stockbridge for Hamilton House and the larger stables of Compton Newbury Berkshire which he purchased half from Mr. W.G, Stevens. Thomas Cannon Junior lived at Compton in Berkshire at Hamilton House to which he owned more than 150 acres of land as listed in Kelly's directory of 1931. He is listed as a private resident but also as a commercial resident. Tom Jnr moved to Compton to set up as private trainer to Leopold De-Rothschild.

In 1908 Tom Junior now at Compton Stables in Berkshire was set up as trainer to Leopold De Rothschild and some of the stables winnings are as below:

1908	2 winners	£208.00
1909	9 winners	£1119.00
1910	8 winners	£1446.00
1911	6 winners	£1022.00
1912	13 winners	£3472.00
1913	12 winners	£2022.00[362]

I visited Hamilton House back in 2002, it is was in the occupation of Mr. Peter Cundle and family he was very gracious and welcoming host and introduced me to his father Mr. Ken Cundle who knew the Cannons. The Cundles are a well-known name in racing as well Mr. Ken Cundle said he put Lester Piggott on one of his first horses. I promised to send him a copy of this book when it is finished and I will.

My Great Uncle Tom moved from Hamilton House to retire in Sway in the Newforest and purchased a large estate there known as Sway Wood. Great Aunty Dorothy also held a suite of rooms in the Chewton Glen Hotel there. I went to visit Sway in 2004 and Great Uncle Tom's house keepers who also lived in Sway. Mrs Gwen Bootle who was part of the staff for a long time, she was a maid with Tom Junior and her husband was the Chauffer. There were many staff in their employment. Mrs Bootle described my Great Uncle and the Cannons as lovely people.

In 1936, aged 64 years, my great uncle Tom Cannon Junior announced his retirement after more than 50 years as a jockey and trainer *"Tom Cannon is to retire at 64 years of age after more than half a century first as a jockey then as a trainer. His training Establishment at Hamilton House Compton Newbury together with several Downs Training Gallops will come into the market to be sold by private treaty Cannon has trained there for many years principally for Anthony De Rothschild and Sir Walter Gilbey."* [363] Uncle Tom retired to Sway Woods, a country estate at Sway in the New Forest where he lived with his wife Dorothy. I went there in 2003 and visited some of the surviving house maids and chauffer's who were really lovely and had been with the Cannon family for many years they told me how they used to clean the big silver racing cups.

My great uncle Tom died there in 1942 aged 71 and is buried in the local church.

---

362 Rothschild Family Archive Training Fee Amounts and Race Winnings Tom Cannon Junior from the Rothschild's 1908-1913 (Accessed in London 2002
363 Gloucestershire Citizen Trainer to Retire 11th August 1936,

Hounds, Harriers and a Hunt Wedding

Figure 122Tom Cannon on Eruption 1872 Watercolour by William Sextie

Hunting was always a big thing in my family, and has been recorded as early as the 1780's. Hunting with dogs has been banned in modern times but in their day it was most certainly considered a social event. All across Hampshire would have been heard the barking of hounds and the blasting of the bugle. The Day family kept their own pack of hunting hounds but were more famous for their pack of harriers the first record I have of them is in the early 1800's, John Day 1767-1828, used to breed the hounds and harriers when he first came to Stockbridge in the late eighteenth century, he seems to have become quite famous for his dogs. John Day of Danebury even sold a pack of 20 of them to Prince Albert Sax De Coburg husband of Queen Victoria in 1841.[364]

Figure 121Danebury Harriers by William Sextie

John Barham Day at Danebury continued the tradition and formed his own hunt and pack that were called the Danebury Harriers. They too became quite famous in Hampshire at the time, and the descendants of that pack were sold in 1861, and went to Austria *"Mr. John day the well-known trainer of Danebury kept a very neat pack of harriers, which afforded great sport. He*

---

364 *Sporting Magazine* "Prince Albert recently purchased 20 couple of beautiful harriers mostly bred by Mr. J.Day of Stockbridge", Rogerson and Tuxford, London, 1842 p.549

Figure 123 Pyrography by great auntie Alice dining room Grosvenor Hotel Stockbridge
hunted them himself, and was whipped into it by his son and little Judd, who has since distinguished himself by winning several races for the Danebury stable. This pack was given up in 1860-61 and I believe, went to Austria." [365]

Tom Cannon of Danebury revived the pack after 1882 and renamed it the Danebury Harriers. There was a picture painted by Sextie that he had commissioned showing him and his four sons hunting. John Day Junior and Mr. Saddler also kept a pack of Beagles called the Stockbridge Union, and as recalled by the writer *"they are Lilliputian fox-hounds, and show more dash and courage than I ever witnessed before in such little creatures."*[366]

There were many hunting pictures that used to hang in the Grosvenor Hotel in Stockbridge, but they have all since disappeared well stolen. This is such a shame as they also showed the hounds meeting outside of the Grosvenor Hotel in Stockbridge around 1890. Tom Cannon was the master of the Danebury Hunt, he had his harriers painted in another picture *Figure 121Danebury Harriers by William Sextie* and they look amazing.

In the dining room of the Grosvenor Hotel Stockbridge there are pyro graphic images burnt into the oak panelling, in the dining room showing Tom Cannon with his hunting horn in mouth riding off to the hunt. The poker work was produced by his daughter Alice, using a hot poker in the style called pyrography. Alice was an artist and to commemorate her father Tom's Retirement from racing in 1892 she completed all of them including his major Classic race wins. Originally the poker panelling was fixed in the dining room at Tom's Garlogs estate along with many other pictures and memorabilia but was moved to the Grosvenor sometime after 1908 where it resides today in the dining room.[443] Appendix 2: Tom Cannon Garlogs (Family Book).

Not only horse racing but hunting was also an obsession of my ancestors and it was part of their tradition as can be seen when in 1883 Tom

365 AESOP, *Sporting reminiscences Of Hampshire* 1745-1862,(Chapman and Hall, London (1864 p.344)
366 AESOP, *Sporting reminiscences Of Hampshire* 1745-1862, 1864,p.233)

THOMAS LEONARD GILBERT CANNON 1872-1942

Cannon's eldest daughter Alice who had produced the poker work was married. The marriage was a hunt wedding and in the interest of tradition, as I believe no one has these weddings anymore, I wish to show the descriptions of the wedding here from press cuttings of the day:-"A charming hunt wedding took place yesterday at Nether Wallop Church where Miss Alice Cannon daughter of Mr. Tom Cannon of Danebury was married to Mr. Charles Compton Martin eldest son of Mr. W.B.Martin of Paulsgrove Hants.

The Bride wore a green habit with gold hunt buttons, a black hat and brown top boots and a hunting tie fastened by a diamond pin. Instead of the orthodox bouquet Miss Cannon carried a Gold Hunting Crop, surmounted by a bunch of Orange Blossoms. The bridesmaids were attired in covert shirts, with scarlet waistcoats and hunt buttons, brown boots and Spats, and soft felt hats with trim black toke feathers. The bridegroom presented them with Gold Horn and Fox Head Rings and Horseshoes of Scarlet and white flowers. The Bridegroom and the father and the brothers of the bride also wore hunt dress."[367]

How charming, not sure I liked the bit about the poor foxes though, but that was then, this is now, I will include the full wedding later on. What I found interesting though was that even in 1883, a hunt wedding was considered rare and old even then, you could almost imagine it in comparison to today's modern theme wedding but I think the couple were married in the church. Tom Cannon Junior was best man by the way.

Tom Cannon Junior was breeding basset hounds in 1891 at Danebury as seen, "The first couple of basset hounds we ever possessed were given to us by Captain Peacock (late M.F.H. Hertfordshire, Isle of Wight, etc.), in 1890, and with four or five couples we used to chivvy about, but in April 1891, we purchased 9½ couples from Mr. T. Cannon, Junior, of Danebury"[368] not sure of the basset hounds but he gave up his pack of Danebury Harriers

---

367 Tom Cannon Garlogs 1898
368 H. A. Bryden *Hare Hunting and Harriers*, (Grant Richards London, 1903 p.296) (H.A.Bryden, 1903)

Figure 124 Tom Cannon Jnr in Hunt dress 1883 (Family Collection)

in 1895. Kempton Cannon, his brother, revived the hunt in Newmarket sometime in the early 1900's.

I must add an amusing story surrounding hunting but the hunting of a very different animal a tiger and the tiger was hunted at Danebury. *"I made one of a shooting party entertained by Tom Cannon Peerless Horseman and a good fellow who at that time resided and trained at Danebury near Stockbridge. We had capital sport and after a big luncheon were waking up the birds in a big field. All of a sudden the most agonizing cries were heard in the difference of "The Tiger, The Tiger," and two stablemen rushed up breathless and apparently terror stricken, "what nonsense" said brother Joe "Tigers don't grow in Hampshire "In another few seconds the Tiger was distinctly seen bounding through a belt of firs and making straight for our party. I never saw men run so fast anywhere out of reach of the furious monster. Nearer and nearer came the tiger I held my fire, anon he stopped and sat up on his haunches and barked! Barked pearls of laughter came from the party the Tiger was Tom Cannons yard dog an enormous Mastiff who had been painted in Black and White for the occasion."* [369]

The brothers played many other sports together boxing golf hunting and cricket as can be seen from the picture overleaf with Morny, Kempton, Tom and Charles in 1905 in a match called Jockeys Vs Athletes at the Oval, these were predominantly charity matches and were sponsored with the winnings going to a designated charity, the proceeds of the ticket sales for

---

369 The Liverpool Echo May 4th 1914

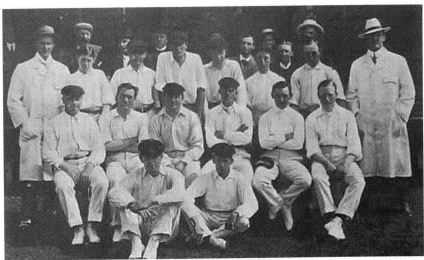

Figure 125 Jockeys Vs Athletes at the Oval 1905 Kempton Charles Standing row Mornington Tom Seated Row (Bystander July 12th 1905)

the match went to the Belgrave Children's Hospital, I don't know who won but it would have been interesting to find out.

Such was their love of Hunting they had many paintings commissioned, below a painting by William Sextie 1904 showing Tom Cannon Senior with Tom Junior and Morny out hunting with the Danebury Harriers at Danebury, the pack are in full chase with the riders in hot pursuit.

Danebury Harriers with Tom Senior, Tom Junior, and Morny, by William Sextie

HERBERT MORNINGTON CANNON 1873-1962

Figure 126Mornington Cannon (Racing Illustrated 1895)

CLASSIC WINS AS A JOCKEY

TABLE 4 CLASSIC RACES WON AS A JOCKEY

Morny Cannon	Horse	Year	Owner
2,000 guineas	Flying Fox	1899	Duke Of Westminster
1,000 guineas			
Epsom Oaks	La Roche	1900	6th Duke Of Portland
	Our Lassie	1903	Jack.B.Joel
Epsom Derby	Flying Fox	1899	Duke Of Westminster
St Ledger Stakes	Throstle	1894	Harry McCalmont
	Flying Fox	1899	Henry Greer

Champion Jockey	Number Of Wins	Year
	137	1891
	182	1892
	167	1894
	184	1895
	164	1896
	145	1897

Figure 127 Morny 1883 aged 10 (Family Collection)

HERBERT MORNINGTON CANNON THE SECOND BORN son to Tom and Kate was of course destined to be a jockey he rode at a weight of 8st 7lb. Mornington was born in Stockbridge on the 25th May 1873. I have found a passage, from a noted expert of the turf at the time, Grace the Duke Of Beaufort in 1893, and other top jockeys of the time, to best describe him:-

"Mornington Cannon, second son of Tom Cannon of Danebury, who, profiting by the teaching and example of his father, speedily made his way to the front rank of his profession to the leading place, indeed, in the front rank, for having begun to ride in 1887, the fifth season of his career found him at the head of the list of winning jockeys, and in the year following, 1892, his name again came first with 182 successful mounts, his nearest rival following with 154. The lad was only eighteen years of age he first topped the list, a remarkable instance of an old head on young shoulders. Patience when patience is necessary, extraordinary judgment and alertness, great strength and invincible resolution are the characteristics of this admirable young horseman. Mornington Cannon should be a born jockey."[370]

Figure 128 Morny Cannon Kings Colours 1900 Family *Collection*

According to family oral tradition, this story has been told many times, his name was given by his father Thomas, the day he won on a horse in Bath. His father had telegraphed home a message containing the name of the winning horse, but at the same time one of the servants had sent a message to the course requesting Thomas to provide a name for the new son. The rest was history as the maid thought Thomas had answered the request with the name Mornington, so Mornington it would be.

---

370 Henry Charles Howard Earl of Suffolk and Berkshire, William George Craven, Arthur George Coventry Arthur Alfred Thomas Watson, *Racing And Steeple Chasing*, (1893, p.246)

HERBERT MORNINGTON CANNON 1873-1962

Mornington was privately educated at Queenwood College in Hampshire like his brothers Tom, Kempton and Charles[400] and was reputed to have been a very lazy boy and his father often referred to him as "Lazy Beggar". But this could not be said about his riding career, as he was soon to flourish as an extremely fine and world famous jockey. He was ranked among the greatest jockeys to appear on the turf, and some even referred to him in the same breath as the greatest of all time *"Morny Cannon, who on one occasion rode for me, and I still hold the opinion that next to Archer there has been none to equal him."*[371] Between 1890 and 1900 in just 10 years Morny rode 1524 winning races[372]. On average that's 152 wins per year, to win that much he must have been tired of it. His father Tom rode 1544 winning horses over 32 years, so you can see the comparison.

Figure 129 Mornington Cannon 1898 (Family Collection) Picture

Morny was apprenticed to his father Thomas Cannon at Danebury his career took off a day before his fourteenth birthday. As recalled by Morny *"my first race; it was Coralline in a five furlong stretch at Kempton Park in 86. I came in last."* [373] Morny further laments on his early years. "When I was fourteen, riding began in earnest and I was apprenticed to my father for seven years. I left school, but we were taught by a tutor each afternoon. At least four hours a day of horseback was the rule, and even after I had begun riding in public, and considered myself no end a big man, the lessons were kept up. Duke of Parma winner of the Cesarewitch in 1875 was my school master and the first thoroughbred I ever rode-only of course as a hack. The first trial I ever rode in was on Jolly Sir John. Those were well filled days. Riding trials in the morning study in the afternoon, and more riding after study. Moreover we had got together a pack of basset hounds which fully occupied our leisure time. No end of fun did we have with that pack, which still survives in the New Forest under the care of Mr Heseltine, brother of the well-known cricketer."[373]

---

371 John McGuigan *A Trainers Memories Being Sixty Years Turf Reminiscences and Experiences at home and abroad*, (Heath Cranton Madison 1946, p.84)

372 Theodore Andrea Cook, *A History of The English Turf*,1901-1904,Vol III p.539

373 C. B. Fry *C. B. Fry's Magazine of Sports, Riding a racehorse by Mornington Cannon*,1904, p.168)

Figure 130Morny Cannon Flying Fox Guinness Book of Jockeys

In 1887 he won a race on a horse called Flint, belonging to Mr. H.E Tidy at Salisbury he won the Bowl and this is where Morny's career is considered to have started. [374] The renowned trainer of the horse Mr. Charles Morton gave him a sovereign to buy sweets as was the custom then. That same year proved a good one for Morny as he then went on to win the Stewards Cup in July at Goodwood, riding a horse called Upset, beating his father's horse called Tib by three lengths which his brother Tom Junior was riding, this all helped to launch his career in the saddle and there was no stopping him.

Figure 131Morny Cannon Duke of Westminster Flying Fox

Morny managed to obtain the title of Champion Jockey in 1891 at the age of 18 winning a total of 137 winners. He did not stop there.

In 1894 Morny was asked to become first jockey to the powerful stable of John Porter in Kingsclere, a good friend of his father's, and Porter was apprenticed under John Barham Day Morny's grandfather, in position of First Jockey would have been a great honour because it meant riding all the best horses and also for the King. Mornington managed to gain many wins and his first Classic success was the St Leger on Lord Alington's Throstle in 1894, aged 21 he was one year older than his father had been at the time of his first Classic. The next time he won a Classic was in 1899 and what a Classic that would be to win. In 1899 Flying

---

[374] Henry Smurthwaite, *Racing Illustrated, The Sportsman* Vol 1, 1895) "Morny Cannons career as a successful jockey began in 1887, at Salisbury, where on the afternoon of May 20th, he won the Bowl on Mr. H.E. Tidy's flint."

Figure 133 Morny Cannon winning the Triple Crown on Flying Fox 1899 after John Alexander Harrington Bird

Fox and Morny Cannon would make history together, being in small elite of jockeys and horses to win the coveted Triple Crown which is awarded to

those who complete the near impossible task of winning the 2,000 Guineas, St Leger and Derby in the same year on the same horse. Morny would in 1899 be the 8th person ever to win it. Flying Fox was trained by John Porter a Kingsclere trainer who had been apprenticed to John Barham Day and was a close friend of the family. Cannon would ride at 8st 6 and he had already won the 2,000 Guineas and the St Leger, when he snatched the Derby on Flying Fox, who was then sold for £39,375 to Mr. M Edmond Blanc and by all accounts the English buyers gave a moan of discontent as the horse passed out of England.[375]

Figure 132 Morny Cannon Caricature in his father's colours by Spy

Morny held the title of Champion Jockey six times, in 1892 a year in which he had a total of 182 wins. Again in 1894 with 167, 1895 with 184, in

---

375 (Cook, 1901-1904 p. 668)

1896 with 164 wins, to end in 1897 with 145. Over six years total of 979 wins with an average of 163.

There appeared to be no end to this amazing career and Cannon nearly completed the impossible, *Figure 134* never achieved then or since, he would have won a second Triple Crown the following year for King Edward VII in 1900 if it was not for a bad tempered horse, Diamond Jubilee. *"Cannon was leading him back to the yard after a gallop prior to the 2,000 guineas. Diamond Jubilee seized him in his teeth and rolled on him until help came thus making it plain that a change of riding arrangements was necessary."*[376]

Diamond Jubilee proved too troublesome for Cannon as told in his own words "Another Horse that I found difficult to ride was the Kings Horse Diamond Jubilee. I was to ride him in the Derby and all the classic races, and I went down to Newmarket in March to get accustomed to him. I rode him in a gallop, and went quietly and well before I got off to change, and put the stable boy back on him. I was no sooner away from him then he savaged me in the left arm, threw me down and knelt on me, he fell over on his side and as he righted himself, Jones his boy jumped on his back. It was one of the smartest things I had ever seen. Later on I tried to approach Diamond Jubilee again, but though in his box he was perfectly quiet, as soon as I walked in he became very excited and, pouring with perspiration, came at me like a dog on a chain. I cleared. I had one more attempt at riding him, but on that occasion he tore his breast cloth to pieces, and showed generally that he preferred my room to my company. It was some consolation to me that I was not the only man he took a dislike to; he bit Jack Watts in the leg when he was only two years old." [377]

The Cannons style of riding was the same as all the other jockeys of the day it was the classic upright style this had been the same since racing began, however at the end of the 19th Century and the start of the 20th Century this style of racing was about to change for good.

---

376 (the Jockey Club)
377 C. B. Fry C. B. Fry's *Magazine of Sports, Riding a racehorse by Mornington Cannon,*1904, p.165)

MONKEY UP A STICK THE AMERICAN STYLE

Figure 135Morny Cannon Old Seat

At the beginning of the Twentieth Century there was an event that became known as the American invasion. [378] Where- by the style of the classic English seat, the seat being the way in which you sit on a horse, was becoming old fashioned and the new American style of riding, which was shorter stirrups and perched on the saddle, introduced by Tod Sloan was producing more winners, as can be seen in 1900 at Ascot where 17 of the 28 races for that year went to American riders. However by 1902 in comparison Morny was still in the top ten of winning jockeys in seventh place, and had a winning percentage of 17.7%.[379]

The impact of the change in style can be seen from the improved race times between 1899-1909 when compared to the preceding decade of 1888-1899, for the Epsom Derby the time had improved by 4.3 seconds, St Leger 8.2 seconds, and the Ascot Gold Cup 14.1 seconds, so in other words the English jockeys would have to either adopt this new style of racing, or lose their races.[380]

Figure 136Morny Cannon American Seat

Most of the English jockeys did adopt this style, but it wasn't well received by some, as accounted by one famous jockey and friend of the Cannons George Lambton *"You cannot like it but it has come to stay and we must make the best of it."* [381] Charles Cannon my Gandfather and Kempton, Morny's brothers were among the first English

378 Michael Tanner *Guinness Book Of Great Jockeys Of The Flat*, p.110 "In 1900 as many as 17 of the 28 races at Royal Ascot went to American Riders"
379 (A History of The English Turf)
380 Michael Tanner *Guinness Book of Great Jockeys of the flat*, 1992, p.110 "The average derby time improved by 4.3 seconds, the average St Leger time improved by 8.2 seconds, with the Ascot Gold cup by 14.1 seconds."
381 Michael Tanner *Guinness Book Of Great Jockeys Of The Flat*, 1992, p.110

Figure 137 Morny Cannons seat 1904 a compromise

jockeys to adopt this new style.[411] I have read that my 16 year old grandfather was the first.[412] There was one English jockey however, who completely refused the new style. It was Morny Cannon, he was a traditionalist and in my family it was known as one of the reasons he gave up horse racing.

Morny hated the American style of riding and is quoted as saying the American style was riding like a "Monkey on a stick". On one occasion it was reported that Morny had the American jockey Tod Sloan who was responsible for introducing the style stood down at a race meeting in Doncaster in 1900 for foul riding. In the end Morny did concede by hitching his leathers and stirrups up a little.

The position of the rider using the "American style" on the horse was much the same as we can see today in modern racing, where the stirrups are

Figure 138Morny Cannons Seat

hitched up higher, instead of being long, and thus elevating the body in a more forward position almost like a crouch, this also meant that the rein was shortened, but I am no expert, it apparently makes the transfer of weight better, allowing more movement in the hind of the horse Morny was an expert and some years later after his retirement he concedes *"The short Stirrup is best for racing, you should not sit on the Horses back when galloping; you should sit practically on nothing, and the short stirrup enables you to do this It also shifts the weight from the Horses back and throws it on the withers, thus giving absolute action to the hind action whence the pace comes."* [382]

382 CB Fry's Magazine1904 page167

Morny Cannon's seat was that in the style of the Classic English rider every jockey used prior to Todd Sloan and the "American Invasion". Morny did concede that the hitching up of the leathers was better for racing as recalled in his own words [383] *"As to the seat I always used to ride with ordinary long stirrups, and this is undoubtedly the right way for ordinary riding, hunting etc. But when the new American seat was introduced into this country by Tod Sloan we all tried it, and I arrived at the conclusion that the exaggerated position with the short stirrup was no good. I became convinced however that the short stirrup is best*

Figure 139Morny Cannon Photo 1900 Family Collection

for racing, provided it is not to short."

History shows that Morny Cannon started to drift away from racing after 1900 the last Classic race for Morny Cannon was in 1903 at the Oaks. He won the race on Mr. J.B. Joel's Our Lassie, trained by Charles Morton. In 1900 Morny lived at Ridgeway House in Pear Tree Avenue Southampton with his wife, it was a lavish manor house. By 1904 Morny had moved to a new property at Bletchley Park the final notable race for Mornington Cannon was won in 1905 at the Royal meeting for the Gold Cup. He won on Lord Howard de Walden's Zinfandel trained by Charles Beatty.

Figure 140 Morny Cannon golf at the Worlington

Morny did not renew his jockey license after 1908 due mainly to poor health he suffered with intermittent rheumatism in his legs, probably due to too much riding. [384] His last race was on 31 October 1907 on Marozzo in the Houghton Handicap at Newmarket a

383 CB Fry's Magazine 1904 page167
384 Manchester Courier and Lancashire General Advertiser 1st April 1908, p.2 "Mornington Cannon has not been in the best of Health Lately suffering from Rheumatism and his doctor has advised him to exercise due care during the present treacherous weather, Hence the popular Danebury Horseman has not applied for a renewal of his license"

Figure 141 Ridgeway House Unknown Watercolour circa 1910

winner at 100/14 that's the way to go out Morny. He retired at only 34 years of age, having made enough money from the sport, he retired to Brighton to have some fun, and he was a keen golfer which he played with his cousin, Boxer Cannon, Joe Cannon's son, and his brother Kempton Cannon. The name of Cannon was very famous at the Royal Worlington and Newmarket Golf Club a very exclusive club near Newmarket and is well known for being a 9 hole course, Joe Cannon and his sons Noel and Boxer were all presidents.

In 1894 Morny was married, the bride's name was Miss Nellie-Grey Dennett, and the date was initially set for 1st Feb 1894. They were married at St Mary Abbot's church in Kensington, to all accounts the wedding was a closed affair, away from the public eye. This was due to the recent death of the bride's father. Morny was 21 and Nellie was 25, a toy boy, Nellie and Morny had no children together. Due to the death of the bride's father they married early on 1st January 1894. *"My good friend Mornington Cannon [whose unblemished record as one of our very foremost jockeys is an enviable one] was "tied up" in, perhaps, the briefest possible time. "Short and sweet" was the motto of the minister, the Rev W H Bramwell.*

Morny's esteemed father was present, but Morny's brother, Tom, junior, was his best man; while the charming bride was given away by Mr. Frederick Ingle. Tommy Loates looked in at his friend's wedding. Of the three bridesmaids I mustn't breathe which our

Figure 142 Mornington Cannons Home Bletchley Park 1905

artist fell in love with. There is no reason why I should: his pencil has let the cat out of the bag involuntarily. Suffice it to say that, while Miss Cannon, Miss Mabel Cannon, and Miss Penny Blackburn were tastefully garbed in white cloth coats and skirts with bright waistcoats of scarlet brocade and lace cravats, and white felt hats to match, the

Figure 143 Wedding of Mornington Cannon and Miss Dennett Kensington 1894 Penny Illustrated

bridegroom's presents to them being diamond cannon pins and muffs of scarlet and white flowers, the bride herself looked just as nice as a bride should look in white moiré, trimmed with sable and old lace, a tiny capote in the shape of an Alsatian bow in moiré, with sable border and sprays of orange blossom - as a lady journalist informed me."

"The young couple were engaged with the full approval of the greatly respected Nottingham gentleman who was to have given his daughter away. No one could have been prouder than his future son-in-law than the late Mr. Dennett to whom the jockey was greatly attached. To be with the old gentleman in the illness which suddenly took him away, Cannon retired from riding for the season before his death.

But for Mr. Dennett's death the wedding would have been one of the gayest events of the sporting year He will make a start at Lincoln this year with his condition doubly changed. Last year he was a bachelor and an apprentice. This he will be "out of his time" and a Benedick, with a grand income almost ready made, as one may say." [385]

But it became quite the celebrity wedding and was recorded in the Times and many other papers of the day. Many celebrities attended, Tom Cannon

---

385 The Penny Illustrated, Morny Cannons Wedding (13th January 1894)

Figure 144 Morny Cannon Guinness Book of Jockeys of Flat

Junior was best man. But it was just never to last, Nellie Dennet a few years later had filed for divorce. By 1898 they were separated, this was considered a scandal in those days and I think was to go some way to prevent Morny from horse racing. But I should imagine that it angered his father more so, Morny was known as a ladies man so perhaps we can imagine that this may have been the cause behind the divorce but the truth is we do not know and probably never will. In that same year came the closure of the Stockbridge Course.[335]

Morny married again in 1915 this time to Miss Emily Harris, they had their first child Claude Herbert Cannon, Emily was only 16, and this marriage wasn't to last either as Morny was divorced again by 1920. Emily went to America with Claude, who I had the pleasure of speaking to once before he died. Claude had a son who I have spoken to and is a gentleman who lives in Oxford. I have rescued a short story of him from our Family Book.

MORNY CANNONS HEADER

"We do not often hear of jockeys being thrown over the heads of their mounts or if this interesting occurrence does take place then the unfortunate rider is not usually pitched into the lap of bounty and luxury in the shape of two ladies sitting in a carriage having lunch yet this was Mornington Cannon back when mounted on Cordelier. As he was leaving the birdcage for the autumn handicap of 1891 one of the fiercest storm at Newmarket for some years swept over the heath. The hailstones came down like bullets almost cutting ones flesh as they struck, and Cordelier maddened by the stings made for the rails and ran through them getting his head under the second line of posts and pitching Morny over the rails right into a carriage, fortunately for him the door happened to be open right at that moment and he was shot right inside to the astonishment of the occupants who were lunching. The young jockey pulled himself together and assured the two ladies that he was not hurt, and at their kind suggestion accepted a glass of wine, Cannon had been wasting hard to ride victorious

Morny Cannon in the Middle, Joe Cannon Senior 1895

at 7st 12 and had not had time since the Ceasarwitch to lunch. On hearing this the ladies asked their unexpected guest to join them, and while the other jockeys who had been weighed out for the race had been drenched by the storm, Morny was regaling himself with chicken and champagne. It was however a very unusual way of entering a carriage and one that might not always be followed by such good fortune."

Morny retired to Brighton and Hove where he lived out the rest of his days, being joined later by his brother Kempton. Morny died there in 1962 aged 89.

LIEUTENANT WALTER KEMPTON CANNON (1879-1951)

Figure 145 Walter Kempton Cannon, in full racing silks, (Racing Illustrated, 1895)

Classic Wins as a Jockey

Table 5 Classic Races Won as a Jockey

Kempton Cannon	Horse	Year	Owner
2,000 guineas	St Amant	1904	Leopold De Rothschild
1,000 guineas			
Epsom Oaks			
Epsom Derby	St Amant	1904	Leopold De Rothschild
St Ledger Stakes	Doricles	1901	Prince Of Wales

LIEUTENANT WALTER KEMPTON CANNON (1879-1951)

Figure 146 Kempton Cannon 1898 Family Collection

WALTER KEMPTON CANNON: WAS BORN ON 21st November 1879 third son to Tom and Kate. Kempton or Kemy like his other brothers was a lightweight youth, and like his brothers was destined to follow the family profession as a jockey. He was privately educated at Queenwood College in Broughton Hampshire like his brothers Tom Morny and Charles[400]. There was an arrangement that all the boys had with the school to come home on Friday nights ready to ride Saturday morning.[386]

Kempton also served his apprenticeship under his father Tom at Danebury tutored in the classic style of English riding, Kempton along with his brother Charles was among the first jockeys to shorten their leathers and adopt the American style. This change allowed him to carry on into the 20th century.

As a boy Kempton was a good photographer and renowned for his sense of humour. As a jockey he rode his first winner at the age of fourteen, at the Stockbridge races, for his father. Kempton moved firstly to Newmarket to Leopold de Rothschild's trainer Alfred Hayhoe and then on to live with John Watson at Exeter House Newmarket, and can be seen there in the 1901 census as a 21 year old jockey and also unmarried.

Kempton Cannon aged 14 rode his first mount in public on 25th May 1894 on a horse called Poor Box at Kempton Park, owned by Mr. Low[386] His first notable win was on Bunting at the Stockbridge races July 12th 1894 in an aged plate, it was Kempton's third ever ride in public and he was only fourteen years old but the best bit must have been looking over his shoulder to see his famous brother Morny behind him in second.[386]

He was excelling just like the rest of the Cannons and in 1895 he rode 188 races winning 15 times, and was placed second or third 50 times. That is a good start for a very young man. In 1896 he rode in 281 races recording 21 wins, 81 times placed. 1897 brought 432 races winning 32 and being placed 132 times including a large win in the Cambridgeshire. In 1898 Kempton

---

386 A.H.Bailey, *Baileys Magazine of Sporting Past Times*, 1902, p. 467)

took the Goodwood Cup, had 230 mounts 15 wins and placed 55 times. In 1899 Kempton rode 291 races winning 27 of them, being placed 82 times; he won all of his races on a saddle weighing a pound and a half which was half the weight of the normal racing saddle.[386]

Kempton's first major win came in 1896 when he was 17 at the Cesarewitch on St Bris, these races were important handicaps. This was followed shortly in 1897 winning the Cambridgeshire on Comfrey. Again In 1899 with Irish Ivy the last being in 1902 on Black Sand. He was still in the top ten of English jockeys in 1902 as was his brother Morny, with a winning percentage of 13.7%[387]. By 1900 things were changing for Kempton as he grabbed an opportunity to ride for Leopold De Rothschild with whom the Cannon family were already closely associated not just as jockey owner trainer but also as friends and the Rothschild's were also the Cannon family bankers. In 1900 Kempton rode in 600 races doubling his usual quota winning 75 of those races and being placed 245 times. By the end of the season Rothschild's jockey Loates retired leaving Kempton to become first jockey and to eventually only ride for Rothschild.[386]

Kempton had a fondness for Leopold De-Rothschild as he recalled, "When I was a little boy at school Mr. Leopold De-Rothschild gave me a Sovereign, it was the first piece of gold I ever had. And I thought Mr. Rothschild must be an awfully nice man. I made up my mind to keep the Sovereign for always, but after keeping it for a long time the temptation, was too strong and I changed it, It might have been on Silk Worms, I was mad on Silkworms just then. Anyhow from that time I got it was to have three great ambitions in my mind. The first to ride first jockey to Mr. Leopold De-Rothschild, the second to win the Derby for Mr. Rothschild, and the third to be top of the tree in the list of winning jockeys. I don't suppose I am in the least likely to do the last, but I have done the other two."[388]

Cannon won three Classics, firstly the St Leger in 1901 on Doricles-(Florizale II-Rosalie), for the Prince of Wales, and then next was the 2,000 Guineas in 1904 on St Amant.-(St Frusquin-Lady Loverule), for Leopold De-Rothschild.

The most memorable race of his career was when he won the Derby in 1904, again on St Amant, he was 25 years old, and this was the third Derby

---

387 Theodore Andrea Cook, *A History of The English Turf*,1901-1904,Vol III p.538
388 Morning Leader, K .Cannons Story, June 2nd 1904 Care of the Rothschild Family Archive London

LIEUTENANT WALTER KEMPTON CANNON (1879-1951)

Figure 147 Kempton Cannon St Amant 1904 Derby

to be won by the Cannon Family, the first being won on Shotover in 1882 with Tom Senior, Morny with Flying Fox in 1899 who went on that same season to take the Triple Crown.

I have found an account of the St Amant Derby of 1904 in Leopold De-Rothschild's personal Folio that I was allowed to view in the Rothschild family archives. Interestingly the very first horse run by the Rothschild's was called Leopold. There was a complete book made in honour of the race, as it was one of Leopold De-Rothschild's ambitions to win the Derby achieved first with Kempton Cannon and St Amant. The 1904 Derby was run in a thunder storm, King Edward VII was in attendance, and Kempton was racing against his brother Morny. "The lightening was very vivid, and the claps of thunder so loud, that it would not be surprising in the race if the horses were too scared to give their true running."[388]

An account of the race from the words of the jockey Kempton Cannon, "*I wanted the horse on his toes, he went down in a cantor like a bird, but at the post got sleepy again, so I got the man behind to give him a cut with his whip, I hit him myself too and that made him wake up and attend to his business. When the gate went up he jumped into his bridle, and was going right away up to the top of the hill, where I found I was well in front. So I crossed over and took the rails. I steadied him a little at the top of the hill to give him a breather. When I got six furlongs from home I set him going again, and kept him going right the way down the hill to the Tattenham Turn. He came down the hill and around the turn well but slipped on the wet grass just as he got into the straight which put him on the wrong leg. When I got him balanced again I took hold of*

him and drove him home in earnest, I peeped over my shoulder and found the others were nowhere near, and I knew then I had won."388

The account clearly describes the skill that a jockey must have and also the minute alterations that go on unseen in a race. The owner Leopold De Rothschild, so excited by the race took the horse out in the rain after the race and

Figure 148 Kempton Cannon after St Amant 1904 Derby Courtesy Rothschild Archive

completely forgot himself and got soaked to the skin. Here is the 1904 Derby after winning in Kempton Cannons own words:-

"I pulled the horse up halfway across the paddock, I could hear the cheering on the course, the boy who does him came running down the course to meet him, and when he got to him he kissed him, the boy was as white as a sheet. Then we went through the crowd back to the weighing room. When we got halfway Mr. Rothschild met the horse, and the boy put on the white leading rein, and Mr. Rothschild led him. There were roars from the crowd that went right through you. I couldn't possibly tell you what my feelings were. Mr. Rothschild got drenched as the rain was coming down in torrents. When Mr. Rothschild took hold of the horse the crowd were simply fighting with policemen to get near him. Some policemen had hold of the men by their coat tails, but they were all cheering away.

*They were crowding in all around. They were slapping the horse and patting him all over the quarters and on his tail, but he took it well, the only thing he objected to was an umbrella being shoved in his face."*388

I think that goes some way to describe the excitement of both the

Figure 149Finish of the 1904 Derby (Courtesy Rothschild Archive

crowd and the jockey at the turn of the century, much the same I suppose as today. It seems that Kempton had achieved all he had set out to achieve in that race In 1902 Kempton Cannon was to ride for the Viceroy of India, the passage was booked for 28th November 1902.

"Kempton Cannon joins the P. and O. Ship China on his way to India to ride Petridge in the Viceroys Cup at Calcutta, the horse has already arrived in good health, and it is quite a record for a jockey to travel 16,500 miles for a single engagement." [389] I am unsure if he rode in the race as the horse Petridge did not qualify but he travelled to India anyway and as mentioned by the paper 16,500 miles for a single race what an experience.

In August, 1907 Kempton opened a garage in Newmarket, this was a very early garage the motor car by 1907 was new, having only been around for a few years.[390] The cars in those days were amazing not travelling much over 30 Mph so I find it extremely funny that In 1909 Kempton was fined for speeding, as recalled in the paper of the time. *"A fine of £5 with costs has been imposed at Kingston on Thames on Walter Kempton Cannon of Newmarket, for motoring at a speed which the police put at 37mph."* [391] I suppose they were jockeys and they liked to travel fast.

---

389 Yorkshire Evening Post Tuesday 17th November 1902 page 5
390 Luton Times and Advertiser (23rd August 1907) "Kempton Cannon the Jockey has recently opened a Garage in Newmarket"
391 Yorkshire Evening Post From Saddle to Chauffeur Seat (11th June 1909,p.3)

Figure 150Kempton Cannon winning 1904 Derby for Leopold De Rothschild on St Amant
Courtesy Rothschild archive

LIEUTENANT WALTER KEMPTON CANNON (1879-1951)

In 1911 Kempton married the widow of his lifelong friend Jack Watts, who was apprenticed to his father Tom at Stockbridge. Jack had died at 41 years of age and had won the Derby, on that amazing horse Persimmon for Prince Edward on 3rd June 1896. I think Kempton's marriage was one of honour for his friend; .On 1st January 1911 Kempton married Mrs. Letitia Annie Watts and adopted the son Tommie Owen Watts, who was also to try his hand in the saddle. Kempton was married in Newmarket *"The wedding took place at St Mary's parish Church Newmarket of Mr. Walter Kempton Cannon the well-known ex jockey to Mrs. Letitia Annie Watts's widow of Mr. Jack Watts who was at one time the late King Edwards Jockey. The Rev H.B.young rector of the church officiated. The bride who wore a tailor-made costume of cream cloth with Ermine wraps was given away by her stepson Jack Watts, there were no Bridesmaids.*

There was a large attendance in the church, Master Claude Watts's son of the bride. Miss M.H.Hammond her sister, Miss Cannon cousin to the Bridegroom. Mr. and Mrs. Cannon had a hearty greeting from the crowd outside after leaving the ceremony and subsequently held a reception at the belt which is to be their residence in Newmarket. On Saturday Mr. and Mrs. Cannon will leave for St Moritz will stay for a few weeks." [392]

By 1910 Kempton had become interested in flying and was taken for his first flight on 20th September 1910, *"Mr. Kempton Cannon was taken for a good flight in a double seater by Mr. Drexaland upon returning to terra firma exclaimed, winning the Derby on St Amant and that trip are the two finest experiences I have ever had; he is a keen tobogganer and has designs on the championships,"* [393] by October 22nd 1910 he was announced as being a new member of the Royal Aero Club [394] and commenced his flying course at Beaulieu Aerodrome on 29th October 1910. By November 12th 1910, we find Kempton being commended for his abilities as an early aviator, *"Kempton Cannon has more than realized the expectations expressed in these notes three weeks ago the first moment he got into a machine he seemed to get the touch of the control and rudder, his rapid qualification as Pilot Aviator looks certain, there is little doubt that his thorough knowledge of motors stands him in good stead, but lightness of hands ready resource and quickness of action inherent in a good jockey probably contributes toward his astonishing aptitude for aviation than anything else"* [395] By the end of November 1910 Kempton held his pilot's license, but gave up flying on 21st January 1911

---

392 Manchester Courier and Lancashire general advertiser 5th January 1911

393 Flight Royal Aero Club of the United Kingdom, official notices to members, 15th November 1910, p.840

394 Flight Royal Aero Club of the United Kingdom, official notices to members, New Members W. Kempton Cannon 22nd October 1910

395 Flight Royal Aero Club of the United Kingdom, official notices to members, New Forest Aviation School November 5th 1910, p.931

due to getting married, must be due to Mrs. Cannon worrying about him crashing. By 1913 Kempton had enlisted in the RFC and was commissioned as a second lieutenant on 27th August 1916 "special reserve of officers Royal Flying Corps the undermentioned to be 2nd Lieutenants 27th August 1916."[396] his brother Ronald was in the RNAS and Charles went into the 19th Royal Hussars. After the war was over Kempton lived at Rosslyn East Moseley in the county of Surrey.

In 1922 Kempton and his brother Morny had forwarded official applications to become starters for the Jockey Club *"Mornington Cannon and Kempton Cannon have forwarded official applications to become starters to the Jockey Club. The vast experience and splendid records of the brothers Cannon in racing matters would be of inestimable value if the authorities avail themselves or their services in that important and responsible capacity."*[397]

In 1923 Kempton was again making headlines when he had issued a challenge, and by all accounts a very public and important challenge *"An important challenge has been made by Kempton Cannon and should it be accepted a lot of interest will be accepted. The challenge arises out of the statement made by lord Durham in the recent racing case Boam vs Beary, that anyone riding in the old fashioned style would have no chance against the modern style in a flat race. Kempton Cannon does not agree with this and is prepared to back himself with 100.00 of his own money, to ride a match of one mile with anyone of the present leading day jockeys, Steve Donahugh preferred. Cannon is prepared to ride either animal in the old English style taught by his father and practiced by himself and his two brothers."*[398]

Kempton Cannon was the only jockey to ever win the Cesarewitch and two Cambridgeshire twice as reported in "Credit is being given to Kempton Cannon who yesterday joined the ranks of winning owners that he is the only jockey who ever rode the winners of the two Cesarewitch's and two Cambridgeshire."[399]

In 1926, aged 47, Kempton joined his brother Morny in Hove where he retired and died in 1951 at 72 years of age.

396 Supplement to the London Gazette No. 10070 19th October 1916
397 Hull Daily Mail, Sporting Items, 20th (July 1922, p.2)
398 Yorkshire post and Leeds Intelligencer (15th August 1923, p.12)
399 Nottingham evening post 10th November 1909

CAPTAIN CHARLES EDWARD CANNON

Figure 151 Charles Edward Cannon 19th Hussars Family Collection

CAPTAIN CHARLES EDWARD CANNON

Figure 152 Charles Cannon 1892

CHARLES EDWARD CANNON WAS MY GRANDFATHER, by the time he was ready to wear the pigskin his family were already some of the most famous sportsmen in the world, the Stockbridge Racecourse had closed in 1898 and by the time Charles started riding professionally the Cannons were nearing the end of their riding careers. Charles would have had a lot to live up to seeing as three of his brothers were among the finest riding men of their time, and his father was already being called the Master that's without the history of the Day family of jockeys and trainers his grandfathers and uncles bearing down on his young shoulders as well. However I have recorded what is known.

Charles Cannon was born on 26th March 1884 to Tom Cannon and Kate Day and was the youngest boy and the last of the Danebury horse men; he was born in Longstock near Stockbridge. Being born into a family of famous horse men it was preordained what he was going to do with his life, he was to be a jockey. In December of 1892 when Charles was 8 years old his mother Kate passed away. Tom his father remarried the following year in March at South Stoneham to a Scottish woman, named Jessie Catherine Cameron, by all accounts she was the governess to the Cannon family.

This was to be a huge turning point in his life as Charles and the rest of his family hated his new step mother as you can appreciate it's like your dad bringing home your strict teacher, and they all had to call her Madam. Tom Cannon and Madam had a baby boy in 1895 called Ronald Portman Cannon. I grew up exactly the same way, and the same thing happened to me when I was 15 and to my brothers and sisters, I know how this feels it is devastating something inside you dies and you lose all care and control. Recollections of the cold character of Madam have been passed down to me by my uncles, who were told the tales by their father, that she Madam was a strict and unkind woman who they all hated with a passion. Charles turned naughty, probably rebelling and they had put bars on the windows of his room which was in the Castle Tower of a turret at Danebury when he was a child to stop him running away, which he apparently did frequently.

There seems to be something that happened before that, between Tom and Kate, as usually when a census is taken the family are together, history hints at a possible break up in the relationship of his mother and father recorded in the 1891 census. Charles is shown as living with his mother Kate and two sisters Blanche and Ethel at Garlogs and his father is residing at Danebury with Tom Junior and two sister's Alice and Letitia. It seems very odd that a census would show the family living in separate estates. It is strange though as the 1881 census also shows his mother as not being at home either or being with Tom. It was said that Madam was Tom Cannon's mistress, but I doubt it to be true, that gossip was probably fuelled by the hatred towards her.

The life that Charles Cannon was born into was that of landed gentry, the Cannons had amassed a huge fortune as a family throughout the years, and Tom had earnt the equivalent of £6 million in riding fees alone in today's money which he had invested in estates and land. In 1892, after his mother Kate died his father gave up racing and handed over Danebury to his brother Tom Junior. His father then resided at Garlogs a 1,000 acre estate which he had purchased for £10,000 and the family resided there too.

At the time of my grandfather's birth the Cannons lived in Danebury another 1,000 acre estate in Stockbridge. There were many frequent visitors including King Edward VII who would stay as a guest of Tom Cannon. My grandfather Charles used to have to walk King Edward around the grounds and the course. Edward also used to stay at Garlogs one of the Cannon's other estates and would spend that time fishing with Tom Cannon on the River Test or shooting, amongst other things. Besides Edwards's entourage other frequent visitors were Baron Hirsh and Leopold De-Rothschild. Charles Cannon like his brothers Tom, Morny and Kempton was privately educated at Queenwood College in Hampshire.[400] Charles after finishing school went to Handles College in Southampton where he studied the piano of which he went on to be very accomplished. He even played a solo for the King in 1902 at the Royal Albert Hall in London.

The first time we see Charles appearing in the press is when he is 11 years old assisting with the Prince of Wales when attending the Stockbridge races as was custom in our family *"The last day at Stockbridge was generally quiet and today was no exception the attendance was small but the Prince was here, Another distinguished personage was Charlie Cannon, Younger Brother to Tom Morny and Kempton who came over from his school at Southampton to assist at the last scene as used*

---

[400] Yorkshire Post (9th June 1904, p.12)"his dam is Queenwood which is the name of the old school in Hampshire where his owner Alec Taylor was educated. Among others educated there were the brothers Tom Mornington, Kempton and Charlie Cannon."

Figure 153 Charles Cannon with Family 1895 outside Danebury Racing Illustrated

to be the annual custom with each of his elder brothers" [401]

My grandfather's racing debut was announced in the paper on Wednesday 6th July 1898 2:10pm in the Johnstone Plate at Stockbridge, he was 14 years old Charles's patron was his father Tom Cannon, Charles at this time would have been 14 years old about the same age as his father when he first started *"Young Charles Cannon makes his debut in the Johnstone Plate Charlie Cannon the younger brother of Tom, Morny and Kempton Cannon rode his first race his mount being Melanyal he is 14 years old and shaped well."* [402] My grandfather was 6-12 and rode a very good race finishing in 4th place in a field of 10 over a distance of 1 mile. The horse was owned by his father and trained by his brother Tom Junior.

The next race we find him in is the 16:15 Danebury Selling Plate of 5 furlongs with the purse set at £100.00 he is up on a horse called Coral Strand again owned by his father and trained by his brother Tom Junior, he was riding against a field of 12 and in this race were both his accomplished and already famous brothers Morny and Kempton. Another entry has him on Thursday 7th July when he rode in some of the last races at Stockbridge he was only 14 years old and was on a horse called Moon Wave in the All

401 Sheffield Evening Telegraph Racecourse Gossip from Stockbridge (9th July 1896, p.4)
402 Yorkshire Evening Post 6th July 1898.

Figure 154 Charles Cannon 1900 Fathers Colours unknown race Family Collection

Aged Plate of 5 furlongs with a winning purse of £100.00 he was up on a horse called Quassia, 3 years old and owned by his father Tom Cannon, trained by his brother Tom Junior. His first day out he rode against some of the most experienced and skilled jockeys of the turf, there was one more race for my young grandad that day and it was a match and probably the last race of the Stockbridge Course before it closed for good it was between Quassia against Peseta. Quassia and my 14 year old grandfather won.

The closure of the course which we have already covered did not stop the Cannons from racing and in 1899 Charlie wins the Juvenile Plate at Salisbury, new home of the Bibury Club *'The Salisbury two-year-olds was supplied when Madreperla, a daughter of Chelsea and Madrilena, ridden by- little Charles Cannon, the youngest of the famous riding family, carried off a Juvenile Plate the Danebury Youngster rode with great coolness."* [403]

Charles like his brothers was apprenticed to his father Tom and was ready to hitch up his leathers and take his place in the hall of fame besides the rest of his family. Imagine breakfast in their house, I suppose all they did was talk about horses.

---

403 Morning Post - London 10 July 1899 "The Salisbury two-year-olds was supplied when Madreperla, a daughter of Chelsea and Madrilena, ridden by- little Charles Cannon, the youngest of the famous riding family, carried off a Juvenile Plate the Danebury Youngster rode with great coolness,"

Figure 155 Charles Cannon fathers colours Northamptonshire

By 1900 Charles Cannon is starting to ride in bigger races and also winning some too *"C. Cannon rides Admiral Drake in the Liverpool Cup 1900."* [404] as his confidence is building so are the races, next Redcar *"Coastham handicap talent got well away with Pallisburn who was entrusted to the handling of Charles Cannon, youngest of the four brothers bearing that famous name, and he won in a canter the cannons were in strong evidence on Tuesday apart from the success of young Charles, Kempton rode a winner, Mornington by the aid of jurey rose."* [405]

Charles Cannon now 16 years old was riding in the 1900 Cambridgeshire which was a big race, he is now in the elite class of Jockeys and riding against all the big competitors two of whom were his own brothers Kempton and Mornington Cannon. Charles was up on Mr. J. H. Peards Merry Methodist he weighed in at 7 stone 11 and the betting was 100-7[406].

Charles was starting to excel as a jockey and his riding style was being admired as captured in the Morning Post of 1900 after winning the Sandown Park Autumn Handicap of that year *"Charles Cannon whose riding style has been a theme of general admiration lately, accomplished a good performance in driving Blumenaue home a head and a neck in front of Lady Min and May Bruce respectively in the Sandown Park Autumn Handicap, and his talent is such that his services are sure to be in brisk demand for the remainder of the season."* [406] Their father Tom must have been really proud of all four of his sons keeping his name firmly in print. Being Tom Cannon's son meant he had to be successful and the racing world had now started recognizing he was going to be a good jockey *"Young Charles cannon is going to be a jockey worthy of the*

404 Hull Daily Mail 6th November 1900
405 Manchester Courier Lancaster General Advertiser 20th August 1900
406 Morning Post 22nd October 1900, p.2

family. He rode a grand race on Japonica in the Brighton Stakes yesterday holding the rails all the way, and keeping the filly going under pressure from outside the distance [407].

Charles was winning some good races and being quite creative with his riding style *'Gold finger rode hurdle races under national hunt rules. Charlie Cannon who rode the winner had to borrow a jacket owing to the proper colours not being available but he solved the difficulty by turning it inside out.'*[408] Charles also went on to win the Palatine Handicap of 1900 valued at 390 Sovs on board Deep Sea trained by his brother Tom Cannon Junior beating rivals in the race such as L. Reif, D Maher Todd Sloan the cream of the international Jockeys, and was captured by the press of the day:-

"Young Charles Cannon who has fully asserted his right to consideration as a jockey worthy of the famous name he bears, gave two highly credible exhibitions on Saturday in his riding first on Branksome in the Gerard Nursery and next on Deep Sea on who he won the Palatine Handicap in his father's Hoops after a rare set to with Sloan on Zanoni and Maher on Esmerrada II. In each instance the youngster betrayed great strength and skill." [409]

By this time the American Invasion was in full swing and the American jockeys were in high demand but the English jockeys were holding well and Charles Cannon was one of them. *"Except for the Success for Petridge and Holmewood the results are in favour of the Talent, and in the opening races the brothers Mornington and Charles Cannon alone saved the situation from the American Jockeys."* [410]

Charles Cannon at 16 years old was one the first of the English Jockeys the other being his brother Kempton to hitch up his leathers and ride in the American Style as reported in 1900 *"As showing how the American Craze is increasing no more than five American Jockeys were up out of eight horses that went to the post for the Newmarket October Handicap the three English Jockeys being Sam Loates Charlie Cannon and Dalton, the two latter of whom ride in the Yankee Style."* [411]

I think Charles was even the first English jockey to ride in the American style beating Kempton to the post *"I saw several gallops on this bright morning two days ago and was amused to observe that Charlie youngest of the four brothers Cannon had adopted the American Style of riding."* [412] The first record I have found of Charles using it is on 20th July 1900 at Sandown Park *"Murthly raced him out of it*

407 Sunderland Daily Echo and Shipping Gazette 8th August 1900, p.2
408 Sheffield Independent 5th October 1900, p.4
409 Morning Post 24th September 1900, p.2
410 Morning Post 10th October 1900, p.2
411 Sheffield Independent 27th September 1900, p.4
412 Manchester Courier and Lancashire General Advertiser (1st August 1900, p.8)

and won by three parts of a length ridden by young Charlie Cannon who endeavoured to copy the American style."[413]

Charles was excelling at the American style as reported in 1900 on riding at Sandown Park *"Another magnificent piece of riding was that of Charlie Cannon on Blumenauer and to those who believe in the new methods and yet like to see their own countrymen winning, it was gratifying to see the three Chief American Imitators, Haysley and Kempton and Charlie Cannon each having a winning ride."*[414] Charles was riding and training out of Danebury House up until 1901, and was also learning to become a trainer, but after 1901 he moved with his brother Tom Cannon Junior to Chattis Hill a substantial property built for them by their father where they set up as Flat Race Trainers, Danebury was leased to Mr. W.H.Moore for his own training establishment.[358]

1901 had the Cannon brothers retained to ride as follows *"M.Cannon has concluded his arrangements for the next racing season with Kinsclere and Eagerton House Stables as before Kempton Cannon will ride for Mr L. De Rothschild, while Charles Cannon will serve his father and Mr. Fairlie."*[415] Charles Cannon starting to follow in his brothers footsteps and at only 17 years of age he was pitched to ride Royal Rouge in the 1901 Derby but he was changed last minute, *"the only alteration was that J.Thompson had the mount on Royal Rouge and not Charles Cannon."*[416] must have been disappointing but it goes some way to show at how quickly he had come on to ride in larger races.

By 1903 disaster for my grandfather the one thing that all jockeys, boxers and other sports people fear the most the dreaded weight struck, as it had done to his elder brother Tom, due to his increased weight Charles Cannon aged 19 applied for a National Hunt license *"Licenses under rule 93 have been granted to the following jockeys for 1903 Joseph Cain Charles Edward Cannon etc. it will be noted from the list that young Charles Cannon the fourth and youngest son of Tom Cannon whose career as a horseman on the flat was restricted on the account of increasing weight, has been granted a license and his appearance under the changed condition will be watched with interest."*[417] This must have been devastating for my grandfather as flat racing was what the Cannons did, his older brother Tom Junior and his uncle Joe had put weight on to which had forced them to training and steeplechasing.

---

413 Nottingham Evening post 20th July 1900
414 Yorkshire Post and Leeds Inelegance 19th October 1900
415 Dundee Evening Post (27th February 1901, p.5)
416 Yorkshire post Leeds intelligencer (6th June 1901, p.10)
417 Sunderland Daily Echo and Shipping Gazette (11th December 1903, p.4)

But it did not stop Charles like his uncle Joe Cannon he took his National Hunt license and trained to jump hurdles, we see him making his debut before the close of 1903, *"It has been intended that young Charlie Cannon should make his first appearance over Hurdles on a Gelding by Breadknife-Lancarvan but a stupid mistake was made in connection with his entry into the Clifton Hurdle race, a name not having been bestowed upon him prior to nomination."* [418]

In 1904 Charles, rode in a farmer's lightweight race which was restricted to farmers who held land in the area of the Hunt of the Blackmore Vale Hounds or any member of the yeomanry within those limits he was recorded as riding his own horse Queenie and he came in third.

We next find him in 1905 with his debut race over hurdles *"Charles Cannon a younger Brother of the celebrated family made his debut over hurdles on his father's Chrysomela in the three year old hurdle he led to the final obstacle when Shaniboo gave him the go-by."* [419]

In 1906 Charles Cannon is back on the big race scene and what an event he is to ride in the 1906 Derby on Leopold De Rothschild's Minos by St Fresquin-Cratan Belle dark blue and yellow cap, which is great but he has to compete against both his brothers Morny and Kempton who were also in the race [420]. They didn't win but what an amazing experience to have, last time that had been done was when Grandmother Day had seen four of her sons racing in the same race years before back in the 1830's.

By 1907 Charles had gone to France he had been requested to ride for the Pfizer Stables *"Charles Cannon brother to Kempton and Morny Cannon has arrived at Maison Laffitte. He will ride jumping for the Pfizer Stable managed by Campbell."* [421] Charles was declining appearances in the saddle in England as recalled by the press of the time *"Charles Cannon made one of his few appearances in the saddle, when he got up on his father's horse Bertillon for the Ashford selling hurdle."* [422] The same year W.H.Moore vacated Danebury House and it was put up for sale, [437] but the auction bidding never met the reserve so Danebury the family home for the last century was leased out again in 1908 to Mr. Freddy Withington. My grandfather Charles was there as a jockey and assisting as a trainer to Mr Withington who he was also riding for as a

418 Sheffield Daily Telegraph (16th December 1903, p.12)
419 Hull Daily Mail (11th December 1905, p.8)
420 Manchester Courier and Lancashire General Advertiser (30th May 1906, p.9)
421 Sheffield Evening Telegraph (9th March 1907, p.3)
422 Manchester Courier and Lancashire General Advertiser (28th Feb 1907, p.2)

jockey and winning as well as can be seen, *"Madeley Plate 103 Sovs 1 mile on Lord Fitzwilliams foresight by Carbine-Chaffinch C.Cannon winner trained by Withington Stockbridge."* [423]

By1907-1908 he was due to marry a lady of his father's choosing, it was one of his cousins but Charles declined and this caused major problems and rifts in the family which we will pick up on later. Charles was made an offer as a gift from his father upon condition of marriage to take over the Chattis Hill Establishment from his brother Tom Junior who was leaving to go to Compton to set up there to train for Leopold De-Rothschild as private trainer. After declining this offer Charles moved to Llangunllo, Newcastle in Emlyn, Cardiganshire, Wales where he set up training the horses for Sir Marteine and Lady Lloyd who were very well acquainted with the Cannon family. Charles was there in 1911 training their horses and looking after the hunt where Sir Marteine Lloyd kept a pack of Beagles known as the Bronwydd Beagles. Charles was registered as living in the grounds of Bronwydd Castle the Lloyds of Bronwydd were a powerful old Welsh land owning family and the grandparents of Freddy Withington the Jockey turned Trainer who was by 1908 renting Danebury and who Charles was working with before.

Between the years of 1910 and 1913 Charles Cannon was riding in lots of Hurdling Races outside of my interest to record them here, but there was an encounter at Wigston where Charles was riding one of his fathers' horses in an important hurdle race the Wigston Hurdles, but was thrown off. *"Mr. Tom Cannon Senior and Kempton Cannon came to see Leckford run in the Wigston Hurdle race. Charles Cannon was put up on the son of Morganatic, he fell at the first hurdle but was remounted, at the second he suddenly whipped round and unshipped Cannon who was quickly up again but could not get the horse over so returned to the paddock."* [424] He must have been annoyed at that especially in front of his dad and brother. This was perhaps the last time the Cannon colours of scarlet and white hoops were seen on a course.

In 1914 immediately after the outbreak of the First World War Charles, against his father's strong wishes, on September 5th 1914 joined Queen Alexandria's 19th Hussars of the line 3rd Gloucestershire Regiment as a private, he joined for three years with the colours at Tidworth. Charles and Ronald were praised in the paper of the time when speaking about jockeys being recruited into the War, *"It may be of interest the question of recruiting among*

---

423 Nottingham Evening post 11th October 1909
424 Nottingham Evening post 25th November 1913

jockeys to mention that Charles Cannon joined a regiment of Hussars directly the war broke out, and Ronald Cannon has been doing such good work at the front in one of the Flying Corps that he has been sent back to Sheerness to perfect his knowledge of Sea Planes which is a big compliment the Admiralty could pay to anyone who is only 19 years old the two are the youngest sons of Tom Cannon." [425]

Charles was in the 3rd Brigade Glostershire regiment stationed at Bristol, moved on to Abbey Wood Woolwich and then to Gravesend in May 1915. Charles was in the expeditionary force that was sent to France, he fought in some of the early Battles of the Great War.

On 25th August 1915 Charles applied for a commission as an officer he was registered at the Grosvenor Hotel as his permanent address and awarded a temporary commission as reported by the London Gazette, *"Special Reserve of Officers the undermentioned to be Second Lieutenants on (probation) dated 27th August 1915, Royal Field Artillery Charles Edward Cannon"* [426]he had served 356 days as a private and was now a second lieutenant, RFA were horse drawn units responsible for deployment of the medium sized guns and howitzers to the front line.

Charles by 1916 was attached to the IV Division 74th Brigade in Y.4 Trench Mortar Battery, which was a medium size mortar battery. Trench mortar batteries or T.M.Bs: was a new form of artillery developed to meet the conditions of war on the Western Front. The RFA provided the manpower for the heavier mortars; a T.M.B was made up of (4 mortars of the same type) 2 Officers, 1 Sergeant, 4 Corporals or Lance-Corporals, 16 Privates, 2 Batmen.

On the 29th August 1915 Charles Cannon in the 74th Brigade of the R.F.A entered the theatre of war landing at Le Havre as soon as the division landed it became part of the New Guards Division. Charles Y.4 Mortar Battery joined the 4th Division in Feb 1916

Charles was walking in the shadow of the valley of death he was about to embark on the first battle of the Somme a battle that would be his last.

By 16th July 1916 belonging to R.F.A 74 Brigade Y.4 T.M.Battery Charles had contracted trench fever; (later to be shellshock) he left his unit on 16th July 1916 leaving France (Calais) aboard a hospital ship arriving in Dover July 24th. I researched trench fever as I had never heard of it before. The

425 Yorkshire Post and Leeds Intelligencer 19th December 1914, p.12
426 Supplement to the London Gazette 8706 1st September 1915

disease is categorized as a 5-day fever. The onset of symptoms is sudden with high fever, severe headache, back pain and leg pain and a fleeting rash contracted in the trenches of the First World War from louse bites. Trench fever can last for weeks and even months and some after effects are neurasthenia or shellshock. By 16th September 1916 Charles had recovered from his trench fever but had lost many of his teeth to which he received dentures.

Orders dated 08th December 1916 refer "Second Lieutenant C.E.Cannon R.F.A reported for duty with the 66th Divisional Artillery Colchester on the 15th instant and has been   posted to the 330th Brigade, R.F.A"[427] On 8th December 1916 Charles is home on Medical Board. Leave. By 1st of July 1917 Charles was promoted to Lieutenant on 14th May 1918 Charles was placed on the retired list of active service.

On 2nd May 1918 Charles aged 34 had served a total of 44/12 34/12 at home 10/12 abroad he was invalided out of the army with neurasthenia *"This officer was returned from France in July 1916 with Trench Fever after six weeks in Hospital developed stomach trouble, carried on 8 months in 1917 on active service then taken ill with Neurasthenia and chronic Dyspepsia admitted to Helena Hospital 07/01/18"* the Doctor treating my Grandfather wrote this of his condition, *"He suffers with fits of depression vomiting of a purely functional mature alternating with days of comparative fitness. In the opinion of the board his state of health is so unstable as to make it impossible that he will ever be fit for further Military Services."* [427]

I did not know what neurasthenia was until I researched it, it is shell shock I felt so sorry for my grandfather and for the other soldiers that had contracted this. He became injured in the Battle of the Somme receiving shell shock, shot through the head and mustard gassed; additionally Charles Cannon was buried alive. He once told my uncle Peter how he had been riding the horses pulling the gun carriages to the front, it was not uncommon to glance around and see his comrades riding beside him without a head. He, like many others, rarely spoke of the war, but they could never forget the experiences. We can however mention that he received the Silver War Badge, the 1914-15 Star, Victory Medal and British War Medal for his services.

During the Great War Charles met and fell in love with my grandmother Miss Dorothy Thrush who was 15 years old at the time, she was supposedly descended from the Earl of Berkley, who was hung for treason.

---

427 National Archives WO339/37881 dated 19th Dec 1916 Eastern Command

Dorothy was a singer and had trained her voice with the famous Gracie Fields, she came from Bristol where her father Thomas Thrush was a boot maker, and like his father before him that was their family business and quite a contrasting life it would have been Charles from glitz and glamour, Dorothy from a quiet village in Fishponds Bristol.

Charles Cannon's father Tom had wished and planned for Charles to marry a girl from the Day family, Leonard Day's daughter Miss Annie Florence Day which would have been his first cousin, I think it had all been arranged since they were young. Against his father's strong wishes Charles and Dorothy married in December 1916 at Bristol and like his brother Mornington, who had divorced already, Charles was going against his father. For this we were told he was disinherited by his father.

Tom Charles's father died at the Grosvenor Hotel, Stockbridge on 13th July 1917 and left a personal estate of £5,000 none of Tom's sons from his first marriage with Kate received anything, this could partly be due to the fact that they had already earnt enough money of their own, and Tom Junior had a large training ground in Compton, Berkshire. Kempton and

Figure 156 Charles Cannon at Auntie Nina's wedding

Morny had earnt enough in jockey fees. That left Charles and Ronald, Tom Cannon his father had left his entire estate to Ronald Portman Cannon, Charles received nothing, reputed as punishment for marrying my grandmother Dorothy and not the lady of his father's choosing.

After the war Charles had seen it all and spent two years recovering in various hospitals including Netley Abbey in Southampton, the injuries he received during the Great War ensured his career as a jockey and public life would never be the same. Charles was invalided out of the army in the early part of 1918, with neurasthenia or shell shock, prior to this he had caught trench fever in France and was ill with it for three months. He had, like many other men of that day, sacrificed much and received so little in return.

After the war Charles moved to Newmarket with his family. Charles set up as a trainer of horses and was soon sending out winners, on 30th June 1923 "Wolsey Handicap, Dowser, Sir Walter Gilbey Winner trained by C.Cannon. One of Charles Cannons Patrons was Sir Walter Gilbey "he carried on training in Newmarket until 1926 he was by now 42 years old."

Charles next moved to Wiltshire where he worked for the Duke of Beaufort his regimental Colonel in the Royal Hussars, Gloucestershire Regiment. The Duke used to ride with the Cannons on hunts with his father at Danebury when Tom was Master of the Danebury Harriers and with John Day before him. Among other guests that rode with the Cannons was King Edward VII. Charles looked after the hunters when they rode, in the Dukes famous Badminton Hunt. In 1926 Dorothy gave birth to Peter Charles Cannon, they lived at West Littleton near Chippen Sideburg, South Gloucestershire and still with the Beaufort Hunt that would use the village green as a meeting place.

Charles was a very talented pianist, and once played for King Edward VII in the Royal Albert hall before the Great War broke out. Charles then moved to Fritham in the New Forest to stay with the priest who was attached to his regiment in the war.

By 1930 he was still training horses as can be seen on 30th October 1930 *"cowling claiming and selling plate of 200 sovereigns for 2 year olds Clare House Mr. J.M.Clayton trainer C.Cannon, jockey J.Leach."*[428] But the training was nothing like it was before, perhaps this was due to the injuries sustained in the Great War. These injuries eventually meant Charles could not work properly anymore and had to rely on his army pension of £7 and 9 shillings a month and as many others did after the war he suffered with nerves, which stopped him going out much so he withdrew and retired from public life.

In 1942 Tom Cannon Junior, his brother, died and left Charles £500 in his will, Charlie decided to buy the house that he lived in for £230. From all accounts the family and childhood of my mother was a happy one, a hard one but full of stories. She was the youngest of nine children and would

---

428 Dundee Courier (30th October 1930, p.8)

recount how her father would spend his days repairing watches and fixing clocks, or playing the piano while my grandmother Dorothy sang, it sounded like a happy home.

Charles and Dorothy had their first child in 1916 in Bristol but the child died at birth, due to it being 16Ib, they called her Evelyn. Joan was next in 1919, she

Figure 157 Charles and Dorothy with Uncle Morny and Connie at their Wedding

was born in Newmarket, then Nina Gladys 1921 also in Newmarket, Thomas Mornington, also born in Newmarket 1923, then Peter born West Chipenham Wiltshire 1926, all the children had a good army education, next came Margarete, in West Wellow 1930, then Mornington Kempton 1931, Sheila Mary in 1939, Terrence Leonard, my uncle Terry, in 1942, and finally my beautiful mother Patricia in1944.

Charlie's sister Margaret Kate Piggott and Ernest Piggott used to visit at Christmas to which Ernest would call my Uncles Tom and Peter to box on the front lawn. The first person to draw blood would win a sovereign. Uncle Peter went to visit Mornington Cannon in Hove around 1957, to which Mornington said "he did not think he would live this long. "He did not arrange his finances right and it was lucky that Lester came along when he did." My Uncle Tom was apprenticed as a jockey and went on to ride many races, he knew Lester and Lester's father Keith was his first cousin.

Charles Edward Cannon was the last of the Cannons of Danebury, and in June 1968 he said he was just going upstairs to lie down and not long after he had passed away peacefully in his sleep. All his papers and books like his brothers and fathers before him were burnt. I presume in accordance with his instructions. My Auntie saved one of the books which was very thin on contents as people had unfortunately removed much of the inside over the years, and kept it secretly, that was the book that started all of this Appendix 2: Tom Cannon Garlogs (Family Book)

CAPTAIN RONALD PORTMAN CANNON R.N.A.S

Ronald was born 22nd August 1894 in Bournemouth and was the fifth and final son of Thomas Cannon from his marriage with Madam Jessie Cameron. Ronald escued the turf being more interested in flying, when young his father Tom sent him to flying school, he was recorded as an aviation pupil with Hewlett and Blondean an early flying school in Luton prior to World War 1. He was recorded as working there in Civilian Life. Although he had no direct influence on Horse Racing he was quite amazing as a Pilot in the Great War and I wanted to remember him here.

As soon as the war broke out in 1914 Ronald joined up with his brother Charles who had already joined the Hussars. *'It may be of interest the question of recruiting among jockeys to mention that Charles Cannon joined a regiment of Hussars directly the war broke out, and Ronald Cannon has been doing such good work at the front in one of the Flying Corps that he has been sent back to Sheerness to perfect his knowledge of Sea Planes which is a big compliment the Admiralty could pay to anyone who is only 19 years old the two are the youngest sons of Tom Cannon.'* [425] Ronald joined the R.N.A.S Royal Naval Air Service, a for runner for the R.A.F and could already fly planes prior to the war but entered the C.F.S or Central Flying School based at Upavon Aerodrome in September of 1914. The Central Flying School trained Pilot Instructors, so Ronald at only 19 years old was to become a Pilot Instructor.

During Sep 1914 the Navy, had conducted two of the first ever Ariel bombing raids in history. The Pilots were tasked with flying from Amsterdam to bomb the Zeppelin Hangers in Cologne and Dusseldorf Germany. Those hangers housed the Zeppelins that were conducting deadly bombing missions. Churchill and Captain Murray Suerter who were in charge of Air operations for the Navy did not know how to attack a Zeppelin in the air so they were attacked on the ground. This mission was a first for aviation anywhere and had never been tried before so extremely dangerous. By all accounts the attacks were not a success and only one plane managed to deliver its bombs.

Ronald Portman Cannon must have been an exceptional pilot as by November 1914 he was picked to conduct a secret raid on the Zeppelin base at Friedrichshafen in Germany. On his service records[429] we can see that he transferred to Belfort in France via Le Harve the unit to which he

---

[429] National Archives, PRO, London, R.N.A.S Pilot Service RecordsGBM_075_0_0456

was transferring to was "Special Services Belfort" Belfort was the destination that the raid was launched from as told by Flight magazine of the time. "A special flight of four Avro 504s had been formed at Manchester under squadron commander P. Shepard and the pilots were Sqn. Cdr. E. F. Briggs, Flt. Cdr. J. T. Babbington, Flt. L T. S. V. Sippe and Flt. Sub-Lt R. P. Cannon the Avro's officers and eleven air mechanics arrived at Belfort by night on November 13th 1914."[430] They settled in and made their preparations.

On the 21st November Four Avro 504 Biplanes took part in the raid on the Zeppelin Hangers at Friedrichshafen and left the R.N.A.S station at Ostend. *"The Avro's left Belfort at five minute intervals, Sqn. Cdr Briggs were first to go on No 873, followed by Babbington on 875 and Sippe on 874: Cannon's machine broke its tail skid and was unable to take off."*[430]. The mission was rendered a success.

After that mission and in Dec 1914 Ronald was posted to the Isle of Grain in Kent where he was to test pilot the Sea Planes he was only 19 years old. Shortly after he was transferred to the Dover Sea Plane Station where he would remain for two years. By 27 October 1916 he was transferred to Dundee and then on 22 February 1917 he was moved back to Calshot where the South Coast Sea Plane Station was.

---

[430] Flight Magazine 9th July 1954 p.43

Ronald was next commissioned as one of the officers to form No 6 Wing of the R. N. A. S. A newly formed unit whose task was solely to prevent submarine activity in the Adriatic and Mediterranean Sea. Ronald moved to Tranto Southern Italy to where No 6 Wing RNAS was formed on the 10 March 1917, 6 Wing was then split to form No.66 and 67 Wing Ronald was attached to 66 wing who supported the allied offensive in the attack of Durazzo dropping an estimated 5 tons of Bombs, the bombing ability seems to have advanced such a long way in such a short time. Ronald Stayed in the Middle East until 22nd March 1919 at which point he fell ill and was transferred to the Cairo Hospital. He was transferred on the 13th June to Alexandria Royal Hospital and then on the 22nd June to Netley Hospital in Southampton then on the 8th November 1919 he was retired from the service. Ronald was injured in the War like his brother Charles they like so many others were lucky to return home, but also like so many others had to carry horrific memories and injuries throughout the rest of their lives.

Ronald Died at his home in St Albans1951 aged 56.

Joseph Cannon 1849-1933

Figure 158 Joe Cannon Lordship House Racing Illustrated 1895

Joseph Cannon 1849-1933

When speaking of so many great horsemen in one family it is easy to get lost, Joseph Cannon was younger brother to Tom by two years, and like Tom had been provided with the upbringing of a horseman by their father Thomas Hopkins Cannon who was a horse trader[431]. Joseph excelled at was much more the trainer of horses than a jockey and he would go on to have a large number of horses under his care at Newmarket, although as a rider he did win some great races his robust frame was considered more suitable to that of a steeple chase rider than a flat jockey.

Figure 159 Joe Cannon Heroes and Heroines p.223

Joseph Cannon was born on 10th December 1849 at 12:20 young brother to my great grandfather Tom Cannon of Danebury Joe was first educated at Eton by Dr. Hawtrys School the Provost of Eton College then by Dr. Powney also at Eton. Son of a Windsor horse dealer, Joe had his life cut out for him. Before Joe Cannon was ten years old he was already well known by Etonians as a fierce rider in the Queen's Staghounds as was his older brother Tom *"Joe had started racing proper at the age of 12 and had entered a stable"*

Joe Cannon unlike his older brother Tom had turned to training and started at Kentford House near Newmarket, it was said that to this he was better suited but also like many jockeys he had put on the dreaded weight which was no good for the flat. He first started training for Captain Machel who had sent his jumping horses to Joe Cannon at Kentford where he was based then.

Joseph aged 27 years established himself as one of the country's leading jump jockeys and opened his racing career by winning the Grand National for Captain Machell on Regal in 1876, I have a commentary on the race below, the horse was 5 years old which was exceptional:- *"Chandos, however, the immaculate hurdle-jumper, was less skilful over a country. After breaking a thick*

---

431 Henry Charles Howard Earl of Suffolk and Berkshire, William George Craven, Arthur George Coventry Arthur Alfred Thomas Watson, Racing And Steeple Chasing, (1893, p.371)"Joseph Cannon, brother of the perhaps still more famous Tom, both of whom, sons of a horse-dealer, had been almost brought up in the saddle"

rail with such violence that a piece of it flew back and nearly knocked Robert I'Anson, who was riding Shifnal, out of his saddle, Chandos fell, just after Jewitt had shouted to Cannon that he was going on to win; but the second string was much better than had been generally supposed, and, riding with much vigour and judgment — as, indeed, he always did Cannon got the hors-e safely home a neck in front of Congress. Regal was, it may be remarked, the second five-year-old that had won the race." [431]After winning that race there was no stopping him and

Figure 160 Young Joe and Morny Cannon Joe Senior Lordship Farm 1896 Racing Illustrated

Cannon assumed total control of Captain Machells Bedford Lodge Stables Newmarket, where he sent out the Petrarch the same year to win the 2,000 Guineas.

Two years later in in 1878 Joseph Cannon encouraged Lord Lonsdale to buy the horse Pilgrimage, and Pilgrimage was added to the stable That same year Cannon brought home the 1,000 Guineas with Pilgrimage, if that was not enough he added another Classic the same year by winning the 2,000 Guineas, both times ridden by his brother Tom Cannon, it was a credit to the family that both brothers brought home a double together and with the same horse. Another two years passed and Joseph sent out Petronal to win the 2,000 Guineas of 1880, amazing.

In 1882 Joseph was asked by Lord Lonsdale to be his trainer, the same year it was done. Joe was now the private trainer to Lord Roseberry and had moved to Lordship House where he was assisted by his son young Joe at that time the stables were packed having about 80 horses in training, Joe won for the Lord the Great Metropolitan with Roysterer and also the Manchester November Handicap no less than 4 times.

JOSEPH CANNON 1849-1933

Joe left Lord Roseberry and set up at Grafton House with Patrons such as George Lambton, author of "Men and Racehorses I have known", Charles Kinsky and Baron Max de Tuyll.

As a trainer they had their own specific diet for the horses to eat, I have detailed the diet the Cannons used for their horses and also when they were fed:-"*His light-pressure diet consists of a feed, crushed oats and chaff — not long hay — at 7 a.m.; a snack at noon, and another feed when done up at 5 p.m. This is one course less than we fancy is given by most trainers. In all that appertains to teaching the chaser his business, English trainers such as Tom Cannon, his brother Joseph, Richard Marsh, James Jewitt, Mr. Arthur Yates, and others, have no superiors in the world.*"[432]

His Grace the Duke of Beaufort thought extremely highly of the Danebury school of Horsemen and of the Cannon brothers Joseph and Tom, with regard to training as well as riding. See racing and steeple chase riding.

Joe had a love of boxing as did Joe Junior or Boxer as he was known along with Morny and my grandfather. Joe Cannon and his sons were also dab hands at golf, first Joe Senior then Joe Junior and finally Noel Cannon were presidents of the Royal Worlington and Newmarket Golf Club a very exclusive nine hole course. Noel Cannon and James Herbert or "Boxer" was like the rest of the Cannons he was going to be in horse racing.

NOEL VICTOR SHARP CANNON

Noel Victor Sharp was the most accomplished horseman of Joseph's children and was born at Lordship in 1897 Noel was like his father to become an accomplished trainer. In 1936 he set up as trainer in Bedford House Stables Newmarket where his father had started in 1874. Noel Cannon moved into the famous Druids Lodge Stables on Salisbury Plain with a millionaire owner of flour Mr. James Voase Rank owner of Rank Hovis as his patron. In 1938 Noel Cannon sent out Scottish Union for Mr. Rank with Jimmy Carslake as jockey to win the St Leger Stakes that was his first Classic in the bag. A few years later Noel was at it again and in 1943 he sent out Why Hurry winning the Epsom Oaks ridden by Charlie Elliot and owned by Jimmy Rank

In 1949 Noel Cannon was responsible for bringing Scobie Breasley over to England to race for him. After two years in the United Kingdom Breasley was homesick and he returned to Australia in 1951 with his wife. This was

---

432 Henry Charles Howard Earl of Suffolk and Berkshire, William George Craven, Arthur George Coventry Arthur Alfred Thomas Watson, Racing And Steeple Chasing, (1893, p.126)

Figure 161 Noel 23, Joe 71 and Boxer Cannon 29 summer 1920 Lordship Farm Noel Cannon Family Collection

not to last and by 1953 they were back and Noel Cannon had another Patron a Mr. Jack Dewar who was in the business of whiskey.

In 1954 Noel Cannon sent out Festoon with Breasley on-board winning the 1,000 Guineas, and his third Classic Race as trainer. That same year 1954 Breasly was about to bang heads with the wonder boy Lester Piggott 21 years his junior starting the most confrontational relationship between Jockeys the turf would ever see famously telling Breasley in a race to "move over grandad". Noel had a family tie in this and was cousin to Lester's grandmother and my great auntie Margaret Cannon.

There is a race named after Noel Cannon at Salisbury called the Noel Cannon Memorial Handicap run over 1 mile, Noel was the last member of the Cannon family to train horses.

THE PROPERTIES OF TOM CANNON:

THE PROPERTIES OF TOM CANNON

Tom Cannon was known for investing his money heavily in land and properties, some people have accounted that he had earnt the equivalent of six million in today's money from riding fees alone and that was without his business ventures. In this section we will explore what my great grandfather owned. Most of the properties were purchased after 1890 once he had left Danebury and handed over the reins to his son Tom Junior; by 1908 he had amassed a huge portfolio not just in Stockbridge but in the surrounding Nether Wallop and Broughton area as well. 1908 saw a change, something happened to cause him to draw up an Abstract of Title[433] for his free hold lands in Nether Wallop and Broughton. He had control in 1892 of nearly, 2,340 acres of land and nearly most of it, he owned as free hold.

You will see in this section that being an owner and trainer consisted of a great deal more than knowledge of the horse, money, influence, connections, it was not just a job it was a way of life built over many years and in the case of Danebury, it was an empire handed from father to son.

Above all things trainers needed land for the horses to train on and it needed to be secure land and if it could be avoided not the type that could be rented. Racing was a cut throat business, you could invest years building up your business and then have it taken away the next day when the lease ran out on the land and was not renewed. As had been so painfully seen in 1898 and the closure of the Stockbridge Course.

Danebury and the Cannons and the Days were not just jockeys and trainers they also had the racecourse to consider, so for them in addition to the land required for the horses, lavish houses and estates were also needed to both entertain their guests and patrons and also to provide accommodation for royalty who when they visited, would have many servants to accommodate. On top of all this you would need a reliable network of suppliers and retained cooks to feed both the workers and guests. The retinue to run Danebury would have been huge as seen in the1840's when John Barham Day gave evidence at the gaming committee on the size of his business. He counted every day that 35 people would sit down to dinner with him and he would employ over 100 people in the running of the establishment.

---

433 Hampshire Record Office, 50M81/E/T27 ,1908 "Abstract of title of Mr. Thomas Cannon to freehold hereditaments and premises situate in the parishes of Broughton and Nether Wallop The premises comprise: Chattis Hill Farm (also known as The Down or Seven Barrow Farm), citing from 1847-1890; land later known as Darfield farm, citing from 1755-1890; Garlogs House and Nine Mile Water Farm (313 acres) in Broughton and Nether Wallop, citing 1888; other land in Broughton, citing from 1888-1889'

Since his time, Danebury had grown and so had the number of horses trained there and with it the tastes of the individual patrons and on many occasions Tom Cannon would find himself having to cater to such distinguished and powerful individuals as the future King Edward VII so the properties were both lavish and fashionable. Tom needed to be the most gracious and entertaining of hosts with a well-stocked wine cellar. I would like to take the reader on a trip around some of the properties that the Days and then Tom Cannon owned, this is not all of them but this provides an idea of the scale of the operation.

THE ELMS OR SNAILS CREEP

Figure 162 the Elms Stockbridge 1870 Family Pictures

The Elms which is situated in Longstock opposite the Book Inn is where Tom Cannon first lived and was probably a gift by his father in law and employer John Day of Danebury upon marrying his daughter Kate. *"At the close of this year 1860 Cannon removed to Marlborough where he remained until 1865 with on his marriage with one of John Day's Daughters he settles himself on Houghton Down in a Cottage called the Elms."* [307] King Edward when he was Prince of Wales used to have his dinner here sometimes after the races, and many of Tom and Kate's children were born here.

Tom Cannon also owned a substantial amount of land in Houghton one piece was called Home Meadow which was in and around the Boot Inn. Cannon purchased Home Meadow as recorded in the Deeds of the Boot on 13th December 1876 from William Lywood, and then purchased more on December 24th 1878. By April the fourth 1899 Cannon sold it to William White. [434]

---

[434] Hampshire Record Office Deeds Boot Inn 4M92/D7/8

DANEBURY:

Figure 163 Danebury 1895 Racing Illustrated

Danebury House was my family's home where generations of my ancestors lived, my grandfather Charles lived in the Turret or Tower. Danebury remained one of the most successful breeding and training establishment in the country, I have included a brief description of the establishment below as we have already covered it in previous chapter. It consisted in 1907 of approximately 998 acres of land and many out buildings and tenements. Part of the sale was Place Farm which included 312 of those 998 acres. Danebury did not always look like this the first image we have of Danebury that was painted in 1848 painted by Abraham Cooper titled Danebury a

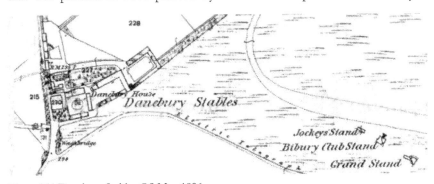

Figure 164 Danebury Stables OS Map 1896

Figure 24 Landscape of Danebury viewed from Chattershill by Abraham Cooper R.A 1848

view from Chattishill. The below is captured from the sale advertisement.

"Of picturesque appearance reached by a gravelled drive and overlooking Home Yard which is also gravelled and the centre laid out in flower beds and shaded by a finely grown chestnut with a lawn at the west end. Entered through a lobby with tiled floor and stained glass lights it contains, on the ground floor, spacious entrance hall heated by a radiator, drawing room 21ft by 19ft including bay, fitted with marble mantel, modern tile stove hearth and French casement window. A well-proportioned dining room 24ft by 16ft including bay, morning or business room 15ftby 12ft 3in, lavatory and WC.

On the first floor seven beds and dressing rooms bath room H&C and WC. There are two rooms used as day and night nurseries and two servants bedrooms shut off from the foregoing and reached by a separate stair. In the tower is an additional bedchamber."

"Amongst the patrons of the Danebury Stable, may be mentioned, Lord George Bentinck, the Duke of Athol, Viscount Palmerston, Lords Dorchester, Sligo and Howth, Sir J.B.Mills, Bart, Sir E.B.Baker, Sir L.Glyn, Messrs. Gully, Biggs, Farquharson, Wreford, Etwall, and in the more recent times the Maruess of Hastings, the Marquis of Anglesey, the Duke of Beaufort, Sir F. Johnston and many others." [437]

Some of the amazing horses trained and bred in Danebury, over the years and captured in the Sale Particulars, "Amongst the Numerous Winners of Classic Races Trained here were the following, Viz: Pussy, winner of the Oaks 1824, Bay Middleton, winner of the Derby 1836, Ellis winner of the

Figure 165 Danebury House after the Refurb 1884 Family Collection

St Leger 1836, Venison, Cardinal Puff, Spume, Crucifix, winner of the Oaks 1840, Pyrrhus 1st the winner of the Derby 1846, Mendicant, winner of the Oaks 1846 Cossack winner of the Derby 1847m Cymba, winner of the Oaks 1848, Andover winner of the Derby 1854, Mince pie, winner of the Oaks 1856, Siberia winner of the 1000 Guineas, Siberia winner of the 1000 Guineas 1865, Repulse winner of the 1000 Guineas 1866, Hero winner of the Goodwood Cup, Ceylon winner of the Grand Prix, Lecturer winner of the Ceasarwitch 1866, Gold Cup and Alexandria plate Ascot, 1867, Vauban winner of the Newmarket Biennial 2000 Guineas Prince of Wales Stakes 1867, Saucebox winner of the St Leger, Trumpeter-Lady Elizabeth, The Earl, Duke-Athena, Mameluke, Rustic, Europa and many more."[437]

Danebury House was first a cottage constructed by James Blunt prior to 1831 then John Barham added to it later. By 1848 we have our first image, **Figure 24 Landscape of Danebury viewed from Chattershill by Abraham Cooper R.A 1848**John Day further added stables, and after all that Tom Cannon pulled most of it down in 1883 and rebuilt it as shown in a picture above taken the same year.

'By the way it may be here mentioned that the new Tenant has decided to pull the house down with the exception of the kitchen and its offices and the premises will be considerably enlarged when rebuilt. This step will of course render Coopers landscape of Danebury from Chattershill all the more interesting and valuable, and at the price it must be on account of old associations be considered a bargain To its late owner successor.

Already the repairs and general overhauling of the stabling are going to assume a somewhat dilapidated aspect it has been nearly completed. And it will not now be long before the large racing stud under the care of Tom Cannon will be sheltered under one roof

at Danebury. Though of course considerable time must necessarily elapse before the Dwelling house is ready for Habitation. The shrubbery in front is to be all together remodelled and by the way it may here be noted that the old paddock on the ace course is to be converted into a promenade lawn, tastefully laid out with flower beads, and the

Figure 166 Danebury Lodge 1883 (Family Collection)

saddling enclosure will in future be on the other side, so it will be seen." [435]

Tom Cannon also put large underground water tanks in for the horses as previously there was only a well to which I feel sorry for the stable lad who would have to run to the well all day for water for 100 horses, that must have been a full time job.

The remodelling works to Danebury were completed a year later on 2nd July 1884, and Tom Cannon was as usual throwing a party to celebrate and inviting everybody to it, as captured by the press "Danebury the New Danebury I mean is now finished and very perfect in all its details of Luxury and Comfort is Tom Cannons new home, he kept open house these three days and to lunch was everyone's duty, the club enclosure was crowded but as by a new rule a member can only introduce one lady, there was a great searching for unattached men all Hampshire was there and a good many London faces too." [435]

The Danebury Estate was advertised as 9 lots, 6 of those lots were under mortgage including the house, and they were consolidated into one mortgage by 1866. The remaining 3 lots of the 998 acre estate were owned by James Blunt who was the son of Walter Blunt, in turn son of Sir Henry Blunt 2nd Baronet of Wallop House. James Blunt died in 1832 it appears he owned a small part of the estate consisting of 3 cottages with 38 and 26 acre parcels of land. [436]

---

435 Hampshire Advertiser 5th July 1884
436 Hampshire Record Office, 46M84/F67/3, "Danebury Nether Wallop(998 acres 6th May 1907) properties include: stables complete with racecourse, Danebury House, corn and grist mill, three cottages and a detached tenement"

THE GRAVEYARD, DANEBURY.
The graves of Bay Middleton (ob. 1856) and Crucifix (ob. 1857).

Figure 167 Danebury Horse Cemetery

By 1898 the ownership of the Danebury Estate was split between Tom Cannon who owned a large portion of the land and house. Vaudrey Barker Mill who owned land on the Longstock side that ran across the straight mile and the part of the downs known as the bush. The rest of Danebury was owned by the descendants of Walter Blunt or the Blunt family Mrs. Bigwood and Miss Blunt.[334]

In September 1898 Tom Cannon Senior vacated Danebury for good and moved permanently to his mansion Garlogs leaving Tom Junior there but by all accounts he was still training horses out of Danebury and was there in 1901. Danebury staged the marriage of Tom Junior in 1908, after which it was leased to Mr. W.H.Moore who took up the stables for his own racing purposes. For the Cannons many guests there was a private Lodge built within the grounds. Tom Junior had moved into Chattishill by now to train his horses which had been built by Tom Senior. It would be interesting to know what arrangement the owners of the land had come to with. Tom Cannon regarding the Dwelling House as a few years earlier in 1883 Cannon spent a fortune having the existing house pulled down and rebuilt and that is the house that is there today.

Danebury came up for auction on 28th August 1901 and then again on 6th May 1907 with 998 [437] acres, but it never reached its reserve so was kept. The highest bid was £12,000 which did not make the reserve so was not sold. Danebury remained leased. In 1915 Danebury, was put up for sale, and eventually purchased. It was to become the home of Lord Glanely, who was using it for his stud [438], it is unclear if he purchased the house or even lived there because by all accounts it was still rented to Freddy Withington.[439] Danebury was advertised for sale again in 27th June 1918 [440]

---

437 Hampshire Record Office, 46M84/F67/8, "Danebury Nether Wallop(350 acres) Properties include: Danebury House, training grounds and stabling for race horses and stands and accommodation for jockeys"
438 Newmarket, *Chapters From Turf History*, 1922 "This Property was put up for sale and brought by Lord Glanley" (Chapters From Turf History, 1922)
439 *The Badminton Magazine Of Sports And Past Times*, Mr. Fred Withington is now the tenant

with 350 acres of land. Danebury stables and residence was sold with 555 acres of land in 1958 for £36,500. Finally in 1958 Danebury was sold with 555 acres of land for £36,800.

Danebury has a horse cemetery which is located in the Danebury Yard very near to the house previously marked by an old chestnut tree that it was said was planted by Mrs. Day my 5 times grandmother when they moved there prior to 1831, Under that tree is buried many famous horses Bay Middleton,Crucifix.

---

of Danebury, long associated with Tom Cannon who succeeded his father in law John Day 1916 p. 319
440 Hampshire Record Office, 46M84/F67/8 Danebury Nether Wallop (350 acres) 27th June 1918 Properties include: Danebury House, training grounds and stabling for race horses and stands and accommodation for jockeys.

GARLOGS ESTATE

Figure 168 Approach to Garlogs Racing Illustrated 1895

Tom Cannon purchased Garlogs estate for £10,700 on 19th August 1889[441] it included the Nine Mile Water Farm of 313 acres, the combined estate was about 900 acres. It was purchased for Tom Cannon as perhaps his retirement home with Kate, but sadly Kate died in 1892 and Garlogs was set up as a breeding stud.[442] I have rescued a write up on Garlogs in the press of the day, it sounds amazing. *"Tom Cannon is probably unique, inasmuch as he undoubtedly knows more about, race riding, horse-training, and jockey-making than any man breathing. It was to find out some interesting facts with regard to the making of jockeys that I recently paid the renowned jockey a visit at his magnificent residence at Garlogs, with its well-stocked trout stream and game preserves. The interior of the house is reminiscent of a shop of the Goldsmiths' Company, as many of the rooms are dotted over with silver cups, and other examples of the silversmith's art, won by his own racehorses in some of the most important events on the turf. It is not to be wondered at that the place teems with exceedingly interesting mementoes and priceless pictures of equine racing celebrities and racing plates, horseshoes worn by famous racers—a veritable*

441 Hampshire Record Office, 50M81/E/T27, Abstract of the Title of Thomas Cannon 1908
442 Lancashire Evening Post 2nd December 1901

Figure 169 Garlogs House view across the ornamental lake 1895 Racing Illustrated

"turf museum. The library is probably the only room of its kind in England. A wooden fresco runs round the walls, and on it Miss Cannon, who shines as an artist, has executed in poker work remarkably good likenesses of some of the best horses ridden by her father—Shotover (Derby), Geheimness (Oaks), Busybody (Oaks), Ormonde, Ackworth, Pilgrimage, Isonomy, Robert the Devil (St. Leger), and Humewood." [443]

After 1901 Tom Cannon put Garlogs up for sale but it did not sell and he tried to sell it again in 1902 by which time it had been changed dramatically from when he first purchased it and now included a stud-farm.[444] Cannon had also diverted the Wallop Brook and installed two large lakes which unfortunately one of his daughters Blanche drowned in. Garlogs was announced as sold in September of 1902, *"the sale of the Garlogs Estate at Stockbridge comprising an area of about 600 acres for many years in the occupation of Mr. Tom Cannon. The residence which is situated in a nicely timbered park is intersected by a trout stream which in front of the house forms two large lakes the property offers considerable accommodation for blood stock, Messer's Edmund smith and Co do not give particulars of the price"*. It was strangely still in Tom Cannon's possession in 1908.[433]

---

443 The London Magazine 1902-1903, Vol 9, p.76
444 Hampshire Record Office, 46M84/F67/2 Garlogs Estate Nether Wallop 31st August 1903Properties include: stud farm and Nine Mile Water Farm (313 acres)

Figure 170 Garlogs House Viewed over the Ornamental Lakes 1890's

The approach to Garlogs House was intended to be, very impressive to his guests. Tom Cannon invested heavily in remodelling works to his properties

as at Danebury, he did the same spending thousands at Garlogs with ornamental lakes laid out flanking the driveway with bridges he even diverted the wallop brook to provide water to the lakes his enthusiasm knew no bounds, the pictures demonstrate a residence that would have been made for show to have created an impact on the many visitors. Tom Cannon can just be seen by the entrance Figure 169 **Garlogs House view across the ornamental lake 1895 Racing Illustrated** from the pond flanked by two sculptures that have long since disappeared, the gardens are

Figure 171 Front View of Garlogs before Cannons remodelling works 1880's

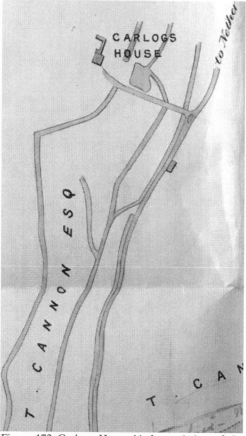

beautiful. The grounds are beautiful to walk around.

Tom Cannon became a keen Gardener after retirement and also Chairman of the Houghton Horticultural Society, he even grew Scarlet and White (his racing colours) flowers all over the front of Danebury House, and Garlogs talk about marketing, unfortunately for the modern day visitor all of that has now gone and a more modern look replaces it. I can imagine how amazing that must have looked to an approaching visitor, total branding.

Figure 172 Garlogs House kind permission of the Hampshire Record Office[456]

GROSVENOR HOTEL

Figure 173 Grosvenor Hotel 1910

The Stockbridge Manorial Rights or rights to the Manor of Stockbridge appear to exist with the Grosvenor Hotel grounds, it is perhaps the original Stockbridge Manor *"Stockbridge Hants the Manor of Stockbridge and the Grosvenor Arms Hotel a valuable property comprising this first class Family and Posting Hotel, situate in the town with tap house, yard stabling premises and other outbuildings, also with meadow at the rear together with the Manor of Stockbridge with its rights privileges appurtenances and the fair tolls rising out of the annual Sheep and Lamb fairs in the rear of the Hotel*[445] The Manorial Rights of Stockbridge were held by Joseph Forster Barham, then to Earl Grosvenor in 1822 when it was sold, then to the Earl of Clarendon, through his widow, then to G.Gammie Maitland.

John Barham Day Clerk of the Stockbridge Races 1828 1829, 1830 prior to the Bibury Club move used to have the horses entered for the race in the Grosvenor Arms *'the horses to be entered in the Grosvenor Arms Hotel between the hours of two and four Tuesday 15th June."* [446] The Steward's Table was also held at the Grosvenor and it stayed like this when the Bibury Club moved in to town as well.

The Grosvenor Hotel, or Grosvenor Arms, as it was known then was owned by the Marquis of Westminster Lord Grosvenor. Sometime after 1835 Lord Grosvenor had built the market room called the Marky Room in

---

445 Salisbury and Winchester Journal 25th June 1870
446 Salisbury and Winchester Journal 14th June 1830

1835 The market, on Thursday, is well attended; and a large and handsome market-room, adjoining the Grosvenor Arms, has been built, at the expense of the Marquis of Westminster .He had the room built as they used to have the sheep fayres on the land behind the Grosvenor Hotel as afforded by part of the Manorial Rights.

The Club Room was added, the Bibury Club's head offices were to be based there and at the Bibury Club Race Stand on the Stockbridge Course. John Day proprietor rented out the Grosvenor Arms in 1861 to Sam Scott [447] his nephew by his sister Ann Scott Day and Henry Scott who had previously been in Ascot *'At Stockbridge also people need not be afraid to stay in here to as much as Sam Scott the new Tenant under John Day of the Grosvenor Arms."* [448]. Sam Scott was also a trainer and was renting Houghton Down House and Stables at the time. *After retiring from Houghton Down he became John Days Tenant of the Grosvenor Arms* [447]. A further record refers to Sam Scott as being landlord at the Grosvenor for many years as well *"Mrs. Scott Hostess for many years of the Grosvenor Hotel Stockbridge, and widow of the late Sam Scott Trainer at Houghton Down died last week at Whitchurch"* [449] In 1861 there was a ball held at the Grosvenor. [450]

In 1867 the Lord of the Manor and proprietor of the Grosvenor Hotel was G.Gammie Maitland Esq who had purchased it from the estate sale of the 4th Earl of Clarendon and had gifted the land that the new St Peters church was built upon situated next to the Grosvenor, the church was consecrated 28th Dec 1867"*The part on which the church stands was partly parish property and the smaller half as much as required given by the Lord of the Manor G.Gammie Maitland Esq. from the yard of the Grosvenor Hotel. Mrs. Scott the Landlady generously resigning her interests in any part of the land."* [451]

447 A.H.Bailey, Baileys Magazine Sports and Pastimes (Vol IX1865 November, p.54)
448 Morning Post 26th June 1861
449 Nottinghamshire Guardian 14th January 1881
450 Bells life in London Sporting Chronicle 31st March 1861"
451 Hampshire Chronicle Stockbridge Consecration of a New Church 5th January 1867, p.5

THE PROPERTIES OF TOM CANNON

Tom Cannon purchased the Grosvenor Hotel on 6th July 1885[452], his idea was obviously to use it when the race meetings were on to provide accommodation for the visiting guests and his intentions were also to display the many trophies and racing memorabilia and build a little museum to the Days and the Cannons I presume to impress the visiting patrons.

Tom Cannon died at the Grosvenor in 1917, after a long illness, and after his death the hotel, was willed to Ronald Portman Cannon in 1917, and was up for sale in 1919 but no buyer was found, by 1949 Strong and Co Brewery were in possession. The Houghton Fishing club has for ages past had their head office at the Club Room, in the big annex that surmounts the front, and they always held it on a pepperbox or very low rent agreement. The layout of the Grosvenor has changed considerably over the years, the figure below shows how it was in 1885 prior to Tom Cannon purchasing it where the bar is now was a billiard room and the dining room was a coffee room it is very different with good stabling and grounds attached to it.

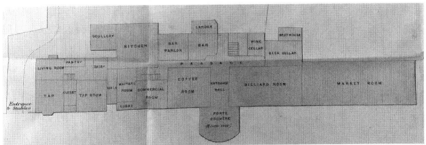

Figure 174 Grosvenor Hotel layout in 1885 kind permission Hampshire Records Office[452]

452 Hampshire Record Office, 93M92/E7 6th July 1885 Sale particular for the Grosvenor Hotel, Stockbridge

GROSVENOR HOUSE AND COTTAGE

Figure 175 White House or (Grosvenor House)

Grosvenor House or White House as it has been renamed was named after its occupier Lord Grosvenor 1st Marquis of Westminster he lived here in the early 19th century and still owned it in 1842 when the Tythe map was drawn[453]. The Day family owned this after and by 1885 it was in the hands of Thomas Cannon The same year he made an Indenture of Conveyance with the Stockbridge Fishery Association to secure the fishing rights in that part of the River Test. The house was used for guests visiting the racecourse and for those wishing to fish the river. After Cannon's death in 1917 it passed to my great uncle Ronald Portman Cannon who put it up for auction on 9th October 1919 it was purchased by Mary Carr Johnstone for £1000. The sale particulars describe the house as *"Ground Floor attractive freehold property ground floor three reception rooms, entrance hall, dining room 16ft x14ft overlooking the river, drawing room 20ft into bay by 15ft, morning room 16ft x 10ft overlooking the river, small conservatory. Upper Floor six bedrooms the principal measuring 16ft x 15ft and 14ft by 13ft. The Domestic Offices Kitchen with range*

---

[453] Hampshire Record Office Tithe Map of Stockbridge 21M65/f7224/2 dated 1842

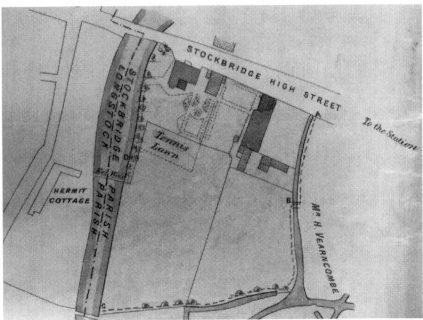

Figure 176 Grosvenor House plan view 1919 kind permission Hampshire Record Office[454]
Scullery with sink hot and cold water Butler's pantry, Larder, Cellarage in basement. The stabling for two horses' lofts over includes harness room coach or motor house knife or boot house coal shed larder etc. Well-timbered pleasure grounds bounded by the west by the River Test with spacious lawns

Sundial, brick built, ha-ha wall, excellent walled garden, well stocked fruit trees etc.; small lean to Vinery. Adjoining is a well-built Brick and Tile Cottage containing two sitting rooms, three bedrooms, kitchen, with range, sink. Let to Dr. W. K. Loveless on a monthly tenancy of 5s per week but can be estimated to be worth £26 per annum" [454]
As can be seen in the figure below, the Grosvenor House plot was much more substantial when Cannon held it, and even more so when the Day family held it., there were even tennis courts there as shown in the plan of 1912.

---

[454] Hampshire Record Office 46M84/C33/1/3 Farebrother, Ellis & Co Sale Particulars 31/12/1919

SEVEN BARROW FARM

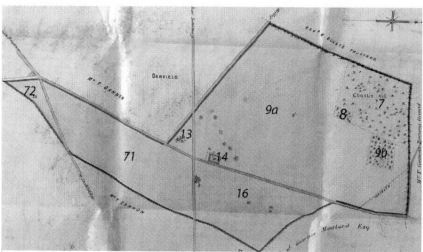

Figure 177 Seven Barrows Farm or Chattis Hill Down kind permission of Hampshire Record Office[455]

Seven Barrow Farm or Chattis Hill Down Conveyance consisted of 363.2 acres of land Tom Cannon purchased it on 29th March 1891 from the Briton Medical and General Life Association Limited for £2,000.some of the land was later used to build Chattis Hill Stables on. The 363 acres of land included in the Conveyance of 1891 amalgamated other farms with it so Seven Barrow and Down farm became part, the allotted land in the schedule was referred as; "6 Plantation 3.11 acres, 7 Down Farm 32.24 Acres, Plantation 1.2 Acres, 9a Arable 183.31Acres, 9b Plantation 5.32 Acres, Pasture 4.2 Acres, 14 Two Cotton farm buildings 0.324 Acres, 16 Arable 54.3 Acres, 17 Pond 0.26 Acres, Arable 69.3 Acres, Rough pasture 6.22 Acres total of 363.02 Acres".[455]Chattis Hill House was built over the original Seven Barrow Farm House as can be seen on the 1872 Ordinance Survey map.

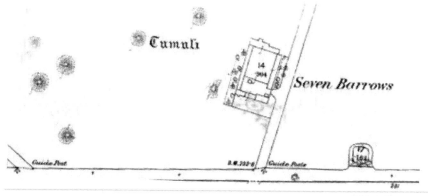

DARFEILD FARM

Figure 179 Darfield Farmhouse kind permission the owners

Darfield Farm or Southovers was purchased on 30th January1890 by Tom Cannon for £2,400. From a Mrs. Anne Maria Payne, the land package included Kent's Ditch (61.3 Acres) Old Ditch (180 Acres) and Down Farm 12 Acres a combined Total of 254.1 Acres [456]

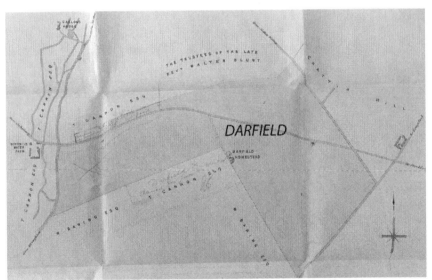

Figure 178 Darfield Farm kind permission of the Hampshire Record Office456

456 Hampshire Record Office, Conveyance was called "A farm called Darfield in Broughton Hants containing 254.1.14 Acres50M81/E/T13 Conveyance: land allotted to Thomas Edwards, deceased, under the Broughton Enclosure Award of 1790, namely Kent's Ditch (61 acres) Old Down (180 acres), Down (12 acres), a barn and a small parcel of ground (as in 50M81/E/T10), now described as Darfield Farm

NINE MILE WATER FARM

Figure 181 Nine Mile Water Farm produced with kind permission of the owner

Nine Mile Water Farm was purchased by Tom Cannon in 1888[457] and consisted of 383 acres the farm originally adjoined the Garlogs Estate it had good stabling to which the owner has tastefully converted into mixed use buildings.

Figure 180 Nine Mile Water Farm kind permission Hampshire Record Office

---

[457] Hampshire Record Office 50M81/E/T27

HOUGHTON DOWN FARM

In 1809 the Houghton Down Farm consisted of 383 acres of land and the Houghton House. On 31st July 1809 Joseph Foster Barham had to surrender certain copyhold or leasehold estates in Stockbridge to James Forbes of Stanmore Middlesex, as he had purchased them under mortgage,[458]by definition of the copyhold means they were registered in a manorial court i.e. a copy of the tenure or the lease for the land the Tenant was holding also had a copy of this held in the Manorial Court and the land was held according to the customs of the Manor, this practice had been normal in Manors since the middle ages.

Copy Hold leases were usually passed from father to son, but Forster Barham took the name of Barham from his step father Henry who held the estate under either copyhold or freehold and had passed it to Joseph his step son upon his demise. The land was leased on 25th September 1809 by John Day for £383 for a period of 21 years from the "tenure", not ownership, of Thomas Gudgeon Esq.'

In 1832 Joseph Foster Barham died and his will left the estates to his children, and in Stockbridge the lands were left to John Foster Barham and Sackville Tufton his brother in law for their pleasure. On receipt of these lands John Foster Barham under one of the clauses of the will had to pay £5,000 to each of his brothers and sisters, of which there were four. In the

---

458 Hampshire Record Office Surrender of Certain Copy Hold Lands by Joseph Forster Barham 8m52/36

life time of the will of which was only six years he had only managed to pay one, which was to Charles Barham his brother. Prior to this his wife had agreed in her marriage settlement to him that the legacies should be paid within six months. The problem was now he had died intestate without a will, and he had taken possession of the lands and there was no way possible to pay his wife.

In 1870 the Houghton Down Farm is up for sale and so is the Manor of Stockbridge after the death of the 4th Earl of Clarendon, and was reputed to have sold for between £10-15,000. The contents of the sale was "*999 acres of land 22 lots including racing stables training grounds and breeding paddocks occupied by John Day also the Grosvenor Arms Hotel the Manor of Stockbridge and fair tolls the Cossack pub and 2 beer houses*" Within the Houghton Down Estate sale it refers to the "Houghton Down Estate 389 acres the training grounds of Houghton Down 130 acres are leased to John Day, the Paddocks Stabling and residence of Houghton Down are let to Mr. Day for 14 years from 25th December 1866 for 210 per anum, shooting on Houghton Down is also letting to John Day for £25 per annum."[150]

By 1880 Tom Cannon had paid £500 in railway stocks for the lease in, part codicil to John Day's will. Cannon had Houghton Down Farm in 1890 [459] to which Mr. Chandler was a tenant. The farm was up for sale in 1907, Seven Barrows Farm and Chattis Hill 1847-1890The Days owned Seven Barrows farm from 1809, near Chattis Hill and was referred to as Grandfather Day's 1767-1828 favourite Gallops. In 1856 they still owned it, I have not been able to find the deeds, but I did find a reference in a book.[460]

---

459 Alfred E. T. Watson, *A Great Year, Lord Glanleys Horses*, 1921, p.206) "Tom Cannon was not on good terms with his tenant Chandler, the trainer, who occupied the Houghton Downs Farm, the reason being that Chandler was in the habit of taking out his gun without permission from his landlord; but Amphion was in the Houghton Downs stables, Tom Cannon declared that he must have a ride on this charming chestnut, and for a time the quarrel was patched up.
460 On Seven Barrow farm in the distance all is life, with Alfred Day on Stonehenge

HERMIT LODGE AND 15 ACRES

Figure 183 Hermit Lodge early 20th Century kind permission Hampshire Record Office

Named after the Derby winner Hermit, this property was in the Day family first, and used to be rented out to the Duke of Beaufort on his week's stay at the races The famous horse Hero is also buried in the garden, *"Hero was vanned down to Hermit lodge where his grace the Duke of Beaufort stayed during the Stockbridge week, and shot Hero and buried him in the Garden"* [461] this was a practice of the family there are many famous horses buried in the gardens of their properties. The Cannons later owned Hermit Lodge for the same purpose of providing accommodation to their guests and many others would have stayed there, John Day Junior lived there for a while in the 1870's.

Figure 182 Hermit Lodge or Langtry House front view kind permission of the owners

461 H.H.Dixon, Silk and Scarlett, (1859, p.119)

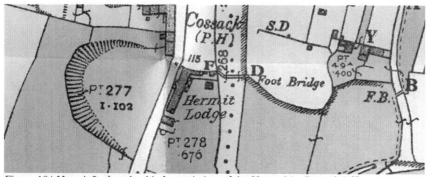

Figure 184 Hermit Lodge plan kind permission of the Hampshire Record Office

The house was described as such and came with 15 acres of land "On the Ground Floor entrance hall opening to inner hall about 15ft 9" x 10ft 6" open brick fire place with French windows to lawn. Cloakroom fitted basin and separate WC. Lounge 24ft x 16ft having two French casements to lawn. Dining Room about 17ft 6" by 12ft 6 having large French windows to conservatory. Study about 11ft 6 by 10ft 6. On the First Floor approached by principal and secondary staircases are, Eight bedrooms measuring respectively about 17ft 6" by13ft 6" Bathroom fitted bath basin separate WC The Domestic Offices Large Kitchen fitted dresser, Garage two stall stable and harness room."

Figure 185 Hermit Lodge rear view kind permission of the owners

CHATTIS HILL

Figure 186 Chattis Hill House 2004 Kind permission of the owners.

Chattis Hill or "Chatters Hill" as it was known in 1790 [462] consisted of 32.2 acres and was purchased by Cannon in 1891 from the Briton Medical Life Assurance Company as part of a 363 Acre Conveyance. [455] The site of Chattis Hill House was built over the original Seven Barrows Farm House as can be seen in the 1872 Ordinance Survey map **Figure 179.**

The Chattis Hill House we see today was built by Cannon around 1891 for one of his four sons to live in and train from in later years and as an overspill from Danebury. Due to the closure of the Stockbridge Course in 1898 Tom Cannon immediately started work on building new stabling at Chattis Hill not far away from the House, the stabling was extensive no expense was spared resulting in the stables being considered state of the art *"At Chattis Hill not more than a mile away from the House a range of perfectly appointed stables has sprung up. Here both men and beast are carefully looked after. Well ventilated stalls and boxes shelter the steeds and their attendants, vicariously termed boys have equally good accommodation, and although buried so to speak in the country*

---

[462] Hampshire Record Office Copy of Isaac Taylor Map 1790 87M97/B5/1

Figure 187 Chattis Hill Stables now houses kind permission of an owner
and up-to date luxury in the shape of an electric light installation have been arranged.'[463]

Tom his eldest son was supposed to continue at Danebury so did not move into Chattis Hill House but remained at Garlogs. Chattis Hill was Grandfather Days 1767-1828 favourite Gallop. [464] Tom Cannon Junior used Chattis Hill as his major stabling from 1898 until 1908 after which he removed his horses to Hamilton House Stables in Compton in Newbury, Berkshire. By 1902 my grandfather Charles was living there. By 1908 the Chattis Hill House and stables were leased to Attey Pearse on 23rd Dec 1908, [465]Chattis Hill House came with Down or Seven Barrow Farm of 383 acres of land. Atty Persse the trainer of the future Tetrarch a horse also known as the spotted wonder drew up a draft mortgage[466] between Tom Cannon and Henry Seymour Persse in 1908 for Chattis Hill House and Seven Barrow Farm for the sum of £6,500. [467]Henry Persse held a joint mortgage with a Mr. Edwin Sandilands, the mortgage was £32.10s.

463 Manchester Courier and Lancaster General Advertiser Wednesday August 1st 1900
464 H.H.Dixon, *Silk And Scarlett*, 1859, p.123, "Chattis Hill That Hill was Grandfather Days favourite Gallop"
465Hampshire Record Office, 50M81/E/T26 Further requisitions on title T.Cannon Esq. to HS Persse Esq. 23rd Dec 1908
466 Hampshire Record Office, 50M81/E/T30Letter from Edwin Sandilands to Messrs. Frere Cholmeley and Co £32 10s as interest on his mortgage, and requests a deed or other evidence that he is a part-mortgagee of Mr. Persse's property at Chattis Hill
467 Hampshire Record Office, 50m81/E//T28Draft mortgage to secure £6,500 and interest: Chattis Hill House, The Down or Seven Barrow Farm (363 acres)

PYRRHUS COTTAGE (SARUM)

Pyrrhus Cottage was originally owned by the Day family. Pyrrhus the First was the winner of the Epsom Derby 1846. The building consists of three cottages joined into one, located on the end of the Stockbridge High Street, today it has been renamed as Sarum. John Gully of Danebury Confederacy stayed here quite a lot. In Cannon's time the cottage would have more than likely been used to house employees and rented out during race week to visiting patrons. I am sure that the famous Race Horse Pyrrhus the First is buried somewhere in the garden as this was the custom of my ancestors.

SPRINGFIELD: (CANNON HOUSE)

Figure 188Springfield House now Cannon House front view kind permission of the owners

Springfield House renamed Cannon House was purchased by Tom Cannon from W. Squire in 1895 [468] for his new wife the governess to live in. Incidentally the year of purchase was the same year that Ronald Portman Cannon was born, Tom Cannon's last son.

There were two naval cannons that were outside of Danebury for many years, they were mounted on the gatepost, the cannons were said to have come from a naval ancestor and from HMS Victory, Nelson's war ship. Alfred Day owner of Fontwell Park racecourse had Nelson's sword, and another relative had his signet ring. However, they were there in early 2000 but I think they have since been removed by an unknown. The House served as a hospital for the wounded in the Great War and is now renamed Cannon House, the house has been extensively and tastefully restored by

---

468 Hampshire Record Office, 46M84/F87/5, Purchased by Tom Cannon 7th May 1895

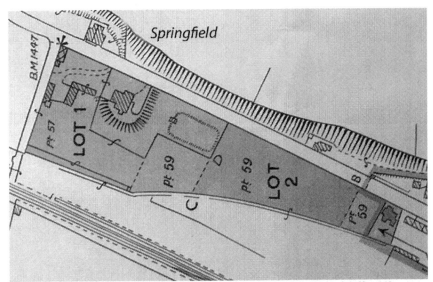

Figure 189 Springfield Sale Particulars kind permission Hampshire Record Office469

the current owners. Springfield originally came with 12.56 acres of land and extensive stabling to the side and was described as such;

LOT ONE

"Ground Floor-Entrance Porch. Entrance Hall about 12ft by 11ft with open brick fireplace. Staircase Hall opening of which are dining room south and east 15ft 6" by 15ft. handsome drawing room south and west about 27ft into bay 16ft with fireplace, overlooking pleasure lawns and tennis court with French windows giving direct access to the garden.

The First Floor is approached by an easy staircase to 5 bedroom and dressing rooms No.1 North East about 12ft by 12ft; No2. 12ft by 12ft No3 15ft by 13ft No.4 12ft by 11ft No.5 13ft 8" by 16ft. above are maid's room and box room. Gardens and Grounds 1 and ¾ Acres comprise informal lawns, Enclosed Tennis Lawns splendid Kitchen and fruit partially walled."469

The description goes on to include Lots One House Garden and Paddocks 1.750 Acres Lots two Accommodation or building land .848 Acres, Lot Three A detached cottage Garden and Paddock .250 acres, Lot Four Accommodation or building land 9.719 acres totalling 12.567 acres.

---

469 Hampshire Record Office 46M84/F87/25 Springfield conditions of sale

Figure 190 Cannon House side view kind permission of the owners

Epilogue-The Final Furlong

A good friend of mine once told me you never finish a story you just abandon it. After 14 years it is that abandoning I am finding so difficult. The writing of this book has been the most challenging adventure I have ever undertaken in my entire existence. Rescuing a story from a world that has disappeared and long been forgotten, that was dominated by those who have gone before me, forgotten? Not now, they have been remembered and I hope I have done my best to honour their memory in these pages.

As my Uncle Terry used to say, this is the Final Furlong. In the will of my great uncle Thomas Cannon Junior Appendix 16 **Will of Thomas Cannon (Jnr)**the sporting memorabilia, silver racing cups, oil paintings etc. should go to the Grosvenor Hotel to remain there as a memory to his father along with other sporting items placed there on loan in years past.[470] That memorabilia has vanished from the Grosvenor Hotel and they received only printed copies of those oil paintings. Ronald Portman Cannon the youngest son of Tom from his second wife died 1951 St Albans he was in possession of Tom Cannon's antiques and pictures which were put in the Grosvenor but those items have also vanished, this pilfering of bequeathed items is just unacceptable.

In 2001 an elderly lady Binda (Dorothy Lillian) Bilsborough died, Binda was a cousin of the children of Alfred Day, Fontwell Park, whose father was William Day of Danebury. Alfred owned and set up the Fontwell Park race course that Binda had inherited and lived in the house called Hermitage purchased by him in 1887, renamed (Days). It was her dying wish that the proceeds obtained from the sale of Fontwell Park and Hermitage would be used to fund a museum to house the horse racing memorabilia amassed by the Days over a life time. This was told to me in 2002 by someone who was selling a diary and other possessions from that estate as I was an interested party. To date I have not seen a museum but I did notice that all the memorabilia

---

[470] Will of Thomas Cannon Junior 1942 Administered 1979 *"I except out of the absolute bequest to my said wife by clause 4 (a) hereof all my oil paintings of the cannon family hunting and sporting pictures and the Silver Stockbridge Common Down Cup 16th June 1866 and the Silver Cup given to my father by the Earl of Cadogan in 1892 all of which upon my wife's death I give and bequeath free of duty in memory of my father to the owner or the owners for the time being of the Grosvenor Hotel Stockbridge in the County of Hants with my wish and desire that the same shall be placed and maintained with other pictures relating to the Cannon family which have already been at the Grosvenor Hotel aforesaid for many years."*

was sold at auction in 2013 and the Museum remains but a lost wish.

I wonder what happened to the commemorative plaque for John Day in 1867 for his gift of the entire East Window to the Church in the centre of Stockbridge, perhaps Vaudrey Barker Mill requested the Church to remove it after she closed the racecourse down in 1898 perhaps the Church would be kind enough to put the plaque back?

My hope in the writing of this book is to provide an alternative version of the truth, for my family who were celebrated and admired in their lives and whose image and reputation as of late is acquiring the undeserved name, of crook cheat, and swindler by authors who are desperate to frame my ancestor's in a bid to sell more books such as Nicholas Foulkes or establishment writers such as Jack Waterman, Henry Cecil should be proud to be named beside my ancestors Jack.

Perhaps those Authors found it far easier to assign the blame of scandals to a family long since dead who can offer no resistance, than to invite corruption to the door of the Jockey Club and its celebrated members. Perhaps access to precious research records wouldn't be granted for those not perpetuating the official line?

THE FINAL POST

It was never, and has never, been the establishment that made horse racing the Sport of Kings, they just wrote the records. It was the hard work of the trainers, the wasting and sacrifice of the jockeys, and the support of the public, that made horse racing great.

It is my hope that next time somebody writes about my family, they will be equipped with this alternative version of history of those forgotten horsemen that version has now been told, *"The fame of great jockeys, like that of great actors, rests upon tradition. They leave nothing behind them by which future generations can judge their excellence"* Well now they have, they have left their story.

I am sitting at a table in the garden of the White Hart Inn Stockbridge on 11th July 2015 pondering time and its passage as I write the close of this book. Staring back at me across the table in the garden where I am sat are my ancestors. I cannot see them and they cannot see me but we are here sitting together, occupying the same space we are just separated by 225 years of time. They are walking and talking through this very space where we sit, over this same ground. I look up at the window of the White Hart and see Grandmother Day in her crunch bonnet opening the curtains, a quick glance to the stables I find Grandfather Day grooming the racehorses ready for sale. On the tips of the wind I can hear their laughter and tears. I walk the pathway through Stockbridge to Houghton knowing full well that my feet are treading in the same steps of those who made me. I stare at the race horses pass the Grosvenor Hotel and catch a glimpse of the Prince Regent, Nelson and then Lord Palmerston with the parade of history's most famous and fashionable people on their way to the races past Danebury where my Grandfather is entertaining Prince Edward. I am sitting outside the Boot Inn staring across at Church Lane to 1865 and watching my great grandfather Tom Cannon carry his new bride Kate Day over the threshold of the Elms their new home and into the start of their lives, it is a strange feeling reader as they don't know what's to come in their lives but I do. They never left me money or possessions but I found something far more valuable I found the story that made me, and the racing story of this town of Stockbridge has now been told.

As for me I have done my job, I have made my contribution to the turf, I have taken my family's skeleton from the closet where it uncomfortably sat, I have defended the memory of my ancestors and set them free, and in doing so honoured my promise. So now I will leave them to rest where they belong in History, forever protected and always defended in these pages.

I believe, as we were taught as children by my beautiful mother Patricia Cannon, the truth is always the right course and in the pursuit of it, and only in that pursuit has this story of my ancestors revealed itself and finally been placed in history.

"VeritasVos Liberabit" The Truth Shall Set You Free

I would like to close this story as I began with the words of my great-great - great-great- grandmother Mrs. Anne Day.

"Fear Thy God, Speak Evil Of None, Stick To The Truth, And Don't Be Done."

Bibliography

AESOP. 1864. *Sporting reminicences Of Hampshire 1745-1862.* London, 193 Piccadilly : Chapman & Hall, 1864. Vol. 1.

Barry, William Frederick. 1895. *Times Law Reports and Commercial Cases.* Vol11. London : The times, 1895. Vol. 11.

Beresford, Dorothy. 1989. *Nether Wallop In Hampshire.* Winchester : R.N.K. Beresford, 1989. Vol. I.

Black, Robert. 1891. *The Jockey Club And Its Foundees In Three Periods.* London : Smith Elder & Co , 1891.

Bosville, Godfrey. 1908. *Horses, Horsemen and Stable management.* London : George Routledge & Sons, 1908.

Buckley, Parke. 1902-1903. *The Harmsworth London Magazine.* London : The Almalgamated Press, 1902-1903. Vol. IX.

Burke, Sir Bernard. 1863. *Geneological and Dictionary of the Landed Gentry of Great Britain and Nothern Ireland.* London : Harrison Pall Mall, 1863. Vol. 4.

Byles, Tony. 2011. *In Search of Running Rein the amazing fraud of the 1844 Derby.* London : Apex Publishing, 2011.

C.B.Fry. 1904. Mornington Cannon Riding a RaceHorse. *C.B.Frys Magazine.* 1904, Vols. i-22, pp. 162-170.

C.F.Greville, Charles. 1885. *A Journal Of The Reign Of Queen Victoria From 1837-1852.* London : Longman, Green, and Co, 1885. p. 455.

Cannon, Tom. 1898. Family Scrapbook of "Tom Cannon Garlogs". Stockbridge : s.n., 1898. Vol. 1.

Co, Kelly and. 1931. *Kellys Directory of Berkshire Bucks and Oxon.* London : Kellys and Co, 1931.

Co, Saunders Otley and. 1863. *Horse Racing Its History and Early Records of the Principal and Other Race Meetings.* London : Saunders Otley & Co Brook Street, Hanover Square, 1863.

Cook, Theodore Andrea. 1901-1904. *A History of The English Turf.* London : H.Virtue & Company, 1901-1904. Vol. III.

Corbet, Henry. 1864. *Tails And Traits Of A Sporting Life*. London : Rogerson And Tuxford, , 1864. Vol. I.

Cranham, Michael Tanner And Gerry. 1992. *The Guiness Book Of Great Jockeys Of The Flat*. London : Guiness Publishing, 1992.

Creswell, Richard Vaughan Barnwell & Creswell. 1826. *Cases Argued and Determined in The Court Of Kings Bench*. London : A.Strahan, 1826.

Cross, Thomas. 1861. *The Autobiography Of A Stage-Coachman*. 1. London : Hurst And Blackett, Publishers, successors to Henry Coburn, 13 Great Marborough Street, 1861. Vol. II.

Curzon, Louis Henry. 1892. *Or the MacHinery of Horse Racing Revealed: Showing the Sport of Kings As It Is Tod*. London : Chapman And Hall, 1892.

Day, Alfred Day William. 1925. *The Racehorse in Training*. London : Cassel and Company, 1925.

Day, William. 1891. *Reminiscences Of The Turf, with Anecdotes And Recollections of its Principal Celebrities*. London : Richard Bently And Son, 1891. Vol. I.

—. 1880. *The Race Horse in Training*. London : Chapman & Hall, 1880.

Dixon, Druid Henry Hall. 1856. *Post And Paddock Hunting Edition*. London : Piper Stephenson & Co, 1856.

Dixon, Enrique Hall. 1914. *Scott And Seabright*. II. London and New York : Frederick Warne And Co, 1914.

Dixon, Henry Hall. 1862. *Post And The Paddock with recollections of George IV Sam Chifney and other Turf Celebrities*. 1. London : Rogerson and Tuxford 246 The Strand, 1862. Vol. I.

—. 1862. *Scott and Sebright*. London : Frederick Warne and co, 1862.

—. 1859. *Silk And Scarlett*. London : Frederick Warne And Co., 1859.

—. 1856. *The Druid Post and Paddock*. London : Vinton and Co. Ltd, 1856.

Dixon, Sydenham. 1901. *From Gladiateur to Persimmon, Turf Memories Of Thirty Years*. London : Grant Richards, 9 Henrietta Street, Covent Garden W.C., 1901. Vol. I.

Dixon, Thormanby Willmott. 1882. *Famous Racing Men*. London : James

Hogg Exeter Street, 1882.

—. **1898.** *Kings of the Turf: Memoirs and Anecdotes of Distinguished Owners, Backers, Trainers, and Jockeys.* London : Hutchinson, 1898.

East, Edward Hyde. 1845. *Reports of Cases Argued And Determined In The Court Of The Kings Bench.* Philadelphia : Lea & Blanchard, 1845.

Faulk, Bernard. 1950. *The Dukes of Graton Through Four Centuries.* 1st. London : Hutchinson and Co, 1950.

Foulkes, Nicholas. 2010. *Genlemen and Blackguards.* London : Orion, 2010.

Frederic Madden, Bulkeley Bandenel, John Gough Nicolas. 1841. *Collectania Topographica and Genealogica.* London : John Bowyer Nichols and Son, 1841. Vol. 5.

George James Cawthorne, Richard S.Heron. 1902. *Royal Ascot and its Associations.* Revised. London : A.Treherne, 1902.

Gifford, William. 1833. *The Quarterly Review.* XLIXX. London : John Murray, 1833.

H.A.Bryden. 1903. *Hare Hunting and Harriers.* London : Grant Richards, 1903.

Hare, Thomas. 1855. *Reports Of The Cases High Court Of Chancery.* London : W.Maxwell, 1855. Vol. 10.

Henry Charles Howard Earl of Suffolk and Berkshire, William George Craven, Arthur George Coventry Arthur Alfred Thomas Watson. 1893. *Racing and Steeple Chasing.* 1st. London : Longmans and Green, 1893.

Huggins, Mike. 2004. *The Victorians and Sport.* London : A & C Black, 2004.

Hyde, Sir Edward. 1845. *Reports of cases argued and determined in The Court Of The Kings Bench, 1845.* II. London : Lea and Blanchard, 1845.

J.D.Parry. 1833. *An Historical and Discriptive Account of the Coast of Sussex.* London : Wright and Son Longman and Co, 1833.

J.G.F.Rivington. 1838. *The Anual Register.* London : Thomas Curzon Hansard, 1838.

James, Wetherby Edward and. 1832. *The Racing Calendar.* 1832, Vol. sixtieth.

John Kent, Edited by (Hon) Francis Lawley. 1892. *The Racing Life Of Lord George Cavendish Bentinck MP.* London : William Balkavood And Sons, 1892.

Kay, Wray Vamplew and Joyce. 2005. *Encyclopedia of British Horse Racing.* Oxford : Routledge, 2005.

Lambton, Hon George. 1930. *Men And Horses I Have Known.* London : Butterworth, 1930.

—. 1891. *Turf Celebrities I have Known.* London : White, 1891.

Lecomber, Tessa. 2000. *The Barker Mill Story, A Hampshire Family Since the 16th Century.* Southampton : Trustees of the Barker Mill Family, 2000.

Lee, Sir Sidney. 1885. *Dictionary of National Biography second supplement.* London : Smith Elder and Co, 1885.

Lenox, William Pitt. 1877. *Celebrities I Have Known, With Episodes, Political, Social, Sporting And Theatrical.* London : Hurst And Blacknett, 1877. Vol. 1.

Lewis, Samuel. 1835. *A Topographical Dictionary Of England.* London : S.Lewis & Co, 1835. Vol. IV.

Lords, House of. 1844. *The sessional papers (reports on gaming evidence for the select comitee and the House of Lords).* london : House of Lords, 1844. Vol. XIX.

Lybb-Powys, Mrs. 1756-1808. *Passages from the Diary of Mrs Phillip Lybb-Poweys of Hardwick House Oxon.* London : Longmans Green and Co, 1756-1808.

McGuigan, John. 1946. *A Trainers Memories Being Sixty Years Turf Reminicences And Experiences.* London : Heath Cranton, 1946.

Moorhouse, John Porter & Edward. 1915. *John Porter an Autobiography.* London : Grant Richards Limited, 1915.

Mortimer, Roger. 1958. *The Jockey Club.* London : Cassell, 1958.

Mortimer, Roger,Onslow R, and Willet. 1978. *Biographical Encyclopedia Of British Flat Racing.* 1. London : Macdonald and Jane's, 1978.

Newmarket. 1922. *Chapters From Turf History.* London : The National Review Office, 43 Dukes Street, 1922.

Nimrod. 1850. *The Chace The Turf And The Road.* London : John Murray Albemarle Street, 1850. Vol. New Edition.

Office, Post. 1855. *Post Office Directory Of Hampshire Wiltshire And Dorsetshire.* London : Kelly And Co, 1855.

Osbaldeston, George. 1926. *Squire Osbaldeston his Autobiography.* London : John Lane, 1926.

Parry, John Docwra. 1833. *An Historical and Descriptive Account of the Coast of Sussex.* London : Longman and Co, 1833.

1867. *Piggotts directory.* London : Piggotts, 1867.

Radcliffe, John B. 1905. *The Life and Times of John Osborne.* London : Sands and Co, 1905.

Rice, James. 1879. *History Of The British Turf.* 1. London : Sampson Low, Marston And Rivington, 1879. Vol. 8.

Richardson, Charles. 1901. *The English Turf A Record Of Horses And Courses.* [ed.] E.T.Sachs. London : Methuen & Co 36 Essex Street, 1901.

Robert Weir, James Morray Brown. 1891. *Badmington Library of Sports and Past Times.* II. London : Longmans, 1891.

Rous, Henry John. 1866. *On the Laws and Practice of Horse Racing.* London : A.H.Bailey and Co, 1866.

Skinner, John Stuart. 1833. *American Turf Register and Sporting Magazing.* IV, 1833, Vol. IV.

Skinner, John Stuart. 1840. *American Turf Register And Sporting Magazine.* 1840.

—. 1837. *American Turf Register And Sporting Magazine.* 1837, Vol. 8.

Smith, George,. 1882. John Day. [ed.] Sir Sidney Lee. *Dictionary of National Biography.* London : oxford University Press, 1882.

Smurthwaite, Henry. 1895. *Racing Illustrated.* 1. London : The Sportsman, 1895.

Society, Hampshire Geneological. 2008. Hampshire Baptisms-CD ROM Ref: HCD012 1752-1812. Cosham : Hampshire Geneological Society, 2008.

Tattersall, George. 1850. *The Pictorial Gallery Of The English Racehorse.* London : Henry G Bohn, York St Covent Garden, 1850.

1830. *The Law Advertiser Vol VIII.* London : J.W.Paget Quality Court Chancery Lane, 1830.

Tiballs, Geoff. 2003. *Great Sporting Scandals.* London : Robson Books, 2003.

W.H.Jacobb. 1905. *Hampshire At The Opening Of The Twentieth Century.* London : W.T.Pike, 1905.

W.H.Langley. 1854. *Ruffs Guide To The Turf.* London : Piper Stephenson and Spence, 1854.

Watson, Alfred E.T. 1921. *A Great Year, Lord Glanleys Horses.* London Paternastor Row : Longmans Green and Co, 1921.

—. **1883.** *Racecourse and Covert Side.* London : Richard Bentley and Son, 1883.

—. **1904.** *The Racing World and its Inhabitants.* London : MacMillan & Co, 1904.

Weatherby, Charles and James. 1847. *The Racing Calender.* London : Reynell and Weight, 1847. Vol. 75.
Weatherby, Edward and James. 1808. *Racing Calender.* London : H.Reynall, 1808. Vol. 35.
—. **1800.** *The Racing Calender.* London : H.Reynell, 1800.
—. **1804.** *The Racing Calender.* London : C.Reynell, 1804.
—. **1805.** *The Racing Calender.* London : H.Reynell, 1805.
—. **1801.** *The Racing Calender.* London : H.Reynell, 1801. Vol. 28.
—. **1825.** *The Racing Calender.* London : H.Reynell, 1825. Vol. 53.
—. **1793-1795.** *The Racing Calender.* London : C.Reynell, 1793-1795.
—. **1796-1799.** *The Racing Calender.* London : H.Reynell, 1796-1799. Vol. 23.
—. **1806.** *The Racing Calender.* London : H.Reynell No 21 Piccadilly, 1806.
—. **1810.** *The Racing Calender.* London : H.Reynall, 1810. Vol. 38.
Whyte, James Christie. 1840. *History Of The British Turf, from the earliest period to the present day.* London : Henry Colburn, 1840. Vol. 2.
William George Craven Duke of Beaufort, Arthur Coventry, Thomas Watson. 1893. *Racing And Steeple Chasing.* London : Longmans Green & Co, 1893.

MAGAZINES

American Turf Register and Sporting Magazine
Bells Life in London Sporting Chronicle.
Bentleys Miscellany
The Gentleman's Magazine
C. B. Fry's Magazine
Badminton Magazine of Sports and Past Times
Baileys Magazine of Sports and Past Times
John Bull
The Illustrated Sporting Theatrical News.
Monthly Magazine sporting transactions of the turf
The New Sporting Magazine
The Newcastle Magazine
Racing Illustrated
Frasers Magazine
The Sporting Review
The London Magazine
Flight Royal Aero Club

NEWS PAPERS

Lancashire Evening Post
Bury and Norwich Post
Berkshire Chronicle
Daily Telegraph
Exeter Flying Post
Manchester Courier
Morning Chronicle
Hampshire Advertiser
The Standard
The Times
The London Morning Post
Lancashire General Advertiser
Edinburgh evening News
Birmingham Daily Post
Sheffield Daily Telegraph
Salisbury and Winchester Journal
The Press
Sunderland Daily Echo
Morning Leader
Nottinghamshire Guardian
Western Gazette
Liverpool Daily Post
Birmingham Daily Post
Yorkshire Evening Post

Hull Daily Mail
Bath Chronicle and Weekly Gazette
Cheltenham Chronicle
Dundee Evening Post
The Illustrated London News
Reading Mercury
Hampshire Chronicle
The Tatler
The Sketcher
The London Gazette (Supplement)
London Standard
Lancashire Evening Post
Aberdeen Journal
Nottingham Evening Post
Sheffield Independent
The Observer (Argus Eye)
Gloucestershire Citizen
Sheffield Evening Telegraph
Nottingham Evening Post
Windsor and Eton Express
London Morning Post
Liverpool Echo
Yorkshire Post Leeds Intelligencer
Luton Times and Advertiser

SPECIAL COLLECTION AND OFFICIAL DOCUMENTATION

Newmarket Racing Museum Library
Stockbridge Archives Hampshire Record Office (HCRO)
Portland Collection, University of Nottingham
Rothschild Family Archive London
Gloucestershire Record Office (GCRO)
National Archives (PRO)
Hampshire, Genealogical Society
Somerset County Record Office (SCRO)
Tom Cannon Family Archive
Noel Cannon Family Archive
Houghton Fishing Club Archive
Annual Register 1838
Hansard Parliamentary Debates
House of Lords Select Committee; the Laws Respecting Gaming 1844
Imperial War Museum
Southampton Aviation Museum

WEBSITES

Race news online
Thorough bred heritage
British history online

Index

Problem, 62
Promised Land, 59
Pussy Horse, 48, 90
Pyrrhus Cottage, 321
Pyrrhus the 1st, 49, 122

Q

Qui Tam, 112–15, 144

R

Rattan Affair, 119–23, 144
Red Rover Horse, 47
Repulse Horse, 191
Rice, James, 46, 95
Robert the Devil, 197
Robinson, Jem, 46
Rogers, Sam, 119, 144
Rous, Admiral, 146, 157, 158
Running Reign, 144
Running Rein, 149
Running Rein 1844 Derby Fraud, 116–18

S

Sadler, William, 146
Sam Rogers, 121
Scott, Henry, 46
Seven Barrow Farm, 312
Sextie, William, 187
Ship Inn Stockbridge, 27
Shotover Horse, 197
Sloan, Tod, 202
Smallman Frank, 24
Smallman, Frank, 55
Snails Creep, 190
Somerset, Lord Charles Henry, 74
Spider and Fly Letters, 158–61
Springfield House, 322–24
Spye Park, 106
St Hubert Horse, 125

St Peters Church Stockbridge, 153
Star Hotel, 88
Starkey, John Bayton, 107
Stebbings, Mr, 134
Stockbridge Racecourse, 215, 210–17
Sunningdale Ascot, 48
Sweats, 85

T

Tarver, Mary Wilkins, 132
The Bibury Club, 22, 77
The Dukes Head Stockbridge, 27
The Elms, 296
The Jockey Club, 24
The Swan Inn Stockbridge, 27
Thurio, 195
Tom Cannon, 231
Tooke, Jane Eleanor Cheval, 102
Townsend, Harriet, 185
Trent Horse, 194
Trumpator, 27

U

Ugly Buck, 116

V

Vaudrey Barker Mill, 153
Virago, 123–28

W

Watts, Jack, 224
White Hart Inn Stockbridge, 26, 28
Winchester Racecourse, 26
Witchcraft Horse 1804, 30
Wood, Henry, 193
Woodyates, 56, 60, 125, 126, 166
Wormwood Scrubs, 88

APPENDIX 1: ALICE MARY CANNON PYROGRAPHY OF HER FATHER

The Pyrography shown is created by burning the panels with a hot poker; the panels are of English sawn oak. Further and more specialist reading has been prepared on these panels by the Alice Mary Alice Mary Cannon, Tom Cannon's eldest daughter and child, created these for her father one for every time he won a major race. The panels were originally located in Garlogs House but were relocated to the Grosvenor Arms Hotel after Garlogs was sold in 1902. *"The Library is probably the only room of its kind in England A wooden*

fresco runs round the walls, and on it Miss Cannon, who shines as an artist, has executed in poker work remarkably good likenesses of some of the best horses ridden by her father—Shotover (Derby), Geheimness (Oaks), Busybody (Oaks), Ormonde, Ackworth, Pilgrimage, Isonomy, Robert the Devil (St. Leger), and Humewood.[443] Three further panels are in the possession of my cousins and her granddaughters the descendants of my Great Aunt Alice in America.

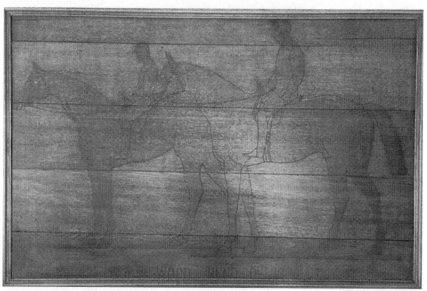

Figure 191 Humewood and Bendigo 1886 and 1887

Figure 193Tom Cannon on his Hunter 1893

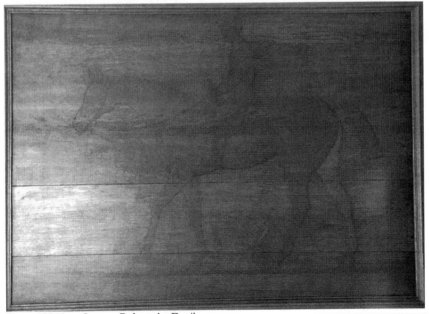

Figure 192 Tom Cannon Robert the Devil

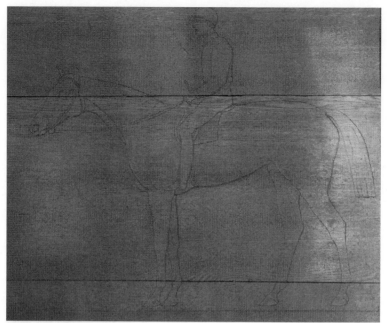

Figure 195 Pilgrimage 1876

Figure 194 Tom Cannon Shotover 1882

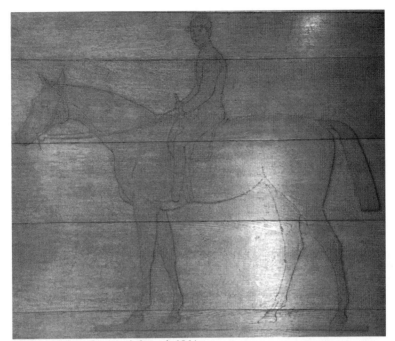

Figure 197 Tom Cannon Ackworth 1864

Figure 196 Amphion 1890

APPENDIX 2: TOM CANNON GARLOGS (FAMILY BOOK)

This was a scrap book of Tom Cannon's I believe this book was intended to be published by Tom Cannon there are only 10 pages of paper cuttings left inside of it and they are recollections with memories from his mouth this book was borrowed by an anonymous writer years before and was returned with many pages missing from it.

Figure 198 Family Book Tom Cannon of Garlogs

Appendix 3: Bibury Club Rules

Amended rules of the Bibury Club.[471]

The importance of Bibury Races has very much increased of late years. Originally the horses were all the property of, and rode by, members of the Club, no others being allowed: but latterly jockeys have been permitted to ride. Early in the present season several members having suggested the propriety of revising the Rules of the Club, a general Meeting of the members was held at Stockbridge ; when the following Rules were adopted, subject to confirmation at the meeting next year, except the Sixth Rule, which was unanimously passed, and ordered to be acted on immediately :—

1. To meet annually to dine at Stockbridge on the clay before the Races commence.
2. That the Steward fix the hour of starting for 1 each race by ten o'clock the evening before running, allowing a quarter of an hour from one race to the time of saddling for the next, and a quarter of an hour from that time to the time of starting.
3. That every groom shall have his horse at the post ready to start within five minutes of the time appointed by the Steward. And every jockey is to be there ready to start within the same time. And every groom and jockey making default herein shall forfeit to be paid to Mr. Weatherby, and by him accounted for to the Club.
4. That every member of the Club, excepting those abroad, subscribe Four Guineas annually to be paid, to Mr. Weatherby, in London, on the first of May.
5. That any person desirous of belonging to the Club must be proposed by a member; and be balloted for at an ensuing meeting:—ten members to make a ballot, and two black balls to exclude.
6. That a person, though chosen, shall not be considered as a member of the Club, until he shall have paid the usual sum for the admission and subscription of a new member. And the name of every member whose subscription shall be in arrears at the time of the races shall, on the second day of the races, be placed! over the chimney-piece at the place of Meeting, and afterwards in Mr. Weatherby's Office; and if such arrear be not paid by the end of the following meeting, he shall cease to be a member, and shall not be again admitted as a member until his arrears be paid, and until he be again chosen by ballot; but he shall always be considered liable for the

---

471 Extracted from- (Sporting Magazine Or Monthly Transactions Of The Turf, The Chase, 1832)

arrears left unpaid at the time of his name being struck out.

7. That all new members pay Five Guineas on their admission, exclusively of the subscription of Four Guineas for the year; and that they are requested to sign an order on their banker or agent, in London, for the annual payment of the subscription of Four Guineas to Mr. Weatherby.

8. That all horses &c. that starts for any of the Bibury Plates, Sweepstakes, or Subscriptions, be bona fide the property of the members of the Club.

9. That no individual member, or joint confederates, be allowed to start more than one horse, &c. for any of the Bibury Plate, Sweepstakes, or Subscriptions; and that, in cane of confederacy, all the parties concerned are members of the Club.

10. That all Stakes and Forfeits be paid to Mr. Weatherby before starting ; and that they be made in Cash, Bank Bills, Bank Post Bills properly endorsed, Bankers' Notes payable to bearer, or Bankers' Notes payable to order, also properly endorsed ; and for the due execution of this rule Mr. Weatherby be held responsible.

11. That no horse & c. be allowed to start, either for Matches or Sweepstakes unless his owner shall have previously made his Stake.

12. That no person be allowed to start or ride any Horse, Mare, or Gelding, for Plate, Subscription, Match, or Sweepstakes, unless he shall have paid all former Subscriptions, Stakes, and Forfeits, by eight o'clock the evening before running.

13. That for all prizes, where particular qualifications ore required, the colour, age, and pedigree of the horses named be specified; and in case the pedigree and age cannot be ascertained, the person's name of whom the horse was bought be expressed.

14. That any member who shall be discovered, though at any distance of time, to have started an unqualified horse, &c. for any Plate, Subscription, or Sweepstakes, shall forfeit Ten Guineas to the Club; and, if a' winner, refund the Prize to the owner of the first horse disqualified: but in case of such disqualification, all bets are to be paid as if the horse who went in first was entitled to the Prize.

15. That when any Match or Sweepstakes shall be made, and no weight specified, the horses, &c. shall carry, if jockeys ride, 8st. 7lb., and, if Gentlemen ride, list. 7lb.; and if no distance be specified, they shall run two miles; and if weight is given, the highest weight shall be 8st. 7lb. or list. 7lb.

16. That no race be run with heats.

17. That Gen. Grosvenor, Lord Jersey, Mr. Dundas, Mr. Pryse, Mr. Rawlinson, Mr. Thornhill, and the Steward for the time being, be a Committee for managing the affairs of the Club.

18. That the Committee be responsible for all money collected (including

the forfeits) for the use of the Club: that they annually appoint a Steward, not being one of their own body; and that they, or any three of them, determine all disputes. The following Noblemen and Gentlemen have recently become Members:—Duke of Richmond Col. Gilbert, Marquis of Worcester Major Cosby, Lord Wilton Mr. Farquharson, Lord Chesterfield Mr. W. Wyndhara, Lord Mountcharlcs Mr. Knatchbull, Lord Southampton Mr. Payne, Lord Ranelagh Mr. C. W. Codrington, Hon. Capt. Roué Mr. J. Bayley, and Sir Lewin Glyn Mr. H. Peyton. Sir Mark Wood.

APPENDIX 4: List of Members of the Bibury Club 1798-1832

The below list has been compiled from a number of sources, the best source was the Sporting magazine of 1832, where it disclosed most of the new members, the committee members and the old members were sourced from William Pitt Lenox, and other sources.

Prince Regent, later King George, Sovereign (Patron)
MP for Chester 1790-1802 (Founder and head of the committee)
George Child Villiers, 1773-1859 5th Earl of Jersey, (principal shareholder of the bank child & co). (Committee member)
Mr. William Dundas 1762-1845 Lord Commissioner for the Admiralty (Committee Member)
Mr. Pryse Pryse Loveden M.P 1774-1849 (Committee Member)
Sir Henry Rawlinson 1st Baronet 1810-1895
Duke of Wellington (Steward)
John Day (Clerk)
Charles Lenox 1764-1819 4th Duke of Richmond KG
Lord Palmerston (Prime Minister)
Robert Grosvenor 1767-1845 2nd Earl Grosvenor, 1st Marquis of Westminster
George John Frederick Sackville, 1745-1815 Lord 4th Duke of Dorset
George William Frederick Villiers1800-1870 4th Earl of Clarendon (Lord Lieutenant of Ireland) (Later lord of the Manor of Stockbridge)
William Henry Cavendish Cavendish-Scott-Bentinck, 4th Duke of Portland PC (24 June 1768 – 27 March 1854 Baronet MP
Joseph Foster Barham 1759-1832 West Indies Merchant & MP (Member)
Henry Charles Somerset, 1766-1835 6th Duke Of Beaufort
Lord Charles Henry Somerset 1767-1831 Governor of South Africa
Sir John Shelly 6th 1771-1849 Baronet Michaelgrove
Duke of Bedford
Charles James Fox MP
Colonel J.R.Lumley
Mr. Peter Delme
Major Charles Rooke Dragoons
Colonel Cooper
Captain Robert Parkhurst
Richard Edward Erle Drax Grosvenor
Sir Charles Talbot 1751-1812
Marquis of Worcester
Lord Wilton
Lord Chesterfield
Lord Mount Charles, Lord Southampton, Lord Ranelagh

Appendix 5 the Instruction of Jockeys Tom Cannon

Page 9:

Riders:

Until all chances of winning be passed. Many who ought to have known better have been caught in this trap. As this manoeuvre is accomplished without any crossing or jostling, it does not come under the head of foul riding according to racing law.

It is generally considered dangerous to try to get through on the inside, for some men won't give way or pull out, while it is anything but pleasant to be shoved up against a post, or against the railings.

When carrying a heavy weight one should never allow a dangerous light weight to get too far in front.

A jockey ought to pay due attention to the ....
The ground over which he has to go, and to a..............
Linarites possessed by his mount. Thus if a particular course be heavy or hilly, he might ease hi.................
While he might rattle him along downhill,
Ground was sound, always supposing that the feet could _can_ stand it.
Horses with short upper......................
Are most unsuited to go down a hill-...................
Vauban, the Two Thousand winner, in.....................
Good example of this fact- neither did particularly ......
Well on hard ground; while the...........................
Pasterns generally like to hear their feet.....................
Not get their legs jarred when going down an incline.
Horses with rather high action and good hocks are the best to climb a hill. The possession of large broad feet is most useful on a heavy course, from the mechanical advantage they have over small feet. A compact, quick striding horse, like what Freeman was, is best for a cramped course, like the Rodee at Chester, while a big long striding animal requires a straight level course, like that at Doncaster, on which to display his powers.
Unsound horses, as a rule, act best on a soft course especially those with any tendency to laminitis or muscular disease. Old horses, which are somewhat stiff on their legs, should have a steady preliminary canter to warm them up before starting. Certain horses appear to have a special liking for certain courses and varieties of ground. Game honest horses are often

several pounds better when facing a hill, than one with a suspicion of "softness" though they might be as nearly equal as possible on the flat.

The Seat when Finishing. - When a jockey wants to finish, he should sit down in the centre of his saddle with his seat as much under him as possible. He should catch a good hold of the horse's head so as to collect him at each stride; he should lean slightly back; should grip the flaps of the saddle tightly with his knees, and should draw his feet well back, so that the weight, at each stroke of the horse's hind legs may not come with a jerk on the stirrups, which would cause it, by reaction, to be thrown to the rear, and would thus increase the work the horse has to do. The hands and arms should yield to the extension of the horse's neck at each stride, without, however, slackening the reins in the slightest.

Page 10:

The hands should be brought within five or six inches of each other and should be kept low, say- not more than six inches above the withers. The rider having assumed the position should conform to the movements of the horse; so that the weight may impede him as little as possible. The seat and thighs of the rider should appear as if they are glued to the saddle, while there should not be the slightest approach to any bumping up and down. While the jockey can or cannot relieve the horse, by giving a forward impulse to his body when the hind legs on the ground is a question that does not concern us here nor is it one of practical application. It is sufficient for us to know that when a man sits down and finishes in proper style, the horse is enabled to travel faster than he can do when any other kind of seat is adopted. We know that "dead weight," over which the muscles of the jockey cannot exercise any influence, is particularly disadvantageous at a finish, however well placed it may be. We are also aware that if a man be tired or weak, however "still" he may sit; his horse will not be able to gallop by any means as fast as he would do, were the rider fresh and strong. These facts seem to indicate that the jockey can afford a certain amount of mechanical assistance, which cannot be derived from the reins, for, although they may serve to "collect" him, or to retard his speed, they are powerless to give him any onward impulse. As the legs of the rider are the only other parts which connect him to the horse, the "lift" if there be one - must proceed from them, and may be the result of the weight being, more or less, taken of the horses back at each instant, as his hind feet make their stroke. Colonel Greenwood, in his excellent book "Hints on Horsemanship," considers that such mechanical assistance can be given. We know that the rider may aid the horse by adjusting his weight, during each stride, so that it may impede the animal's movements as little as possible

Page 11

But whether he can give him any further assistance or not is a question which I am unable to decide.

A man requires a great deal of practice to finish well, while, if he does it badly, he is certain to impede the horses movements by rolling about in the saddle; hence, if he be not expert in the art, he should not attempt to practice it, but should endeavour to sit as still as possible, catch a good hold of his horse's head, and should assume the position which he finds to be the easiest one for the horse and for himself. As the action of finishing is very fatiguing to the jockey, he does not, as a rule, "sit down" before he comes to the distance post.

On Finishing.-At a finish it is always best to be on the whip hand of one's most dangerous opponent, who might, if one was on his near side, close in, either intentionally or by his horse swerving, and might thus prevent one from using the whip with the right hand.

Besides this, as many horses have a tendency, especially under punishment, to swerve of to the outside of a course, it is just as well to have something on the near side, so as to keep ones owns horse straight.

Before sitting down to finish, it is generally advisable, especially if the race has been run at a strong pace, to take a pull at one's horse for a few strides, so as to enable him to catch his wind, and to collect himself before he makes his effort.

It is a dangerous and often fatal mistake for a jockey to ease his horse, or to cease riding him, when leading and close to the winning-post, for by doing so he may make him "stop," and may then be unable to get him to stride again, in time to "stall off a rush" from one of the others.

At a finish, if one finds that the leader has the race easy, one might get directly behind him, on the chance of his slackening speed to look around, or to look at his boots, or at the stand, and then one may, with a rush on the side away from which the other's head is turned, manage to beat him on the post, before he can set his horse going again.

Many an important event has been lost from over-confidence *of the rider* of the leading horse, who, when winning easily, has tried to make a race of it for "the gallery," or has been cajoled into slackening his speed by one of the other riders jockeys, and has then been unable to make effort in time when required to do so.

As a last piece of advice, I would recommend the tyro never to be too anxious "to get home," and never "to draw it to fine."

Page 12:

On Riding Rogues.-As the generality of "rogues" will run kindly enough until they are pressed or hustled, a jockey when riding one of this sort, as a rule, make the running , or at least keep with the leaders, and, if he finds that he is winning easily at the finish, should he on no account, take a pull, or allow any of the others, if he can help it, to close up on him, for many rogues will either not try a yard, or win by " the length of a street." The jockey should sit still, ride as quietly as possible, and should do all he can to persuade the Jady one that he is running away.

It often happens that the more the rider pulls, the faster will the "rogue" go. The jockey should allow him to make his own running and effort while interfering with him as little as possible. Horses learn so quickly what a race means that I believe better results than we often get would be obtained, were we to trust more to their judgment than we do, as to how they should be ridden in their races. Rogues run very much better in a match or in a very small field than they do in a crowd; hence if a Jady horse manages to run a dead heat in a race for which there are several starters, the chances are in favour of winning the deciding heat, supposing that he has not had much punishment.

One may try the effect of giving the rogue, a quarter of an hour before his race, half a bottle (not more) of port or sherry in order to make him run kindly. Though horses can take, comparatively, enormous quantities of certain drugs with impunity, still they cannot take drink much more than twice the amount that an ordinary man can without becoming intoxicated.

On Riding Pullers. - Although a curb is objectionable from its tendency to make a horse go "round" and high, still if the jockey cannot hold the horse in any kind of snaffle, it is better for him to use a curb, taking care to put it low down in his mouth, than to take the chance of running himself to a standstill, or to be obliged to saw his mouth or pull his head about, so as to keep him in his place. Speaking to and humouring a horse a little will often make him stop pulling. The remarks I have made on p. about dropping the hands when a horse gets his head up, and taking a pull the moment he lowers it may, be referred to here. I have remarked on p. that their thin snaffles have a tendency to make horses pull. If possible, a large smooth snaffle should be used. If that does not prove sufficient to hold a horse, a chain snaffle may be tried. We may take for granted, especially as the pace will hold most of them, that it is the fault of the jockey if a horse run away in a race. Allowance should of course be made for small weak lads.

Page 13:

As the majority of hard, determined pullers are done running, when they stop pulling, being then left without the power of making an effort, a jockey ought to be particularly careful to "keep a bit in hand" with a horse of this sort.

That hard pullers often fail to stay is frequently the fault of their riders. I quite agree with Hiram Woodruff, the celebrated American trainer, when he remarks that, "It is often said that a horse cannot pull hard and last; and this is contrary to the facts that I am about to mention. Trustee lasted; and was a hard puller. Captain McGowan lasted; and he was the hardest pulling horse in America, I suppose. Dexter pulls a pound or two, I can assure you; and he has shown his capacity to go on. The truth is, that the pulling horses last well enough, but the riders do not last so long. It is just so with the runners."

Orders.- When giving orders it is injudicious to lay down to precise directions, such as to keep a certain number of lengths behind the leading horse who may be sent from the start to cut out the running for another at a pace which may cause him to collapse long before the distance post is reached ; or to wait on some particular horse- a proceeding which has been the cause of many a mistake, for the dreaded one may turn out a rank duffer which is unable to go fast, so that the jockey, by waiting on him, may have in the meantime allowed the others to get so far ahead that he will not be able to catch them before it is too late ; or he may run himself to a standstill in endeavouring to keep the lead all through. If a jockey capable of carrying out minute instructions, he will certainly be clever enough to accomplish the far easier and more profitable task of acting up to the spirit of broad general directions. As a rule it is far much better to ride a race so as to suit the capabilities of one's own horse (with which one ought to be fully acquainted), than to devote one's entire attention to the weak points of the supposed dangerous horse or horses which must be naturally problematical ; for this reason I would never hamper a jockey's judgment by laying out the program cut and dry, but would simply tell him my horse's peculiarities, and what kind of running would most likely bring him home.

For instance, with a fast horse in a one-and-a-half-mile-race, instead of telling; him to wait so many lengths behind, I might say, "Get off well and keep a good bit in hand for half the journey, gradually get up within a couple of lengths of the horses which are going strongest in front of you at the distance post, take a pull for a few strides if you find your horse at all distressed, and make your effort the moment you think you can get home." If the animal then gets beaten, the probability is that the winner was the better horse of the two at the weights and the distance run- a fact which owners of defeated horses often overlooked.

Page 14:

On the Use of Spurs during a Race.- Spurs ought to be put on for a race, unless the horse runs unkindly when they are used, or the jockey is such a bad rider that he cannot spur properly at a finish, or cannot help touching his horse with them. After taking one's spurs off to ride a rogue, it may be just as well, in the preliminary canter, to touch him a couple of times with one's heels in order to show him that he need not fear punishment from them. Some horses, on the contrary, will not extend themselves unless spurs are on.

The proper way to use the spurs is to turn out the toes and strike as close behind the girth as possible, without raising the heels in the slightest when doing so. The feet should on no account be swung back. Nothing is more unworkmanlike then scouring of the horse's sides with the spurs by raising or drawing back the heels. Bad riders not unfrequently spur a horse about the shoulders; while men, who never ought to have been given a mount, have been known to spur a horse on his stifles. When inferior horsemen use spurs, they ought to have them as short as possible.

As a rule, a horse should not be touched with the spurs until the jockey sits down to finish, when three or four digs will be quite enough to make any ordinary animal exert himself to the utmost. An inexperienced rider ought to endeavour to make his horse go fast at a finish by catching a good hold of his head and riding him out, then and not by spurring or flogging him.

On the Use of the Whip.-When hands and spurs fail to make a horse go fast enough to win his race, we may use the whip, if it be a very "near thing," to squeeze the last ounce out of the horse. Horses, when ridden by a workman, will undoubtedly, under the whip, make a last effort which cannot be obtained by any other means of punishment. This effort, speaking in general terms, may make a difference of a length, perhaps even of two lengths, in some rare cases letting the risk we run of spoiling a horse's temper for the rest of his life by flogging him, we may take it for granted that we should not use the whip, if we have to trust it to make up more than two lengths to secure the judge's verdict. A horse, as Mr. Edwin Martin, the well-known Newmarket trainer remarked once to me, cannot, at the end of a race, go farther than a hundred yards at his very utmost speed without beginning to shorten his stride and go slower; hence we may conclude that our last resource, the whip, should not be used until we are within a hundred yards of the winning post.

Page 15:

Practically speaking, the whip should be very rarely indeed "picked up" until within before the last thirty or forty yards, nor should more than two or three cuts be given.

When a jockey begins to flag, as many of them do, two or three hundred yards from home, we need not be surprised at seeing his horse, after answering the call for ten or a dozen strides, go slower and slower as he nears the judge's box. The horse is then probably condemned as a rogue, while the jockey is praised as a resolute finisher.

Some of our best jockeys, now and then, flourish the whip at a finish without hitting the horse, as a "bit of kid," or to make him travel faster than he is doing without punishing him.

A jockey should strike a horse with the whip nowhere else except just behind the girth, unless when preventing him from swerving, etc. When he is hit in this manner, the side away from the whip hand will, if anything, be hurt more than the other, so that the horse will not be so liable to swerve as he would be, were he hit in any other way. Besides, hitting him thus on the centre of the body will not "double him up," nor will make him change his leg, as striking him on the flank or shoulder might do. A jockey who punishes a horse about the sheath, or rips his sides with the spurs, is a disgrace to his profession.

During a race, the whip should be held lash down, for if it be kept up, the horse will often watch it, expecting a cut every moment, and his attention will thereby be distracted from his work. When the moment comes to use the whip, it should be quickly "picked up," while the reins are grasped firmly in the other hand; the rider should sit well down in his saddle, should keep his shoulders square, should lean back, draw his feet back, and keep his body as steady as possible, so that it may not get any sway that from the arm which might interfere with the motion of the horse.

Page 16:

If the whip is to be used by the right hand, the left hand – of course supposing that both hands are on the reins see Fig. - should let go the slack of the off rein, should then slide forward on the near rein, and grasp the off rein in the full of the hand, as shown in Fig. When doing this, the left hand should go forward in a somewhat circular manner, and not directly to the front, so as to preserve that on both reins may be preserved the whole time. It is necessary to shorten the reins in this way, for, when catching hold of a horse's head with one hand, the reins should naturally be shorter than when they are held in both hands. Both reins being now grasped in the left hand, the right hand which holds the whip quits them, and swings the whip slightly forward; so as to bring it between the first and second fingers, see Fig. The whip is now quickly swung round to the rear and brought up into the position shown in Fig. The first finger slips round it, and it is then caught firmly in the hand, and the cuts, which should rarely exceed two or three, are given straight down behind the leg, without any backward swing. Should be timed so that the horse may be struck just as his hind legs make their stroke.

Although explaining how to change the reins and pick up the whip has occupied some space, these actions can be performed, after a little practice, with the utmost rapidity. *The moment for using the whip is such a critical one, that trial a well- practiced motion adopted, so that the rider may have no chance of making a fatal muddle with the reins. Such mistakes, which would appear to be barley excusable in an amateur, are not unfrequently committed professionals who fancy themselves not a little. How often do we see jockeys "let go the reins" the moment they use the whip. It always strikes me that the reason they commit this unpardonable event is that they do not slide the bridle hand forward to shorten the reins before the whip hand grips them, as ought to be done. When there is little time to act and none to think, the mere knowledge of this proper method of doing a thing enough cannot be utilized. An action however, which has been sufficiently repeated to become automatic (forgive me this word) will be instinctively performed without the necessity of reflection on ourselves receiving the required signal.*

When the whip has to be changed from the right to the left hand, the former should grasp the reins in front of the latter, in the latter, in the manner before described. The left hand should now quit the reins, seize the whip, Fig. And draw it through the right hand a novice should not use a whip, for none but a good rider can sit still, hold his horse together with one hand, and flog at the same time. Though spurs do not present these difficulties, they are much less efficient than a whip in the hand of a "Workman."

Effect of Punishment on Horses.- Without wishing to be "hard" on a very meritorious class of men, I must say that a large number of horses are annually ruined for life by needless punishment. Jockeys are apt to attach too much weight to the opinion of the public, and consequently often "ride a horse to pieces" is very different to the one held by a humane owner. Still it is a difficult point to decide whether a jockey is always justified in punishing a horse to the utmost of his power, if he thinks that by so doing he has any chance of winning.

Page 17:

If he knows that he has no chance, and persists in using whip and spur, he ought never to get another mount. Regarding the matter as an owner and racing man, I hold that a jockey should not "knock about" a young promising horse or valuable old one, for an unimportant event, on a mere off chance of winning. He should be most particular not to "squeeze" one which has any suspicion of jadedness. Though it is too much to expect that a jockey should take a sentimental view of punishment, still he ought to regard the interest of his employer, within honourable limits, and should be averse to ruin the noble animal by whose exertions he earns his bread. The most forcible argument I can use against punishment is that, in nine cases out of ten, it defeats its own object.

Page 18:

CHAPTER II

STEEPLECHASE RIDING.

Before riding a chase, the jockey should go round and carefully examine the course, if it is strange to him, in order to find out the easiest and safest parts of the fences, which knowledge may be most useful to him when his horse is tired ; to mark where the "taking off" and "landing" is soundest ; and to observe the nature of the ground, so that he may know when to go fast, where the "going" is good, when to take a pull at his horse, where it is heavy, or where, as may occur over a natural line of country, he might make a slight detour with advantage.

He should above all things, make up his mind to go straight, and should never allow his horse the chance of even trying to refuse. If he knows that his mount is incapable of making a wilful mistake, he should merely regulate the pace, and should on no account, interfere with his fencing; for a pull at his mouth, or a touch of the whip or spurs, at a critical moment, can only tend to make him shorten or lengthen his stride, and, consequently, to blunder. If the horse be dangerously impetuous, he should "drop his hands," speak soothingly to him, and sit as still as possible. If he be liable to chance his fences, and not jump big enough, the jockey should take a good hold of his head and should rouse him when approaching them. He should, however, avoid, unless obliged to do so, hitting the horse with the whip when in the act of jumping, as the sight of it is apt to distract his attention, and may make him blunder over the fence, or to refuse, which he can easily do when the rider has only one hand on the reins. Pressure of the legs and the voice should always be used as a stimulus in preference to the spurs, and the spurs to the whip. It sometimes happens, however, that in the last stride we instinctively feel that the horse is not going to jump big enough, whereupon our heels close, or our whip comes down in response to the thought which flashes in a moment.

APPENDIX 6 INSTRUCTION OF HOW TO RIDE A HORSE

MORNY CANNON

Riding a racehorse is quite a distinct thing from riding an ordinary horse. In the first place the animals are different To the person who knows nothing of horses there is not much to choose between a racehorse and a Hunter, but to the initiated the difference is every bit as marked as that between a Greyhound and a Foxhound. The racehorse has a higher Temperament; its nerves are more finely strung; it is altogether a more delicate creature. But apart from the question of breeding and appearance, there is the matter of age. An ordinary Horse is not ridden until it is four or five years old, whereas a racehorse gets well into the thick of things when it is two. That is where the chief distinction lies. A two year old is quite a baby and it has to be treated with all the care that one bestows on a child; you have to humour it- use it as you would almost use a very delicate instrument; the least little thing upsets it. I have known for instance a two year old to become almost unmanageable while being exercised, merely because it happened to catch sight of a white pocket handkerchief in my hand. Even a three year old is extra tender and irritable. Generally speaking, stallions get worse as they grow older and mares better.

One can recall plenty of instances of the curious tempers of racehorses. Here was Worcester belonging to the late Mr. Barny Banarto; I rode him for the Brighton Cup. As soon as I arrived and caught sight of him I knew I was in for a ticklish job. He was, muzzled and had a blanket over his head, and when I went near him he roared like a lion. We daren't take him into the Paddock, so he was saddled by special permission at the post. Then all went well I rode him won the race by 10 lengths, and was almost congratulating myself I had got well out of it when a Policeman, who was clearing the crowd for me to pass riled him. Just before I got him to the paddock he reared up and came down on a Whelk stall; two people were knocked over, and they sent about ten more spinning. That cleared the air so far as Worcester was concerned, but it started a fresh storm in the owner of the Whelk Stall. This good Gentlemen raved about for some time, and finally sent a bill for the damages for whelks; Mr. Barny Banarto refused to pay, declaring that it was the man's own fault for being in the way, but eventually the case was settled at a cost of two pounds.

Another Horse that I found difficult to ride was the Kings Horse Diamond Jubilee. I was to ride him in the Derby and all the classic races, and I went down to Newmarket in March to get accustomed to him. I rode him in a gallop, and went quietly and well before I got off to change, and put the stable boy back on him. I was no sooner away from him then he savaged me in the left arm, threw me down and knelt on me, he fell over on his side and as he righted himself, Jones his boy jumped on his back. It was one of the smartest things I had ever seen. Later on I tried to approach Diamond Jubilee again, but though in his box he was perfectly quiet, as soon as I walked in he became very excited and, pouring with perspiration, came at me like a dog on a chain. I cleared. I had one more attempt at riding him, but on that occasion he tore his breast cloth to pieces, and showed generally that he preferred my room to my company. After that I had to give it up although I was naturally disappointed, as I never quite abandoned the idea that I should be able to make friends with him; still it was obviously wiser to put up someone to whom he hadn't unreasonable antipathy. It was perhaps some consolation to me to know that I was not the only man he took a dislike to; he bit Jack Watts on the leg when he was only two years old.

Mr. George Edwards's Santoi was another Horse that gave me some trouble. I was on him at the Epsom Cup at Epsom, and I had never ridden him before. When I went into his box the sight was a trifle formidable; two men, were holding him, one on each side, he was muzzled he had a blanket over his head and his forelegs were tied together with a rubber. The trainer was anxious to put the best face on things; he said "you need have no fear he is as quiet as a Lamb. I can do anything with him." I had a peep, and thought to myself, "It's lucky for him he hasn't got to do it." When the time came to mount the trainer advised me to just walk in quietly and jump on his back without speaking. Well I did it, and they pulled the blanket off. As soon as they let go his head he reared bolt upright in the box- his forelegs were still tie, mind-and pawed the air like a pump handle. After a lot of trouble they got the rubber of his legs, and I was led down to the post. He ran all right but I was beaten; principally, I think because Santoi was annoyed with one of the mounted Police. After the race I had got permission for the stable boy to take the saddle of; the animal wouldn't let me do it. Subsequently, San Toi was ridden by a steeple chase jockey, E. Piggott.

But all race-horses are not like this. Many of them are perfectly delightful to ride. Sundridge for instance was one of the kindest horses I ever had to deal with, and Eager was much the same; Flying Fox was quiet till anything upset him, but when that happened, which was very rare, he was very awkward.

Another very striking distinction between riding a racehorse and a Hunter is in the Gear. It is difficult to appreciate the difference between the ordinary hunting saddle, which weighs 12 lbs. and the light racing saddle that weighs 1lb, until you have seen the two side by side; while the hunting saddle gives you a good, comfortable seat the racing saddle is merely a tiny perch amounting to little more than a thing to hang the stirrups from. So small is it that one is practically next to the Horse- almost like riding bare backed; there are, in fact some racing saddles which consist of nothing but the tree and a soft pad.

The whole racing kit, when one is riding ones lightest, weighs exactly 3lbs. This includes the saddle, the pads which go under the pommel and protect the horse's withers, breeches boots, colours (cap and jacket) and silk stockings. These last I frequently leave off, and save thereby half oz. The whip is not included in the 3lbs kit, because the whip is not weighed, either "out" or "in" with them.

The racing boots are enumerated as part of the kit. They come from Palmers at Newmarket. I do not know whether correct article can be got in London. They are all made by a woman, and are so pliable you can fold up the whole boot, sole and all, and put it in your breast pocket.

The kit is made with a view of saving weight in every possible direction. The value of every insignificant detail will perhaps be appreciated when I say that a whiskey and Soda will put on nearly as much weight as the entire kit when a jockey has been "wasting" is of course a serious matter. I have occasionally gone two days without solid food if I wanted to bring my weight down for some important race. Generally however I begin training the day before; I eat half a dinner on the previous evening, take a light breakfast on the day, and do a ten mile walk. That is usually sufficient.

Now for the question of the actual riding. When mounting for a race the jockey is "thrown up" that is to say a man gives him a leg up, grasping him halfway down the shin. But it may happen on occasion that you have to get on without assistance; you may lose your seat, for instance when cantering to the post. You have then no one to help you, and you must resort to another method- a method by the way which is very helpful in the hunting field.

Standing close to the near shoulder, take the left reign very short in the left hand, thus bringing the horses head towards you- the reason for this being that when you jump the horse must come towards you and can move only in a circle- then place the left hand on the neck and the right hand on the pommel of the saddle; next take a spring and get the left elbow over the neck, keeping the right hand on the pommel to prevent you overleaping yourself and toppling over. Many people in mounting a horse make the mistake of putting both elbows over, a practice which tends to land them on their heads on the far side. Others don't put their elbows over at all but rely on their spring to seat them; this is equally risky. In mounting a racehorse one takes no risks. When you have the left elbow over the right hand on the pommel, take one more spring, and throw the leg over and you are on.

When riding the hands should be on the withers and fairly close together, the knuckles of the thumbs uppermost. The mistake is frequently made of holding the hands to far apart and sticking the elbows out.

As to the seat I always used to ride with ordinary long stirrups, and this is undoubtedly the right way for ordinary riding, hunting etc. But when the new American seat was introduced into this country by Tod Sloan we all tried it, and I arrived at the conclusion that the exaggerated position with the short stirrup was no good. I became convinced however that the short stirrup is best for racing, provided it is not to short. You should not sit on the horses back when galloping; you should sit practically on nothing, and the short stirrup enables you to do this. It also shifts the weight from the horses back and throws it on to the withers, thus giving absolute freedom to the hind action whence the pace comes.

The successful riding of a race is obviously a matter of experience, but it is useful to give one or two useful hints. In pulling a horse round a turn, for instance, the following dodge is often valuable; say the horse is going to the right, you put the left reign across his neck and pull to the right with that, and not with the right rein. This method keeps the horse from changing on the wrong leg, and, as every jockey knows, many a race has been lost by a neck or a head owing to the horse changing his legs at a critical moment. It is of course frequently necessary to effect this change, and I am afraid I cannot describe how this is done; it is a question of knowledge and sympathy. I can only say that you first steady your horse and then make him feel by hand and knee that you want him to go on the other leg.

Here is another useful tip that has saved me many a fall. It is frequently difficult with a small saddle to keep your seat when a horse is whipping round; you are always liable to be thrown in the opposite direction to that in which the horse is whipping. In these circumstances if you put out a stiff arm with your hand against the horses neck, on the side on which he comes round, he gives you a kind of purchase, and takes you round with him. This sounds rather like holding on, but in reality is nothing of the sort, for you are keeping your balance all the time.

These are just one or two little tricks that come to my mind and can be told. There are probably dozens more that I am in the habit of employing, but one doesn't think of them until they are wanted. Some people imagine that there is nothing in riding a racehorse beyond ordinary Horsemanship. I have even heard trainers say they have stable boys that can ride as well as any man living; and that there is only 3lbs difference between an experienced jockey and a stable boy. I have noticed however that these very trainers are the ones that are keen on having the services of the best jockeys for their particular stable. From which it may be seen that trainers as the saying is "know a thing or two." They don't give themselves away. There is not the slightest doubt that jockeyship invariably tells. It probably tells more in a long race than in a short one, but tell it always does. This is why my father put me up on a crook to ride my first race; it was Coralline in a five furlong stretch at Kempton Park in 86. I came in last and disappointed a good many backers, who never suspected that my father would start me on anything but the best. He knew better. He knew that there is more in a race than mere riding, and that I should see how others won first before I should win myself. A race does not consist of just getting away well at the start.

APPENDIX 7: WILL OF JOHN BARHAM OF TITCHFIELD YEOMAN 1708[472]

In the name of God Amen, I John Barram of the Parish of Titchfield in the county of Southampton yeoman being sick and weak of body but of sound and perfect mind and memory do make and declare this my last will and testament, form following first and principally second my soul into the hands of almighty God who gave it hoping through the merits death and passion of my saviour Jesus Christ to rise full and for pardon and forgive us of all my sins and to everlasting life my body I commit to the earth to be decently buried at the discretion of my executors…..named and for such worldly effects as if hath pleased almighty god to bless me with all in this life I give and dispose thereof as following. First I will that my debts and funeral expenses be duly paid and discharged. Then I give and bequeath unto my son William Barham and my daughter Ann Barham fifty pounds apiece to be paid to them by executors as they shall attain the age of one and twenty years. And my will is that my executors shall provide for and good my said son William and my said daughter Ann until they are able or can provide for themselves without making any demand out of this said fifty pounds apiece. Then I give and bequeath unto my daughter Elizabeth the wife of Charles Shaw One Shilling. Then I give and bequeath unto my daughter Mary Barham One Hundred pounds to be paid to her by my executors when she shall attain the age of one and twenty years. Then I give and bequeath unto my daughter Eloise Barham One Hundred pounds to be paid to her by my executors when she shall attain the age of one and twenty years. Then all the rest and residue of my goods and chattels and ready money I give and bequeath unto my sobbing wife Eliouse and my two sons Hugh Barram and John Barram whom I do hereby make joint and full and sole executors of this my last will and testament and I do hereby revoke annul and make void all former and other wills by me made and ask this to be my last will and testament in witness whereof I have here into set my hand and seals this eighth day of September anno 1708 and in this years of the reigns of our sovereign lady the grace of god Queen of Britain.

---

472 Hampshire Record Office1709a/006Will of John Barham of Titchfield Yeoman 08/09/1708 Winchester Record Office1709a/006

Appendix 8: Inventory of John Barham of Funtley Fareham Yeoman 1743[473]

Died without a will Intestate, letters of administration were granted to his son Richard Barham of Fareham of Knowle in the parish of Southampton yeoman. Richard divided the estate between his brothers William Barham of Titchfield Miller, and John Barham of Gosport Brewer,

Inventory:-

And for Inventory of all and singular ...... chattels and credits of John Barham late of Funtley in the parish of Fareham in the county of Southampton and Bishop of Winchester his guidance deserved taken and appointed by us whole names hereunto subscribed this twenty seventh day of July in the year of our lord 1742:-

Eighteen quarters of wheat at 1:4g Quarter at Knowle Farm 21:12:01
Twenty four quarters of ditto at Mayles Farm at ditto 28:16:01
Seventeen Quarters of Barley at Knowle Farm at 1g a quart 17:00
Half quarter of Oates at Mayles at 16g quarter 8:00
Hay in a rook at Knowle 10:00
Sire Horses one Colt and 45:00
Twenty one bullocks 69:00
Four yearling bullocks 8:00
Six milk cows 22:00
Hogs and pigs at Knowle and Mayles 14:14:6
Sixty eight Sheep at ... 19:19:0
Two Wagons Van and Bushey 12:00
Two plow's two drags two harnesses 13:00
Four old harrows 0:60:00
Chapel Coppice and wood 18:2:0
Birch fike cops and wood 15:00
Two dung carts 3:00

Total 323:13:6

For ripping and binding 24 3/4 acres of wheat at 4.6 g an acre 6:9:4
For cutting and raking 1g Acre of Barley 1:19:0
For ditto 5 acres of Oats 0:10:0

---

473 Hampshire Record Office 1743ad/017Will of John Barham of Fareham Funtley Yeoman 06/06/1743 Winchester Record Office 1743ad/017

For Four Acres of …..
To be deducted 9:6:4
Remainder 314:7:3

Signed Thomas Smith Assessors
The Sixteenth day of June 1743 On which day administration of all singular goods chattels credits of John Barham late of Funtley in the parish of Fareham in the county of Southampton and diocese of Winchester Husbandman deceased intestate was granted and permitted unto Richard Barham the lawful son of the said deceased and the said Richard Barham was duly sworn administrator of the said deceased.

Administration letter were granted to Richard Barham of Knowle in the parish of Fareham Yeoman, and William Barham of Titchfield Miller and John Barham of Gosport Brewer the estate was thus divided equally.[474]

---

474 Hampshire Record Office Administration Letters of John Barham of Fareham Yeoman 16/06/1743 21m65/d4/1743/8

APPENDIX 9: WILL OF JOHN BARHAM OF ROMSEY

GENT 1781[475]

In the name of God Amen I john Barham of Romsey in the county of Southampton Gentleman being weak in the body but of sound disposing mind and memory and –

Understanding proved be God do make and declare this to be my last will and testament in revoking in the manner allowing that this to be my first will and declare that all my just debts and funery expenses to be paid and discharged and after payment thereof I give to my son James Barham the sum of one Guinea having already advanced for him as much as my circumstances would admit of whereas by indenture of six parts being date the twenty fifth day of November One Thousand Seven Hundred and Eighty Eight and made between Richard Barham Late of Knowle of the county of Southampton but then of Curdridge in parish of Bishops Waltham in the county of Southampton Yeoman of the first part. I the said John Barham of the second part James Barham late of Ashton but then of Kimbridge in the said county of Southampton Miller Eldest Son and Heir at Law of the said John Barham of the third part John Brookes of Gosport brewer of the fourth part Charles Bedford of Gosport in the said county of Southampton Gentlemen of the fifth part and William Bedford of Gosport aforesaid Gentlemen and the Reverend Thomas Bedford fellow of New College Oxford of the sixth part the sum of One Thousand Pounds part of the sum of Three Thousand Six Hundred Pounds being the purchase money for the vestal Estates therein mentioned and received in the hands of the said John Brookes by way of security against the claim of my wife Sarah Barham of and in the same Estates which were conveyed upon the ….. And for the sum proven therein particularly approved and whereas

Page 2

I have since the Execution of the said Indentures received a part of the said sum of One Thousand Pounds and the residue thereof now remains in the hands of the proprietor of the said Estates subject to such….. And conditions as and declared in the said Indentures concerning the same. Now I do hereby give and bequeath all my resulting and beneficial Right Claim and Interest of and in the … Residue of the said Sum of One Thousand Pounds and in every part thereof after the several trusts where to

475 Will of John Barham of Romsey Gentleman 04/06/1781 Winchester Record Office 1781B/03

the same is liable and fully accomplished to my Son Richard Barham his executor Administrator or after give shall there out fully pay and satisfy my just debts and after payment and satisfaction thereof .... I give and bequeath and bequeath unto the said Richard Barham his executors administrators and assigns all the surplus money that shall remain of the residue of the said One Thousand Pounds for his and their own use and disposal and all the rest and residue of my goods chattels effects monies and personal Estate II give and bequeath unto my said son Richard Barham and I do appoint him sole executor of this my will and I do revoke all former wills by me hereafter made. In witness where of I have here unto set my hand, and seal the fourth day of June in the year of our Lord 1781.

Page 3

August 30 1781 on which day the within named Richard Barham came before me and duly proved the within will and made oath that the effects of the within name testator and under the value of one hundred pounds as he believes and the said Richard Barham was duly .... Executor before me Sir Henry Norman.

APPENDIX 10: THE WILL OF JOHN DAY OF HOUGHTON DOWN 1768-1828

This is the last Will and Testament of me John Day of North Houghton in the county of Southampton Yeoman. I first pay my just debts and finery and testamentary expenses to be fully paid and satisfied as is soon as the value......... may be after my death. I bequeath all my Estate and effects whatsoever and wheresoever unto my said wife Anne Day upon trust to invest the value in or upon Government or other good.............investments. And the dividends and annual proceeds thereof I give and bequeath to my said wife for and during the term of her natural life, independent of and not subject to the debts or......... of any future husband which she may have or take and it is my will that she shall throughout maintain and ..... with of my children as shall not be of the age of twenty one years until they attain that age and from and immediately after that date I give and bequeath the amount principal trust monies and all and .... The said trust estate and effects unto and equally amongst all and every of my eight children John, James, Ann Scott, Henry Thomas, Samuel, William, Charles and Frederick.'[476]

---

476 Will of John Day of North Houghton extracted from the original 1828

APPENDIX 11: THE WILL OF JOHN BARHAM DAY OF DANEBURY 1790-1860

On the Ninth day of July 1860 the Will with a Codicil thereto of John Barham Day late of East Woodyates in the Parish of Pentridge in the Country of Dorset Gentlemen. Deceased who died on the 21st day march 1860 at East Woodyates aforesaid was proved in the principal Registry of her Majesty's Court of Probate by the Oaths of Joseph Parker of no' 19 Queens Road Gloucester Gate Regents Park in the Country of Middlesex Gentlemen and William Day of East Woodyates aforesaid Gentlemen and Alfred Day of Longstock in the County of Southampton Gentlemen.

This is the last will and Testament of me John Barham Day of Woodyates in the county of Dorset Gentlemen. First I order all my just debts funeral and testamentary expenses to be paid and discharged by my Executors hereinafter named as soon as conveniently may be after my decease I give and bequeath to my dear Wife Jane Ann Barham Day all my household goods and furniture plate linen china and household effects (except pictures) which shall be in and about my dwelling house at the time of my decease for her own use during her life or Widowhood and as a home for my single Daughter Emma Day so long as she shall remain unmarried and from and after the decease or marriage of my said Wife whichever shall first happen I give and bequeath the said household goods and furniture plate linen china and household effects except the pictures unto my said daughter for her use during her life or so long as she shall remain unmarried and in the event of her marrying or in her death then I direct that the said household goods and furniture plate linen china and household effects shall be sold by auction and the proceeds therefor divided equally among all my sons and daughters then living share and share alike. I also give and bequeath unto my said wife the sum of two hundred and fifty pounds owing to me from Mr. John Pester and secured by way of way of mortgage on property at Chiderck in the county of Dorset and also the security for the same for her own absolute use and benefit I give and bequeath unto my daughter Harriet the wife of William Sadler all the household goods furniture and household effects now in her possession at Winchester which belong to me for her use during her life and after her decease I give and bequeath the same household goods furniture and household effects unto all her children then living equally to be divided between them share and share alike and as to all my freehold leasehold and real-estate and also all the rest residue and remainder of my personal estate and effects of every description of which I am enabled to appoint or dispose of by this my will I give devise and bequeath the same and every part thereof respectively unto my friend Joseph Parker of No 19 Queens Road Gloucester Gate Regents Park London and my two sons William Day and Alfred Day their heirs executors administrators and assigns upon the following trusts,

That is to say upon trust as soon as conveniently may be after my decease to call in and convert into money my said personal estate or such part thereof as shall not consist of money and absolutely to sell and dispose of my said real estate either together or in parcels by public auction or by private contract to any person or persons willing to purchase the same and for such price or prices as to my said trustees or trustee for the time being shall seem reasonable with however to buy in the same at any such auction and afterwards to resell the same at any future auction or by private contract without being answerable for any loss or any divination in price to be incurred thereby. And for facilitating such sale or sales to enter into make and execute all such contracts conveyances assignments surrenders and assurances acts deeds matters and things which to my said Trustees or the survivor of them by his heirs executors administrators or assigns shall seem reasonable and I declare that the receipt and receipts of my said trustees or trustee for the time being for any money payable to them or him under this my will shall effectively discharge the persons or person paying the same from being answerable or accountable for the misapplication or no application thereof or of any part thereof or from being obliged to see to the application of the same or of or to enquire into the necessity or propriety of any sale that may be made by virtue of this my will and I do declare that my said trustees and the survivor of them and the executors administrators and assigns of such survivor do and shall stand and be possessed of and interested in all the money to arise from the sale or sales of my said real estate and also of my said personal estate and the money to arise and be produced therefrom upon the following trusts that is to say upon trust as to the sum of two thousand pounds part thereof to lay out and invest the same in their or his names or name in the parliamentary stocks or public funds of Great Britain or at interest upon Government or real security in England or Wales with power to alter and vary the same for and into other securities of a like nature at their and his discretion and to pay the interest dividends and annual proceeds thereof unto or permit the same to be received by my said Wife Jane Ann Barham Day and her assigns for and during the term of her natural life or Widowhood and for and after her decease or marriage of my said Wife upon trust to pay the interest dividends.

And annual proceeds of the said sum of Two Thousand pounds unto my said Daughter Emma Day and her assigns during her natural life in case she shall remain single and unmarried and from and after the death or marriage of my said daughter Emma Day upon trust to allow the said principal sum of Two Thousand Pounds to sink into and form part of my residuary personal estate upon trust to invest the same in their or his names or name in the Parliamentary Stocks or Public Funds of Great Britain or at interest upon Government or Real Security in England or Wales with forever to alter and vary the same for and into other securities of a like nature at their and his discretion and to pay the interest dividends and annual thereof unto my said Daughter Emma Day during her natural life free from debt duties interference or engagements of any husband with whom she may intermarry and without being liable for anticipation and her receipt alone to my said trustees to be the only good discharge for the same and after her decease upon trust to pay and divide the said principal sum of one thousand pounds unto and among all and every the child and children of my said daughter Emma Day and the issue of any deceased child or children if any, share and share alike such issue however only taking among them the share his her or their parent or parents would have taken if living but in case my said daughter Emma Day shall die without leaving any child or children surviving then upon trust to pay and divide the said principal sum of one thousand pounds unto and among all and every the brothers and sisters of the said Emma Day as shall then be living and the issue of such as shall be then dead share and share alike such issue however taking such share only as his or their parent or parents would have taken if living and after making the several investments aforesaid upon trust out of my said residuary personal estate to pay the following legacies that is to say to my son William Day the sum of One thousand pounds and two hundred pounds, to my son Alfred Day the sum of One thousand Pounds to my daughter Hope Dixon the sum of One Thousand Four Hundred and Fifty pounds, to my son Edward the sum of One Thousand Two Hundred Pounds, To my daughter Ann the wife of Mr. Aaron Dibben.

The sum of One Thousand Four Hundred and Fifty Pounds. To my Daughter the said Emma Day the sum of Five Hundred Pounds over and above the sum of One Thousand Pounds before directed to be invested for her benefit as aforesaid Provided and I do hereby declare that in case my said residuary Estate shall not be sufficient for the said last mentioned legacies in full then I direct that the same shall abate pro rata in proportion to their respective amounts but in case there shall be any residue either on my death or after the death of my said Wife after making the several investments and payments aforesaid I do hereby direct my said trustees or trustee for the time being to divide and I do give and bequeath the same unto and equally among all my children that is to say John, Harriet the wife of William Sadler , Elizabeth wife of William French, William, Henry, Hope the wife of John George Dixon , Alfred, Edward, Ann the wife of the said

Aaron Dibben and Emma Day share and share alike and to their respective executors administrators and assigns . But I do hereby expressly declare and direct that the share of my said daughter Harriet Sadler shall not be paid to her or to her said husband but shall be retained by my said trustees and held by them upon the following trusts (that is to say) Upon Trust to lay out and invest the same in their own names in the Parliamentary Stocks or Public Funds of Great Britain or at interest upon Government or real Security in England or Wales with forever to alter and vary the same at their discretion and to pay the interest dividends and annual proceeds therefor unto my said daughter Harriet Saddler for and during her natural life the same to be free from the debts control interference of her present or any future husband but without power of anticipation and her receipt alone to be the only good discharge to my said trustees for the same and from after the decease of the said Harriet Sadler upon trust to pay the principal of the said trust monies and unto and among all and every child children of the said Harriet Saddler and the issue of any deceased child or children share and share alike such issue however taking among them the share or shares his her or their parent parents would have taken if living, and I do also expressly declare and direct that the share of my said daughter Elizabeth French should not be paid to her or her husband but shall be retained by my said trustees and held by them upon the following trust that is to say to invest the same as above directed with respect to the share of the said Elizabeth French and to pay the interest dividends and annual proceeds thereof unto my said daughter Elizabeth French for and during her natural life the same to be free from the debts control interference of her present or any future husband but without power of anticipation and her receipt alone to be the only good discharge to my said trustees for the same and from after the decease of the said Elizabeth French upon trust to pay the principal of the said trust monies and unto and among all and every child children of the said Elizabeth French and the issue of any deceased child or children share and share alike such issue however taking among them the share or shares his her or their parent parents would have taken if living. Provided lastly and I hereby declare that on the death refusal or incapacity to act the said Joseph Parker William Day and Alfred Day or any trustee or trustees to be appointed in his or their place or stead it shall be lawful for the surviving or last acting trustee or trustees for the time being of this my will or the executors or administrators of the surviving or last acting trustee to appoint a new trustee or trustees in the place or stead of such trustee so dying or refusing or becoming incapable to act as aforesaid and therefor the said here dements trust estate monies and premises shall be conveyed assigned and assured so that the same may rest in such new trustee or trustees jointly with the surviving or continuing or last acting trustee or solely as the case may require and in his her or their heirs administrators executors and assigns to the use upon the trusts and for the ends intents and purposes here for declared and that every such new trustee either before or after such conveyance assignment or insurance shall have and may exercise the same powers or authorities as if he had been appointed a trustee by this my Will and that none of the trustees appointed or to be appointed as aforesaid shall be answerable for the other of them or for the acts deeds or defaults of the other of them nor for the involuntary losses nor for money received

Under receipts which they shall join in only for conformity and that the present and every future trustee may reimburse themselves and each other out of the said trust premises or out of any monies that may come into their hands by virtue of this my Will and all losses and expenses to be incurred by them in the execution of the trusts aforesaid or anywise in relation thereto And I hereby nominate and appoint the said Joseph Parker and my two sons the said William Day and Alfred Day joint executors of this my Will hereby revoking all former Wills by me at any time heretofore made and I do declare this alone to be and contain my last Will and Testament in Witness Whereof I the said John Barham Day Testator have to this my last will and testament contained in six sheets of paper set my hand this fifth day of September in the year of our lord one thousand eight hundred and fifty nine.

Signed published and declared by the said John Barham Day the Testator as and for his last Will and Testament in the presence of us who in his presence at his request and in the presence of each other have together at the same time subscribed our names as witness.

Codicil

This is a codicil to me John Barham Day of Woodyates in the county of Dorset Gentlemen which bears the date the fifth day of September One Thousand Eight Hundred and Fifty Nine. Whereas I have by my said Will directed my trustees therein named to invest a sum of two thousand in their own names in Parliamentary Stocks or Public Funds of Great Britain or at interest upon Government or real security in England and Wales and to pay the interest,

Dividends or annual proceeds thereof and to pay the proceeds thereof unto and permit the same to be received by my wife Jane Ann Barham Day and her assigns for and during the term of her natural life or Widowhood. Now it is my wish that my said wife should have and be entitled to the interest dividends and annual proceeds of the said sum of Two Thousand Pounds for and during her life, I do therefor hereby expressly desire and direct my said trustees or trustee for the time being to pay the interest dividends and annual proceeds of the said sum of Two Thousand Pounds or permit the same to be received by my said wife and assigns for and during the full term of her natural life and from and after her decease to pay the dividends interest and annual proceeds of the said sum of Two Thousand Pounds to my daughter Emma Day and her assigns during her natural life in case she should remain single and from and after the death or marriage of my said daughter Emma Day the said principal sum of Two Thousand pounds shall sink into and form part of my residuary and personal estate and be applied and disposed of as in my said Will provided in Witness I have hereof set my hand this second day of December one thousand eight hundred and fifty nine

Signed published and declared by the said John Barham Day the Testator as and for his last Will and Testament in the presence of us who in his presence at his request and in the presence of each other have together at the same time subscribed our names as witness.

APPENDIX 12: THE WILL OF JOHN DAY OF DANEBURY 1815-1882

This is the last Will and Testament of me John Day of Danebury near Stockbridge in the county of Southampton trainer. I appoint my son Leonard Day now residing with me at Danebury aforesaid trainer and my son Thomas Lamb of the Elms Andover in the said county Solicitor Trustees and Executors of this my Will. I give devise and bequeath all of my real and personal estate of every tenure and of what nature and kind sever and wheresoever situate of which I shall be subject of or entitled to at the time of my decease unto and to the use of my trustees and executors the said Leonard Day and Thomas Lamb their heirs executors and administrators respectively upon trust that they the said Leonard Day and Thomas Lamb or the survivors of them or the heirs executors or administrators of such survivors respectively shall sell and convert into money the same either together or in parcels and either by public Auction or private contract and with power to make any stipulations as to title or evidence or commencement of title or otherwise which they or he shall think fit and may buy in or receive or vary any contract for sale or resale without being answerable for any loss occasioned there by and may for the purposes aforesaid or any of them execute and do all such assurances and things that they or he shall think fit. And I direct that the said Leonard Day and Thomas Lamb and the survivors of them or the executors or administrators of such survivors shall be and out of the monies to arise from such sale calling in and conversion as aforesaid in the first place pay all my just debts and funeral and testamentary expenses and to all the rest residue and remainder thereof shall pay the same unto my four children John Day the younger Leonard Day Kate the wife of Thomas Cannon and Harry Day equally between them share and share alike provided always and I do hereby declare that if my daughter Kate Cannon should die in my lifetime the share as before given her shall go and be paid to her husband the said Thomas Cannon for his own use and benefit absolutely. And I do hereby declare that the receipt of the said Leonard Day and Thomas Lamb or the survivors of them or the heirs executors or administrators for such survivor for the purchase monies of any property hereby directed or authorized to be sold and for any other monies paid and for any stocks funds shares or securities transferred to them or him by the virtue of this my Will or in the execution of any of the trusts or peeves hereof shall effectively discharge the person or persons paying or transferring the same there from and from being bound to see to the application or from being answerable for the loss misapplication or non-application thereof Provided always and I do hereby declare that if the said trustees hereby constituted or either of them shall die in my lifetime or if they or either of them should die after my death or be abroad or desire to be discharged or refuse to become incapable to act the provisions of the Act 23 and 24 C.145 as to the appointment of new trustees shall be applicable to and shall be deemed to be incorporated with this my will and such powers shall be exercised in the manner therein authorized and directed provided always and I do hereby declare that the trustees for the time being of this my Will shall be respectively chargeable only for such monies stocks funds shares and securities as they shall respectively actually receive notwithstanding their respectively signing any receipt for the sake of conformity and shall be answerable or accountable only for their own acts receipts neglects and defaults respectively and not for those of each other nor for any banker broker auctioneer or other person with whom or into whose hands any trust monies or securities may be deposited or come. And also that the said trustees or trustee for the time being may reimburse themselves or himself or pay and discharge out of the trust premises all expenses incurred in or about the execution of the trust or powers of this my Will. And hereby revoking all former wills made by me at any time heretofore made. I declare this to be and contain my last Will and Testament in witness whereof I have signed my name at the foot or end of this my will this eighteenth day of March one thousand nine hundred and eighty. Signed by the said John Day.

This is a codicil to the last will of me John Day of Danebury whereas I have this day received from my son in law Thomas Cannon the sum of five hundred pounds for the purchase of the interest of my lease of Longstock Down from Lady Mill and I have invested the said sum in the purchase of London and South Western Railway Stock in the names of myself and Mr. Thomas Lamb of Andover now I do hereby bequeath the said sum of five hundred pounds so invested as aforesaid and the accumulation of dividends which may from time to time arise therefrom up to the date of my death to my two sons Leonard Day and Harry Day equally to be divided between themselves and share alike and in case of the death of either the said Leonard Day or Harry Day in the lifetime of the other before my death then I bequeath the whole of the said sum of stock and the accumulations thereof to the survivor. I have Hereunto set my hand this twenty eighth day of March one thousand eight hundred and eighty one.

This is a second codicil to my last will bearing date the eighteenth day of March one thousand eight hundred and eighty. Whereas since the date of my said will my said son John Day has died now therefor I bequeath the residue of my said estate to my other children named in my said will equally between them as if the name of my said son John Day had not been named therein. And whereas in the first codicil to my said will I have given the accumulations of the dividends on the sum of the London and South Western stock purchased with the sum of five hundred pounds received from Mr. Cannon to my two sons Leonard and Harry Day now I revoke the gift of the accumulations of the dividends to them giving them the fund exclusive of the dividends to the day of my death. And in every other respect I confirm my said will in witness whereof I have hereunto set my hand this twenty first day of August one thousand eight hundred and eighty one.

Personal Estate
£3, 558, 18.0 Gross
£2, 140, 12.2 Net

Appendix 13 List of Sporting Pictures Sold from John Days Estate 1883

"The sale of the entire effects of the late John Day of which we gave notice some few days since took place at Danebury on Wednesday or Thursday last, under the personal superintendence of Mr. Frederick Ellen of Ellen and Sons of Andover and the result was highly satisfactory to all parties concerned. There was a good attendance of buyers and full prices were realized for the various lots. The pictures were of course the most important items in the whole catalogue and at a glance at the appended return will show the majority of them were purchased by Tom Cannon, so that they will still continue to decorate the walls of Danebury. By the way it may be here mentioned that the new Tenant has decided to pull the house down with the exception of the kitchen and its offices and the premises will be considerably enlarged when rebuilt. This step will of course render Coopers landscape of Danebury from Chattershill all the more interesting and valuable, and at the price it must be on account of old associations be considered a bargain To its late owner successor.

Already the repairs and general overhauling of the stabling are going to assume a somewhat dilapidated aspect it has been nearly completed and it will not now be long before the large racing stud under the care of Tom Cannon will be sheltered under one roof at Danebury. Though of course considerable time must necessarily elapse before the dwelling house is ready for Habitation. The shrubbery in front is to be all together remodelled and by the way it may here be noted that the old paddock on the ace course is to be converted into a promenade lawn, tastefully laid out with flower beads, and the saddling enclosure will in future be on the other side, so it will be seen. But the new (clerk of the course) is determined(to go with the times).Stockbridge meeting is always regarded as being the most enjoyable of the entire season, and Cannon is evidently bent on making the three days reunion even more pleasant.

It might have been expected on Wednesday that the highest priced picture was that by, A. Cooper of Andover (*A. Day Hermit Wells*) a portrait of the then "Leviathan, Gully and sundry members of the Day family". Cannon was a purchaser, and to his final nod was also knocked down "Harry Halls painting of Crucifix and junior Portraits of Auburn Vaun with Fordham up by the same band now still in death, and decisive with portraits of Tollard and the late Master of Danebury were likewise amongst the paintings secured by Tom Cannon. Mr. Toovey was a conspicuous bidder and bought Coopers picture winner of the Oaks and virtually the foundation of the Late Sir Josephs Hawley's great succession on the turf. As after the Kentish Baronet had purchased her from Mr.' Gulley daughter of Touchstone had turned out a veritable goldmine at the stud amongst her produce, being beadsmen in addition to winning the derby, was the Sire of many other good horses that carried the cherry black cap to victory at important races. At the time of his decease John Day had only two thoroughbreds in his property, and confessor and prince Edward were purchased by Mr. Sidney Jacobs at a very moderate outlay below will be found particulars of the sale. "

ABRAHAM. COOPER

Lot 1 Oil paintings in handsome guilt frames by A. Cooper. A very fine oil painting, Andover and Hermit, with A. Day and Wells Mr. Gully and members of the Day family portraits 1854. Mr. Tom Cannon purchased that for £77.14s

Lot 2 A very fine Oil painting Pyrrhus the first winner of the Derby in 1846 Mr. Toovey purchased it for £23.2s

Lot 3 A very fine Oil painting Mendicant winner of the Oaks 1846 purchased by Mr. Toovey for £47.5s

Lot 4 A very fine Oil Painting Cossack winner of the Derby 1847 purchased by Mr. Turner for £11.11s

Lot 5 A very fine oil painting Cimba winner of the Oaks 1848 purchased by Mr. Toovey for £11.13s

Lot 6 A very fine oil painting Hero winner of the Goodwood Cup that was purchased by Mr. Cannon for £18.18s

Lot 7 A very fine oil painting Surplice winner of the Derby and St. Ledger 1848 purchased by Mr. Wolfe for £11.11s

Lot 8 A very fine oil painting Mango winner of St Ledger 1837 ridden by Samuel Day purchased by Mr. William Day for £21.00

Lot 9 A very fine oil painting Spume ridden by John Day 1837 purchased by Mr. Cannon £15.00

HARRY HALL

Lot 1 Oil painting Lecturer ridden by S. Hibbard purchased by Mr. Toovey for £29.08s

Lot 2 Oil painting Vauban ridden by Fordham purchased by Mr. Cannon for £28.07s

Lot 3 Oil painting Aqua ridden by Tom Cannon purchased by Mr. Turner for £27.6s

Lot 4 Oil painting Crucifix with John Day Senior and John Day Junior portraits purchased by Mr. Cannon for £65.2s

Lot 5 Oil painting Hero with Alfred Day up purchased by Mr. Turner for £16.6s

Lot 6 Oil painting Pussy winner of the Oaks 1824 with William Day trainer and John Day Jockey portraits purchased by Mr. Toovey for £39.18s

DAVIS
Lot 1 Oil painting H.R.H the Price of Wales Maria winner of the Somerset stakes at Bath 1828 ridden by John Day purchased by Mr. William Day for £8.8s

G. COLE
Lot 1 Oil painting Decisive with Tollard and J Day portraits 1843 purchased by Mr. Cannon for £31.10s

BRETLAND
Lot 1 Oil painting St Lawrence winner of the Chester Cup 1847 purchased by Mr. S Jacob Senior £5.5s

HOPKINS
Lot 1 Oil painting Trumpeter 1868 purchased by Mr. William Day £10.10s

VARIOUS
Lot 1 Oil painting Ellis winner of the St Ledger 1836 with Mr. John Day Senior purchased by Mr. Lee £5.5s

Lot 2 Oil painting finish of a memorable race at New Market Cardinal Puff and two others a portrait of a pony purchased by Mr. Cannon for £7.7s

Lot 3 A portrait of Eclipse purchased by Mr. Cannon for £8.8s

Lot 4 Oil painting Not Yet Caught purchased by Mr. Cannon for £6.6s

COOPER JUNIOR
Lot 1 Oil painting Landscape view of Danebury from Chatters Hill purchased by Mr. Cannon for £32.11s

R LINDSEY
Lot 1 Oil Painting Flower Girl purchased by Mr. L Day for £12.12s

COLE
Lot 1 Oil painting Venison purchased by Mr. S Jacobs for £3.3s

McDONALD
Lot 1 Oil painting Game Cock purchased by Mr. S Tovey £4.4s

SALE OF HORSES IN TRAINING
Lot 1 Confessor BH Aged by the Palmer Secret purchased by Mr. S Jacobs for £22.1s

Lot 2 Prince Edward BC 3 years Lowlander Margret purchased by Mr. S Jacobs for £17.17s

Appendix 14: Hunt Wedding and List of Guests and Presents

Date of the Wedding **December Eighth 1893**

Danebury was in fate on Wednesday upon the occasion of Tom Cannon's eldest daughter Alice, to Mr. Charles Compton Martin. A large number of Guests assembled to see the happy couple turned off. Additional interest attached to the ceremony which took the novel form of a hunting wedding. The master of the Danebury hounds with his huntsman and the first whip as represented by Tom Cannon (Young Tom). Young Tom and Mornington Cannon happily recovered from his indisposition attending in full dress and supported by several Gentlemen in Pink, inclusive of the Master of Tedworth Mr. Shrub. It was altogether a picturesque affair and will be long remembered by the inhabitants generally who turned out in great force. The pretty church at Nether Wallop being crowded to its upmost holding capacity the service which was fully choral was conducted by the Vicar of the parish Reverend E Blaken, and the Reverend Bolton Smith of Wymering Vicarage, and everything passed off as merrily as a proverbial wedding bell. A large company was entertained at Breakfast at Danebury, after which the Hounds met and soon found in Danbury Paddocks, and during the afternoon killed twice after good sport. In the evening Mr. and Mrs. Compton Martin posted to London on route to Manchester where they will spend a few days prior to finishing their honeymoon at Brighton. They will return to Danebury to spend Christmas and on the sixth of January will start by the good ship the Scott form Southampton to Johannesburg the Cape of Good Hope, where it is their intention to set up home. A few days later Mornington Cannon will lead Miss Denuet to the Alter at St Mary Abbotts Kensington, but the Wedding will be of very quiet character, owing to the recent and much regretted death of the Bride's father.

Marriage of Miss Alice Cannon (Tom Cannon Jnr was the best Man)

A charming hunt wedding took place yesterday at Nether Wallop Church where Miss Alice Cannon daughter of Mr. Tom Cannon of Danebury was married to Mr. Charles Compton Martin eldest son of Mr. W.B.Martin of Paulsgrove Hants. The Bride wore a green habit with gold hunt buttons, a black hat and brown top boots and a hunting tie fastened by a diamond pin. Instead of the orthodox bouquet Miss Cannon carried a Gold Hunting Crop, surmounted by a bunch of Orange Blossoms. The bridesmaids were attired in covert shirts, with scarlet waistcoats and hunt buttons, brown boots and Spats, and soft felt hats with trim black toke feathers. The bridegroom presented them with Gold Horn and Fox Head Rings and Horseshoes of Scarlet and white flowers. The Bridegroom and the father and the brothers of the bride also wore hunt dress.

ANOTHER SECTION ON THE WEDDING "EXTRACT 3", LIST OF PRESENTS

Captain Jessop gave a drawing room suite, Mr. and Mrs. Geddington gold enamelled Diamond and Pearl heart bracelet , Mr. and Mrs. Groom silver button hook and shoehorn , Miss Denuet Chrysler phrase and pearl heart pendent and gold chain, Dr. and Mrs. Claperton and family set of silver teaspoons and cheque, Mr. Dennett Luncheon Basket, Mr. and Mrs. Lamb set of ivory brushes in case, Mrs. Cook solid silver Muffineers ,Mr. and Mrs. Martin gold curb chain watch bracelet and eider down, Mr. and Mrs. Sheppard gold pencil, Mr. and Mrs. Deverell ivory toilet box, Mr. and Mrs. Beckett Servants at Garlogs china teapot, Miss Lettie and Mable Cannon gold horse shoe bracelet engraved (A. from L. and M, December 6th 1893) also they gave a night dress, case and sideboard cloth. The Bridegroom gave Emerald and Diamond ring, gold lettered bracelet and sable tie. Messer's J. A and H.A Forsythe solid silver butter dishes shell shape. Mr. and Mrs. Crabtree silver mustard pot and muffineers, Mr. and Mrs. T. Redford silver butter dish, Mr. and Mrs. Leonard Day two bronze figures and a shawl, Mrs. Agnes Day set of Doyle's, Mrs. Alexander nightdress case and comb bag, Mr. A. Wolf set of silver spoons, Mr. and Mrs. J.H.Smith two silver candlesticks Mr. S.C.Williams silver tea urn, Mr. Shrub silver gilt cut glass smelting bottle, Mr. R. Fidges silver backed hair brushes, Mr. Robinson gave a cheque, Mrs. Cannon silver tea and coffee service, Mr. S and Mrs. Harper two silver candlesticks Mrs. Hirsh triple mirror, Mr. Leopold De Rothschild Bracelet Mr. Dick March gold pencil Bracelet with Alice inscribed in Diamonds.

APPENDIX 15 WILL OF THOMAS CANNON (SNR)

Death On or After 1st January 1898

Will

Be it known that "Thomas Cannon of the Grosvenor Hotel Stockbridge in the county of Hants, died on the 13th day of July 1917 at the Grosvenor Hotel aforesaid. And be it further known that at the date hereunder written the last Will and Testament, of the said deceased was proved and registered in the Principal Probate Registry of his Majesty's High Court of Justice, and that administration of all the estate which by law devolves to and vests in the personal representative of the said deceased was granted by the aforesaid Court to "Walter Kempton Cannon of Rosslyn East Mosley in the County of Surrey Lieutenant in H.M. Army son of the deceased and Walter King Loveless of Steepleton Stockbridge in the County of Hants M.D. the executors, named in the said will.

Dated the 21st day of September 1917, gross value of Estate 5,306-12-07, Net value of Personal Estate 992-9-2

This is the last will and Testament of me Thomas Cannon of the Grosvenor Hotel Stockbridge in the County of Hampshire made this second day of May in the year of our Lord one thousand nine hundred and sixteen. I hereby revoke all wills heretofore made by me I appoint Walter Kempton Cannon of Rosslyn East Mosely in the County of Surrey and Dr. W K Loveless of Stockbridge in the county of Hampshire to be executors of this my Will I direct that all my debts funeral and testamentary expenses shall be paid as soon as conveniently may be after my decease. I give devise and bequeath unto the above named executors 100 (one hundred pounds) to my daughter Ethel (Mrs. Tennison) & 100 (one hundred pounds) to my housekeeper Miss Minnie Reid I wish to be buried in my wife's grave at Stockbridge the rest of my estate including everything to my son Ronald Portman and advise him to make his will. Should like Miss Minnie Reid to stay till the Grosvenor Hotel is either sold or let.

Thomas Cannon- Signed by the said testator as and for his last will and testament in the presence of us who at his request in his presence and in the presence of each other have hereunto subscribed our names as witnesses. Florence Elizabeth Stockly Grosvenor Hotel Stockbridge-Laura Philpot Grosvenor Hotel Stockbridge on the 21st Day of September 1917 Probate of this Will was granted to Walter Kempton Cannon and Walter King Loveless the Executors.

Appendix 16 Will of Thomas Cannon (Jnr)

I Thomas Leonard Gilbert Cannon late of Hamilton House Compton in the County of Berks Trainer but now of Sway Wood Sway in the County of Hants hereby revoke all Wills and testamentary dispositions therefor made by me and declare this to be my last Will.

I Appoint the National Provincial Bank Limited and my Wife Dorothy Cannon(hereinafter called " my Trustees')to be Executors and Trustees of this my Will and I declare that the said National Provincial Bank Limited (hereinafter called the Bank) may act as Executor and Trustee on the terms and conditions including the right to remuneration and the incidence thereof as set forth in the Banks Trustee and Executorship Regulations in force at the date hereof and if such terms and conditions were here set out. And in any case which a solicitor is employed the firm of Messrs. Bouch Belcher & Company of Newbury shall if possible be employed without prejudice to the right of the bank to consult its own Solicitor in any case in which it shall think fit to do so.

I direct my Trustees to pay my just debts funeral and testamentary expenses as soon as they are conveniently able after my death.

I bequeath to my brother Herbert Mornington Cannon my collection of Day Pictures viz: "John Day on Crucifix" by J.F. Herring "John Day on White Cob" and "Decision" by Geo. Cole and also the "Danebury Picture" and "Danebury Downs" and "Stockbridge Racecourse" by W. Sextie and also the Stockbridge Cup in Silver.

I bequeath to my said wife free of all duties (a)All my household furniture plate linen china glass books the remainder of my pictures prints musical instruments wines provisions jewellery silver (except as provided by clause 5 hereof) and also my carriages horses and motor cars belonging to me at my death. (b) The sum of Five Hundred Pounds to be paid to her as soon as possible after my death. (c) The annuity secured to me on the life of my said wife under contract number 3406 in the Clerical Medical and General Life Assurance Society. Provided nevertheless that if my said wife shall be proved not to have survived me for the period of one month the forgoing bequests shall follow the trusts declared in favour of my brothers and sisters as specified in clause 6 hereof.

I except out of the absolute bequest to my said wife by clause 4 (a) hereof all my oil paintings of the cannon family hunting and sporting pictures and the Silver Stockbridge Common Down Cup 16th June 1866 and the Silver

Cup given to my father by the Earl of Cadogan in 1892 all of which upon my wife's death I give and bequeath free of duty in memory of my father to the owner or the owners for the time being of the Grosvenor Hotel Stockbridge in the County of Hants with my wish and desire that the same shall be placed and maintained with other pictures relating to the Cannon family which have already been at the Grosvenor Hotel aforesaid for many years.

I bequeath to my Trustees the following sums of Stock and Shares:

£5000 4% Funding Loan 1960/90 Post Office Issue.

> £5000 3½% Conversion Loan 1961.
> £2000 2½% Consolidated Registered Stock.
> £1500 3% Local Loans Registered Stock
> £2000 2½% London County Council Stock.
> £2500 4% London Midland and Scottish Railway Preference Stock.
> £1200 National Provincial Bank Limited "B" Shares of £5 each £1 paid.
> 500 Unilever Limited 7% Cumulative Preference Shares of £1 each
> 600 British American Tobacco 5% Preference Shares if £1 each
> 625 Imperial Chemical Industries 7% Cumulative Preference Shares of £1 each.

And also (subject to the provisions of clause 7 hereof) the proceeds of sale of my freehold property known as Sway Wood aforesaid.

Upon trust to retain such sums of Stock and Shares in their names and to pay the annual income and dividends thereof to my said wife during her life and from and after her death Upon trust to realize the same and to pay and divide the net proceeds thereof as follows: As to one Half thereof to my brother Walter Kempton Cannon absolutely and as to the remaining one half thereof unto and equally between my sisters and brothers Alys Mary Martin the said Herbert Mornington Cannon Agnes Mable McAlister Margaret Kate Piggott Ethel Cecilia Louise Tenison and Charles Edward Cannon absolutely. But in the event of the said Walter Kempton Cannon predeceasing me the half share hereinbefore given to him shall go in augmentation of the shares given to my said other brothers and sisters.

I give devise and bequeath my freehold property known as Sway Wood aforesaid to my said wife for her life Provided always that my said wife shall be under no obligations with regard to repairs to the property but shall only be responsible for keeping the dwelling house and buildings insured against loss or damage by fire in the full value thereof and from and after the death of my said wife I give devise and bequeath the said freehold property unto my Trustees Upon Trust to sell the same and to hold the net proceeds of sale upon the same trusts as are declared concerning the Stocks and Shares set out in Clause 6 hereof.

I bequeath the following pecuniary legacies all free of duty to my said brother Walter Kempton Cannon the sum of Eight Hundred Pounds to each of my said sisters Alys Mary Martin Agnes Mabel McAllister Margret Kate Piggott and Ethel Cecilia Louise Tennison the sum of Five Hundred Pounds respectively to my said Brother Charles Edward Cannon the sum of Five Hundred Pounds And I declare that the legacies bequeathed by this Clause shall only be paid after the bequest of the sums of Stock and Shares mentioned in Clause 6 hereof to be retained in trust for my said Wife shall have been satisfied and that my said property known as Sway Wood shall not during the lifetime of my said wife be resorted to for payment of the legacies bequeathed by this clause and that if after satisfying the bequest contained in clause 6 and the devise of my said property known as Sway Wood contained in Clause 7 it shall be found that my Estate is insufficient to satisfy the legacies bequeathed by this clause then such legacies shall abate proportionately or payment thereof in full be postponed until after the death of my said wife as circumstances may require.-

I declare that in the event of any of the said brothers or sisters predeceasing me or my said wife leaving issue living at the date of my death or the death of my said Wife such issue shall take and if more than one equally between them the legacy and share in the proceeds of sale of the sums of stock and shares and of my property Sway Wood aforesaid respectively which his or her parent survived me and my said wife respectively.

I give devise and bequeath all the residue of my estate both real and personal unto my said wife for her own use and benefit absolutely subject nevertheless to the same proviso as is contained in Clause 4 hereof.

I empower my Trustees at their absolute discretion to retain in their then state of investment any of the investments held by me at the time of my death whether the same shall be authorized Trustee investment or not without being answerable for any involuntary losses which shall occur by reason only of such retention My Trustees shall nevertheless at their discretion have power to realise all or any of the said investments and to invest the proceeds thereof in any investments for the time being authorized by law for the investment of trust funds.

In witness whereof I have to this my will in this and the proceeding two sheets of paper contained set my hand this Eighth day of May One thousand nine hundred and forty two.

Signed by the said Thomas Leonard Gilbert Cannon as for his last will in the presence of us both.

APPENDIX 17: WILL OF WALTER KEMPTON CANNON

In Her Majesty's High Court of Justice. The District Probate Registry at Lewes

Be it known that Walter Kempton Cannon of 8 Princes Avenue Hove Sussex, died there on the 2nd day of December 1951.

And be it further Known that at the date hereunder written the last Will and Testament(a copy whereof is hereunto annexed) of the said deceased was proved and registered in the District Probate Registry of her Majesty's High Court of Justice at Lewes and that Administration of all the Estate which by Law devolves to and vests in the personal representative of the said deceased was granted by the aforesaid Court to "Tommy Owen Watts of Persimmon 151 Maple Road Surbiton Surrey Company Director the sole executor named in the said will"

And it is hereby certified that an affidavit for the Inland Revenue has been delivered wherein it is shewn that the gross value of the said estate in Great Britain (exclusive of what the said deceased may have been possessed of or entitled to as a trustee and not beneficially) amounts to 14,131-17-7, and the net value of the estate amounts to 12,804-18-4. And it is further certified that it appears by a receipt signed by an Inland Revenue Officer on the said Affidavit that 474-1-8 on such duty has been paid Dated 16th day of February 1952…..signed W.K. Cannon

I Walter Kempton Cannon of 8 Princess Avenue Hove 3 in the county of Sussex Hereby Revoke all former testamentary instruments made by me and declare this to be my last will.

I appoint Tommy Owen Watts of Persimmon 151 Maple Road Surbiton in the county of Surrey to be the sole executor of this my will.

I give to the said Tommy Owen Watts all my furniture and articles of personal domestic and household use or ornamental and all my pictures not otherwise disposed of by this my will free of all the death duties

I give the following legacies all free of all death duties

(a) To my Sister Alys Mary Martin of Jersey Avenue Stanmore Middlesex the sum of two hundred and fifty pounds but if she shall predecease me then I give the same to her daughter Mrs. Vixen Thompson.

(b) To my sister Margaret Kate Piggott of 103 Southall Road Oxford the sum of two hundred and fifty pounds if she shall survive me.

(c) To my Brother Herbert Mornington Cannon of 10 Scott Road Hove the sum of two hundred and fifty pounds if he shall survive me

(d) To my Brother Charles Edward Cannon of Coppice House West Willow near Romsey Hampshire the sum of two hundred and fifty pounds if he shall survive me.

(e) To my Cousin Hilda Cannon of Crosstrees Bram Heath Woodbridge Suffolk the sum of one hundred pounds in recognition of her kindness to me at Newmarket in my single days thirty eight years ago if she shall survive me.

(f) To Charlotte Elizabeth Wilde my honest and faithful maid of 8 Princess Avenue Hove aforesaid the sum of Five Hundred pounds in recognition of her twenty eight years' service to my late Wife and myself together with her bed the mahogany Wardrobe and the two mahogany chests of drawers which are in my Dressing Room.

I give the residue of my estate whatsoever and whosesoever (subject to and after payment of my funeral and testamentary expenses and debts and the legacies given by this my Will and the duties therein and on the specific legacies bequeathed by clause 3 hereof) to the said Tommy Owen Watts absolutely.

It is my desire that the said Tommy Owen Watts will use his best endeavours to see that the said Charlotte Elizabeth Wylde shall have sufficient furniture for her reasonable needs to enable her to furnish a room but without imposing any legal obligation upon the said Tommy Owen Watts to do or creating any trust or equity in favour of the said Charlotte Elizabeth Wylde.

In witness whereof I the said Walter Kempton Cannon have to this my will set my hand this Fourth Day of February One Thousand nine hundred and forty eight.

Proved 16th day of February 1952.

Authors Biography

Figure 199Author with his Wife Wahida and son Charles at the family home 2016

Andrew Ager grandson to Charles Cannon great-grandson to Tom Cannon great-great-grandson to John Day of Danebury was born in 1974 to Patricia Cannon and Leslie Walter Haskell. Leslie unfortunately died 16 months later. Patricia then remarried to Keith Ager Andrew's father and Mark Jaine Andrew and Anthony all had a wonderful childhood together in the New Forest Hampshire.

Andrew's passion for history began at a young age with his love of horse racing he wanted to become a jockey but his mother was against the idea stating that her "father Charles and her uncles Morny and Kempton had broken too many bones in their body" so unable to ride the horse he decided like his ancestor's to contribute to the turf by writing the complete unwritten history of his family.

Andrew studied Retail Design Management Ba Hons Degree at London Institute Bond Street, and then further studied Interior Design Ba Hons at Bournemouth University. After graduating Andrew commenced his career as a project manager in London for a few years, moving abroad to Hong Kong and then China spending a year in Thailand, after moving to Qatar and then to Dubai for 10 years and eventually returning to the UK where he met his wife Wahida and his son Charles was born.